Communications in Computer and Information Science   1212

Commenced Publication in 2007
Founding and Former Series Editors:
Simone Diniz Junqueira Barbosa, Phoebe Chen, Alfredo Cuzzocrea,
Xiaoyong Du, Orhun Kara, Ting Liu, Krishna M. Sivalingam,
Dominik Ślęzak, Takashi Washio, Xiaokang Yang, and Junsong Yuan

Editorial Board Members

More information about this series at http://www.springer.com/series/7899

Wataru Ohyama · Soon Ki Jung (Eds.)

Frontiers of Computer Vision

26th International Workshop, IW-FCV 2020
Ibusuki, Kagoshima, Japan, February 20–22, 2020
Revised Selected Papers

 Springer

Editors
Wataru Ohyama 🆔
Saitama Institute of Technology
Saitama, Japan

Soon Ki Jung
Kyungpook National University
Daegu, Korea (Republic of)

ISSN 1865-0929   ISSN 1865-0937 (electronic)
Communications in Computer and Information Science
ISBN 978-981-15-4817-8   ISBN 978-981-15-4818-5 (eBook)
https://doi.org/10.1007/978-981-15-4818-5

This Springer imprint is published by the registered company Springer Nature Singapore Pte Ltd.
The registered company address is: 152 Beach Road, #21-01/04 Gateway East, Singapore 189721, Singapore

Preface

It is our great pleasure to present the proceedings of the International Workshop on Frontiers of Computer Vision (IW-FCV 2020), held during February 20–22, 2020, in Ibusuki, Kagoshima, Japan.

IW-FCV started as the Japan-Korea Joint Workshop on Computer Vision (FCV 1995), held for the first time in Daejon, South Korea. The workshop alternated between South Korea and Japan, annually, and IW-FCV 2020 was hosted in Japan. Although the workshop is hosted by a different country each year, the basic policy has been decided upon by the Steering Committee in order to ensure continuous operation. This year, we put efforts into making the workshop more attractive. First, we decided to publish several high-quality papers as post-proceedings from Springer. Second, we made the workshop more international. Papers from seven countries, mainly researchers visiting Japan or South Korea, were accepted. Finally, we introduced a demo session, which gave researchers a chance to showcase their interesting applications even if it was not published yet.

As a result, the number of submissions increased from last year to 68. Each paper was reviewed by three reviewers from the Program Committee members in a single-blind manner. After presentation at the workshop, 27 high-quality full papers were selected for this post-workshop proceedings.

The all the committee members made a great effort in planning and holding the event. The Program Committee and publication chair were dedicated to creating a wonderful program and the booklet. Grants from Kyushu University and IEEE Fukuoka Section as well as project support from Iwasaki International Academic Exchange Foundation were helpful to maintain the high-quality workshop. We also thank the continuous support by the Institute of Electrical Engineers of Japan as organizers.

March 2020

Hiroshi Kawasaki
Kanghyun Jo
Wataru Ohyama
Soon Ki Jung

Organizing Committee

General Chairs

Hiroshi Kawasaki — Kyushu University, Japan
Kanghyun Jo — University of Ulsan, South Korea

Program Chairs

Wataru Ohyama — Saitama Institute of Technology, Japan
Soon Ki Jung — Kyungpook National University, South Korea

Publicity Chair

Masashi Toda — Kumamoto University, Japan

Local Arrangement Chairs

Satoshi Ono — Kagoshima University, Japan
Noritaka Shigei — Kagoshima University, Japan

Financial Chair

Tsubasa Minematsu — Kyushu University, Japan

Web Chair

Takafumi Iwaguchi — Kyushu University, Japan

Steering Committee

Kazuhiko Yamamoto — Gifu University, Japan
Hiroyasu Koshimizu — Chukyo University, Japan
Rin-ichiro Taniguchi — Kyushu University, Japan
Kunihito Kato — Gifu University, Japan
Yoshimitsu Aoki — Keio University, Japan
Chikahito Nakajima — CRIEPI, Japan
Makoto Niwakawa — Meidensha, Japan
Jun-ichiro Hayashi — Kagawa University, Japan
Kanghyun Jo — University of Ulsan, South Korea
Inso Kweon — KAIST, South Korea
Kiryong Kwon — Pukyong National University, South Korea
Chilwoo Lee — Chonnam National University, South Korea

Weon-Geun Oh	ETRI, South Korea
Jong-Il Park	Hanyang University, South Korea
Yongduek Seo	Sogang University, South Korea
Kyunghyun Yoon	Chung-Ang University, South Korea

Program Committee

Shuichi Akizuki	Chukyo University, Japan
Saumik Bhattacharya	IITK, India
Kyoung Ho Choi	Mokpo National University, South Korea
Wahyono Doank	University of Ulsan, South Korea
Takayuki Fujiwara	Hokkaido Information University, Japan
Hironobu Fujiyoshi	Chubu University, Japan
Hitoshi Habe	Kinki University, Japan
Van-Dung Hoang	Quang Binh Uni, Vietnam
Maiya Hori	Kyushu University, Japan
Md Zahidul Islam	Islamic University, Bangladesh
Masakazu Iwamura	Osaka Prefecture University, Japan
Wenjing Jia	University of Technology Sydney, Australia
Hyun-Deok Kang	Ulsan National Institute of Science and Technology, South Korea
Yasutomo Kawanishi	Nagoya University, Japan
Jaeil Kim	Kyungpook National University, South Korea
Soo-Hyung Kim	Chonnam National University, South Korea
Wonjun Kim	Konkuk University, South Korea
Yoshinori Kuno	Saitama University, Japan
Chul Lee	Dongguk University, South Korea
Suk Hwan Lee	Tongmyong University, South Korea
Jongwoo Lim	Hanyang University, South Korea
Michihiro Mikamo	Kagoshima University, Japan
Masashi Nishiyama	Tottori University, Japan
Takahiro Okabe	Kyushu Institute of Technology, Japan
Umapada Pal	Indian Statistical Institute, India
Soon-Yong Park	Kyungpook National University, South Korea
Kaushik Roy	West Bengal State University, India
Hideo Saito	Keio University, Japan
Atsushi Shimada	Kyushu University, Japan
P. Shivakumara	University of Malaya, Malaysia
Kazuhiko Sumi	Aoyama Gakuin University, Japan
Toru Tamaki	Hiroshima University, Japan
Hiroshi Tanaka	Fujitsu Laboratories Ltd., Japan
Kenji Terada	Tokushima University, Japan
Kengo Terasawa	Future University Hakodate, Japan
Diego Thomas	Kyushu University, Japan
Kwanghee Won	Dakota State University, USA
Takayoshi Yamashita	Chubu University, Japan

Keiji Yanai   The University of Electro-Communications, Japan
Ming-Hsuan Yang   University of California at Merced, USA
Byoung-Ju Yun   Kyungpook National University, South Korea

Main Sponsor

Sponsors and Supporters

Contents

Object Detection and Tracking

Inspection and Diagnosis

Camera, 3D and Imaging

Real-World Applications

Efficient and Fast Traffic Congestion Classification Based on Video Dynamics and Deep Residual Network

Mohamed A. Abdelwahab[1]([⊠]) [iD], Mohamed Abdel-Nasser[2,3] [iD],
and Rin-ichiro Taniguchi[4] [iD]

[1] Electrical Engineering Department, Faculty of Energy Engineering,
Aswan University, Aswan 81542, Egypt
abdelwahab@aswu.edu.eg
[2] Department of Computer Engineering and Mathematics,
Rovira i Virgili University, 43007 Tarragona, Spain
[3] Electrical Engineering Department, Faculty of Engineering,
Aswan University, Aswan 81542, Egypt
[4] Graduate School of Information Science and Electrical Engineering,
Kyushu University, Fukuoka 819-0395, Japan

Abstract. Real-time implementation and robustness against illumination variation are two essential issues for traffic congestion classification systems, which are still challenging issues. This paper proposes an efficient automated system for traffic congestion classification based on compact image representation and deep residual networks. Specifically, the proposed system comprises three steps: video dynamics extraction, feature extraction, and classification. In the first step, we propose two approaches for modeling the dynamics of each video and produce a compact representation. In the first approach, we aggregate the optical flow in front direction, while in the second approach, we use a temporal pooling method to generate a dynamic image describing the input video. In the second step, we use a deep residual neural network to extract texture features from the compact representation of each video. In the third step, we build a classification model to discriminate between the classes of traffic congestion (low, medium, or high). We use the UCSD and NU1 traffic congestion datasets to assess the performance of the proposed method. The two datasets contain different illumination and shadow variations. The proposed method gives excellent results compared to state-of-the-art methods. It also can classify the input video in a short time (37 fps), and thus, we can use it with real-time applications.

Keywords: Traffic congestion · Dynamic image · Optical flow · Deep learning

1 Introduction

Automated traffic monitoring systems become essential due to the increasing of road networks and the number of vehicles. Road traffic congestion is a severe

© Springer Nature Singapore Pte Ltd. 2020
W. Ohyama and S. K. Jung (Eds.): IW-FCV 2020, CCIS 1212, pp. 3–17, 2020.
https://doi.org/10.1007/978-981-15-4818-5_1

problem that has its economically and ecologically adverse effects. Vehicle accidents are one of the most problems due to bad traffic management, which yields many deaths every day. Traffic congestion can also cause at least a long delay in time. There is an expeditious development in the Intelligent Transportation System (ITS) technologies to realize better traffic management. The spread in CCTV cameras and the enormous development in the platforms have strengthened the development of various vision-based methods for traffic monitoring [8]. Traffic flow measuring in real-time helps in avoiding or decreasing the congestion probability. Discerning if the traffic is fluid or jams in real-time is vital information that can help authorities re-route traffic and thus reduce congestion. Additionally, this information can be beneficial for guiding the drivers to the best routes and avoiding the congested ones.

In short, researchers have categorized automated traffic congestion systems into vehicle-based and holistic methods. In the vehicle-based methods, researchers suggested methods for detecting and tracking vehicles using computer vision techniques, and then they compute vehicle trajectories and use them to discriminate between traffic congestion levels (low, medium, or heavy). Other researchers have adopted the number of vehicles on a particular road as an indicator of the level of traffic congestion. The authors of [12] detect the moving objects based on frame differences and adaptive thresholding. They extracted wavelet coefficients from moving regions to track vehicles, and to train a neural network for recognizing vehicles in the moving object areas. Mo et al. [15] used the scale-invariant feature transform (SIFT) for detecting vehicles. In the training phase, they extracted SIFT features for creating a codebook. In the detection stage, they used the trained codebook in the vehicle detection process. Finally, they track the detected vehicles and use the trajectories information to classify the traffic. The authors of [11] presented a solution to overcome the problem of occlusions by proposing two distinct techniques in case of low and high occlusions. In the case of objects under occlusion, they employ local features in vehicle detection and tracking. In the case of high occlusion, they employ color probability besides the local features to separate the occlusion areas and to make the tracking of individual vehicles easier.

Numerous researchers have used the number of vehicles as an indicator of the level of traffic congestion [1,3,4,23]. For example, the authors of [1] introduced a fast technique for counting vehicles. They create a background model for a narrow region instead of the whole frame. Within this region, they detect moving vehicles that are detected as foreground objects and counted without any need for a tracking step. Yang et al. [23] used a low-rank decomposition technique for separating the moving object from the background, where they described the background by the low-rank component and the moving purposes by the outliers component. Ultimately, they used the Kalman filter to track vehicles. The authors of [3] use the region convolution neural network (R-CNN) and KLT tracker to count vehicles. They detect vehicle bounding boxes by the R-CNN and then obtain corner points within the detected bounding boxes. In addition to that, they compute vehicle trajectories by tracking these corner points and propose an algorithm for assigning a unique label for each vehicle.

In holistic methods, researchers extract global features to describe the whole scene. These features may represent motion, texture, or both. The authors of [16] proposed a congestion estimation method based on the MPEG compressed domain. They extract features from motion vectors and discrete cosine transform (DCT) coefficients. Then, they use these features to train a hidden Markov model. Unfortunately, we can use this method with only the MPEG video format. Asmaa *et al.* [6] presented two approaches for estimating the traffic density, namely microscopic and macroscopic. In the microscopic approach, they detect and track vehicles and then get three distinct motion features: traffic flow, velocity, and the rate of road occupancy. In the macroscopic approach, they split video frames into small blocks. In each frame, they employ a block matching algorithm to search around every block to find the best-matched one in the subsequent frame and then compute a motion vector. Also, they compute the average flow velocity and density from all block motion vectors. Finally, the authors performed different combinations of the microscopic and macroscopic features to find the best features, remarking that such combination yields the highest accuracy. Yet, the block matching algorithm makes the computational complexity of this method high, and therefore it is inappropriate for real-time applications.

Riaz *et al.* [17] used motion features to describe the traffic flow, where they track sparse feature points to form motion vectors. They exclude motion vectors that have low displacements or directions drafted from the main direction of vehicles (vectors containing noise). Then, they compute mean velocity, standard deviation velocity, number of motion vectors for each video, and the average length of motion vectors. Notably, the main limitation of this method is that the mean velocity of the motion vectors is determined for the whole video and not considering the difference in flow between road regions and the stopped car motion vectors, and thus, they do not contribute in determining the traffic congestion. The authors of [14] extracted different texture features from video frames without considering any motion information. They assessed two texture analysis approaches: codebook descriptors and CNN-based extracted features. In the codebook approach, they compute four visual codebooks based on SIFT features, namely locally aggregated descriptors, improved fisher vector, locality-constrained linear coding, and a bag of visual words. In the CNN-based approach, they utilized the last fully connected layer of a pre-trained network to extract a feature vector from every video frame.

Figure 1 presents frames of three videos representing diverse traffic congestion classes: light, medium, and heavy, where we represent each video by three frames (videos taken from UCSD dataset [7]). As we can see, there is a remarkable variability on the number of vehicles and the vehicle motion pattern (vehicle displacements) between the three frames. Therefore, the extracted features should describe both the number of vehicles as well as their motions to obtain an accurate classification. With such videos, the use of only one feature type has some

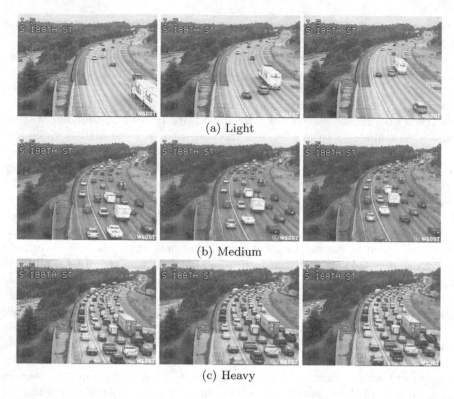

(a) Light

(b) Medium

(c) Heavy

Fig. 1. Frame samples of three videos having different traffic congestion classes. We show three frames from each video (11th, 21th and 31th from left to right, UCSD dataset).

shortcomings. For instance, if motion features are only exploited in the traffic measuring [17], fully stopped vehicles in a jam traffic scene can be mistakenly classified as an empty roadway. In turn, the texture features (appearance) [14] may not discriminate between two scenes of different flow having the same vehicle numbers. Indeed, most of the existing traffic classification methods are not robust against the illumination conditions, or they have a high computational complexity, which makes these methods hard to be used in practical systems.

In this paper, we propose a fast and efficient automated system for traffic congestion classification. The related work extracts features from the whole video or a single frame. Differently, we propose two approaches for modeling the dynamics of each video (or a batch of $L-$frames in case of an online system) and generate a compact representation for it. In the first approach, we propose to aggregate the optical flow in front direction. In the second approach, we propose the use of a temporal pooling method to generate a dynamic image summarizing the whole video. After we obtain the compact representation of each video, we use a pre-trained deep residual neural network (ResNet101) to extract texture features from it. Finally, we train a support vector machine (SVM) to discriminate

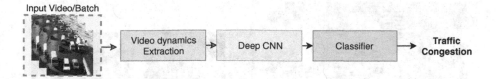

Fig. 2. The steps of the proposed system.

between the classes of traffic congestion (low, medium, or high). The proposed system can classify the input video in a short time, and thus, we can use it with real-time applications.

We organize the rest of this paper as follows: Sect. 2 presents the proposed system. Section 3 discusses the results, and Sect. 4 summarizes the paper and gives some lines of future work.

2 The Proposed System

Figure 2 presents the steps of the proposed system: video dynamics extraction, feature extraction using deep CNN, and classification. We explain the detailed steps of the proposed method in the next sections.

2.1 Video Dynamics Extraction

Here, we propose the use of two approaches for extracting the dynamics of each video and generate a compact representation for an input video or a batch of frames (i.e., $L-$frames). The two approaches are aggregating of optical flow and temporal pooling. The importance of creating such compact representation is to save the processing time i,e., instead of extracting texture features from each frame in a video, features are extracted from only the compact image. In addition, if features are extracted independently from each frame, they are not correlated to each other, i.e., the evolution of features from one frame to the next one is not taken into account. Below, we explain each approach in detail.

Aggregation of Optical Flow. Following [2], we compute the optical flow for input video frames with a size of $(m \times n \times k)$, then we obtain the aggregation of optical flow (AOF) by aggregating the magnitude of the obtained optical flow volume (V) in front direction as described in Eq. (1). However, the authors of [2] split the optical flow volume into layers based on its angles; we utilize it in our experiments without partition. In [2], optical flow aggregations in front and side directions were employed, however, we believe that the frontal aggregation of optical flow is more representative for vehicle motion; thus, we use it to extract the dynamic of traffic video and generate a compact representation of the whole sequence.

Fig. 3. Examples for generating a compact representation for a 30 input frames. (a) The original input video (b) representation obtained by frontal aggregation of the optical flow, (c) and (d) representations obtained by the forward and reverse temporal pooling, respectively.

$$AOF = \sum_{i=1}^{k} V_{m,n,i} \qquad (1)$$

Figure 3 (a) presents a 30 input frames, and Fig. 3 (b) shows the corresponding compact representation obtained by the AOF. As we can see, AOF can represent the dynamic of traffic in the input frames. It has the same size as a single frame, and thus using AOF in the next steps of the proposed method reduces the computational complexity without losing the core information about traffic congestion.

Temporal Pooling. We use the temporal pooling method proposed in [9] to produce a compact representation of a sequence of frames. This representation has the same size of one frame and describes the temporal dynamics of the traffic inside the sequence of frames. Assume that we have L frames which are represented by $X = [x_1, x_2, \ldots, x_L]$ where $x_i \in \mathbb{R}^D$ represents the pixel raw values for a frame i. First, the smoothed vectors $V = [v_1, v_2, \ldots, v_L]$ are obtained from X. The authors of [9] introduced three alternative ways to obtain the smoothed vectors: (1) the use of independent frame representation, (2) the use of moving average, and (3) the use of time-varying mean.

The dynamics $\mathcal{D}$ of the smoothed vectors V is encoded using a linear function $\Psi_u = \Psi(V; u)$ parametrized by u, where $\mathcal{D}$ reflects the way that smoothed vector values change from time t to $t+1$ for all t. The parameter $u \in \mathbb{R}^D$ is used as a new representation for the $L-$frames, which captures the appearance evolution through frames. The learning to rank model [13] is used to capture the dynamics $\mathcal{D}$ by optimizing the ranking function $\Psi(t, V_{1:t}; u)$. Three methods can be used to solve such an optimization problem: (1) a point-wise, (2) a pair-wise, and (3) a sequence-based ranking. If v_{t+1} succeeds v_t, it can be represented as $v_{t+1} \succ v_t$, by the end, we can obtain the order constraints $v_L \succ \cdots \succ v_t \succ \cdots \succ v_1$. A constrained minimization pairwise-learning to-rank [13] formulation is solved such that preserving the frame order constraints as shown in equation (2).

$$\arg\min_u \quad \frac{1}{2}\|u\|^2 + C \sum_{\forall i,j, v_{t_i} \succ v_{t_j}} \epsilon_{ij},$$
$$s.t. \quad u^T(v_{t_i} - v_{t_j}) \geq 1 - \epsilon_{ij},$$
$$\epsilon_{ij} \geq 0. \tag{2}$$

where C is the regularization parameter, and ϵ is the margin of tolerance.

In the proposed traffic congestion classification system, we exploit the obtained u to represent the dynamic changes through an input $L-$frames. We obtain forward or reverse representations of the dynamic of traffic videos on the basis of the direction of determining the evolution of the textures through the video frames. If the temporal information is captured from the first frame to the next one in a forward direction, the feature is known as a forward dynamic sequence (FDS). In turn, if the process starts from the last frame of the input video, the feature is defined as a reverse dynamic sequence (RDS).

2.2 Feature Extraction Using Deep CNN

After we obtain a compact representation for each input video (or a batch of $L-$frames), we extract one feature vector from it. This feature vector should efficiently represent the textures of the compact representation. To do so, various pre-trained deep convolutional neural networks (CNNs) are exploited: VGG19 [19], GoogleNet [20], ResNet101 [10] and inceptionv3 [21], which are previously trained with numerous illumination conditions and object sizes. With each CNN network, the feature vector is taken from the last layer of the network. The length of the extracted feature vector depends on the type the utilized network. With VGG19, GoogleNet, ResNet101, and inceptionv3 networks, the length of vectors are 4096, 1024, 2048, and 2048 for using respectively.

VGG19 [19]. The VGG19 is composed of 47 layers. These layers constitute several serial convolution layers, and each layer is followed by a rectified linear unit (ReLU) layer. The network is ended by a three fully connected (FC) layers. The convolutional kernels of the VGG19 networks have small sizes which help in reducing the number of parameters of the network. The input image should be re-sized to $224 \times 224 \times 3$. The length of the first and the second FC layers is 4096, while the final FC layer has a length of 1000, which gives the probabilities for the output classes.

GoogleNet [20]. Unlike VGG19 that has a single path, GoogleNet has several paths and thus the processing is performed in parallel rather than sequential. In this network, the "Inception Module" is the basic block, in which many convolution processes are performed in parallel. In inception modules, different filter sizes are used (e.g., $1 \times 1, 3 \times 3, 5 \times 5$) to extract different features. A dimensional reduction is applied to the extracted features from different passes then they are combined.

ResNet101 [10]. The unique feature of this network is its ability to train very deep CNN easier than the other CNN networks. With other networks, the accuracy is saturated and even decreased if the depth is increased. However, the ResNet101 has a skip connections property across their residual blocks. This property enables the network to overcome the degradation problem.

Inceptionv3 [21]. In Inceptionv3, the inception architecture is modified in order to reduce the network parameters and enhance the computational efficiency. Inceptionv3 has 11 inception modules, and each one includes pooling layers and convolutional filters. ReLUs is used as an activation function. By this rebuilding of the network architecture, the network can have similar complexity to the VGG network but with more deep layers.

2.3   Classification Step

We feed the extracted feature vectors into an SVM classifier to discriminate between the levels of traffic conestions: low, medium, or heavy. Note that we extract the CNN features from three different compact representations of input videos: AOF, FDS, and RDS. We assess the performance of several combinations, namely AOF & FDS, AOF & FDS, and FDS & RDS. We build an SVM model using features extracted from AOF, FDS, and RDS, separately. Then we aggregate the output posteriors of two SVM classifiers and determine the final class label based on the maximum class posterior.

3   Experimental Results and Discussion

In this section, we analyze the proposed system with two traffic congestion datasets: UCSD and NU1 video. The main aim of the proposed system is to achieve a robust and fast system for traffic classification that can be adopted for real-time applications. We perform two experiments to demonstrate that the proposed system can achieve the desired goal. In the first experiment, we use the UCSD dataset to compare the results of the proposed system with those of

Table 1. The classification accuracy (%) of different combinations of AOF, FDS, RDS, and CNN models for the SVM and k-NN classifiers (UCSD dataset)

Method	VGG19 (4096)	GoogleNet (1024)	ResNet101 (2048)	Inceptionv3 (2048)
AOF - KNN	89.76	91.40	94.09	87.40
FDS - KNN	88.58	86.61	92.91	87.40
RDS - KNN	90.94	90.55	94.49	90.16
AOF - SVM	94.09	92.91	94.49	92.52
FDS - SVM	92.52	88.19	96.85	90.55
RDS - SVM	94.49	90.55	95.28	94.49

Table 2. The classification accuracy (%) of different combinations between AOF, FDS and RDS using posteriors of their SVM classifiers (UCSD dataset)

Combination	VGG19 (4096)	GoogleNet (1024)	ResNet101 (2048)	Inceptionv3 (2048)
AOF-FDS	96.06	92.91	96.46	93.31
AOF-RDS	94.88	93.31	96.06	95.28
FDS-RDS	93.31	92.52	**97.64**	94.09
AOF-FDS-RDS	95.28	94.49	97.24	95.28

state-of-the-art methods. In the second experiment, we use the NU1 video (long video, 45 min) to simulate a practical situation for online traffic monitoring. The proposed system outputs the classification decision for every 15 frames.

3.1 Analyzing the Performance of the Proposed System with UCSD Dataset

The UCSD dataset [7] contains 254 for highway videos. These videos are recorded during the day time under various conditions such as clear, overcast, and raining weather. Many of these videos are difficult to classify due to their lousy illumination. For the sake of comparison, we use the whole frames of each input video to create a compact representation. In this experiment, we compare the performance of different techniques (AOF, FDS, and RDS) for obtaining compact representation. Then, we use pre-trained networks (VGG19, GoogleNet, ResNet101, and inceptionv3) to extract one feature vector from the compact representations. We compare the results of these networks to select the best CNN model. In each case, we build a separate classifier for classifying the traffic videos. SVM and k nearest neighbor (k-NN) classifiers, with $k = 5$, are used in this experiment. Table 1 shows the accuracy of each combination of AOF, FDS, and RDS and each of the CNN models for the SVM and k-NN classifiers. As shown in this table, the ResNet101 model gives the highest accuracies with all compact representations and classifiers. Also, accuracies obtained by the SVM classifier are higher than those obtained by the k-NN classifier.

From analyzing the results, we can conclude that the FDS and RDS features are more representative than the AOF feature. This is due to the FDS and RDS

Table 3. Confusion matrix when using FDS

		Predicted		
		Heavy	Medium	Light
GT	Heavy	41	3	0
	Medium	2	42	1
	Light	0	2	163

Table 4. Confusion matrix when using RDS

		Predicted		
		Heavy	Medium	Light
GT	Heavy	41	3	0
	Medium	6	37	2
	Light	0	1	164

Table 5. Confusion matrix when aggregating FDS and RDS

		Predicted		
		Heavy	Medium	Light
GT	Heavy	42	2	0
	Medium	2	42	1
	Light	0	1	164

represent both texture and motion features, however, the optical flow lacks the texture information.

Next, we perform a combination of different SVM classifiers based on their posteriors. Table 2 summarizes the results obtained by these combinations. We obtain the highest accuracy (97.64%) when using a combination of FDS and RDS with the ResNet101 model. Tables 3, 4, and 5 present the confusion matrices of FDS, RDS and FDS+RDS, respectively, when using ResNet101 as a feature extractor. As we can see in the confusion matrices, there are no miss-classified videos between light and heavy classes (no video with a light class is wrongly classified as a heavy class and vice versa). This is an excellent feature of the proposed system because, with many traffic congestion classification methods, heavy traffic videos in which vehicles are almost not moving, are wrongly classified as light traffic as the extracted features of non-moving vehicles are very similar to those of an empty road (i.e., light class). With a total of 254 videos, our system wrongly classifies 6 videos only.

Table 6 shows a comparison between the proposed system and the state-of-the-art methods: [6,14,17,18,22]. As shown the proposed system gives results better than the ones of compared methods.

Methods	Video frame samples		
	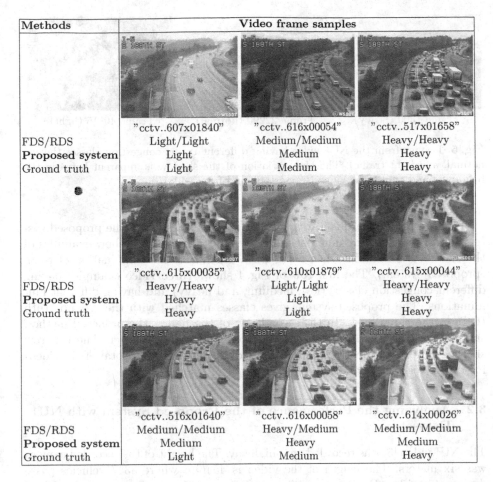		
	"cctv..607x01840"	"cctv..616x00054"	"cctv..517x01658"
FDS/RDS	Light/Light	Medium/Medium	Heavy/Heavy
Proposed system	Light	Medium	Heavy
Ground truth	Light	Medium	Heavy
	"cctv..615x00035"	"cctv..610x01879"	"cctv..615x00044"
FDS/RDS	Heavy/Heavy	Light/Light	Heavy/Heavy
Proposed system	Heavy	Light	Heavy
Ground truth	Heavy	Light	Heavy
	"cctv..516x01640"	"cctv..616x00058"	"cctv..614x00026"
FDS/RDS	Medium/Medium	Heavy/Medium	Medium/Medium
Proposed system	Medium	Heavy	Medium
Ground truth	Light	Medium	Heavy

Fig. 4. Results of the proposed system with the UCSD dataset under different illumination conditions.

Table 6. Comparison between the proposed method and the state-of-the-art methods with the UCSD dataset

Method	Accuracy (%)
Asmaa [6]	95.58
Riaz [17]	95.28
Luo [14]	96.90
Ribas [18]	96.06
Wang [22]	93.30
Proposed system	**97.64**

Frame 1500 (heavy)   Frame 22290 (normal)   Frame 40815 (light)

Fig. 5. Frames from the NU1 video having different traffic congestion classes (heavy, normal, and light traffic). The high variation of the shadow is apparent between the beginning and end of the video (frame 1500 and frame 40815).

Figure 4 presents a qualitative evaluation of the results of the proposed system with frames having different illumination conditions. We show examples of the classification results when using FDS, RDS, and the combination of them (proposed system). The first row of Fig. 4 shows three video examples having different congestion classes (low, medium, and heavy) and having different illuminations. The proposed system gives classes matched with the ground truth (GT) in the three cases. In the second row of the figure, the proposed method success to correctly classify videos captured under bad weather. The last row shows examples of incorrectly classified videos (three from a total of six videos incorrectly classified videos).

3.2 Analyzing the Performance of the Proposed System with NU1 Dataset

The NUI video [5] was recorded on a highway. The height of the recorded camera was six meters. The length of the video is 45 min, where 3337 vehicles passe during this video. During this video, traffic congestion is changed between low, normal, and heavy many times. Figure 5 presents three frames from this video, in which the large shadow variation is obvious between frames. Notably, this video manifests two main challenges to any traffic congestion classification method: (1) vehicles do not follow any lanes or fixed pattern, and (2) high variations of shadow and bad illumination exist on all frames.

With the NU1 video, we extract both FSD, and RDS features every $L-$frames $L = 15$. It is worth mentioning that we do not perform new training for the SVM models in this experiment. Instead, we use the SVM models already trained on the UCSD features (FDS and RDS). We perform the classification decision every $L-$frames to simulate an online situation. The extracted FDS and RDS features are fed to its SVM classifier every $L-$frames, and then the two classifier decisions are combined to obtain the final class label. As there is no traffic congestion ground truth for this video, we visually analyze samples of the obtained results. Figure 6 presents examples of classification results of the proposed system with the NU1 video, where each frame is the last frame of the input batch. We provide the traffic congestion results of each method (FDS, RDS, and the combined

Methods	Frame samples		
	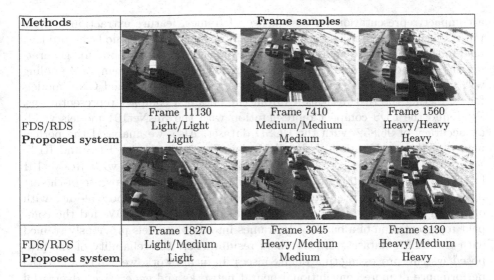		
FDS/RDS **Proposed system**	Frame 11130 Light/Light Light	Frame 7410 Medium/Medium Medium	Frame 1560 Heavy/Heavy Heavy
FDS/RDS **Proposed system**	Frame 18270 Light/Medium Light	Frame 3045 Heavy/Medium Medium	Frame 8130 Heavy/Medium Heavy

Fig. 6. Classification results of the proposed system with the NU1 video.

classifiers) under each example. This analysis demonstrates the reliability of the proposed system as it gives accurate traffic congestion classification results with models trained on videos of a different dataset (i.e., UCSD dataset).

3.3 Analyzing the Processing Time of the Proposed System

In our experiments, we used pre-trained CNN models. Thus here we show the inference time only of each step of the proposed system. With a batch of 15 frames, the average processing times for FDS creation, CNN feature extraction and SVM prediction are 105, 80, and 16 msec, respectively. The average processing time per frame is 13.4 msec. In the case of using the combination of FDS and RDS features, the processing time becomes 26.8 msec. All experiments were carried out on MATLAB 2019b with a CPU (i7 1.8 GHz) and a 16 GB RAM. This analysis demonstrates that the proposed system can classify the input sequences of frames in a short time, and thus it can be adopted for real-time applications.

It is worth noting that the proposed method can be implemented as an end-to-end system by combining the feature extraction and classification in one network instead of using a separable SVM classifier. However, such a system needs a large congestion traffic dataset to be trained which are currently hardly available.

4   Conclusion

In this paper, we have proposed a robust automated system for the classification of traffic congestion. The system includes three main steps: the generation of a compact representation for a sequence of frames, feature extraction using a pre-trained deep neural network, and classification of input traffic level into low, medium, or heavy. We analyzed the performance of two methods for generating the compact representation: optical flow aggregation and temporal pooling with its two directions (FDS and RDS), and various pre-trained CNN models for extracting the texture features from the obtained compact representations. We found the FDS compact representation with the ResNet101 models yields an accuracy of 96.85% with the UCSD dataset. Also, we analyzed the performance of the combination of the SVM classifiers trained with FDS and RDS, separately. We found that the combination of FDS and RDS with ResNet101 features yields an accuracy of 97.64%, which is higher than the state-of-the-art methods. Besides, we evaluated the proposed system for the possible use with online applications by utilizing the long video NU1 (45 min). We fed the compact representation of a batch of 15 frames into SVM models previously trained with the UCSD dataset. The obtained results assert the reliability of the proposed system (processing time of 26.8 msec). In future work, we will evaluate the performance of more convolutional neural networks and generative adversarial networks to improve the classification results.

References

1. Abdelwahab, M.A.: Fast approach for efficient vehicle counting. Electron. Lett. **55**(1), 20–22 (2019)
2. Abdelwahab, M.A., Abdelwahab, M.M.: Human action recognition and analysis algorithm for fixed and moving cameras. Electron. Lett. **51**(23), 1869–1871 (2015)
3. Abdelwahab, M.A.: Accurate vehicle counting approach based on deep neural networks. In: 2019 International Conference on Innovative Trends in Computer Engineering (ITCE), pp. 1–5. IEEE (2019)
4. Abdelwahab, M.A., Abdelwahab, M.M.: A novel algorithm for vehicle detection and tracking in airborne videos. In: IEEE International Symposium on Multimedia (ISM), pp. 65–68 (2015)
5. Aly, S.A., Mamdouh, A., Abdelwahab, M.: Vehicles detection and tracking in videos for very crowded scenes. In: MVA, pp. 311–314 (2013)
6. Asmaa, O., Mokhtar, K., Abdelaziz, O.: Road traffic density estimation using microscopic and macroscopic parameters. Image Vis. Comput. **31**(11), 887–894 (2013)
7. Chan, A.B., Vasconcelos, N.: Classification and retrieval of traffic video using autoregressive stochastic processes. In: Intelligent Vehicles Symposium, 2005. Proceedings. IEEE, pp. 771–776. IEEE (2005)
8. Datondji, S.R.E., Dupuis, Y., Subirats, P., Vasseur, P.: A survey of vision-based traffic monitoring of road intersections. IEEE Trans. Intell. Transp. Syst. **17**(10), 2681–2698 (2016)
9. Fernando, B., Gavves, E., Oramas, J., Ghodrati, A., Tuytelaars, T.: Rank pooling for action recognition. IEEE Trans. Pattern Anal. Mach. Intell. **39**(4), 773–787 (2016)
10. He, K., Zhang, X., Ren, S., Sun, J.: Deep residual learning for image recognition. In: Proceedings of the IEEE Conference on Computer Vision and Pattern Recognition, pp. 770–778 (2016)

11. Huang, L., Barth, M.: Real-time multi-vehicle tracking based on feature detection and color probability model. In: 2010 IEEE Intelligent Vehicles Symposium, pp. 981–986. IEEE (2010)
12. Kim, J., Lee, C.W., Lee, K., Yun, T., Kim, H.: Wavelet-based vehicle tracking for automatic traffic surveillance. In: Proceedings of IEEE Region 10 International Conference on Electrical and Electronic Technology. TENCON 2001 (Cat. No. 01CH37239), vol. 1, pp. 313–316. IEEE (2001)
13. Liu, T.Y., et al.: Learning to rank for information retrieval. Found. Trends® Inf. Retriev. 3(3), 225–331 (2009)
14. Luo, Z., Jodoin, P.M., Li, S.Z., Su, S.Z.: Traffic analysis without motion features. In: 2015 IEEE International Conference on Image Processing (ICIP), pp. 3290–3294. IEEE (2015)
15. Mo, G., Zhang, S.: Vehicles detection in traffic flow. In: 2010 Sixth International Conference on Natural Computation, vol. 2, pp. 751–754. IEEE (2010)
16. Porikli, F., Li, X.: Traffic congestion estimation using HMM models without vehicle tracking. In: Intelligent Vehicles Symposium, 2004 IEEE, pp. 188–193. IEEE (2004)
17. Riaz, A., Khan, S.A.: Traffic congestion classification using motion vector statistical features. In: Sixth International Conference on Machine Vision (ICMV 2013), vol. 9067, p. 90671A. International Society for Optics and Photonics (2013)
18. Ribas, L.C., Goncalves, W.N., Bruno, O.M.: Dynamic texture analysis with diffusion in networks (2018). arXiv preprint arXiv:1806.10681
19. Simonyan, K., Zisserman, A.: Very deep convolutional networks for large-scale image recognition (2014). arXiv preprint arXiv:1409.1556
20. Szegedy, C., et al.: Going deeper with convolutions. In: Proceedings of the IEEE Conference on Computer Vision and Pattern Recognition, pp. 1–9 (2015)
21. Szegedy, C., Vanhoucke, V., Ioffe, S., Shlens, J., Wojna, Z.: Rethinking the inception architecture for computer vision. In: Proceedings of the IEEE Conference on Computer Vision and Pattern Recognition, pp. 2818–2826 (2016)
22. Wang, Y., Wang, L., Kong, D., Yin, B.: Extrinsic least squares regression with closed-form solution on product grassmann manifold for video-based recognition. Math. Probl. Eng. 2018 (2018)
23. Yang, H., Qu, S.: Real-time vehicle detection and counting in complex traffic scenes using background subtraction model with low-rank decomposition. IET Intell. Transp. Syst. 12(1), 75–85 (2017)

Early Wildfire Detection Using Convolutional Neural Network

Seon Ho Oh[1]⬥, Sang Won Ghyme[1], Soon Ki Jung[2]⬥, and Geon-Woo Kim[1](✉)

[1] Electronics and Telecommunications Research Institute, Daejon, Republic of Korea
{seonho,ghyme,kimgw}@etri.re.kr
[2] School of Computer Science and Engineering, Kyungpook National University,
Daegu, Republic of Korea
skjung@knu.ac.kr

Abstract. Wildfires are one of the disasters that are difficult to detect early and cause significant damage to human life, ecological systems, and infrastructure. There have been several research attempts to detect wildfires based on convolutional neural networks (CNNs) in video surveillance systems. However, most of these methods only focus on flame detection, thus they are still not sufficient to prevent loss of life and reduce economic and material damage. To tackle this issue, we present a deep learning-based method for detecting wildfires at an early stage by identifying flames and smokes at once. To realize the proposed idea, a large dataset for wildfire is acquired from the web. A light-weight yet powerful architecture is adopted to balance efficiency and accuracy. And focal loss is utilized to deal with the imbalance issue between classes. Experimental results demonstrate the effectiveness of the proposed method and validate its suitability for early wildfire detection in a video surveillance system.

Keywords: Early wildfire detection · Video surveillance · Deep learning

1 Introduction

Wildfire is a global problem causing devastating damage every year [24]. According to the National Interagency Fire Center (NIFC), 46,706 wildfires occurred between January 1 and November 22, 2019, burning about 4.6 million acres [8]. However, existing fire detection studies focused on flame detection can only work after the fire has spread over a large area. And it makes the control of the fire difficult or sometimes impossible to stop in time. As a result, wildfires can cause catastrophic damage to the atmosphere and the environment. Another problem

This work was supported by Institute for Information & communications Technology Promotion (IITP) grant funded by Korea government (MSIT) (No. 2019-0-00203, Development of Predictive Visual Security Technology for Preemptive Threat Response).

ⓒ Springer Nature Singapore Pte Ltd. 2020
W. Ohyama and S. K. Jung (Eds.): IW-FCV 2020, CCIS 1212, pp. 18–30, 2020.
https://doi.org/10.1007/978-981-15-4818-5_2

caused by wildfires is a long-term disaster, such as impacts on local weather patterns, global warming, and extinction of rare species of the flora and fauna. Therefore, developing an effective method to detect wildfire at an early stage is very important.

Most early studies attempted to explorer color, texture, shape, and motion features for fire detection. For instance, Chen et al. [1] proposed a decision rule-assisted fire detection method that examines the dynamic behavior and irregularity of flame in both RGB and HSI color spaces. Later works considered machine learning-based classification approaches such as support vector machine (SVM) [11] or neural networks [2,26]. Chenebert et al. [2] presented a shallow neural network classifier using the color-texture feature. Recently, Foggia et al. [4] introduced a multi-expert framework that combines shape, color, and motion properties.

Thanks to the recent advances of deep learning, further developments based on the CNNs now perform more robustly compared to earlier works. For instance, Sharma et al. [19] used well-known CNN architectures such as VGG16 [20] and ResNet [6]. And Muhammad et al. [14] adopted other architectures like AlexNet [12] and Inception [21] architectures to detect flame more efficiently and robustly. There was also an attempts to design dedicated architectures for fire detection. Namozov and Cho [15] presented a VGG16 based novel deep convolutional neural network, and an effective training strategy on a limited number of images by increasing the number of training images using a Generative Adversarial Networks (GAN) [5] and data augmentation techniques. Meanwhile, Jadon et al. [9] proposed a light-weight neural network that ensures real-time inference on low-powered devices such as Raspberry Pi.

In this work, we present a method for detecting wildfires at the early stage using deep CNNs. Due to the lack of data that meets the scale and diversity, we collect a large dataset including smokes, flames, etc. Also, we use a light-weight yet powerful architecture to balances efficiency and accuracy. And, to overcome the class imbalance issues, we also use Focal loss [13]. Finally, our experiments demonstrate that the effectiveness of the proposed method and suitability for early wildfire detection in a video surveillance system.

The rest of the paper is organized as follows. The next section describes the collection of dataset for detecting wildfires at an early stage. In Sect. 3, we present our method for early wildfire detection in surveillance video. Experimental results and discussion are given in Sect. 4. Conclusion and future work are given in Sect. 5.

2   Dataset Collection

Since the dataset previously used for fire detection only considers flame or smoke, there exists a potential to cause many errors in real-world video surveillance environments. Another problem is that the scale and diversity of the datasets previously used for wildfire detection are limited, which is insufficient to train deep CNNs. To address this issue, we collect a large set of data containing initial smoke or flame on the rural areas for early wildfire detection. Also, to take complexities and ambiguities on real-world video surveillance environment into consideration when collecting data for wildfire, we include not only smokes and flames but also subjects having visual similarities such as clouds, fogs, snows, waves, waterfalls, etc. More specifically, in order to detect wildfire in an early stage, we first separated flame or smoke-like things having particles and others like solid, however, there are a variety of things like clouds, fog, waterfalls, waves, snow, and flock of birds, which has a flame or smoke-like feature, so it was a necessity to distinguish between them. Moreover, since fires can occur not only natural objects such as mountains adjacent to the coast, lakesides but also man-made structures such as ski slope, town border (rural), all of these places should be considered. Therefore, we summarized the dataset into three groups: solid (rural), smoke or flame, and smoke-like objects having particles. Then we categorized the dataset into six classes such as cloud, snow, rural, fire, wave, and waterfall. Further details to determine the dataset categories are discussed later.

Rest of this section, we present a multi-stage strategy to collect a large early wildfire detection dataset including: how candidate images were collected; and how the dataset was cleaned up both automatically and manually. Table 1 summarizes each stages and corresponding statistics. Individual stages are discussed in detail in the following paragraphs.

Table 1. Dataset statistics after each stage of processing.

Stage	Description	# images
1	Automatic image crawling	152,996
2	Automatic and manual cleanup	16,410
3	Final patch and class labeling	14,741

2.1 Automatic Image Crawling

Images could be easily collected from an image search site. An image crawling tool helps to collect images automatically from such sites. Here the image crawling tools were very useful, and most tools supported common image search engines such as Google, Bing, and Baidu. With such a tool, all we have to do is finding proper keywords. An image crawling tool collects only several hundred images for each keyword. Therefore a lot of keywords are required. For instance, keywords such as bushfire, forest fire, wildfire, etc. were selected for the 'fire' class. To obtain more images, we used keywords from various languages, including English, Korean, Chinese, and Japanese. A total of 101 keywords were selected for all classes and finally 152,996 images were collected.

Fig. 1. Examples of images for test set. From the left, each column shows images corresponding to cloud, snow, rural, fire, wave, and waterfall.

2.2 Automatic and Manual Cleanup

Although a large number of images were collected at the first stage, most of the images were not related to our problem. For example, most images from the keyword 'wave' were related to hair-style. Therefore it is required for removing irrelevant images manually. After removal, only 18,929 images were left alive.

Another problem was exact or near duplication between images. It has been observed that exact duplication due to the same images being found at different locations, or near duplications caused by geometric transformations such as mirror, rotation, cropping, or color adjustments and JPEG artifacts. Most image duplicates can be removed automatically with a duplicate removing tool, and finally, only 16,410 images were survived.

At this point, two types of issues may still remain; first, some images are too small to use; and second, some classes have an insufficient number of images compared to others. Thus, we filtered out all images having a smaller resolution than 300 × 300 pixels. And classes with fewer than 200 images were discarded. In addition, some classes like 'fog' that are difficult to distinguish from others were removed. As a result, a total of 13,051 images of six classes remained.

2.3   Final Patch and Class Labeling

In this stage, part of the image was manually labeled with a specific class. To this end, we used the image labeling tool. One image can have one or more patches, and patches can be mapped into different classes even if they are obtained from the same image. All patches cropped from images are resized with a regular size of 512 × 512 pixels. Finally, our dataset consists of a total of 14,741 patches in six classes including cloud, snow, rural, fire, wave, and waterfall.

Table 2 summarizes the number of images in each class. Figure 1 shows examples of images for each class of clouds, snows, rural, fires, waves, waterfalls. The 'rural' class contains images of mountains, seas, lakes, rivers, etc. And the 'fire' class consists of images of the flame and smoke in rural areas.

Table 2. Dataset statistics summary.

Class	Cloud	Snow	Rural	Fire	Wave	Waterfall	Total
# images	2,503	605	6,832	1,901	1,888	1,012	14,741

3   Proposed Framework

In this section, we will describe the selection of network architecture suitable for a video surveillance systems, and present our training strategy in detail.

3.1   Network Architecture Selection

Current state of the art CNN models, such as AlexNet [12], VGG16 [20], Inception [21], and ResNet [6] have been adjusted and demonstrated promising performance in numerous computer vision issues and applications, such as object detection, image segmentation, super-resolution, and classification. However, these deep CNN models are not suitable for real-time wildfire detection in a video surveillance system due to their computational costs and resource requirements.

Recently, Tan and Le introduced EfficientNet [23]. They systematically studied the impact of scaling different dimensions of the model and presented a family of models called EfficientNet which improve overall performance while balancing all dimensions of the network – width, depth, and image resolution. Surprisingly, these models offer significant gains for speed and resource efficiency. Especially, their baseline model, EfficientNet-B0, allows real-time inference on a low-powered device such as Raspberry Pi. Thus we adopt EfficientNet-B0 as our baseline network architecture. Table 3 illustrates EfficientNet-B0 as our baseline network structure. The mobile inverted bottleneck convolution called MBConv [17,22] is the main building block for EfficientNet. In EfficientNet's MBConv, direct shortcuts between the bottlenecks that connect much fewer channels compared to the expansion layer of the residual block [6] and combined depthwise separable convolution effectively reduce computation by a factor of spatial resolution, and squeeze-and-excitation optimization [7] was also added.

Table 3. Network architecture: EfficientNet-B0 [23].

Stage	Operator	Input resolution	Output channels	# layers
1	Conv (3 × 3)	224 × 224	32	1
2	MBConv (3 × 3)	112 × 112	16	1
3	MBConv (3 × 3)	112 × 112	24	2
4	MBConv (5 × 5)	56 × 56	40	2
5	MBConv (3 × 3)	28 × 28	80	3
6	MBConv (5 × 5)	14 × 14	112	3
7	MBConv (5 × 5)	14 × 14	192	4
8	MBConv (3 × 3)	7 × 7	320	1
9	Conv (1 × 1) & Pooling & FC	7 × 7	1280	1

3.2 Class Imbalance

The fire detection dataset has an inherent imbalance due to its rarity. Such class imbalance causes two problems: Training is inefficient as most samples are non-fire that contribute no useful learning signal; The non-fire samples can overwhelm training and lead to degenerate models.

To address the inherent class imbalance issue, we use Focal loss [13]. The focal loss is designed to resolve the class imbalance problem by weighting the contribution of easy example smaller even if their number is large. As a result, it focuses on training a sparse set of hard examples.

The original focal loss for binary classification defined as:

$$\text{FL}(p_t) = -(1 - p_t)^\gamma \log(p_t), \tag{1}$$

where

$$p_t = \begin{cases} p & \text{if } y = 1 \\ 1 - p & \text{otherwise,} \end{cases} \tag{2}$$

and $p \in [0, 1]$ is model's estimated probability for the class with label $y = 1$. Based on this, we can rewrite the multi-class form as:

$$\text{FL}(p_t) = -\sum_{i=1}^{C} (1 - p_t(i))^\gamma \log(p_t(i)), \tag{3}$$

and

$$p_t(i) = \begin{cases} p & \text{if } y = i \\ 1 - p & \text{otherwise,} \end{cases} \tag{4}$$

where C is the number of classes. The focusing parameter γ was set to 2.0 in our experiment.

3.3 Training

We used a 7:1:2 split between the training, validation and test sets. And stratified sampling was used to partitioning the dataset so that each set had evenly balanced classes. In order to increase the diversity in our train dataset, we used image augmentations such as random cropping, resizing, and flipping. Random cropping produces a patch having a random size $\in [0.08, 1.0]$ and random aspect ratio $\in [3/4, 4/3]$ of the original image. This patch is resized to 224×224 and finally flipped horizontally at random.

We train and fine-tuned ImageNet [3] pre-trained neural network model using a transfer learning strategy. Instead of fine-tuning only the last layer of the neural network, we trained all the layers using different learning rates. The learning rate for pre-trained convolutional layers was set to a factor of 0.1 than of the last dense layers. For regularization, we used dropout between convolutional layers and dense layers with probability of 0.2.

Our model was trained using the Adam optimizer [10] with β_1 0.9 and β_2 0.99; weight decay 1e−4; initial learning rate 0.001. The learning rate was decayed by a factor of 0.1 every 30 epochs. The batch size and total epochs were set to 256 and 90, respectively.

3.4 Implementation Details

The proposed method was implemented with PyTorch [16]. And the neural network trained and evaluated on a workstation equipped with Intel Core i7-6950X 3.0 GHz CPU, 128 GB memory, and two NVIDIA GeForce GTX 1080 GPUs.

4 Experimental Results and Discussion

In this section, we will first evaluate our model on multi-class classification and binary wildfire detection. Additionally, we also describe how to extend patch classification to frame-level detection.

4.1 Multi-class Classification

The primary multi-class classification accuracies on the validation and test sets are 99.46% and 98.58%, respectively. Figure 2 draws the normalized confusion matrix for each class. As can be seen in Fig. 2, the model trained achieved higher and balanced accuracy for individual classes. This means that focal loss effectively alleviated class imbalance by increasing loss contribution from hard examples.

4.2 Binary Projection

For the binary wildfire detection, we projected multi-class classification into binary classification, either fire or non-fire. The validation set is composed of

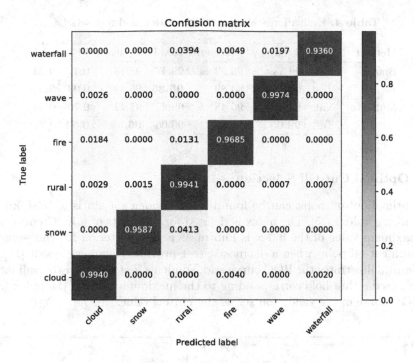

Fig. 2. Confusion matrix on test set.

190 fire images and 1,284 non-fire images, so a total of 1,474 images. And the test set consists of 381 positive images and 2,570 negative images, so 2,951 images in total.

To determine either fire or non-fire, a cut-off threshold obtained from receiver operating characteristic (ROC) analysis in the validation set is adopted. The details of finding the optimum cut-off point will be discussed next subsection.

Table 4 shows evaluation statistics for validation and test sets. We have used six different metrics (accuracy, precision, recall, F_1-score, FPR, and FNR) in order to present a complete and reliable analysis. The FPR and FNR denote false positive rate and false negative rate, respectively. As can be seen in Table 4, the results obtained for each metric is encouraging. It is also noted that the result gives balanced FPR and FNR since the cut-off threshold adopted from the Youden's index.

To investigate the effectiveness of the binary projection, we also compared binary fire vs non-fire classifier. The 'binary' and 'multi-proj.' represent simple binary classification and multi-class classification with binary projection, respectively. As shown in the test set metrics, although binary classification gives better validation set performance, however, our binary projection following the multi-class classification provided better generalization performance.

Table 4. Evaluation statistics on validation and test sets (%)

Method	Split	Accuracy	Precision	Recall	F_1-score	FPR	FNR
Binary	Val.	99.53	96.92	99.47	98.18	0.47	0.53
	Test	98.78	93.89	**96.85**	95.35	0.93	**3.15**
Mult-proj.	Val.	99.32	95.45	99.47	97.42	0.70	0.53
	Test	**99.05**	**96.57**	96.06	**96.32**	**0.51**	3.94

4.3   Optimal Cut-Off Selection

The optimal cut-off point can be found from Youden's J statistic (also known as Youden's index) [25]. The index is defined for all points of a ROC curve, and the maximum value of the index is known as a good criterion for choosing the optimum cut-off point when a diagnostic test provides a numeric result [18].

Figure 3 illustrates the ROC curve and Youden's J statistic on the validation set. We used a threshold corresponding to the maximum value of the index from the ROC curve of the validation set as the cut-off value.

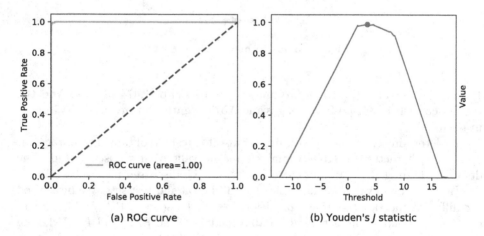

(a) ROC curve   (b) Youden's J statistic

Fig. 3. Receiver operating characteristic curve (a) and Youden's J statistic on validation set (b). The red dot on (b) denotes the optimal cut-off threshold point for the validation set. (Color figure online)

4.4   Patch Classification to Frame-Level Detection

Conventional CNNs only take a fixed-sized image patch, for instance, 224×224, as an input. In order to accept variable-sized images as input, therefore, additional modification is required. Inspired by Class Activation Map [27], thus,

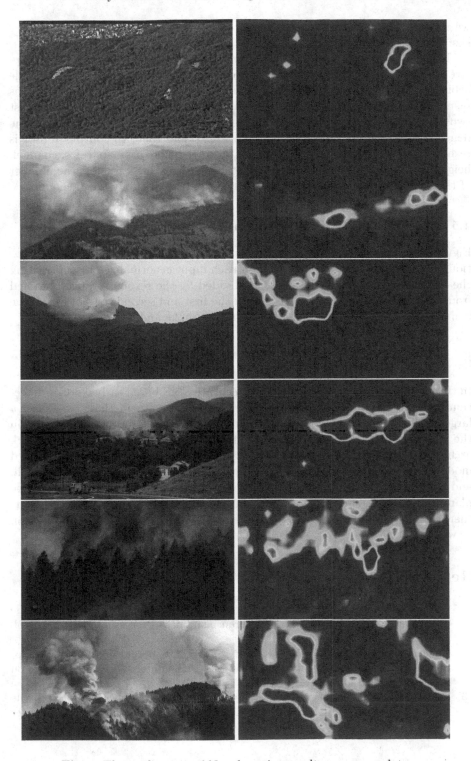

Fig. 4. The qualitative wildfire detection results on unseen data.

we modified the last two layers of the trained model to handling the arbitrary size inputs.

In order to keep all responses from previous layers, first we removed the adaptive average pooling layer. Then we performed the following processes to handle arbitrary-sized tensor in the dense layer First, (B, C, H, W) tensor generated as result of the average pooling layer is reshaped to $(B, C, H \times W)$. Then, the last two axes of the tensor are swapped and reshaped as $(B \times H \times W, C)$. Finally, the dense layer is applied to $(B \times H \times W, 6)$ tensor and then, the output tensor is reshaped into $(B, H, W, 6)$. Here B, C, H, and W denote the batch size, channel, height, and width for feature map. Since the last dense layer reduces the number of the channel for the feature map to 6, the result tensor only has 6 channels.

4.5   Qualitative Wildfire Detection Results on Unseen Data

Figure 4 illustrates the frame-level wildfire detection results using Class Activation Map [27]. Note that the response for each input is normalized by subtracting the optimal cut-off threshold and then divided by the response range obtained from the validation set. As can be seen in the first and second rows of Fig. 4, the trained model successfully detected the initial smoke and flame of wildfire.

5   Conclusions

In this work, we present an efficient and accurate CNN based early wildfire detection methods for video surveillance system. To realize our method, we collect a large dataset for early wildfire detection under the consideration of ambiguity in the real-world video surveillance environments. By adopting an efficient network architecture and sophisticate training strategy, we demonstrate that the learned model not only encouraging in performance in terms of accuracy, precision, recall, and F_1-score but also suitable for a video surveillance system. As future work, we plan to improve the performance of the model even a more diverse dataset. Furthermore, we plan to extend our work to early wildfire detection and localization as well.

References

1. Chen, T.H., Wu, P.H., Chiou, Y.C.: An early fire-detection method based on image processing. In: 2004 International Conference on Image Processing, ICIP 2004, vol. 3, pp. 1707–1710. IEEE (2004)
2. Chenebert, A., Breckon, T.P., Gaszczak, A.: A non-temporal texture driven approach to real-time fire detection. In: 2011 18th IEEE International Conference on Image Processing, pp. 1741–1744. IEEE (2011)
3. Deng, J., Dong, W., Socher, R., Li, L.J., Li, K., Fei-Fei, L.: ImageNet: a large-scale hierarchical image database. In: Proceedings of the IEEE Conference on Computer Vision and Pattern Recognition (2009)

4. Foggia, P., Saggese, A., Vento, M.: Real-time fire detection for video-surveillance applications using a combination of experts based on color, shape, and motion. IEEE Trans. Circuits Syst. Video Technol. **25**(9), 1545–1556 (2015)
5. Goodfellow, I., et al.: Generative adversarial nets. In: Advances in Neural Information Processing Systems, pp. 2672–2680 (2014)
6. He, K., Zhang, X., Ren, S., Sun, J.: Deep residual learning for image recognition. In: Proceedings of the IEEE Conference on Computer Vision and Pattern Recognition, pp. 770–778 (2016)
7. Hu, J., Shen, L., Sun, G.: Squeeze-and-excitation networks. In: Proceedings of the IEEE Conference on Computer Vision and Pattern Recognition, pp. 7132–7141 (2018)
8. Insurance Information Institute, Inc.: Facts + statistics: Wildfires (2019). https://www.iii.org/fact-statistic/facts-statistics-wildfires. Accessed 9 Dec 2019
9. Jadon, A., Omama, M., Varshney, A., Ansari, M.S., Sharma, R.: FireNet: a specialized lightweight fire & smoke detection model for real-time IoT applications. arXiv preprint arXiv:1905.11922 (2019)
10. Kingma, D.P., Ba, J.: Adam: a method for stochastic optimization. arXiv preprint arXiv:1412.6980 (2014)
11. Ko, B.C., Cheong, K.H., Nam, J.Y.: Fire detection based on vision sensor and support vector machines. Fire Saf. J. **44**(3), 322–329 (2009)
12. Krizhevsky, A., Sutskever, I., Hinton, G.E.: ImageNet classification with deep convolutional neural networks. In: Advances in Neural Information Processing Systems, pp. 1097–1105 (2012)
13. Lin, T.Y., Goyal, P., Girshick, R., He, K., Dollár, P.: Focal loss for dense object detection. In: Proceedings of the IEEE International Conference on Computer Vision, pp. 2980–2988 (2017)
14. Muhammad, K., Ahmad, J., Mehmood, I., Rho, S., Baik, S.W.: Convolutional neural networks based fire detection in surveillance videos. IEEE Access **6**, 18174–18183 (2018)
15. Namozov, A., Cho, Y.: An efficient deep learning algorithm for fire and smoke detection with limited data. Adv. Electr. Comput. Eng. **18**, 121–128 (2018). https://doi.org/10.4316/AECE.2018.04015
16. Paszke, A., et al.: PyTorch: an imperative style, high-performance deep learning library. In: Wallach, H., Larochelle, H., Beygelzimer, A., d'Alché-Buc, F., Fox, E., Garnett, R. (eds.) Advances in Neural Information Processing Systems 32, pp. 8024–8035. Curran Associates, Inc. (2019)
17. Sandler, M., Howard, A., Zhu, M., Zhmoginov, A., Chen, L.C.: MobileNetV 2: inverted residuals and linear bottlenecks. In: Proceedings of the IEEE Conference on Computer Vision and Pattern Recognition, pp. 4510–4520 (2018)
18. Schisterman, E.F., Perkins, N.J., Liu, A., Bondell, H.: Optimal cut-point and its corresponding Youden index to discriminate individuals using pooled blood samples. Epidemiology, 73–81 (2005)
19. Sharma, J., Granmo, O.-C., Goodwin, M., Fidje, J.T.: Deep convolutional neural networks for fire detection in images. In: Boracchi, G., Iliadis, L., Jayne, C., Likas, A. (eds.) EANN 2017. CCIS, vol. 744, pp. 183–193. Springer, Cham (2017). https://doi.org/10.1007/978-3-319-65172-9_16
20. Simonyan, K., Zisserman, A.: Very deep convolutional networks for large-scale image recognition. arXiv preprint arXiv:1409.1556 (2014)
21. Szegedy, C., et al.: Going deeper with convolutions. In: Proceedings of the IEEE Conference on Computer Vision and Pattern Recognition, pp. 1–9 (2015)

22. Tan, M., et al.: MnasNet: platform-aware neural architecture search for mobile. In: Proceedings of the IEEE Conference on Computer Vision and Pattern Recognition, pp. 2820–2828 (2019)

23. Tan, M., Le, Q.V.: EfficientNet: rethinking model scaling for convolutional neural networks. arXiv preprint arXiv:1905.11946 (2019)

24. Wikipedia: List of wildfires – Wikipedia, the free encyclopedia (2019).. https://en.wikipedia.org/wiki/List_of_wildfires. Accessed 9 Dec 2019

25. Youden, W.J.: Index for rating diagnostic tests. Cancer **3**(1), 32–35 (1950)

26. Zhang, D., et al.: Image based forest fire detection using dynamic characteristics with artificial neural networks. In: 2009 International Joint Conference on Artificial Intelligence, pp. 290–293. IEEE (2009)

27. Zhou, B., Khosla, A., Lapedriza, A., Oliva, A., Torralba, A.: Learning deep features for discriminative localization. In: Proceedings of the IEEE Conference on Computer Vision and Pattern Recognition, pp. 2921–2929 (2016)

Deep Matting for AR Based Interior Design

Maryam Sultana⬛, In Su Kim, and Soon Ki Jung$^{(\boxtimes)}$⬛

Kyungpook National University, Daegu, South Korea
`maryam@vr.knu.ac.kr, kiminsu69@gmail.com, skjung@knu.ac.kr`

Abstract. In the applications of interior and architectural design, there are various tasks range from ensuring desired floor colors/textures plans, to deciding furnishing arrangement styles: all depending upon the choices of designers themselves. Thus in this modern era of artificial intelligence, computer vision based applications are very popular. Many research studies have been conducted to address different interior design applications using virtual reality technology. However, VR based applications do not provide a realistic experience to the user for interior design. Therefore in this study, we present an Augmented Reality (AR) based end-to-end systematic approach for interior design initialized by deep matting of an indoor scene. In our proposed application, the user has the authority to choose various colors/textures to change the interior of the region of interest in an indoor environment. Our proposed application has different modules working jointly for efficient interactive interior design. It allows the user to select its region of interest (wall or floor) and then give options to choose a color/texture to map on ROI for interior design experience. The final results of our proposed approach give realistic experience to the users as we estimate the global illumination changes on the ROI in our joint modules. Hence in this way, our presented interactive interior design application is user-friendly and works efficiently with realistic looking outputs.

Keywords: Interior design · Deep object segmentation · Illumination estimation · Deep Alpha-Matting

1 Introduction

Augmented reality based interior design is also known as Interactive Interior Design (IID) and it refers to the interior of the indoor scenes with different decors in a generalized standpoint. The application of IID is quite interesting as it works on the choice of users/humans creatively. Its been over a decade since many interesting research studies have been conducted on IID application [1,7,14]. The most conventional techniques for IID are virtual reality based, working by placing artificial/virtual objects in real environments is an effective way for users to participate in IID [8,13,15]. Phan *et al.* [15] proposed a technique for the IID application based on augmented reality. The proposed method

© Springer Nature Singapore Pte Ltd. 2020
W. Ohyama and S. K. Jung (Eds.): IW-FCV 2020, CCIS 1212, pp. 31–42, 2020.
https://doi.org/10.1007/978-981-15-4818-5_3

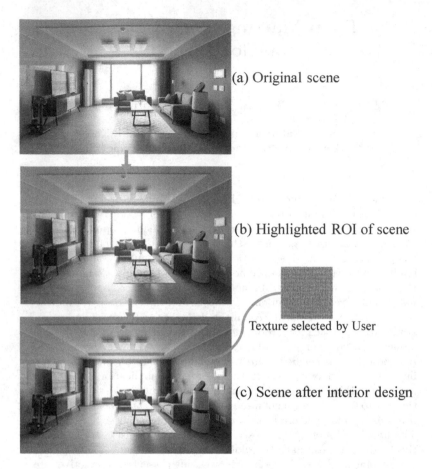

(a) Original scene

(b) Highlighted ROI of scene

Texture selected by User

(c) Scene after interior design

Fig. 1. IID example (a) Original scene, (b) Highlighted ROI with blue color which is a wall in the given scene (c) Scene after user selected wallpaper texture. (Color figure online)

is novel in the context of applying augmented reality to IID application in which user can visualize artificial/virtual furniture in a 3D environment with a flexible interface. Moreover, in this method, the properties of the virtual objects are updated using occlusion-based interaction method for Tangible augmented reality. However, despite the good performance in real-time environments, augmented reality based IID methods with virtual objects placement do not have real experience for the user. From human perception, it is more pleasant to experience the application of IID with real objects or color/texture changes in different indoor scenes.

IID application has a variety of aspects with different modules like wallpaper changing, floor matting, decor addition or placement, furniture setting or color change of frames on windows. The Fig. 1 (dataset Source *2Hae Lifestyle*[1]) shows an example of an indoor scene in which user has selected the texture of the wall to experience a realistic environment IID rather than playing with artificial or virtual objects.

In this proposed method, We aim to integrate an application of IID where user can select the options given by the proposed system to change wallpapers and floor matting in an indoor scene with various colors and textures in a user-friendly way. The main characteristics of our proposed study for the application of IID in real scenes are summarized as follows:

- Our proposed IID system is efficient and effective in a user-friendly way, facilitating the users to do interior design without any complexity.
- The final output of our AR system is realistic rather than virtual/artificial objects placement as in the case of virtual reality based methods.
- For realistic output, we have incorporated the global illumination effects in given indoor scenes which are mapped accordingly on the new interior design selected by the user interactively.
- Our proposed system is a fusion of different modules based on classical and deep learning based methods for realistic IID experience.

The rest of the paper is arranged as follows: Sect. 2 introduces previous research studies on IID. In Sect. 3 we briefly discusses about our proposed system based on different modules, while Sect. 4 contains experimental evaluations. We have concluded our proposed system discussion in Sect. 5.

2   Related Work

Many extensive studies have been conducted on IID application over the past few years [1,2,17,20]. Recently an interesting technique has been proposed in the literature for the application of IID using diminished reality [17]. The novel proposed method works by exploiting an inpainting method performing best even if there is no prior knowledge of the textures of the background objects subjected to be diminished. The inpainting process in this proposed method has an additional capacity to handle the illumination variations on the given input information resulting in realistic outputs for indoor scenes for IID application. Another interesting method is also proposed in the literature for IID application using Convolutional Neural Networks (CNN) [1]. The proposed technique is an embedded architecture learned for the purpose of visual search in the application of IID. This embedded architecture has two domains of product sample images; the first one has cropped given data from various scenes taken, however, the second one contains their iconic form. The main benefit of the multi-domain embedding architecture is that it is useful in various applications of visual search for instance identification of different products in scenes with similar given data. The model of embedding works on CNN architecture trained using a pair of

---

[1] http://mrgongan.2hae.net/.

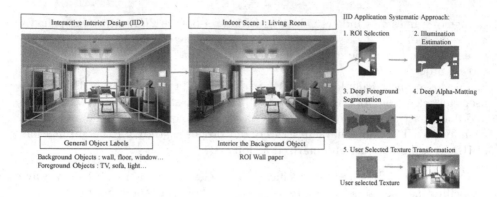

Fig. 2. Systematic overview of our proposed Interactive interior design application. The qualitative evaluation is done on custom dataset provided by *2Hae Lifestyle* as mentioned in Sect. 1.

given image samples. The visual search in this method demonstrated that best results can be obtained for searching multiple visual domains within the model, thus it enables new applications in the domain of IID.

3 Proposed Methodology

Our Proposed IID system works on the fusion various modules shown in Fig. 2. The details of each module is discussed in the following sections:

3.1 ROI Selection

We have designed an IID application where the user has the authority to change the interior of an indoor scene. For instance, in the living room scene layout, the user selects ROI by detecting four points on the regions like walls or floor matting in the indoor scene layout as shown in Fig. 2.

3.2 Handling Illumination Changes

Since the goal of our proposed IID system is to achieve realistic interior design effects in indoor scenes therefore we need to estimate varying illumination changes. To estimate illumination effects and get color consistency we have adopted *CIE-Lab* [11] method. The error function in *CIE-Lab* method provides a significant difference between two different colors in a uniform way with a perceptual approximation. Illumination variation affects the color consistency of the semantics in the indoor scene, hence *CIE-Lab* will estimate the illumination changes from the given input ROI sample. This technique will compute the light intensities of the manually selected ROI from an indoor scene via color system. Once we get the precise knowledge of the scene illumination changes, the given ROI image sample is then corrected to create the color consistency of the indoor scene light resulting in color constant of the given ROI image sample.

3.3   Deep Foreground/Background Objects Segmentation

In this module of our proposed IID application, we aim to segment foreground and background objects by exploiting an efficient semantic segmentation technique known as 'DeepLabv3+' [3]. This method works on the basis of atrous convolution which effectively expands the field of view of CNN filters results in capturing multi-scale context, in the domains of spatial pyramid pooling as well as cascaded modules. DeepLabv3+ architecture is based on atrous convolution with various batch normalization layers and rates that are important for training. This proposed method incorporates the image-level features into the ASPP (Atrous Spatial Pyramid Pooling) module due to the fact that when applying 3×3 atrous convolution on extremely large rate, image boundary effects somehow fails to capture long range information, thus degenerating it to 1×1 convolution effectively works better. For accurate semantic segmentation of foreground and background objects from an indoor scene, atrous convolution is applied to extract dense features. Consider two-dimensional signals, for each location j on the output o and a filter f, atrous convolution is applied over the input feature map x:

$$o[j] = \sum_k x[j + t \cdot k] f[k] \qquad (1)$$

where the t is atrous rate corresponding to the stride operation for sampling the input signal. It is equivalent to the convolutional operation along each spatial dimension with upsampled filters of the input sample x generated by inserting $t - 1$ zeros between two consecutive filter values. Here standard convolution is with rate $t = 1$, while for atrous convolution filter's field of view can be adaptively modified by changing the rate value.

DeepLabv3+ architecture is novel in the context that we can arbitrarily manage the size/resolution of extracted deep features using atrous convolution to swap runtime and precision, which is not attainable with existing encoder-decoder architectures. Also, the Xception model is included in DeepLabv3+ architecture for the task of segmentation by applying depthwise separable convolution operations to both decoder as well as ASPP module for the stronger and faster encoder-decoder network.

In our proposed IID system we exploited the pre-trained model of DeepLabv3+ architecture and used it for Transfer Learning by fine-tuning the network on our custom dataset, so we called this model as $DeepLabv3+^{TL}$. The weights of the pre-trained model are learned using 'Scene Parsing Dataset (ADE20K)' [24].

3.4   Deep Alpha-Matting

Deep alpha-matting is accurate segmentation of objects from a given input image using deep learning based method. In mathematical formulation, the color of pixels in a given image sample is considered as a combination of foreground and background object colors using compositing equation computed as:

$$I_p = \alpha_p F_p + (1 - \alpha_p) B_p, \qquad (2)$$

where F_p and B_p are the foreground and background colors of pixels p with linear combination of α_p in the range $[0, 1]$. Therefore in image samples with pixels values having $\alpha = 0$ belong to the background information while pixels values with $\alpha = 1$ belong to the foreground information.

For our proposed IID application we have exploited *Deep Image Matting* (DIM) [22] technique which uses deep learning methodology to directly estimate the alpha matte of an input image sample and its corresponding trimap. The main advantage of this deep learning based method is that the encoder-decoder network can learn the natural structures in alpha mattes instead of relying only on color information. Therefore deep learning networks are ideal for the representation of these natural structures however, low-level features will not capture this structure. Deep image matting method has two-stage networks including an encoder-decoder stage known as matting network followed by residual CNN method known as refinement network working on novel composition loss. At first, the matting network is trained using a given input image and its corresponding trimap to estimate an alpha matte which is compared with its ground-truth information to compute loss terms. Then the second refinement network which is a convolutional neural network refines the estimated alpha matte from the previous stage to have sharper edges and more accurate alpha. We have initially trained the model using 'Adobe Deep Image Matting Dataset' [22] containing 43100 image samples with their corresponding trimaps and ground-truth alphamatte. Afterwards, we exploited this pre-trained model for Transfer Learning by fine-tuning the network on our custom dataset so we called this model as DIM^{TL}. While we tested the model on another set of our unknown custom dataset.

3.5   User Selected Texture Transformation

The last module of our proposed IID system is to transform/map the user selected color/texture on the ROI. After that with the help of alpha-matte information extracted in module: Deep Alpha-Matting (Sect. 3.4), all the foreground objects are transformed on the newly updated scene with user selected color/texture wallpaper in ROI. Hence this step completes our proposed IID application, implemented with a fusion of various modules, including classical and deep learning based methods. The experimental results with module wise outputs discussion of our proposed IID application are presented in the next section.

4   Experiments

The evaluation is our proposed IID system is done on custom dataset provided by *2Hae Lifestyle*[2] for interior design of indoor scenes. A brief preview of the dataset is shown in Fig. 3 representing two indoor scenes. The evaluation of

---

[2] http://mrgongan.2hae.net/.

(a) Indoor Scene 1   (b) Indoor Scene 2

Fig. 3. Custom dataset overview provided by *2Hae Lifestyle*. (a) Indoor scene 1, a living room, (b) Indoor scene 2, a bed room.

deep image matting is done using mean square error and it is compared with five existing methods including Comprehensive Sampling [16], KNN Matting [4], Global Matting [10], DCNN Matting [5] and Shared Matting [6]. Whereas for segmentation of foreground/background objects we have performed quantitative evaluations on objects segmentation mask captured by $DeepLabv3+^{TL}$. We have also compared our proposed IID application segmentation results with seven existing methods including ForeGAN [19], pix2pix [12], GRASTA [9], RMAMR [23], DECOLOR [25], CNN [21] and DCP [18] using three metrics which are as follows:

– Mean Square Error:

$$MSE = \frac{1}{mn} \sum_{i=0}^{n-1} \sum_{j=0}^{m-1} |GT(i,j) - Fg(i,j)|, \tag{3}$$

– $F1$ measure:

$$P = \frac{TP}{TP + FP}, \qquad R = \frac{TP}{TP + FN}, \tag{4}$$

$$F1 = \frac{2(P \cdot R)}{P + R}, \tag{5}$$

– Intersection Over Union (IOU):

$$IOU = \frac{TP}{TP + FP + FN}, \tag{6}$$

where GT is ground-truth of segmentation mask, Fg is estimated segmentation mask, TN is True Negatives, TP is True Positives, FN is False Negatives, FP is False Positives, P is precision and R is Recall.

Table 1. Quantitative evaluation and comparison of DIM^{TL} for deep image matting with five existing methods. The first highest and the second highest scores are shown in red and green color respectively.

Methods	Mean Square Error (MSE) ↓
Comprehensive Sampling	0.07
KNN Matting	0.10
Global Matting	0.06
DCNN Matting	0.08
Shared Matting	0.09
DIM^{TL}	0.02

4.1   Deep Image Matting Evaluation

Deep Image matting in our proposed AR based interior design application is estimated using DIM^{TL} as explained in Sect. 3.4. It can be seen in Table 1 that DIM^{TL} technique has achieved minimum error value (0.02) as compared to five existing image matting algorithms. However Global Matting method has achieved the second best score for error as compared to all algorithms. The reason behind this fact is DIM^{TL} is trained in a supervised manner with ground-truth alpha-mattes information so that it can learn all the natural structures in alpha mattes. The main goal of this process is to have better pixel values representation at the boundaries of background and foreground separation. It means that if we do not achieve better alpha mattes then in the last step of our proposed IID application the foreground information will not be properly transformed on the updated background of the given image. Thus our system will show performance degradation that's why we have emphasized on high performance image matting technique.

4.2   Deep Foreground Segmentation Evaluation

Deep background/foreground segmentation estimated by $DeepLabv3+^{TL}$ as explained in Sect. 3.3 is evaluated on custom dataset using three metrics. The quantitative evaluations of these three metrics show that for accurate objects segmentation the MSE should achieve minimum value while $F1$ and IOU should be maximum scores. Therefore, it can be seen in the Table 2 that objects segmentation estimated by $DeepLabv3+^{TL}$ has achieved minimum MSE (0.02) as compared all seven existing methods while a GAN based method pix2pix [12] has achieved second best MSE. For the case of $F1$ score again $DeepLabv3+^{TL}$ has achieved the highest value (0.84) while pix2pix has achieved the second best score (0.72). Furthermore, for the third metric evaluation $DeepLabv3+^{TL}$ has also achieved the best IOU sore (0.79) while pix2pix has achieved second best score.

Table 2. Quantitative evaluation and comparison of $DeepLabv3+^{TL}$ for objects segmentation with seven existing methods. The first highest and the second highest scores are shown in red and green color respectively.

Methods	MSE ↓	$F1$ ↑	IOU ↑
RMAMR	4.11	0.29	0.19
GRASTA	4.07	0.37	0.23
DECOLOR	3.83	0.33	0.22
CNN	0.34	0.68	0.46
DCP	0.24	0.51	0.44
ForeGAN	0.32	0.55	0.49
pix2pix	0.20	0.78	0.65
$DeepLabv3+^{TL}$	0.02	0.84	0.72

The reason behind this fact is $DeepLabv3+^{TL}$ is a supervised learning based method using atrous convolution for performing high resolution semantic segmentation. While pix2pix is a conditional generative adversarial method working on the basis of conventional CNN network with U-net architecture (Generator network). However, pix2pix does not work with high resolution segmentation tasks. The Table 2 also shows background subtraction based methods like DCP and ForeGAN with performance degradation for high resolution foreground objects segmentation because of the fact that these methods sometimes contains noisy background pixel values which cause the occurrence of false positives in segmentation masks.

4.3 User's Qualitative IID Experience

We have presented qualitative results of our proposed IID application with respect to each module's output as shown in the Fig. 4 where (a) is an indoor scene 2 input image from our custom dataset given by *2Hae Lifestyle*. In the first step the user will interactively detect ROI to his/her choice in order to change the color/texture of wallpaper on the wall Fig. 4(b) ROI is cropped for further processing. Meanwhile, we get our foreground/background objects segmentation mask using $DeepLabv3+^{TL}$ and used its ROI cropped segmented part for input to our next module. Therefore, in this way we get alpha-mattes of ROI cropped segmented part from the indoor scene by applying deep image matting. Another important module in our proposed IID application is to estimate global illumination variations as our indoor scenes are suffering from illumination changes via *CIE-Lab* and get a color consistency on ROI cropped segmented part of input indoor scene image. Hence now the user chooses the texture to place on the ROI and then on new texture the illumination variations of this indoor environment are mapped back to the new texture (Fig. 4(e)). At the last step of our systematic approach, the estimated alpha-matt using DIM^{TL} will smoothly transform all the foreground information back into the scene, as shown in Fig. 4(f). In this way, by combining all modules we achieved the IID with realistic outputs in an

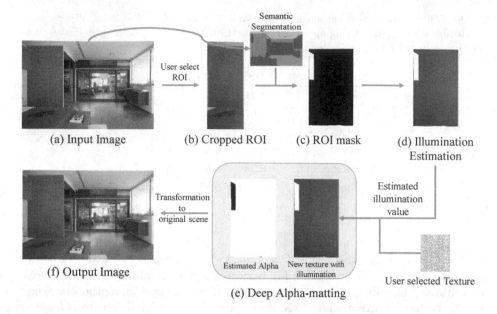

(a) Input Image   (b) Cropped ROI   (c) ROI mask   (d) Illumination Estimation

(f) Output Image   (e) Deep Alpha-matting

Fig. 4. Qualitative outputs of all modules of our proposed IID method on custom dataset provided by *2Hae Lifestyle* in an indoor scene 2.

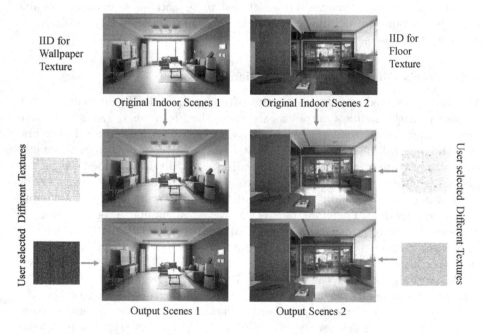

Fig. 5. Qualitative outputs of all of our proposed IID method on custom dataset provided by *2Hae Lifestyle* in two indoor scenes with different textures selected by user for wall and floor texture mapping.

end-to-end fashion. The more qualitative results with floor and wallpaper for IID using various textures selected by the user are presented in Fig. 5.

5   Conclusion

In this work, we have proposed an AR based end-to-end IID application where the user can select background information such as walls or floors and update its color/textures in indoor scenes. Our proposed IID application is a fusion of various modules, working jointly for creating an interactive environment for the user. In this work the user first selects its region of interest (ROI), that can be either wall or floor and afterwards select a color/texture of his/her choice to transform it on ROI for interior designing in indoor scenes. In our proposed IID application systematic approach we have also estimated the global illumination variations on the ROI and mapped it back on the new texture selected by our user, thus in this way our application gives realistic experience to the users for interactive interior design.

Acknowledgement. This study was supported by the BK21 Plus project (SW Human Resource Development Program for Supporting Smart Life) funded by the Ministry of Education, School of Computer Science and Engineering, Kyungpook National University, Korea (21A20131600005).

References

1. Bell, S., Bala, K.: Learning visual similarity for product design with convolutional neural networks. ACM Trans. Graph. (TOG) **34**(4), 98 (2015)
2. Brooker, G., Stone, S.: Re-readings: 2: Interior Architecture and the Principles of Remodelling Existing Buildings. Routledge, London (2019)
3. Chen, L.C., Zhu, Y., Papandreou, G., Schroff, F., Adam, H.: Encoder-decoder with atrous separable convolution for semantic image segmentation. In: Proceedings of the European Conference on Computer Vision (ECCV), pp. 801–818 (2018)
4. Chen, Q., Li, D., Tang, C.K.: KNN matting. IEEE Trans. Pattern Anal. Mach. Intell. **35**(9), 2175–2188 (2013)
5. Cho, D., Tai, Y.-W., Kweon, I.: Natural image matting using deep convolutional neural networks. In: Leibe, B., Matas, J., Sebe, N., Welling, M. (eds.) ECCV 2016. LNCS, vol. 9906, pp. 626–643. Springer, Cham (2016). https://doi.org/10.1007/978-3-319-46475-6_39
6. Gastal, E.S., Oliveira, M.M.: Shared sampling for real-time alpha matting. In: Computer Graphics Forum, vol. 29, pp. 575–584. Wiley Online Library (2010)
7. Grimley, C., Love, M.: The Interior Design Reference & Specification Book Updated & Revised: Everything Interior Designers Need to Know Every Day. Rockport Publishers (2018)
8. Han, T., Seo, Y.H.: Mixed reality system for virtual interior design. Int. J. Smart Home **7**(3), 133–142 (2013)
9. He, J., Balzano, L., Szlam, A.: Incremental gradient on the Grassmannian for online foreground and background separation in subsampled video. In: 2012 IEEE Conference on Computer Vision and Pattern Recognition, pp. 1568–1575. IEEE (2012)

10. He, K., Rhemann, C., Rother, C., Tang, X., Sun, J.: A global sampling method for alpha matting. In: CVPR 2011, pp. 2049–2056. IEEE (2011)
11. Hunt, R.: The Reproduction of Colour, 6th edn. Wiley, Hoboken (2004)
12. Isola, P., Zhu, J.Y., Zhou, T., Efros, A.A.: Image-to-image translation with conditional adversarial networks. In: Proceedings of the IEEE Conference on Computer Vision and Pattern Recognition, pp. 1125–1134 (2017)
13. Nasir, S., Zahid, M.N., Khan, T.A., Kadir, K., Khan, S.: Augmented reality application for architects and interior designers: interno a cost effective solution. In: 2018 IEEE 5th International Conference on Smart Instrumentation, Measurement and Application (ICSIMA), pp. 1–6. IEEE (2018)
14. Park, J., Sil Kim, S., Park, H., Woo, W.: Dreamhouse: NUI-based photo-realistic AR authoring system for interior design. In: Proceedings of the 7th Augmented Human International Conference 2016, p. 14. ACM (2016)
15. Phan, V.T., Choo, S.Y.: Interior design in augmented reality environment. Int. J. Comput. Appl. 5(5), 16–21 (2010)
16. Shahrian, E., Rajan, D., Price, B., Cohen, S.: Improving image matting using comprehensive sampling sets. In: Proceedings of the IEEE Conference on Computer Vision and Pattern Recognition, pp. 636–643 (2013)
17. Siltanen, S.: Diminished reality for augmented reality interior design. Vis. Comput. 33(2), 193–208 (2015). https://doi.org/10.1007/s00371-015-1174-z
18. Sultana, M., Mahmood, A., Javed, S., Jung, S.K.: Unsupervised deep context prediction for background estimation and foreground segmentation. Mach. Vis. Appl. 30(3), 375–395 (2018). https://doi.org/10.1007/s00138-018-0993-0
19. Sultana, M., Mahmood, A., Javed, S., Jung, S.K.: Unsupervised RGBD video object segmentation using GANs. arXiv abs/1811.01526 (2018)
20. Tautkute, I., Trzcinski, T., Skorupa, A., Brocki, L., Marasek, K.: DeepStyle: multimodal search engine for fashion and interior design. IEEE Access 7, 84613–84628 (2019)
21. Wang, Y., Luo, Z., Jodoin, P.M.: Interactive deep learning method for segmenting moving objects. Pattern Recogn. Lett. 96, 66–75 (2017)
22. Xu, N., Price, B., Cohen, S., Huang, T.: Deep image matting. In: Proceedings of the IEEE Conference on Computer Vision and Pattern Recognition, pp. 2970–2979 (2017)
23. Ye, X., Yang, J., Sun, X., Li, K., Hou, C., Wang, Y.: Foreground-background separation from video clips via motion-assisted matrix restoration. IEEE Trans. Circ. Syst. Video Technol. 25(11), 1721–1734 (2015)
24. Zhou, B., Zhao, H., Puig, X., Fidler, S., Barriuso, A., Torralba, A.: Scene parsing through ADE20K dataset. In: Proceedings of the IEEE Conference on Computer Vision and Pattern Recognition, pp. 633–641 (2017)
25. Zhou, X., Yang, C., Yu, W.: Moving object detection by detecting contiguous outliers in the low-rank representation. IEEE Trans. Pattern Anal. Mach. Intell. 35(3), 597–610 (2012)

Examination and Issues of Kumamoto Castle Ishigaki Region Extraction Focusing on Stone Contour Features

Yuuki Yamasaki[1]([✉]), Masahiro Migita[1]([✉]), Go Koutaki[1]([✉]),
Masashi Toda[1]([✉]), and Tsuyoshi Kishigami[2]([✉])

[1] Kumamoto University, 2 Chome-39-1 Kurokami, Chuo, Kumamoto, Japan
yamasaki@st.cs.kumamoto-u.ac.jp, {migita,toda}@cc.kumamoto-u.ac.jp,
koutaki@cs.kumamoto-u.ac.jp
[2] Toppan Printing Co., Ltd., 5-1 Kandaizumicho, Chiyoda, Tokyo, Japan

Abstract. An automated method for extracting stone contours from stone-wall images is examined in the context of the reconstruction of Kumamoto Castle. Various methods are considered: the GrabCut method, which uses a background label for highly-linear parts considered to be features of stone contours, a variant of the GrabCut method that uses low-brightness regions instead of high-linearity parts as background labels, a watershed-based method, and a method combining the GrabCut and watershed methods. In this paper, we report the extraction results obtained by each method. For each stone-wall image, the method yielding the smallest error relative to the ground truth is applied to provide a contour candidate. The results show that the line-segment GrabCut, which considers high linearity, is effective for many stone-wall images. Other methods are also effective, depending on the stone-wall image considered. The best results were obtained with an accuracy of approximately 40% to 50% within the upper limit of the allowable error. Finally, we consider outstanding issues. Owing to the low accuracy of the contour feature extraction, there is contamination of the target region with some of the surrounding region. Another problem is that it is divided extensively by line segments extracted in the texture of the stone surface. In the future, we will seek to improve contour extraction using deep learning and develop an index for matching stone shapes.

Keywords: Restoration assistance · Image segmentation · Contour tracking

1 Introduction

Ishigaki is the stone wall that serves as the foundation of a Japanese castle.

In April 2016, a severe earthquake in Kumamoto, Japan damaged Ishigaki of Kumamoto Castle and caused a substantial number of stones to fall. Here, Ishigaki is the stone wall that serves as the foundation of a Japanese castle. The

W. Ohyama and S. K. Jung (Eds.): IW-FCV 2020, CCIS 1212, pp. 43–53, 2020.
https://doi.org/10.1007/978-981-15-4818-5_4

castle is an important tourist attraction and provides spiritual support to the inhabitants of Kumamoto. The stone walls must therefore be restored urgently. However, the restoration should employ as many of the original fallen stones as possible, as they are a tangible cultural property of Kumamoto. Existing restoration methods for stone walls are expensive, both in terms of time and money, because each individual stone is repositioned visually. This process could be made significantly more efficient through automation. We therefore developed support systems that exploit information and communication technology as part of a project for facilitating recovery from earthquakes. Specifically, using image processing techniques, we developed a system that compares all the stones in a wall before and after a disaster to identify the locations originally occupied by the fallen stones [1]. We also investigated a method for extracting stone contour information, which is important in the matching process [2]. As shown in Fig. 3, this study focuses on extracting stone-contour information as a preprocessing step to the collation process, which allows for the consideration of multiple contour candidates. Therefore, the premise of this study is that multiple contour extraction methods can be employed.

In [3], we proposed several methods for more stable and efficient than conventional methods such as [2] extracting stone-contour information. We evaluated these methods qualitatively and discussed the results and potential related issues. In the present study, we calculate the error between the automatically extracted contours and those manually defined by humans. We summarize the results for the entire dataset of the stone-wall image (Fig. 1).

Fig. 1. Left: Collapsed stones Right: Collapsed stone wall

2   Related Research

The accurate extraction of an object contour, when it is surrounded by similar objects, requires that object to be in the image foreground. To date, various image processing methods have been devised for area extraction, e.g., the region expansion, active contour, mean shift, and graph cuts methods (Fig. 2).

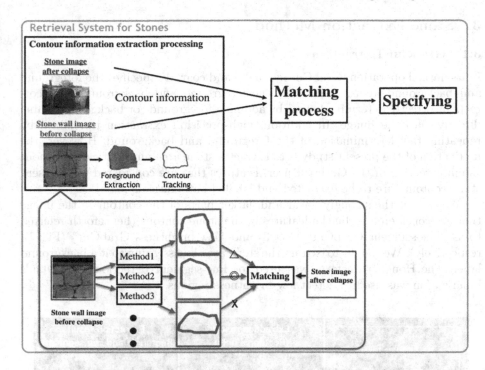

Fig. 2. Outline of the stone retrieval system

Deep learning has opened new possibilities in recent years. U-Net, a kind of all-layer convolutional network mainly used for segmentation, has received much attention for its high accuracy.

In one study on region extraction [4], U-Net was used to extract to extract regions from, e.g., the first thoracic vertebra, and anatomical structures such as the left ventricular shadow, where accurate extraction is typically challenging. The accuracy of the results was evaluated.

In [5], we focused on the fact that the boundaries of regions tend to display sharp color differences. Automatic foreground extraction is then achieved by identifying appropriate boundaries from among boundary-line candidates by over-segmentation and region integration. However, this method does not guarantee a good extraction accuracy when the color difference between the target and non-target regions is small. This makes high-accuracy extraction of the region difficult in the case of the stone-wall images considered here.

In this study, the semi-automatic foreground-extraction method, discussed in [2], which interacts with the user by GrabCut [6], is automated by using the extracted features of the stone-wall contour instead of relying on user input. The discrepancy relative to the ground truth is calculated.

3   Stone Extraction Method

3.1   GrabCut Extraction

In its normal operation, GrabCut manually and coarsely specifies the foreground and background areas, determines the foreground and background, and corrects incorrectly determined areas by adding a foreground (or background) label directly onto the image. In addition, high-precision extraction is realized by repeating the determination of the foreground and background. However, the motivation of the present study is to extract a stone area automatically, without the intervention of the GrabCut user. Features that are considered to represent stone contours are to be extracted and labeled automatically.

We extract the strongly linear and darker parts of the contour in the image that are considered to be the features of the stone contour (henceforth referred to as "line-segment GrabCut" (Fig. 3) and "low-brightness GrabCut" (Fig. 4), respectively). We sought to extract the stone area by assigning to it a background label. The Hough transform was used for line-segment detection, and Otsu's binarization was used to detect low-brightness regions.

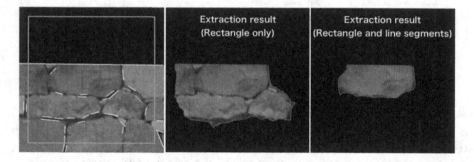

Fig. 3. Rectangle and line-segment GrabCuts

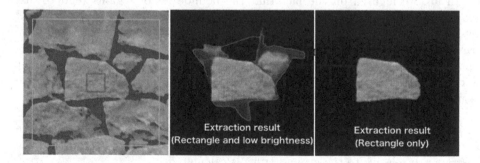

Fig. 4. Low-brightness GrabCut

3.2   Watershed Extraction

Watershed extraction involves extracting the target stone region by dividing each stone in the image with a separate label. Automated foreground extraction using the watershed approach requires the automatic extraction of three types of information from an image, corresponding to regions likely to represent the foreground and background and an undetermined region. A region considered to be a part of each stone contour is extracted, and a clear part of the contour is identified as the background. A background label is then assigned to designate an absolute background. In addition, a different foreground label is assigned to each seed as a region (an initial absolute foreground) that is sufficiently far from the contour. A region that is neither absolute foreground nor absolute background is classified as an undetermined area. The watershed then assigns to it either a background label or multiple foreground labels.

In this study, we assumed that the pit has a lower brightness than stone, and we used Otsu's binarization to detect the contour. To obtain the absolute background from the outline, the white area was expanded using dilation processing applied to this binarized image, and the remaining black area was used as the absolute background. To detect each seed, the binarized image was subjected to distance conversion. The distance of each region was then obtained from the contour, and regions exceeding a certain threshold were used as seeds (Fig. 5).

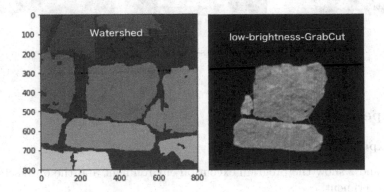

Fig. 5. Watershed

3.3   GrabCut and Watershed Extraction

In the automatic stone-region extraction performed by GrabCut, it is difficult to correctly separate stones when they are exactly fitted and the color contrast is weak, and when the foreground and background regions are erroneously extracted as one region. On the other hand, since watershed-based extraction involves the simultaneous estimation of each stone part, if a seed can be detected for each stone, even if a part of the contour is shared by two stones, a boundary is drawn as a best estimate of the contour. However, a boundary line may be drawn erroneously, depending on the detection accuracy of the contour and the degree of the contour shared by the stones. Based on our experience, when attempting to divide each stone area by the watershed approach, small-scale noise and erroneous detection of the contour part are found to affect the accuracy of the division significantly.

Therefore, we extracted stone regions using GrabCut, and, in the cases where several stones were extracted in combination, we sought to separate the extracted regions by the watershed method. For this purpose, the low-brightness part detected by Otsu's binarization in GrabCut was used to specify the background label. In addition, when applying the watershed to the region extracted by Grab-Cut, Otsu's binarization was used again to detect the contour (Fig. 6).

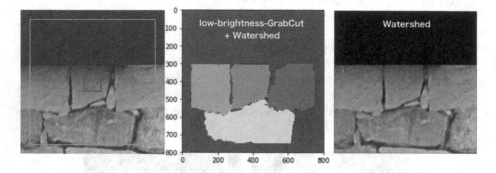

Fig. 6. Low-brightness-GrabCut + watershed

4   Experiment

4.1   Experiment Environment

Tables 1 and 2 show the program execution environment and the data sets used in this experiment.

Table 1. Execution environment

	Details
PC	macOS version: 10.13.6 Processor: 2.2 GHz Core i7 memory: 8 GB
Development environment	Xcode
Library	OpenCV 2.4

Table 2. Execution environment

Dataset name	Class	Size [pixel × pixel]	Number
H268	Iidamaru-gokaiyagura (South side)	2000 × 2000*	311
H269	Iidamaru-gokaiyagura (East side)	2000 × 2000*	159

* In this experiment, each image in the dataset was resized to dimensions 800 pixels × 800 pixels.

4.2 Error Calculation with Ground Truth

We calculated the discrepancy between a manually extracted contour (the "ground truth", GT) and the contour extracted in this study.

First, the details of the GT are described. A human user plots points consecutively on a stone-wall image to define the GT contour. These points are then connected by lines. A smooth contour requires few points. In other words, the stone contour is formed by connecting multiple line segments (or curves). The pairs of x and y coordinates for each of these points constitute the GT contour data.

To calculate the error between the GT and the contour obtained by the proposed method, both of these must have the same scale (in this study, the image size is 800 pixels × 800 pixels and 500 points define the contour after processing is completed). The error L is then calculated with the following formula. (The contour obtained by the proposed method is denoted P and the GT contour Q).

$$L = \sum_{k=1}^{n} \sqrt{(P_{kx} + Q_{kx,nearest})^2 + (P_{ky} + Q_{ky,nearest})^2} \tag{1}$$

where

n is the number of contours (500 in this experiment);
P represents the coordinates of a point on the extracted contour P;
Q represents the coordinates of one point on the contour Q that becomes the GT;

The suffix k denotes an arbitrary point, x and y are the x and y coordinates of the points P and Q, and *nearest* specifies the point on contour Q with the smallest Euclidean distance to a given point on contour P.

The point on contour Q with the smallest Euclidean distance to a given point on contour P is recorded, and this calculation is repeated for all the points on P. L is then defined as the sum of these Euclidean distances, for each recorded P-Q pair. The points on both contours are interpolated to give 500 equally spaced points.

4.3 Extraction Results Obtained by Each Method

Figure 7 shows the extraction results returned by each method, specified on the far left of each row.

GC, L-GC, O-GC, and wshed denote, respectively, GrabCut, Line-segment-GrabCut, Low-brightness-GrabCut, and watershed. O-GC + wshed represents the combination of low-brightness-GrabCut and watershed. The top row shows five types of input stone-wall images. The second and subsequent lines show the results of foreground extraction as obtained by each individual method.

Comparing the images in the second column, L-GC yields the best result from among the methods shown. It is therefore apparent that the quality of the results depends on the chosen method.

4.4 Selecting the Contour Candidate with Minimum Error

The focus of this study, illustrated in Fig. 3f, is to extract stone-contour information as the preprocessing step for the matching operation in the stone-retrieval system. As stated in the Introduction, there may be multiple candidates for the extracted contour at this stage. Therefore, the stone image, in the data set, with the smallest error between the extracted contour and the GT is selected. The overall extraction accuracy is then determined.

Here, the permissible matching error is set to 2 cm per point, and the outline of 500 points in an 800 pixels × 800 pixels image is equivalent to approximately 4000 pixels. Table 3 lists the results with an error within 4000 pixels.

Foreground extraction was performed for the two datasets H268 and H269 in Table 2 using the existing methods (GrabCut, watershed) and our proposed methods (Line-segment-GrabCut, etc.).

Each method can thus be applied in turn to a given stone-wall image. The error in each obtained contour, relative to the GT, is then calculated using Eq. (1). On comparing the different methods, the contour with the smallest error is adopted as the minimum-error contour. The analysis is repeated for each stone-wall image.

Figure 8 shows a histogram of the errors for data set H268 specified in Table 2. The horizontal and vertical axes represent the error rank and the frequency, respectively. The colors in each bar convey the relative error magnitudes associated with the different methods. The colors in each bar convey the relative error magnitudes associated with the different methods. The corresponding results for the H269 dataset are shown in Fig. 9.

4.5 Consideration

According to Fig. 8, in the case of H268, the extraction results of the line-segment GrabCut are widely distributed over the error range. This means that, among the extraction results for each stone image, the line-segment GrabCut method yielded the smallest error. This method is therefore considered to be effective for the H268 dataset. Figure 9 shows that, in the case of H269, the ratio of the minimum was not small even for methods other than line-segment Grab-Cut. Depending on the stone, other methods may thus be more effective. It is necessary to list the contour candidates.

Table 3. Error rate within 4000 pixels

	Total	Number within 4000 pixels	Proportion within 4000 pixels [%]
H268	311	144	46.3
H269	159	69	43.4

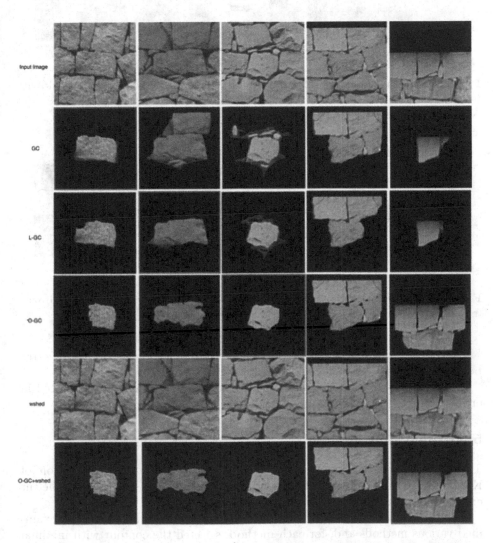

Fig. 7. Comparison of extraction results obtained by each method. GC: GrabCut, L-GC: Line-segment-GrabCut, O-GC: Low-brightness-GrabCut, wshed: watershed, O-GC + wshed: Low-brightness-GrabCut + watershed

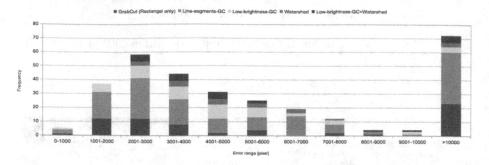

Fig. 8. Error distribution for H268 (horizontal axis: error range [pixel], vertical axis: frequency)

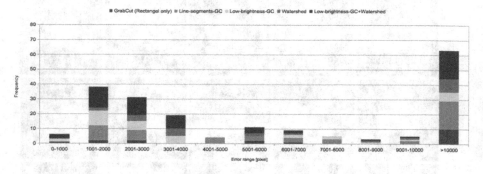

Fig. 9. Error distribution for H269 (horizontal axis: error range [pixel], vertical axis: frequency)

According to Table 3, the proportion of contour candidates with an error below 4000 pixels was 46.3% and 43.4% for H268 and H269, respectively.

The inability to extract contour features accurately might have resulted in errors.

5   Conclusion

The Ishigaki collation system was developed to support the restoration of Kumamoto Castle Ishigaki. This study investigated the automated efficient extraction of contour information from stone shapes.

Since the collation process allows for multiple contour candidates, we examined various methods and, for each method, selected the contour with minimal error relative to the GT. The best results thus obtained generally displayed an accuracy between 40% and 50%. One source of error was the impossibility of extracting the contours of a given stone exclusively and accurately.

Future work will further investigate the following tasks:

1. Refining the image processing to perform further divisions when an extracted contour is not considered to match a stone in the wall from shape evaluation

2. Limiting the position of features used as background labels
3. Creating a more accurate contour extractor (e.g., using deep learning).

Acknowledgment. This research was partially supported by the A-STEP from the Japan Science and Technology Agency (JST).

References

1. Miyazawa, A., Koutaki, G.: Retrieval system for stones of Kumamoto Castle using ISHIGAKI marker. In: The 62nd Annual Conference of the Institute of Systems proceedings (2018)
2. Toda, M., Inoue, K., Koutaki, G., Kishigami, T.: Extraction method of stone contour for support of ISHIGAKI retrieval on Kumamoto Castle. IEEJ Trans. Electron. Inf. Syst. (2018)
3. Yamasaki, Y., Migita, M., Koutaki, G., Toda, M., Kishigami, T.: A study on Kumamoto Castle Ishigaki region extraction using multiscale region division, Technical Group on Media Engineering (2019)
4. Kondo, K., et al.: Analysis of anatomical structure from chest X-ray images using U-Net. The Japan Society for Artificial Intelligence, National conference Proceedings (2018)
5. Matsuo, K.: A non-interactive image segmentation method based on the shape similarity of the Grabcut. In: CVIM, vol. 2010-CVIM-171, no. 19, pp. 1–8, March 2010
6. Rother, C., Kolmogorv, V., Blake, A.: GrabCut: interactive foreground extraction using iterated graph cuts. ACM Trans. Graph. **23**(3), 309–314 (2004)

Detection of Speech Impairments in Parkinson Disease Using Handcrafted Feature-Based Model on Spanish Speech Corpus

Laiba Zahid[1], Muazzam Maqsood[1], Sehar Shahzad Farooq[3], Farhan Aadil[1], Irfan Mehmood[2], Mustansar Fiaz[3], and Soon Ki Jung[3(✉)]

[1] Department of Computer Science, COMSATS University, Attock Campus, Pakistan
muazzam.maqsood@cuiatk.edu.pk
[2] Faculty of Engineering and Information, School of Media Design and Technology, University of Bradford, Bradford, UK
[3] School of Computer Science and Engineering, Kyungpook National University, Daegu, Korea
{sehar146,skjung}@knu.ac.kr

Abstract. Parkinson disease is a neurodestructive disorder. It gradually dismantles the dopamine chemical producing cells in the brain. The symptoms of the disease arise gradually resulting in infects in movements, olfactory, or speech impairments. The cure for disease is important to prevent patients from major motor and non-motor defects. Computer-aided techniques have been introduced for disease detection and is an open research area. In this paper, we present an approach for early diagnosis of Parkinson disease using the Spanish speech dataset. We modeled handcrafted features from different sets of Spanish recordings and classify them using a machine learning model. Several Machine learning algorithms are implemented for significant classification and compared each other's results graphically. The results depict that handcrafted features of vowels are most efficient in Parkinson disease detection.

Keywords: Parkinson disease · Speech recognition · Classification techniques · Handcrafted feature · Speech impairments

1 Introduction

Parkinson Disease (PD) affects thousands of people worldwide. It slowly defects the neurons of brains causing serious motor and non-motor defects. It has been observed from recent studies that the cause of PD is unknown, and its cure is still under research. However, early diagnosis is very useful to prevent patients from major changes in the body [1]. PD slowly progresses without letting know the patient about the disease. Degeneration of dopamine-producing cells causes motor defects such as difficulty in walking, body shivering gait, and tremors, and non-motor symptoms such as speech impairments, loss of sense of smell etc. To prevent the patient from major defects in their body and to increase the life span of the patient a lot of work has been done for early diagnosis of PD and to provide suitable medication to prevent the onset of symptoms [2].

W. Ohyama and S. K. Jung (Eds.): IW-FCV 2020, CCIS 1212, pp. 54–65, 2020.
https://doi.org/10.1007/978-981-15-4818-5_5

In PD, identifying symptoms and severity of disease are difficult as the symptoms appear over time. For early PD detection, a lot of research has been done considering handwriting dataset and speech datasets. Most of the research has considered handwriting tests to detect differences in drawings and writing of Parkinson patients and healthy candidates and considered as a significant biomarker for disease detection. However, many other researches have considered speech recordings for disease detection. PD patients have significant defects in pronunciation of words and sentences as the loss of dopamine cells in brains results in speech impairments causing vocal folds to vibrate more than a normal person. As PD patient produces sounds, there is a significant change in the audio signal of Parkinson patient and healthy candidate. Thus, speech recordings are also considered as important predictors of disease.

Recent research has shown different defects in the phonation of PD patient speech recording and articulation problems in the speech processes affecting intelligibility as well. Phonation and articulation defects can be observed in the continuous speech process of Parkinson patients and in sustained speech pronunciation practices. PD is common among the age group of elderly people so pronunciation in task related to continuous and sustained way is more suitable for which include pronunciation of a common word, normal dialogs, sentences and vowels. Phonation includes the use of vocal folds for the pronunciation of words and articulation is the vibrancy of vocal tract. In regard to articulation task pronunciation of vowels \a\, \e\, \i\, \o\, \u\ are most suitable [3].

In this work, we exhibit an approach to early diagnosis of PD using Spanish speech recording PC-GITA. As patients with PD have speech impairments when they pronounce words and sentences. We utilized Spanish recordings that include signals of words pronunciation, vowels and monologues in Spanish language. The main contribution of our work is to transform speech signals shown in Fig. 1 into handcrafted features. Handcrafted features include a set of different features like spectral as well as statistical features. These features are used as input in our machine learning classifiers k nearest neighbor, random forest, decision trees, etc.

The structure of this paper is divided into the following sections: Sect. 2 presents the related work followed by Sect. 3 that explains the proposed methodology of our work accompanied by Sect. 4 presenting experimental setup and evaluation metrics, dataset utilized. Section 5 provides the details of results acquired using handcrafted features using machine learning models.

2 Related Work

Cai et al. [1] considered enhanced FKNN approach for PD patient diagnosis on vocal speech dataset (Oxford and Istanbul dataset). The proposed methodology used CBFO (chaotic bacterial foraging optimization with gauss mutation) for parameter tuning and FKNN for classification. The author compared CBFO-FKNN results with other FKNN model (PSO, BFO), the proposed methodology proved efficient in clinical decision-making. Hosseini-Kivanani et al. [2] assessed speech signals from three different languages (German, Spanish, and Czech) for intelligibility based automatic speech recognition systems. They proposed a system that is able to distinguish between features that are the most influenced feature for the detection of PD patients. Nilashi et al. [3] make use of an intelligent approach by incorporating incremental SVM for UPDRS (Unified Parkinson's disease rating scale) considering it as the basis for PD assessment. The authors implemented SOM for clustering, NIPALS for data dimensionality reduction and ISVR for predicting total and motor UPDRS. The authors concluded that the proposed method significantly improves the accuracy of PD diagnosis and reduced computation time.

Paisi et al. [4] incorporated a novel approach by making use of the intrinsic feature selection approach instead of using external methods for feature selection (PCA etc.). The authors mentioned that the classifier itself calculates the weights and selects the best features from vocal signals dataset to improve the early diagnosis of PD patients.

The authors observed better accuracy and less computational time as compared to other approaches. Passos et al. [5] implemented deep neural networks Res Net-50 to learn patterns and extract useful features from the drawing of patients (HandPD dataset). The authors used optimum path forest for PD classification and observed a 96% identification rate in it. Moro-Velazquez et al. [6] have incorporated articulation based features in their work and considered Gaussian based densities from different PD datasets. They present gender-based results that male parkinson patients in the Czech language dataset are most suitable for disease detection showing 81% accuracy. Pérez-Toro et al. [7] make use of features like identifying the total number of time a word appeared and a bag of words for the classification process. They observed that language task that include pronunciation of different words like vowels, words, monologues etc. They presented 72% accuracy in their proposed research. Karan et al. [8] incorporated different features from two distinct datasets in which they used 20 Spanish recordings of healthy candidate and PD. Their work accounted for 96% accuracy with random forest and support vector machine.

Arias-Vergara et al. [9] have used extended versions of Spanish speech recordings which include recordings of daily routine phone calls. By using a speech enactment algorithm, they removed noise and presented 84% accuracy in their work. Vásquez-Correa et al. [10] assessed m-FDA using features from Spanish vowels, monologues showing 0.69 correlation in their result. Moro-Velázquez et al. [11] observed kinetic features for PD detection. They used a Gaussian mixture based model and observed 87% accuracy. Orozco-Arroyave et al. [12] considered various features from six different language datasets and assessed three varying diseases including PD. They assessed vowels datasets of PD using a support vector machine and presented 97% of the highest accuracy. Rueda et al. [13] used feature wrapper technique for finding the best features and utilized 15 most suitable features to classify voices using support vector machine and random forest presenting 70% accuracy in their work. Trinh et al. [14] considered spectrograms of Spanish two datasets of speech recordings from Librosa and used these as an input in convolution neural network showing 96.7% accuracy. Shu et al. [15] used EEG (electroencephalogram) signal of 20 PD and 20 healthy individuals for automatic disease diagnosis. The author implemented thirteen layers CNN for classification reducing the need for feature selection stages. The author notices 88.25% accuracy in it.

3 Proposed Methodology

In this paper, we considered the speech impairments of PD patients. We assessed Spanish speech recordings. All these recordings are in Spanish language that includes pronunciation of words, vowels, and monologues in a sustained and continuous manner. These

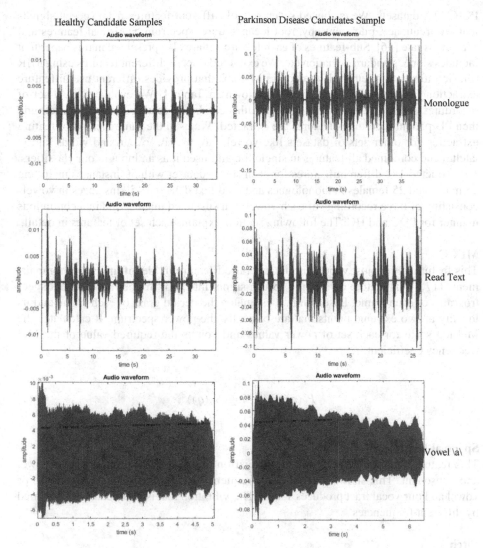

Fig. 1. Spanish speech signal waveform sample.

datasets include healthy candidate recordings that are free of any mispronunciation and Parkinson patient recordings that include mispronunciation at different points in speech signal shown in Fig. 1.

3.1 Handcrafted Feature Extraction

Acoustic features play a significant role in classifying speech impairments. In our work, we used handcrafted acoustic features of Spanish speech recordings for the classification of PD patients. We extracted a suitable number of acoustic features from each set of

PC-GIITA datasets. We evaluated seven sets of different features from speech signals that are frequency, pitch, entropy, root mean square, spectrum, statistical features and zero-cross rate [16]. Sub-features of each feature set are also presented in this paper that includes slope, standard deviation etc. We extracted a set of different features using MIR (music information retrieval) toolbox in Matlab) that provides different useful feature extraction functions from speech signal shown in Table 1. We evaluated each set of recordings separately i.e. monologues healthy candidate features were extracted and then PD patient recordings features are extracted. We used the same method of feature extraction for other sets of datasets like vowels \a\, \e\, \i\, \o\, \u\ and words \apto\, \atelta\ and combined all features in single file and used it as an input in our classifiers. We extracted 122 different features for each set of dataset with 50 instances including 25 males and 25 females in monologues and read text data and 150 instances in vowels consisting of three recordings of each vowel in a sustained manner and in a continuous manner for PDC and HC. The following section explains each set of features in detail.

MFCC
This feature is the most widely used handcrafted feature in identifying speech impairments [17]. This feature divides the speech signal into short frames and account spectrograms of each frame. Based on it, it estimates the period gram of each frame and its locality at two extreme points that are basically the power spectrum. It calculates the Mel log scale for each set of power values and counts the required value of the Mel frequency coefficient.

$$P_n(q) = \frac{1}{N} \log(S_n(q))^2 \tag{1}$$

Spectral Feature
This feature is able to identify the pronunciation problem while pronouncing a vowel and consonant. This shows the values of frequency when we pronounce any word or vowel and our vocal tract produces sound. The vibration that is produced is represented by different frequencies.

Pitch
Pitch represents the vibration caused by our vocal folds when we pronounce a word and speak sentences. The rate at which vocal folds vibrate are represented by differing frequencies, which shows the pitch of vowel. The greater vocal folds vibrate the greater the vibrations are produced resulting in high sound pronunciation. This feature is very important in speech impairments detection because of its ability to differentiate between voice quality of healthy candidate and PD patient candidate.

Zero Cross Rate
This feature is a time-domain feature and represents the total number of times the signal crossed the zero point in a time frame [18]. It shows the values that how the signal

gradually changes its position from peak value to the lowest negative value below zero point. It is considered a discerning feature in speech detection.

Root Mean Square
This feature represents the square root of all sum of the square of the amplitude of all audio signals. It is observed from research that this feature is important in accounting speech impairments.

Entropy and Statistical Features
Entropy is a power distribution of a speech signal. Statistical features represent the statistical values of a speech signal. It calculates mean, standard deviation, slope, etc. of an audio signal. These features play an evident role in the identification of speech impairments of a PD patient.

3.2 Classification

After preprocessing and extracting useful handcrafted features, we classify those features for detecting PD. We use K-Nearest Neighbor (KNN), Support Vector Machine (SVM), Multi-Layer Perceptron (MLP), Naïve Bayes (NB), Random Forest (RF), and Decision Tree (DT) for classification. All these models are trained using five cross-fold validation process instead of separating into training and testing data.

K-Nearest Neighbor (KNN)
It is a widely used classification in computer-assisted diagnosis of speech and emotion impairments and recognition. It performs classification by keeping all instances and classify any new instance by using Euclidean distance [19]. We performed 5 cross-fold validation that means it finds the 5 nearest neighbors by computing similarity measure between them by combining those with smaller distance and predicting the class of new instance on the basis of the majority role of 5 nearest neighbors.

Support Vector Machine (SVM)
It is the most commonly used classification technique in the detection of chronic diseases and an efficient machine learning approaches. In this approach, we input each set of handcrafted features such as vowels \a\, \e\, \i\, \o\, \u\, monologues, words and read the text [20], All these features are inputted into SVM binary classifier. It identifies the linear and non-linear surfaces in the input support vectors by constructing hyperplane, which later classifies the data. The complexity parameters in this model build hyperplane from the class label. The hyperplane that computes the largest distance from the training data has the highest classification result. The parameters like gamma rate are set to 0.01, complexity value is 300000, degree value is 3 and the coefficient is 1. Different kernels of support vector machine have been used in different research. The linear kernel in our research is considered in which configuration parameters are kernel gamma and margin.

Naïve Bayes (NB)
A probabilistic classification approach identifies the relationship between different features. It is widely used in text retrieval, finding spam detection etc. [21]. In the naive Bayes classification approach, we find the chances or probability of a to occur provided that b has also occurred before, where b is evidence and a is the hypothesis that is assumed. It clearly depicts that all the features are purely independent of each other.

$$P(a|b) = \frac{P(b|a) \times P(a)}{P(b)} \tag{2}$$

It means the presence of one specific feature will not influence the other feature that is so is so it is a naive approach.

Random Forest (RF)

It constructs the bootstrap patterns from the random forest original data and develops a raw classification or regression tree for each bootstrap pattern by contemplating instead of each mode choosing the only best disclosure from all predictors. It makes a random selection of predictors and chooses the best split between them. In our study, the total number of iterations is 100. The total number of least instances per leaf is set to default value 1. The seed value for random number is 1 and extreme value for the leaf of a tree is 0 that signifies the unlimited depth of a tree whereas the batch size is set to 100.

Decision Tree (DT

A tree-based classifier that builds a decision tree, which accurately performs the classification task [22]. It computes the information gain for each set of data and utilize it for identification of the highest information gain. It classifies instances into a class that

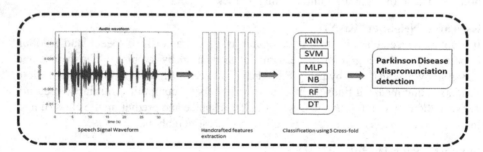

Fig. 2. Proposed methodology. 6 classification algorithms with 5 cross-fold validation

Table 1. Handcrafted features details

Feature	Description
Pitch	Pitch in Hertz
Entropy	Entropy values of signal
RMS	Root mean square values of energy
Statistical	Mean, periodic entropy, standard deviation, slope, periodic frequency, periodic amplitude
Zero-Cross	Number of times signal cross zero point
MFCC	14 Mel-Frequency Coefficient
Spectral	Spectral features

computes the highest gain or entropy. It is the most commonly used iterative development tool J48 that can deal with discrete as well as continuous attributes. It finds the
missing values and attributes of data that have discerning costs (Fig. 2).

Multilayer Perceptron (MLP)
It generally exploited the approach in speech, image, and visual identification system.
It is a feedforward neural network that is consists of an input layer, an output layer and
amongst them is the unseen layer. The input layer receives the input value whereas the
unseen layer refers to information from the input layer to the output layer. An unseen
layer comprises of number of neurons, each of unseen layer neuron i entails information
of its input (Table 2).

Table 2. Dataset details

Dataset			Gender	Age
Monologues			25 Female HC	Female HC 43 to 76 (mean
Read text			25 Female PD	60.7 ± 6 7.7)
			25 Male HC	Female PD 44 to 75 (mean
Words	\atelta\	\apto\	25 Male PD	60.1 ± 6 7.8)
Vowels	\a\	\e\		Male HC 31 to 86 (mean 61.2
				± 6 11.3)
	\i\	\o\ \u\		Male PD to 77 (mean 62.2 ±
				6 11.2)

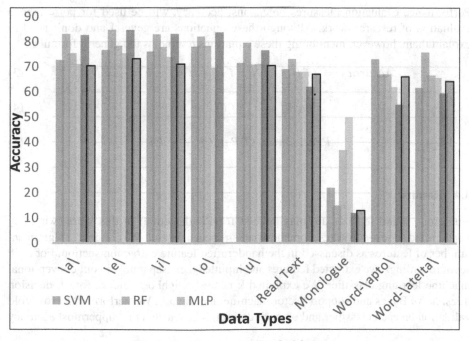

Fig. 3. Results using handcrafted features

4   Experimental Setup and Results

4.1   Experimental Tools

In this work, we have operated HP Core i5-3230 M 2.60 GHz processor with 4 GB random access memory using Matlab 2018a MIR (music information retrieval) toolbox 1.7.2 for feature extraction and Weka 3.9.2 for classification (Fig. 3).

4.2   Spanish Speech Dataset

In this research, we have utilized Spanish speech recordings of PD patient PC-GITA [23].The dataset consist of recordings of 50 PD patient and 50 healthy candidate. The dataset consists of recordings of Spanish vowels \a\, \e\, \i\, \o\, \u\ that are pronounced in a sustained as well as in continuous manner and each vowel is pronounced in three different ways by 25 male candidate and 25 female candidate so total number of recordings for vowel dataset are 150 for both healthy and Parkinson candidates. The other dataset consists of recordings of Spanish monologue that is the pronunciation of sentences in Spanish language, total number of recordings in it are 50. The read text dataset holds recordings of Spanish text reading that are also 50 in number. The dataset also consists of recordings of several Spanish words from 50 candidates each, but in our work, we have only utilized recordings of two words pronunciation \apto\, \atelta\. For each set of recordings, we separately extract handcrafted features for each vowel, words, monologues, read text and used them in our classifiers.

4.3   Evaluation Metrics

Performance evaluation measures precisions, accuracy, will be used for performance evaluation of research work. Although these equations are general and don't need to explain them, however, mentioning these equations remind us the general formulas.

$$Accuracy = (TP + TN)|(TP + TN + FP + FN) \tag{3}$$

$$Recall = (\text{TP})|(\text{TP} + \text{FN}) \tag{4}$$

$$Precison = (TP)|(TP + FP) \tag{5}$$

4.4   Results

Numerous sound features are manipulated for PD detection. In this work, we study handcrafted acoustic features from the Spanish speech dataset. We obtained a significant number of features as discussed in the handcrafted feature extraction section. For each set of recordings, we extracted features and inputted them separately in our conventional machine learning classifier. We exploited k nearest neighbor, random forest, decision trees, naïve Bayes and support vector machine in our work. We performed 5 cross-fold validation on each classifier and on each dataset. It is detected that uppermost accuracy is observed on vowel \e\ that is 84.6% by means of random forest and k-nearest neighbor, vowel \o\ exhibited 83.6% using KNN and 83% using random forest and 82.6% using KNN, vowel \a\ exhibits 83% accuracy with vowel \i\ showing 82.8% accuracy using random forest and 83 using KNN. Minimum accuracy in vowel dataset is observed on vowel \u\ in comparison to other vowels that is highest accuracy is 79.5 using random forest and minimum is 71%. Whether in read text dataset, utmost accuracy 73% is observed using random forest and KNN showed 68% accuracy in it. Monologues dataset displayed very fewer results of 37% using multilayer perceptron and 15% using random forest, highest accuracy in it is observed using decision tree-j48 that is 50%. Thus, it is observed that vowels dataset is efficient in PD detection when handcrafted features are utilized, where random forest and k nearest neighbor classifier showed maximum accuracy in it.

5 Conclusion

Recently, PD is emerging as a major disorder worldwide. Various technique has been presented for detecting onset of disease using gait, kinematic and speech impairments [24, 25]. This work showed that detection of speech impairments is suitable for identifying PD among people. We evaluated handcrafted features of Spanish speech recordings datasets using vowels, monologues, read text and words. The results showed that classifiers like random forest and k nearest neighbor present 84.6% accuracy when handcrafted features are provided as an input. Hence, it is presented that without using any feature selection algorithm we can evaluate better results. Moreover, vowels are most suitable while detecting impairments when pronounced in a sustained manner. However, in future feature selection algorithm can be utilized to enhance accuracies of classifiers and to provide better classification results.

Acknowledgement. This research was supported by Basic Science Research Program through the National Research Foundation of Korea (NRF) funded by the Ministry of Education, Science and Technology (NRF-2019R1A2C1010786).

References

1. Cai, Z., et al.: An intelligent Parkinson's disease diagnostic system based on a chaotic bacterial foraging optimization enhanced fuzzy KNN approach. Comput. Math. Methods Med. **2018**, 1–24 (2018)
2. Hosseini-Kivanani, N., Vásquez-Correa, J.C., Stede, M., Nöth, E.: Automated cross-language intelligibility analysis of Parkinson's disease patients using speech recognition technologies. In: Book Automated Cross-language Intelligibility Analysis of Parkinson's Disease Patients Using Speech Recognition Technologies (edn.), pp. 74–80 (2019)
3. Nilashi, M., Ibrahim, O., Ahmadi, H., Shahmoradi, L., Farahmand, M.: A hybrid intelligent system for the prediction of Parkinson's disease progression using machine learning techniques. Biocybern. Biomed. Eng. **38**(1), 1–15 (2018)
4. Parisi, L., RaviChandran, N., Manaog, M.L.: Feature-driven machine learning to improve early diagnosis of Parkinson's disease. Exp. Syst. Appl. **110**, 182–190 (2018)

5. Passos, L.A., et al.: Parkinson disease identification using residual networks and optimum-path forest. In: Book Parkinson Disease Identification Using Residual Networks and Optimum-Path Forest (IEEE, edn.), pp. 000325–000330 (2018)

6. Moro-Velazquez, L., et al.: A forced gaussians based methodology for the differential evaluation of Parkinson's disease by means of speech processing. Biomed. Signal Process. Control **48**, 205–220 (2019)

7. Pérez-Toro, P.A., Vásquez-Correa, J.C., Strauss, M., Orozco-Arroyave, J.R., Nöth, E.: Natural language analysis to detect Parkinson's disease. In: Ekštein, K. (ed.) TSD 2019. LNCS (LNAI), vol. 11697, pp. 82–90. Springer, Cham (2019). https://doi.org/10.1007/978-3-030-27947-9_7

8. Karan, B., Sahu, S.S., Mahto, K.: Parkinson disease prediction using intrinsic mode function based features from speech signal. Biocybern. Biomed. Eng. **40**(1), 249–264 (2019)

9. Arias-Vergara, T., Vasquez-Correa, J.C., Orozco-Arroyave, J.R., Klumpp, P., Nöth, E.: Unobtrusive monitoring of speech impairments of Parkinson's disease patients through mobile devices. In: Book Unobtrusive Monitoring of Speech Impairments of Parkinson's Disease Patients Through Mobile Devices (IEEE, edn.), pp. 6004–6008 (2018)

10. Vásquez-Correa, J., Orozco-Arroyave, J., Bocklet, T., Nöth, E.: Towards an automatic evaluation of the dysarthria level of patients with Parkinson's disease. J. Commun. Disord. **76**, 21–36 (2018)

11. Moro-Velázquez, L., Gómez-García, J.A., Godino-Llorente, J.I., Villalba, J., Orozco-Arroyave, J.R., Dehak, N.: Analysis of speaker recognition methodologies and the influence of kinetic changes to automatically detect Parkinson's disease. Appl. Soft Comput. **62**, 649–666 (2018)

12. Orozco-Arroyave, J.R., et al.: Characterization methods for the detection of multiple voice disorders: neurological, functional, and laryngeal diseases. IEEE J. Biomed. Health Inform. **19**(6), 1820–1828 (2015)

13. Rueda, A., Vásquez-Correa, J.C., Rios-Urrego, C.D., Orozco-Arroyave, J.R., Krishnan, S., Nöth, E.: Feature representation of pathophysiology of Parkinsonian dysarthria. In: Proceedings of Interspeech 2019, pp. 3048–3052 (2019)

14. Trinh, N., Darragh, O.B.: Pathological speech classification using a convolutional neural network (2019)

15. Shu, M.: Deep learning for image classification on very small datasets using transfer learning (2019)

16. Nazir, F., Majeed, M.N., Ghazanfar, M.A., Maqsood, M.: Mispronunciation detection using deep convolutional neural network features and transfer learning-based model for Arabic phonemes. IEEE Access **7**, 52589–52608 (2019)

17. Chowdhury, A., Ross, A.: Fusing MFCC and LPC features using 1D triplet CNN for speaker recognition in severely degraded audio signals. IEEE Trans. Inf. Forensics Secur. **15**, 1616–1629 (2019)

18. Yue, X., Deng, F., Xu, Y.: Multidimensional zero-crossing interval points: a low sampling rate acoustic fingerprint recognition method. Sci. China Inf. Sci. **62**(1), 19202 (2019)

19. Betrouni, N., et al.: Electroencephalography-based machine learning for cognitive profiling in Parkinson's disease: preliminary results. Mov. Disord. **34**(2), 210–217 (2019)

20. Mostafa, S.A., et al.: Examining multiple feature evaluation and classification methods for improving the diagnosis of Parkinson's disease. Cognit. Syst. Res. **54**, 90–99 (2019)

21. Sakar, C.O., et al.: A comparative analysis of speech signal processing algorithms for Parkinson's disease classification and the use of the tunable Q-factor wavelet transform. Appl. Soft Comput. **74**, 255–263 (2019)

22. Mathur, R., Pathak, V., Bandil, D.: Parkinson disease prediction using machine learning algorithm. In: Rathore, V.S., Worring, M., Mishra, D.K., Joshi, A., Maheshwari, S. (eds.)

Emerging Trends in Expert Applications and Security. AISC, vol. 841, pp. 357–363. Springer, Singapore (2019). https://doi.org/10.1007/978-981-13-2285-3_42

23. Orozco-Arroyave, J.R., Arias-Londoño, J.D., Vargas-Bonilla, J.F., Gonzalez-Rátiva, M.C., Nöth, E.: New Spanish speech corpus database for the analysis of people suffering from Parkinson's disease. In: Book New Spanish Speech Corpus Database for the Analysis of People Suffering from Parkinson's Disease (edn.), pp. 342–347 (2014)

24. Seppi, K., et al.: Update on treatments for nonmotor symptoms of Parkinson's disease—an evidence-based medicine review. Mov. Disord. 34(2), 180–198 (2019)

25. Saikia, A., Majhi, V., Hussain, M., Paul, S., Datta, A.: Tremor identification using machine learning in Parkinson's disease. In: Early Detection of Neurological Disorders Using Machine Learning Systems (IGI Global, 2019), pp. 128–151 (2019)

Face, Pose, and Action Recognition

Short-Term Action Recognition
by 3D Convolutional Neural Network
with Pixel-Wise Evidences

XiaoHan Wang[✉], Junichi Miyao, and Takio Kurita

Department of Information Engineering, Hiroshima University, Hiroshima, Japan
wangxiaohan9416@gmail.com

Abstract. Action recognition in videos is becoming popular these years. The difficulty is how to extract the temporal information, which is important in the target actions. In this paper, we propose a conceptually, simple network for short-term action recognition. The proposed network architecture is extended from standard neural network to Autoencoder, which estimates pixel-wise evidence in frames, and they are integrated to classify the actions in the simple classifier. In the proposed architecture, the standard 2D convolutional layers for image classification are extended to 3D convolutional layers in the Autoencoder to extract the temporal information in the target actions. In the training phase, classifiers are introduced in the middle of layer to let the features of the middle layers are well discriminated. Also, classifiers are introduced at the end of layer to improve performance of the standard classifier. We have performed experiments using UCF101 dataset to evaluate the effectiveness of the proposed architecture. The results show that our methods can get efficient performance in short-term action recognition.

Keywords: Action recognition · Autoencoder · 3D convolution

1 Introduction

In the era of information explosion, more and more videos are uploaded on the internet every day, and the analysis of these videos becomes very important. This encourages the development of algorithms for video analysis, video classification, and video understanding. Computer vision has been developed for decades, and video analysis has solved various problems, such as motion recognition, anomaly detection, and video understanding. Significant achievements have been made on these issues through various methods. Action recognition became popular in recent years.

Convolutional neural networks (CNN) [1] have become a useful model for understanding image content, thanks to the development of more marker data sets and the development of convolutional neural networks. CNN can be used to achieve image recognition, segmentation, detection, and other functions. The successful use of CNN in the field of images has led more researchers to use

© Springer Nature Singapore Pte Ltd. 2020
W. Ohyama and S. K. Jung (Eds.): IW-FCV 2020, CCIS 1212, pp. 69–82, 2020.
https://doi.org/10.1007/978-981-15-4818-5_6

CNN to study video-level recognition. The most significant difference between videos and images is time information. In image issues, 3D data means length, width, and color. However, at the video-level, getting the CNN network to access complex time information is a difficult point for video research.

In large-scale video tasks, it is expected that problems in the short-term action recognition can also be solved through extensions of the existing techniques. Therefore, in this paper, we searched the existing techniques which are useful to extract temporal information in the target actions and to classify actions in videos efficiently. As the results of searching, we propose a network architecture in which 3D CNN [2] is combined with Autoencoder [3]. Autoencoder can extract both high-level features and low-level features, and 3D convolutional neural network can add one more dimension for timing. The usage of these two techniques would help action recognition more efficient.

To accelerate the training, we introduced the auxiliary classifier with softmax activation function in the end of Autoencoder. The auxiliary classifier is to use the output of a final layer for classification. The cross-entropy loss of this auxiliary classifier is integrated with the cross-entropy loss of the middle layer.

The performance of the proposed method is evaluated on UCF101 datasets [4] in which realistic action videos are collected from YouTube. UCF101 dataset consists of 101 classes of actions. In the experiments, videos of UCF101 dataset are split into non-overlapped 16-frame clips, which are then used as input to the proposed networks and the recognition performances are compared.

This paper is organized as follows. In Sect. 2, the related works are reviewed. The details of our proposed method are explained in Sect. 3. In Sect. 4, we explained the experiments and results. Section 5 is for the conclusion.

2   Related Works

2.1   3D Convolutional Neural Network

There is another essential idea to extract the temporal information in the video, called 3D CNN [2]. The 3D CNN adds a temporal dimension in the input of the neural network, and they are used to convolve several consecutive frames with a 3D convolution kernel.

The 3D CNN architecture consists of a hardwired layer, 3 convolutional layers, 2 down-sampling layers, and a fully connected layer. In the original 3D CNN, each 3D convolution kernel convolves 7 consecutive frames, and the patch size of each frame is set to 60×40. They extract five channels of information per frame what are gray-scale, the gradient in x and y directions, and optical flow in x and y directions. They used two $7 \times 7 \times 3$ 3D convolution kernels, here 7×7 is in 2D space, and 3 is the temporal dimension, representing convolve every 3 frames, and then convolved separately on each of the five channels. Then the process of continuous down-sampling and 3D convolution is repeated.

2.2 Autoencoder

Autoencoder is a neural network model. This model collects an image. After receiving this image, the neural network compresses the image and finally restores it from the compressed image. The image uploaded to the Autoencoder model is essentially compressed. Perform a decompression process later. When compressing, the quality of the original picture is reduced (dimensional reduction), and when decompressing, a file with a small amount of information but containing all the information is used to restore the original picture (restore).

The reason for this is that when the neural network needs to input a large amount of information, such as high-definition pictures, the number of input images can reach tens of millions. It is very laborious to learn from the amount of input data directly Flattering work, so researchers thought, why not compress it? Extract the most representative information in the original picture, reduce the amount of information in the input, and then put the reduced information into the neural network to learn, so it becomes easier to learn, so Autoencoder is here. It works at the time, assuming that the information A in the input layer is decompressed to obtain a in the hidden layer, and then the hidden layer a is compared with the input layer A to get the prediction error, and then the reverse transmission is performed, and then gradually To improve the accuracy of Autoencoder, a part of the data a obtained in the intermediate hidden layer after a period of training is the essence of the source data. It can be seen from this model that from the beginning to the end, only this input information A is used. The data label corresponding to data A is not used, so Autoencoder is an unsupervised learning. When we use Autoencoder, we usually only use the first half of Autoencoder. This part is also called EnCode, encoder, encoding. The processor can get the essence of the source data. Then only need to create a small neural network model and then learn the data in this essence, not only can reduce the burden of the neural network, but also can achieve a good effect.

Similarly, if the data is organized by Autoencoder, he can filter and summarize the characteristics of various data from various data. If the type characteristics of this picture are arranged and put on a picture, the data type can be used very well The type of source data is distinguished, and Autoencoder can reduce the dimension of special attributes.

2.3 C3D

The C3D network [9] is proposed as a general-purpose network and can be used in the fields of behavior recognition, scene recognition, and video similarity analysis. The structure of the C3D network is based on 3D convolution operations, with eight convolution layers and four pooling layers. Through experimental research, the authors claimed that it gave the best result when the size of the convolution kernel is $3 \times 3 \times 3$, the stride is $1 \times 1 \times 1$. The size of the pooling kernel is $2 \times 2 \times 2$, and the stride is $2 \times 2 \times 2$, except for the first layer of pooling, the size and stride are replaced by 1×22, which is to gradually increase the length.

Network obtains the final output after passing through the two fully connected layers and the softmax layer.

Because the C3D network is fast and straightforward, it is very suitable for the feature extraction, which is very helpful for the classification of 3D images. The authors evaluated the effectiveness of C3D on the database of behavior recognition, action similarity annotation, scene and object recognition, and all have achieved excellent results.

In this paper, we propose an extended network architecture based on the C3D network.

2.4   GoogLeNet

GoogLeNet [10] first appeared in the ILSVRC 2014 competition and won first place with a significant advantage. Inception Net used in that competition is often called Inception V1, and its most significant feature is that it reduces the amount of calculation and the number of parameters, and obtains outstanding classification performance.

By designing a sparse network structure, but able to generate dense data, it can not only increase the performance of the neural network but also ensure the efficiency of the use of computing resources. Google proposed the basic structure of the original Inception. This structure stacks the convolution and pooling commonly used in CNN, which increases the width of the network and increases the adaptability of the network to the scale. GoogLeNet uses a modular structure, the Inception structure, for easy addition and modification. The network finally adopted the average pooling instead of the fully connected layer. The idea came from NIN [11], which proved to increase the accuracy by 0.6%. However, in practice, a fully connected layer is added at the end, mainly to facilitate flexible adjustment of the output. Although the full connection was removed, Dropout is still used in the network. In order to avoid the gradient vanishing, the network additionally adds 2 auxiliary classifiers with softmax activation functions. The auxiliary classifier uses the outputs of one of the middle layers for classification. The cross-entropy losses of these classifiers are integrated into the loss function with a small weight. This idea is equivalent to model fusion and directly propagates the classification errors to the middle layers. Also, this provides additional regularization, which is beneficial for the training of the entire network.

3   3D CNN with Pixel-Wise Evidences

In action recognition in videos, sequences of frames are usually used as the input of the classifier, and the action class of the videos is estimated. To solve the problem we introduced in Sect. 1, the 2D information in each frame is combined with the temporal information as a 3D information to extract relevant information for action classification in the video. Use this 3D information could solve the time information which is the difficult point for video research.

Autoencoder plays an essential role in feature extraction, and U-Net [8], which is similar to Autoencoder, also could get excellent performance in medical image segmentation.

Therefore, we would like to take advantage of U-Net without the skip-connection part so that the network would be a kind of Autoencoder. Autoencoder could extract both high-level features and low-level features. The high-level features contain spatially rough but abstract information, and the low-level features contain spatially detailed information. The high-level features may contribute to recognizing each action part of people, and low-level features show where the people are to classify actions correctly. It is expected that the combination of the high-level features and the low-level features make the classification better. The architecture of the proposed approach is shown in Fig. 1.

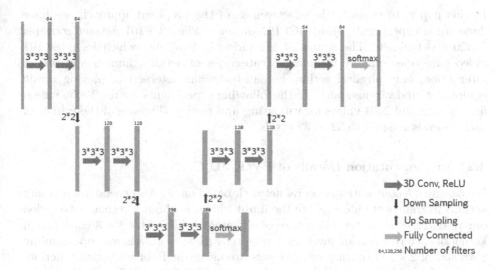

Fig. 1. Architecture of the proposed action classification approach.

The proposed network consists of two parts, the encoding path on the left and the decoding path on the right. The encoding path consists of 2 blocks; each block uses 2 convolution layers and a max-pooling layer to down-sampling. The decoding path is also composed of 2 blocks, which realizes up-sampling. The standard CNN classifier does not have this decoding path. We introduced this decoding path to extract pixel-wise evidence of the class of the short-term action. We call this network 3D CNN with pixel-wise evidences (PWE 3D CNN). In the following experiments, the size of the convolution kernels is all $3 \times 3 \times 3$ size. In the output layer, the classifier with the softmax activation function is attached to estimate the class of the short-term action in the video.

To accelerate the training, we introduced the auxiliary classifier with softmax activation function in the end of the decoding path, which is inspired by GoogLeNet [10]. The auxiliary classifier is to use the output of final layer for classification. The cross-entropy loss of this auxiliary classifier is integrated with the cross-entropy loss of the full network with a smaller weight (0.6). This introduction of the auxiliary classifier is equivalent to doing model fusion. Also, the additional term in the loss function by this auxiliary classifier works as a regularizer, which stabilizes the training and is very useful for the training of the entire network. As a result, it is expected that this classifier promotes to extract the necessary information for action classification in the features of the middle layer, and the accuracy of the recognition accuracy of the full network is improved.

4   Experiments

4.1   Dataset

In this paper, to evaluate the effectiveness of the proposed approach, we have done some experiments using UCF101 dataset. The UCF101 dataset contains 13320 short videos. The source of the video is YouTube, which includes 101 video categories, mainly including 5 categories of actions: human and object interaction, only physical action, human-to-human interaction, playing music equipment, and various sports. In the following experiments, we use 10656 videos for training and 2664 videos for validating and testing. The size of the frames of each video is re-sized to 32×32 pixels.

4.2   Implementation Details of PWE 3D CNN

We designed a convolutional neural network based on 3D Autoencoder to classify actions in frames of videos. Since the input videos is about 1 seconds, we called our research as short-term action recognition. We choose $3 \times 3 \times 3$ convolution kernel of each convolution layer, max pooling with size of 2×2, and up-sampling with size of 2×2. The convolution layers are using the Relu activation function. The number of filters of each convolutional layer is 64, 128, 256, 128, 64. A fully connected layer is at the middle of model which is similar with standard neural network, and the softmax function is used to classify the actions in videos. Due to the decoding part of Autoencoder could extract high-level features, we increased the classifiers from one to two and set the new classifier in the end of decoding part, which is shown in Fig. 1. As the input of the classifier, the outputs of the convolution layer are flattened, and then connected to the fully connected layer of the classifier. In the following experiments, the inputs of the neural network are the 16 continuous frames of videos. The output of the network is the class of the actions in the videos.

To train the model, we used categorical cross-entropy loss as the loss function. We set small weights for each auxiliary classifier to the total loss and integrate them with the final classifier. We have performed experiments with several sets of weights from 0.1 and 0.9 to 0.9 and 0.1. Then, we found that the performance with the weights of 0.6 and 0.4 is the best. We selected SGD as the optimizer and set the learning rate as 0.001, weight decay as 0.001. Dropout with the probability 0.25 is added after every convolution layer to prevent overfitting.

4.3   Performance of the PWE 3D CNN

We randomly divided the dataset into 80% for training and 20% for testing and validating. The learning curves for training and testing are shown in Fig. 2 and Fig. 3, the accuracy and the loss of the trained network are shown in Table 1. In the Table 1, Accuracy_1 and Loss_1 mean the first classifier's performance, which is the classifier located at the end of the encoding path. Accuracy_2 and Loss_2 show the performance of the classifier added at the end of the decoding path. Finally, we get excellent performance with an accuracy of 87.91% by the classifier located at the end of the encoding path and accuracy of 87.31% by the classifier located at the end of the decoding path. It shows that the proposed approach can give excellent performance for the short-term action classification for UCF101 dataset.

Table 1. Performance of proposed method on UCF101 dataset.

Performance	Train	Test
Accuracy_1	99.96%	87.91%
Loss_1	0.0007	0.51
Accuracy_2	99.95%	87.31%
Loss_2	0.0034	0.26

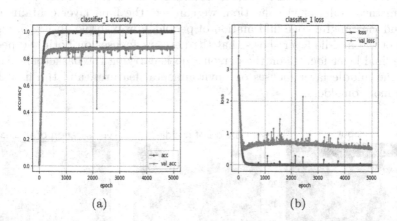

Fig. 2. Action classification results of first classifier on UCF101 dataset with 5000 epochs. (a)The accuracy of both training and testing of the first classifier. (b)The loss of both training and testing of the first classifier.

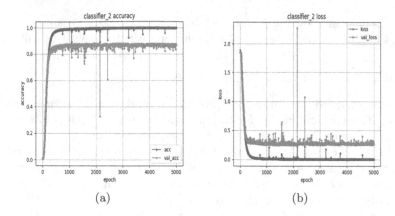

(a)   (b)

Fig. 3. Action classification results of auxiliary classifier on UCF101 dataset with 5000 epochs. (a)The accuracy of both training and testing of the auxiliary classifier. (b)The loss of both training and testing of the auxiliary classifier.

To understand which parts in the frame are considered to be important for action classification, we visualized the feature map in the proposed network. We use Grad-Cam [12] to understand through which pixels the model knows that the input sample belongs to a certain category. As our model is unique in the decoding part, both the feature maps of the middle layer (end of the encoding path but before flatten) and the final layer (end of decoding path before classifier) are extracted and the sum of each pixel values are calculated for visualization. We choose 3 videos from UCF101 dataset as the input video clips. In Fig. 4, a frame in the video clip in which a lady is applying eye makeup. Figure 5 show the result for basketball. In Fig. 6, the results for skiing are shown.

From the results of visualization, we can see, the final layer contains more clear and meaningful edge information of people. For example, in Fig. 5, visualization of the middle layer shows that the network focuses on both two people, but the final layer focuses on the person who is carrying the basketball. And in Fig. 6, the middle layer focuses on environmental features, and the final layer focuses more on skiers.

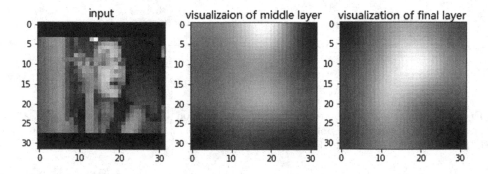

Fig. 4. First input sample visualization.

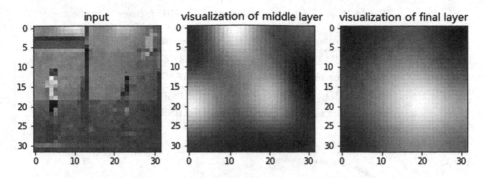

Fig. 5. Second input sample visualization.

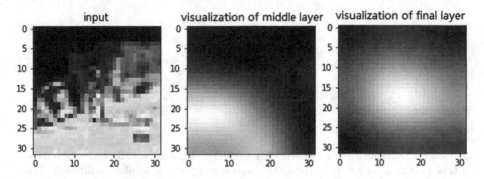

Fig. 6. Third input sample visualization.

4.4   Comparisons with C3D Model

We have also performed several comparison experiments of our PWE 3D CNN to the C3D model [9] on the UCF101 dataset. The C3D model is the same as the network without decoding path of the proposed PWE 3D CNN and can be regarded as the baseline model of the proposed PWE 3D CNN.

To compare with the previous work [9], we set the same parameters of the network and use the same inputs. To make the network complexity equal to C3D, the number of layers of our encoding path to be the same as the C3D model. The decoding path has changed accordingly. Our experiments include fewer filters with 16, 32, 64, 128, and the number of filters with 64, 128, 256, 512 of each convolution layer.

The network parameters are trained by using 10656 videos and 2664 validate videos. Results are shown in Table 2, Fig. 7 and Fig. 8. Since 3D Autoencoder can extract both high-level and low-level features, the classification performance could give a better effect. The proposed model outperforms the C3D models.

Table 2. Action classification on UCF101 dataset.

Methods	Accuracy
C3D (less filters)	79.47%
Our method (less filters)	**82.88%**
C3D (more filters)	83.18%
Our method (more filters)	**84.98%**

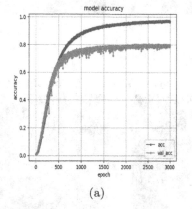 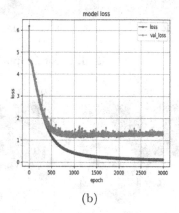

(a)	(b)

Fig. 7. Action classification results on UCF101 dataset based on C3D with less number of filters. (a)The accuracy of both training and testing of less number of filters. (b)The loss of both training and testing of less number of filters.

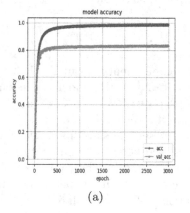 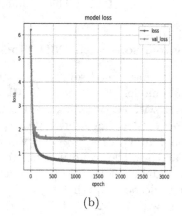

(a)	(b)

Fig. 8. Action classification results on UCF101 dataset based on C3D with more number of filters. (a)The accuracy of both training and testing of more number of filters. (b)The loss of both training and testing of more number of filters.

4.5   Comparison with the State-of-the-art

We have also compared the proposed PWE 3D CNN with the state-of-the-art methods on UCF101 dataset. For the UCF101 dataset, we report the accuracy of classification.

Table 3 shows the results on UCF101 dataset for comparison of the PWE 3D CNN with other RGB based action recognition methods. The proposed PWE 3D CNN model outperforms the RE3DCNN [13], I3D [14] and Spatial Stream-Resnet [17] on UCF101 by 87.91%. As shown in the Table 3, the PWE 3D CNN also performs better than Conv Pooling [15] and Conv Fusion [16] by almost 5% on UCF101.

Table 3. Accuracy performance comparison of PWE 3D CNN with state-of-the-art methods over UCF101 dataset.

Method	Accuracy
3D-ShuffleNet V1 2.0x [13]	84.96%
3D-ShuffleNet V2 2.0x [13]	83.32%
3D-MobileNet V1 2.0x [13]	76.18%
3D-MobileNet V2 1.0x [13]	81.60%
I3D [14]	84.5%
Spatial Stream-Resnet [17]	82.3%
DT+MVSM [18]	83.5%
Conv Pooling [15]	82.6%
Conv Fusion [16]	82.6%
Our method	**87.91%**

4.6   Ablation Experiments

We run a number of ablations to analyze the proposed PWE 3D CNN. Results are shown in Table 4.

Same Architecture Different Weights for Classifiers: At first, we have done the experiments with different weights for the integration of loss functions. The weights are selected from 0.1 and 0.9 to 0.5 and 0.5. Table 4 shows the results of PWE 3D CNN with the results for various weights of the classifiers. We found that the weights 0.4 and 0.6, which is our proposed method performs the best.

Table 4. Ablations.

Method	Accuracy
Same architecture 0.1 and 0.9 weights for classifiers	81.94%
Same architecture 0.2 and 0.8 weights for classifiers	82.09%
Same architecture 0.3 and 0.7 weights for classifiers	82.50%
Same architecture 0.4 and 0.6 weights for classifiers	85.81%
Same architecture 0.5 and 0.5 weights for classifiers	83.41%
Same architecture 0.7 and 0.3 weights for classifiers	87.27%
Same architecture 0.8 and 0.2 weights for classifiers	85.70%
Same architecture 0.9 and 0.1 weights for classifiers	87.42%
Same architecture no weights for classifiers	83.60%
3D Autoencoder with 1 classifier	83.07%
3D Autoencoder with 3 classifiers	82.51%
Omit one decoder layer	84.16%
Our method	**87.91%**

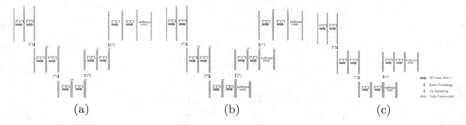

(a)   (b)   (c)

Fig. 9. Three architectures of ablation experiments. (a)Architecture of omit one decoder. (b)Architecture of 3D Autoencoder with 3 classifiers. (c)Architecture of omit one decoder.

3D Autoencoder with 1 Classifier: In the proposed PWE 3D CNN, Autoencoder and classifiers are integrated into one network. By extracting both the high-level features and the low-level features, it is expected that classification performance can be improved. Therefore how to combine Autoencoder with classifier is an interesting. Architecture is shown in Fig. 9 and the result is shown in Table 4.

In Fig. 9, considering the advantage of Autoencoder in feature extraction, we use one classifier to make it useful for action classification. The result shows that the auxiliary classifier which added at the middle of the model does improve performance.

3D Autoencoder with 3 Classifiers: After comparing with condition of 1 classifier, multiple classifier improve the results has been proved. Then we design the model like Fig. 9. For this experiment we use almost the same architecture but add one auxiliary softmax classifier at decoder part. We still make three losses of three classifiers together as the model loss. The results are shown in Table 4.

The result shows that more classifiers does not give better performance. More classifiers do not necessarily lead to better classification results.

Omit One Decoder Layer: Since 3 classifiers do not improve the model, to confirm the role of the decoding part we generate an architecture shown in Fig. 9 which omit one decoder layer but with two classifiers.

In Table 4, we can compare the accuracy of this architecture with our proposed method. This suggests that correspond decoder part can improve the feature extraction for classification.

5   Conclusions

In this paper we proposed to apply autoencoder with 3D convolutional neural network for action classification. By extending the basic CNN structure to autoencoder, and adding a classifier at the end of autoencoder, the extraction of spatial and temporal features is realized, and the classification results are improved. Through experiments using UCF101 dataset, the PWE 3D CNN architecture achieves good performance on action classification in frames of videos.

References

1. LeCun, Y., Bottou, L., Bengio, Y., Haffner, P.: Gradient-based learning applied to document recognition. Proc. IEEE **86**(11), 2278–2324 (1998)
2. Ji, S., Xu, W., Yang, M., Yu, K.: 3D convolutional neural networks for human action recognition. IEEE Trans. Pattern Anal. Mach. Intell. **35**(1), 221–231 (2013)
3. Hinton, G.E., Salakhutdinov, R.R.: Reducing the dimensionality of data with neural networks. Science **313**(5786), 504 (2006)
4. Soomro, K., Zamir, A.R., Shah, M.: UCF101: a dataset of 101 human action classes from videos in the wild. CRCV-TR-12-01, November 2012
5. Simonyan, K., Zisserman, A.: Two-stream convolutional networks for action recognition in videos. arXiv:1406.2199 (2014)
6. Karpathy, A., Toderici, G., Shetty, S., Leung, T., Sukthankar, R., Fei-Fei, L.: Large-scale video classification with convolutional neural networks. In: IEEE Conference on Computer Vision and Pattern Recognition (2014)
7. Rumelhart, D.E., Hinton, G.E., Williams, R.J.: Learning internal representations by error propagation. In: Parallel Distributed Processing: Foundations, vol. 1. MIT Press, Cambridge 1986
8. Ronneberger, O., Fischer, P., Brox, T.: U-Net: convolutional networks for biomedical image segmentation. arXiv:1505.04597 (2015)
9. Tran, D., Bourdev, L., Fergus, R., Torresani, L., Paluri, M.: Learning spatiotemporal features with 3D convolutional networks. arXiv:1412.0767 (2014)
10. Szegedy, C., et al.: Going deeper with convolutions. arXiv:1409.4842 (2014)
11. Lin, M., Chen, Q., Yan, S.: Network In network. arXiv:1312.4400 (2013)

12. Selvaraju, R.R., Cogswell, M., Das, A., Vedantam, R., Parikh, D., Batra, D.: Grad-CAM: visual explanations from deep networks via gradient-based localization. arXiv:1610.02391 (2016)
13. Köpüklü, O., Kose, N., Gunduz, A., Rigoll, G.: Resource efficient 3D convolutional neural networks. arXiv:1904.02422 (2019)
14. Carreira, J., Zisserman, A.: Quo vadis, action recognition? A new model and the kinetics dataset. In: CVPR (2017)
15. Ng, J.Y.-H., Hausknecht, M., Vijayanarasimhan, S., Vinyals, O., Monga, R., Toderici, G.: Beyond short snippets: deep networks for video classification. In: CVPR (2015)
16. Feichtenhofer, C., Pinz, A., Zisserman, A.: Convolutional two-stream network fusion for video action recognition. In: CVPR (2016)
17. Feichtenhofer, C., Pinz, A., Wildes, R.P.: Spatiotemporal residual networks for video action recognition. arXiv:1611.02155 (2016)
18. Cai, Z., Wang, L., Peng, X., Qiao, Y.: Multi-view super vector for action recognition. In: CVPR (2014)

Discriminative Metric Learning with Convolutional Feature Descriptors for Age-Invariant Face Recognition and Verification

Wataru Ohyama[1]([✉]), Yuta Somada[2,3], Nobu C. Shirai[2], and Tetsushi Wakabayashi[2]

[1] Saitama Institute of Technology, Fukaya Saitama, Japan
ohyama@sit.ac.jp
[2] Mie University, Tsu Mie, Japan
[3] Yahoo Japan Corporation, Tokyo, Japan

Abstract. Aging includes internal and external factors that cause variation in appearance of face and, consequently, it is a difficult problem to handle in person identification and verification using face images. In this paper, we propose a method for face recognition and verification that is robust against variation of facial appearance caused by aging. Our proposed method uses discriminative metric learning over convolutional feature descriptors extracted from frontal face images. The results of an experiments for performance evaluation on the FG-Net and CACD face aging datasets empirically clarify that the proposed method is effective for improving the performance of person identification and verification in the scenario where input face images contain appearance variation due to aging.

Keywords: Face recognition · Face verification · Age invariant · Discriminative metric learning · Convolutional feature descriptors

1 Introduction

Recently, the social demands for protecting privacy and personal information have increased. To protect privacy and personal information from unauthorized attacks, authentication based on biometric information has gained much attention because it has inherent robustness against theft and falsification. Of the various modalities in biometric authentication systems, face recognition and authentication have the following advantages: (1) a forgery is expected to be confirmed using a image which is saved previously, (2) Unauthorized access is also expected to be prevented because unauthorized person would not like to be taken a picture of their face.

In the authentication viewpoint, face images have the disadvantage where its performance is easily affected by variation in appearance caused by changes

© Springer Nature Singapore Pte Ltd. 2020
W. Ohyama and S. K. Jung (Eds.): IW-FCV 2020, CCIS 1212, pp. 83–96, 2020.
https://doi.org/10.1007/978-981-15-4818-5_7

Fig. 1. Examples of Face images in the FG-Net aging face database. The above and the below lines in the figure show images of one subject. The ages of each subject are shown at the below of each face image.

of pose, illumination, and facial expression (PIE). Traditionally, several studies for face recognition and verification that handled appearance variations due to change in PIE have been reported. Although these researches proposed some promising techniques, methods for the recognition and verification of faces images that contain appearance variation caused by aging are not mature. The age-invariant face recognition or verification systems are quite important to reduce frequency of updating registered face information, and find persons who are missing for long time using surveillance cameras.

Developing a face recognition method which is robust against appearance variation caused by aging involves challenging problems. First, aging of the facial appearance is affected by not only internal genetic factors but several external factors that come from the living environment of an individual. A Furthermore, whereas developing a face recognition system requires a large dataset of face images for classifier training, acquiring face images including several ages over the long term is not so easy.

Another problem for a dataset is that the image quality of old face images are usually degraded. Because spreading digital cameras to consumers started only approximately past 20 years, the digitization of old photographs requires the scanning of low quality pictures. Old pictures printed on a paper contains a particle-like texture. When we scan these pictures, the texture also appears in the image. Figure 1 shows some examples of actual face images in the FG-Net aging dataset. We can observe that the image at upper-left, in which the person is 4 years old, contains the texture noise from the printing paper. Thus, an age-invariant face recognition method is required to manage both facial appearance changes caused by subjects aging and low image quality.

The authors propose a face recognition method that is robust against facial appearance variation caused by aging. The proposed method matches two input face images and evaluates the similarity between the images in Euclidean space, which is robust against aging. Euclidean space is obtained by discriminative metric learning (DML) in which a nonlinear projection function decreases the distance between samples extracted from face images of the same person and increases the distance between other ones. In the proposed method, the projection function is obtained using a neural network.

The main contributions of this research are as follows:

1. A new method that uses a neural network-based DML combined with a convolutional feature extractor is proposed.
2. For DML, neural network-based optimization is implemented.
3. A comprehensive performance evaluation using two major open datasets, FG-Net and CACD, is performed to confirm the effectiveness of the proposed method.

While a similar concept of DML has been proposed by Hu et al. [6], their method was applied to conventional hand-crafted feature descriptors. In this paper we introduce the convolutional feature extractor and some modifications to their concept.

2   Previous Work

Researches that involve face images have attracted researchers over the past two decades. The research field covers a wide range of topics including face detection, face recognition, facial feature extraction, and recognition and analysis of expression.

Face recognition has been the most active research topic since eigenfaces [16] were reported. Recently, the face recognition performance has been dramatically improved by the introduction of the convolutional neural network (CNN). Some methods, such as Facenet [12] and DeepID [15], demonstrate very high performance that outperforms even human skills.

Face recognition is considered as a special case of object recognition; however, it is distinguished from other object recognition problems in terms of appearance variations, such as PIE and aging. Many methods managing PIE variation have been proposed and have achieved high recognition performance. However, face recognition performance against aging variation is still required for improvement because of a lack of datasets and the low quality of images.

Multiple studies reported methods utilizing age estimation and aging simulation for the aging problem. By contrast, age-invariant face recognition is currently being developed by many researchers. Age-invariant face recognition methods are generally divided into two approaches: generative and discriminative. In generative approaches, the image is transformed to reduce age differences to a comparison image. This approach is closely related to aging simulation. One typical example is a method that matches images transformed by the three-dimensional aging simulation [10] proposed by Park et al. These generative methods are difficult to use in practice because they require optimum parameters and relatively clean training aging samples.

In order to overcome the above problem of generative method, many researches have mainly used a discriminative approach, which extracts features which are less affected by aging. Li et al. [8] proposed multi-feature discriminant analysis that combines scale invariant feature transfer (SIFT) and multi-scale local binary pattern feature descriptors. This was often used as a comparison method in subsequent studies, and the experimental evaluation method was adopted by studies such as Gong et al. [3] and Chen et al. [1]. Gong et al. [3] proposed hidden factor analysis that decomposes an age-invariant identity factor, age factor affected by aging, and noise from histogram of oriented gradients (HOG) features. Moreover, they extended this method to a maximum entropy feature descriptor [4]. By contrast, Chen et al. proposed the adoption of a data-driven approach called cross-age reference coding [1]. This method uses a large-scale cross age reference set collected from the Internet. An another discriminative method for the aging face recognition [14] is also proposed. This method segmented an input face image into three overlapped sub-blocks which contain each facial features (eyes, nose and mouth). Each sub-block is evaluated with them in gallery separately and the results of evaluation are fused to make the final decision.

Recently, CNN-based approaches have emerged. Wen et al. proposed LF-CNN [17], which combines general convolutional layers to extract the pure image features and the fully connected layer to extract age-invariant latent factor features. Xu et al. [18] decomposed identity features, age features, and noise using auto-encoder networks. Face recognition based on CNN promises good results and these methods could obtain high accuracy in evaluation experiments using datasets including small age gap, such as MORPH. However, in datasets such as FG-Net, which has large age gaps and contains childhood images that have appearances that often change because of growth, these methods cannot obtain high accuracy.

In our proposed method, we introduce DML and show that its effectiveness for age-invariant face recognition.

3   DML with Convolutional Feature Descriptors

In this section, we provide an outline of the proposed recognition method for aging faces and detail of each process. The novelties of the method are a method that combines convolutional feature descriptors and DML, and its implementation using a deep neural network.

Figure 2 shows the outline of the proposed method. The process of face image recognition or verification using the proposed method consists of the following four steps:

1. As preprocessing, the face region is extracted by a tight bounding box and image quality enhancement is applied.
2. A convolutional feature descriptor is extracted from input and registered face images using a pre-trained CNN.

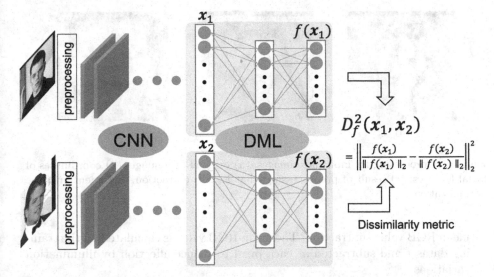

Fig. 2. Outline of the proposed age-invariant face recognition method. The method consists of preprocessing, extraction of convolutional feature descriptors, projection by a nonlinear function obtained by DML, and calculation of dissimilarity.

3. The extracted convolutional feature descriptors are projected into low-dimensional Euclidean space using nonlinear projection function $f(x)$ obtained by DML.
4. The dissimilarity between input and registered face images $D_f^2(x_1, x_2)$ is calculated as the Euclidean distance between them in the transformed space.

3.1 Preprocessing

In usual, face images contain regions that degrade the performance of face recognition, that is, background, hair, and clothes. Therefore, we extract the face region using a tight bounding box determined by the coordinates of facial features (eyes, nose, and mouth) in the original image. In this research, the coordinates of facial features are given as annotation information by datasets. When these annotation information was not given, we can use automatic extraction methods for the face region and coordinates of facial features such as MTCNN [19] and the dlib face detector [7].

After face and facial feature point detection, the following processes are also applied:

– Face alignment: images are aligned so that the positions of eyes are parallel to predetermined coordinates.
– Size normalization: images are resized to a uniform size of 244 × 244 pixels for the feature extraction process.

(a)   (b)   (c)

Fig. 3. Preprocessing for input face images: (a) original face image; (b) coordinates of facial features; (c) result of preprocessing, that is, face extraction, alignment and size normalization.

– mean RGB value subtraction: The mean RGB value is calculated on the training dataset and subtracted at each pixel to reduce affection by illumination variations.

Examples of original images and preprocessed face images are shown in Fig. 3.

3.2   Convolutional Feature Descriptors

As detailed analysis of its high performance and internal behavior has progressed, CNN has become the de facto standard for feature extraction for image recognition. At the present time, several promising CNN models that are pre-trained using very big datasets are available for the research community. Motivated by these developments, the authors use neural network architecture that was originally developed by the Visual Geometry Group (VGG) [13] and trained using over 2 million face images [11].

The convolution layer of the VGG16 architecture inputs an image of three channels with 244×244 pixels and outputs $7 \times 7 \times 512$ convolution values. Although the standard VGG16 architecture inputs this output into the fully connected layer for classification, the authors regard the output as a feature vector whose dimensionality is 25,088.

3.3   Discriminative Metric Learning

The main difficulty in face recognition that includes aging face images is that the matching score, that is, the similarity, between face images of the same person sometimes become smaller than that between different people because of facial appearance change caused by aging. To overcome this problem, the authors propose a method that obtains a nonlinear projection function that provides a discriminative metric using a neural network. The obtained nonlinear projection function projects the input convolutional feature descriptors into a metric space in which the distance between samples extracted from the same person becomes small and, by contrast, that between different people becomes large.

Neural Network for DML. DML in the proposed method consists of an M-layer neural network that has $p^{(m)}$ nodes in the m-th layer. When a convolutional feature descriptor extracted from a face image $\mathbf{x} \in \mathbb{R}^d$ is given, the output of the first layer in the neural network is obtained using $\mathbf{h}^{(1)} = s(\mathbf{W}^{(1)}\mathbf{x}+\mathbf{b}^{(1)}) \in \mathbb{R}^{p^{(1)}}$, where $\mathbf{W}^{(1)} \in \mathbb{R}^{p^{(1)} \times d}$ and $\mathbf{b}^{(1)} \in \mathbb{R}^{p^{(1)}}$ denote a linear projection matrix in the first layer and a weighting vector for the bias term. Function $s(\mathbf{x})$ is a nonlinear activation function; we use the rectified linear unit (ReLU).

Repeating a similar transformation, the output of the final M-th layer is determined using

$$f(\mathbf{x}) = \mathbf{h}^{(M)} = s\left(\mathbf{W}^{(M)}\mathbf{h}^{(M-1)} + \mathbf{b}^{(M)}\right) \in \mathbb{R}^{p^{(M)}}. \tag{1}$$

Function $f(\mathbf{x})$ can be regarded as a nonlinear function that projects a d-dimensional feature vector into $p^{(M)}$-dimensional space using the M-layer neural network. Here, we define $\mathbf{W} = \{\mathbf{W}^{(1)}, \mathbf{W}^{(2)}, \ldots, \mathbf{W}^{(M)}\}$ and $\mathbf{b} = \{\mathbf{b}^{(1)}, \mathbf{b}^{(2)}, \ldots, \mathbf{b}^{(M)}\}$ to simplify the following notations.

We calculate the matching score between feature descriptors $\mathbf{x}_i$, $\mathbf{x}_j$ extracted from two face images as the normalized squared Euclidean distance using function f:

$$D_f^2(\mathbf{x}_i, \mathbf{x}_j) = \left\|\frac{f(\mathbf{x}_i)}{\|f(\mathbf{x}_i)\|_2} - \frac{f(\mathbf{x}_j)}{\|f(\mathbf{x}_j)\|_2}\right\|_2^2. \tag{2}$$

Network Learning. Parameters $\mathbf{W}$ and $\mathbf{b}$ are optimized using the backpropagation algorithm. In the proposed method, using the determined threshold value τ and margin r, the neural network is trained to behave as the projection function that makes the distance between the samples from the same person smaller than $\tau - r$ and that from different people larger than $\tau + r$:

$$l_{ij}\left(\tau - D_f^2(\mathbf{x}_i, \mathbf{x}_j)\right) < r, \tag{3}$$

where $l_{ij} = \{1, -1\}$ when $(\mathbf{x}_i, \mathbf{x}_j)$ are from same and different people, respectively.

To satisfy equation (3), the loss function that is minimized in the neural network is determined as follows:

$$L = \frac{1}{2}\sum_{i,j} g\left(r - l_{ij}\left(\tau - D_f^2(\mathbf{x}_i, \mathbf{x}_j)\right)\right) + \frac{\lambda}{2}\sum_{m=1}^{M}\left(\|\mathbf{W}^{(m)}\|_F^2 + \|\mathbf{b}^{(m)}\|_2^2\right), \tag{4}$$

where function g is regarded as a logistic loss function and determined by $g(z) = \frac{1}{\beta}\log(1+\exp(\beta z))$. The second term of Eq. 4 introduces the weight decay property which implements L_2-norm regularization, where $\|\mathbf{W}\|_F^2$ denotes the Frobenius norm of matrix $\mathbf{W}$. Parameters β and λ control the smoothness and weight of regularization, respectively.

4   Evaluation Experiments

To evaluate the effectiveness of the proposed DML method, we conducted evaluation experiments using two public facial image datasets that include appearance variation caused by aging.

4.1   Datasets

The datasets used for performance evaluation in conventional research that proposes age-invariant face recognition sometimes contains bias regarding the race or age of a person. Consequently, evaluation and comparison using multiple datasets that have different characteristics are requested to perform a fair assessment. From this point of view, the authors conducted evaluation experiments, which evaluated and compared the performance of the proposed method with that of conventional methods using two major public datasets that contain facial appearance variation caused by aging.

We evaluated the performance improvement by introducing DML using two major open datasets: FG-Net and Cross-Age Celebrity Dataset (CACD) [1]. FG-Net contains 1,002 images from 82 subjects and 6–18 images per subject. The age variation of subjects is 0 to 69 years old. Each image is provided with annotations that consist of vertical and horizontal orientations and image quality. The CACD dataset consists of 163,446 images from 2,000 subjects. The age variation of subjects is 12 to 62 years old. All images were taken between 2004 and 2013. The CACD dataset also provides the verification subset (CACD-VS) for the evaluation of verification performance. CACD-VS consists of 4,000 pairs of face images of which 2,000 pairs are of the same subjects and 2,000 pairs are of different subjects.

4.2   Network Implementation

In this section, the implementation of the DML network and detailed process of network training are described.

As described in Sect. 3.2, we use the convolutional layers of the pre-trained VGG16 network for convolutional feature descriptor extraction. To adopt the limited number of training samples, we also use the weight values of fully connected layers in VGG16 as the initial weight of the DML network.

The structure of the DML network is as follows: The numbers of layers M and nodes $p^{(n)}$ are 2 and 4,096, respectively. These values correspond to those in the VGG16 network. Threshold value τ in DML is set to 1.2 from the mean value calculated from the verification dataset. The other parameters λ, β and r are determined as 0.001, 30, and 0.1, respectively, from initial experiments using a small verification dataset.

We use the remaining images obtained removing test images from the CACD for training DML network. The CACD dataset does not include a sufficient

Table 1. Comparison of recognition accuracy for each age group in FG-Net between our proposed method and LF-CNN [17], one of state-of-the-art methods.

Age Group	Amount	LF-CNN	DML (proposed)
0–16	612	76.47%	87.07%
17–69	390	96.93%	100.00%
0–69 (total)	1002	88.10%	91.32%

Table 2. Comparison of verification accuracy on the CACD-VS dataset.

Method	Accuracy
HD-LBP [2] (2013)	81.6%
HFA [5] (2013)	84.4%
CARC [1] (2015)	87.6%
Human, Average	85.7%
Human, Voting	94.2%
without DML (VGG16 [11])	96.5%
with DML (proposed method)	98.4%
LF-CNN [17] (2016)	98.5%

number of images per subject for training the network for the classification task. However, because DML is based on verification, in which the required task is to determine the input pair that comes from the same or different subjects, the lack of an image number for one subject does not cause a problem. For instance, when we have n samples for one subject, we can create $_nC_2$ pairs for the DML.

4.3 Results and Discussion

Evaluation on the FG-Net Dataset. Following the experimental procedure in Li et al. [9], we evaluated the performance of face recognition based on leave-one-person-out (LOPO), where all images of one subject were excluded from the dataset as test subjects and remaining images were used for training.

Figure 4 shows the rank performance of face recognition with and without DML. Face recognition without DML denotes the condition in which the pre-trained VGG16 network was naively applied on the FG-Net dataset. We observed that the Rank-1 recognition accuracy significantly improved from 83.93% to 91.32%.

Table 1 shows the results of comparing our proposed method and LF-CNN [17], which is one of state-of-the-art methods in age-invariant face recognition, for Rank-1 recognition accuracy. Because facial appearance significantly develops during childhood, face recognition for young subjects is more difficult than that for adults. Consequently, we separated the dataset into two age groups: young

(0–16 years old) and adult (17–69)[1]. The proposed DML method outperformed LF-CNN in all age groups. These results suggest that DML successfully suppressed the effect of facial appearance change caused by aging.

Evaluation on the CACD-VS Dataset. The DML is also applicable for verification tasks. We evaluated the verification performance using the CACD-VS dataset, which consists of 4,000 pairs of face images. We adopted 10-fold cross validation for performance evaluation.

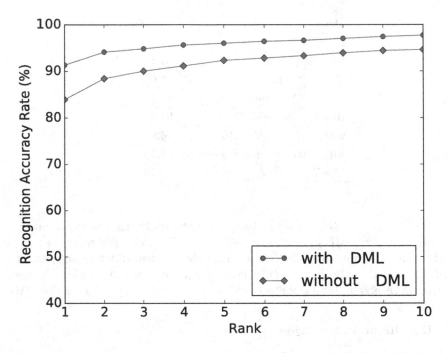

Fig. 4. Improvement of recognition accuracy by introducing DML for FG-Net.

Table 2 shows the comparison between the proposed and conventional method for verification accuracy. Similar to the evaluation on FG-Net, verification without DML denoted a naive application of the pre-trained VGG16 network. Even though the verification performance without DML was relatively high, further improvement was achieved by introducing DML. The performance of the proposed method was slightly lower than that of LF-CNN, but quite competitive against such a state-of-the-art method.

Verification performance against the variation of the threshold value was also evaluated. Figure 5 shows the receiver operating characteristic (ROC) curves of each verification method. LF-CNN was excluded because no information was

---

[1] This separation was also used in [17].

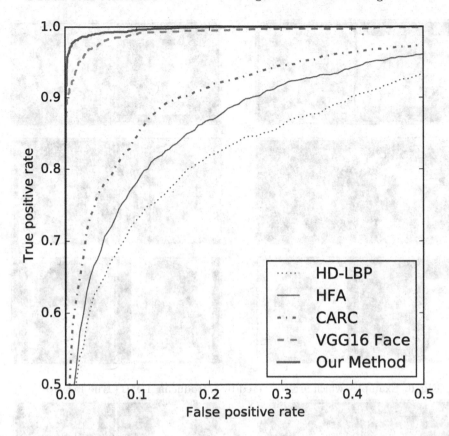

Fig. 5. Comparison of verification performance using the ROC curve among the proposed and conventional methods.

provided in the paper [17]. From the ROC curves, we observed that the verification performance effectively improved by introducing the DML.

Figure 6 shows some examples which are improved by introducing DML. While each pair in Fig. 6 belongs to a same subject, it was verified as belonging to different ones before introducing DML. These failures are corrected by introducing DML and each pair is verified as belonging to the same subject. We can observed that image pairs having a large age gap are handled properly by the proposed method. Similarly, examples in Fig. 7 were originally verified as belonging to the same subjects, but corrected by the proposed method as that they are from different subjects. We can see that the pairs of different persons in similar appearance age are correctly verified.

Fig. 6. Examples which are recovered by introducing DML (True Positive)

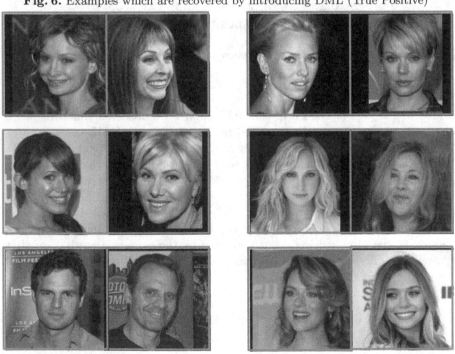

Fig. 7. Examples which are recovered by introducing DML (True Negative)

5 Conclusions

In this paper, we proposed DML for age-invariant face recognition and verification. The proposed DML method used a fully connected neural network to obtain an adaptive nonlinear projection function for samples that included facial appearance change caused by aging.

The effectiveness of the proposed method was empirically evaluated using two major public datasets that contained aging. We confirmed that both recognition and verification performance were effectively improved by introducing DML. Particularly, in the face recognition experiment using the FG-Net database, the proposed method outperformed LF-CNN, which is one of state-of-the-art methods in this field.

By contrast, the verification performance of the proposed method was quite competitive but slightly lower than that of LF-CNN. We need to introduce fine-tuning and careful parameter setting for further performance improvement.

References

1. Chen, B.C., Chen, C.S., Hsu, W.H.: Face recognition and retrieval using cross-age reference coding with cross-age celebrity dataset. IEEE Trans. Multimedia **17**(6), 804–815 (2015). https://doi.org/10.1109/TMM.2015.2420374
2. Chen, D., Cao, X., Wen, F., Sun, J.: Blessing of dimensionality: high-dimensional feature and its efficient compression for face verification. In: 2013 IEEE Conference on Computer Vision and Pattern Recognition, pp. 3025–3032 (2013)
3. Gong, D., Li, Z., Lin, D., Liu, J., Tang, X.: Hidden factor analysis for age invariant face recognition. In: 2013 IEEE International Conference on Computer Vision, pp. 2872–2879, December 2013. https://doi.org/10.1109/ICCV.2013.357
4. Gong, D., Li, Z., Tao, D., Liu, J., Li, X.: A maximum entropy feature descriptor for age invariant face recognition. In: 2015 IEEE Conference on Computer Vision and Pattern Recognition. pp. 5289–5297, June 2015. https://doi.org/10.1109/CVPR.2015.7299166
5. Gong, D., Li, Z., Lin, D., Liu, J., Tang, X.: Hidden factor analysis for age invariant face recognition. In: 2014 IEEE International Conference on Computer Vision, pp. 2872–2879 (2013)
6. Hu, J., Lu, J., Tan, Y.P.: Discriminative deep metric learning for face verification in the wild. In: 2014 IEEE Conference on Computer Vision and Pattern Recognition, pp. 1875–1882 (2014)
7. Kazemi, V., Sullivan, J.: One millisecond face alignment with an ensemble of regression trees. In: 2014 IEEE Conference on Computer Vision and Pattern Recognition, pp. 1867–1874 (2014)
8. Li, Z., Park, U., Jain, A.K.: A discriminative model for age invariant face recognition. IEEE Trans. Inf. Forensics Secur. **6**(3), 1028–1037 (2011). https://doi.org/10.1109/TIFS.2011.2156787
9. Li, Z., Park, U., Jain, A.K.: A discriminative model for age invariant face recognition. IEEE trans. Inf. Forensics Secur. **6**(3), 1028–1037 (2011)
10. Park, U., Tong, Y., Jain, A.K.: Age-invariant face recognition. IEEE Trans. Pattern Anal. Mach. Intell. **32**(5), 947–954 (2010). https://doi.org/10.1109/TPAMI.2010.14

11. Parkhi, O.M., Vedaldi, A., Zisserman, A.: Deep face recognition. In: 2015 British Machine Vision Conference, vol. 1, p. 6 (2015)
12. Schroff, F., Kalenichenko, D., Philbin, J.: FaceNet: a unified embedding for face recognition and clustering. In: 2016 IEEE International Conference on Computer Vision and Pattern Recognition, pp. 815–823. IEEE Computer Society (2015)
13. Simonyan, K., Zisserman, A.: Very deep convolutional networks for large-scale image recognition. arXiv preprint arXiv:1409.1556 (2014)
14. Somada, Y., Ohyama, W., Wakabayashi, T.: Segmented face image verification for age-invariant face recognition. In: 2017 6th International Conference on Informatics, Electronics and Vision, pp. 1–4 (2017)
15. Sun, Y., Liang, D., Wang, X., Tang, X.: DeepID3: face recognition with very deep neural networks. Computing Research Repository (2015). http://arxiv.org/abs/1502.00873
16. Turk, M., Pentland, A.: Eigenfaces for recognition. J. Cogn. Neurosci. 3(1), 71–86 (1991). https://doi.org/10.1162/jocn.1991.3.1.71
17. Wen, Y., Li, Z., Qiao, Y.: Latent factor guided convolutional neural networks for age-invariant face recognition. In: 2016 IEEE Conference on Computer Vision and Pattern Recognition, pp. 4893–4901 (2016)
18. Xu, C., Liu, Q., Ye, M.: Age invariant face recognition and retrieval by coupled auto-encoder networks. Neurocomputing 222, 62–71 (2017). https://doi.org/10.1016/j.neucom.2016.10.010. http://www.sciencedirect.com/science/article/pii/S0925231216311729
19. Zhang, K., Zhang, Z., Li, Z., Qiao, Y.: Joint face detection and alignment using multitask cascaded convolutional networks. IEEE Sig. Process. Lett. 23(10), 1499–1503 (2016)

Dilated CNN Based Human Verifier
for Intrusion Detection

Ajmal Shahbaz[✉] and Kang-Hyun Jo

Graduate School of Electrical Engineering, University of Ulsan, Ulsan 44610, Korea
ajmal@islab.ulsan.ac.kr, acejo@ulsan.ac.kr

Abstract. This paper proposes an intrusion detection algorithm for intelligent surveillance systems. The algorithm detects an intrusion threat via a dual-stage computer vision algorithm. In the first stage, the input of video sequences passes through a probabilistic change detector based on Gaussian Mixture Models to segment intruders from the background. The extracted foreground region is then passed through the second stage to verify if it is human. The second stage is based on a shallow convolutional neural network (CNN) employing dilated convolution. The system sends an alert if there is intrusion detected. The algorithm is validated and compared with a top-ranked change detection algorithms. It outperformed the compared algorithm on the i-LIDS dataset of sterile zone monitoring.

Keywords: Video surveillance systems · CNN · Dual-Camera sensor · Sterile zone monitoring · Change detection · Camouflaged intruder

1   Introduction

Video surveillance systems (VSS) are more relevant than ever. They help to monitor sensitive areas such as airports, bus stops, borders, etc. Conventional VSS are monitored manually by security personnel for possible security risks. Thus, such systems require a high level of concentration at all times. This could result in negligence.

According to an estimate, 60–160 video surveillance systems cover per 1000 people in modern cities. The majority of the systems record videos and check them later for possible breach. The increase in VSS results in an increase in volumes of videos, thereby, the need for automating the surveillance process.

The conventional VSS is being taken over by their intelligent counterparts. They are capable of detecting anomalies automatically and alert the authorities. The intelligent surveillance systems are powered by computer vision algorithms, e.g., change detection.

Change detection algorithms are building blocks of intelligent surveillance systems (ISS). It aims at segmenting moving information (termed as foreground) from static information (background). The definition of foreground varies with the application. It could be human walking on the road, cars running on the

W. Ohyama and S. K. Jung (Eds.): IW-FCV 2020, CCIS 1212, pp. 97–107, 2020.
https://doi.org/10.1007/978-981-15-4818-5_8

street, or a bag left at the train station. High-level ISS tasks such as intrusion detection employ change detection as a pre-processing task. Therefore, the overall performance of ISS is highly dependent on change detection.   \

Change detection, also known as background subtraction or change detection has been widely studied for the past decade. There are many survey papers on the topic [2,3].

Gaussian Mixture Models (GMM) [7] can be considered as the most popular parametric based algorithm in the field of change detection. GMM is an economical with good performance in coping with illumination changes. However, it failed to cope with the camouflage effect in general [2].

Non-parametric models rely on the observation of the pixel values. For example, SuBSENSE [8], PAWCS [9], and WeSamBE [10] exploited spatial information around the pixel to model background. These algorithms showed promising results. WeSamBE [10] improved [8] by introducing a reward/penalty weighting strategy. However, they are cost ineffective and cannot be used for real-time applications [5].

Recently, CNN-based algorithms are popular among computer vision researchers [13]–[16]. Many algorithms have been proposed to tackle the challenge of change detection. The general theme of these algorithms is to train Convolutional Neural Network (CNN) on handpicked frames with ground truth from a certain video.

The trained model would be scene specific i.e. it would fail to perform on other videos. The first-ever deep learning based method [13] used training 50% of video sequences as training and tested on remaining. The method was scene specific and helped researchers to use CNN for foreground segmentation.

DeepBS [14] trained CNN with the background image. The background image was constructed by median filtering on the initial frames of a video sequence. It was trained multiple CNNs with multi-scale input images. DeepBS trained only one model with 5% training frames from all video sequences of change detection dataset (CDnet) [17].

CascadeCNN [15] built three CNN architecture which takes input image in three different resolutions. The authors also made public their handpicked frames with respective ground truth. SemanticBGS [16] took a different approach. It used CNN architecture trained on a different dataset to get the probabilities of objects in the change detection dataset. Using the information, background and foreground model has been built.

This paper proposes the dual-stage intrusion detection algorithm for intelligent surveillance systems. The first stage consists of a GMM based change detector [1,4]. The first stage extracts foreground information, i.e., an intruder. The region of interest (ROI) is fed into dilated convolutions based CNN network for human verification. The proposed algorithm is tested on the i-LIDS dataset [20] and compared with top-ranked change detection algorithms.

The rest of the paper is organized as follows: The proposed method is described in Sect. 2. The effectiveness of the proposed method is proved in Sect. 3. Paper is concluded with future works.

2 Proposed Algorithm

Figure 1 shows an overview of the proposed method. It consists of two main modules as described below:

1. Probabilistic Change Detector: This module is responsible for segmenting out foreground objects from the background.
2. Human Verifier: The region of interest (ROI) of the foreground object is extracted and fed into a dilated CNN based human verifier.

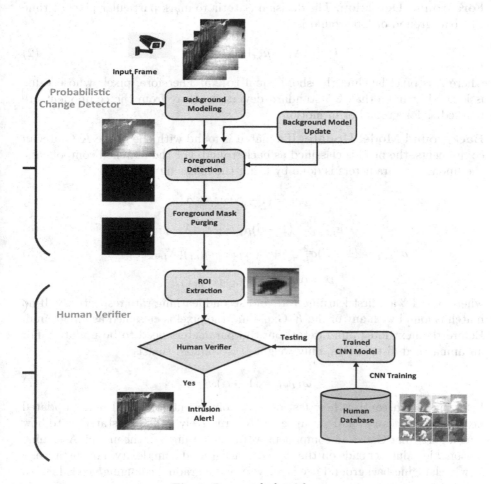

Fig. 1. Proposed algorithm

2.1 Probabilistic Change Detector (PCD)

PCD consists of three steps: background modeling, foreground detection, and background model update as shown in Fig. 2.

Background Modeling. Initial frames are assumed to consist of only background. This is an important assumption. Therefore, each pixel is modeled as a mixture of Gaussian [4]. The probability of observing a particular pixel X at time t is:

$$P(X_t) = \sum_{i=1}^{K} \omega_{i,t}\eta(X_t; \mu_{i,t}, \Sigma_{i,t}) \tag{1}$$

where $\eta, K, \omega_{i,t}, \mu_{i,t}, \Sigma_{i,t}$ are probability density function, number of Gaussian, estimate of weight, mean, covariance of the ith Gaussian in the mixture at time t.

Foreground Detection. The decision criteria to mark particular pixel at time t as background or foreground is:

$$|X_t - \mu_{i,t}| > \lambda\sigma_{i,t} \tag{2}$$

where λ is pixel labeling threshold equal to 2.5. Therefore, pixels whose value is located at more than 2.5 standard deviations away from the component are marked as foreground or in motion.

Background Model Update. If a match is found with one of the K Gaussian components, the pixel is classified as background. For the matched components, the update of parameters is done by using the following equations:

$$\omega_{i,t+1} = (1 - \alpha)\omega_{i,t} + \alpha \tag{3}$$

$$\mu_{i,t+1} = (1 - \beta)\mu_{i,t+1} + \beta X_{t+1} \tag{4}$$

$$\sigma_{i,t+1}^2 = (1 - \beta)\sigma_{i,t+1}^2 + \beta(X_{t+1} - \mu_{i,t})(X_{t+1} - \mu_{i,t})^T \tag{5}$$

$$\beta = \alpha\eta(X_{t+1}; \mu_{i,t+1}, \sigma_{i,t+1}^2) \tag{6}$$

where α and β are first learning rate and second learning rate respectively. If no match is found with any of the K Gaussian, the pixel is classified as foreground. Before the next foreground detection, the parameters need to be updated. For an unmatched distribution, only weight ω is updated that is:

$$\omega_{i,t+1} = (1 - \alpha)\omega_{i,t} \tag{7}$$

Learning rate α controls how fast or slow components of GMM being updated i.e. weight ω, mean μ, and variance σ^2. Alternatively, it can be stated as to how long a particular Gaussian component would be retained in the model. Assigning reasonable value depends on the type of background complexity. For instance, a slowly changing background needs a low α and a gradual changing needs high α.

Foreground Mask Purging (FMP). The foreground mask obtained from PCD has isolated undesirable noise which might result in false positives. FMP employs morphological opening and closing. It has two jobs: First, getting rid of isolated noise in the foreground mask by opening. Secondly, improving the geometry of the foreground object by the closing operation.

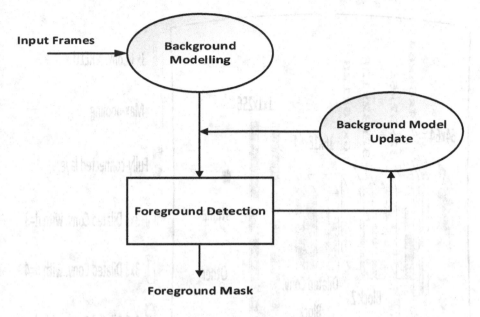

Fig. 2. Overview of probablistic change detector.

2.2 Dilated CNN

The region of interest is extracted and resized to 64×64 for the human verifier stage. This paper proposes a human verifier based on a shallow convolutional neural network which applies dilated convolutions to extract deep features of human. The proposed human verifier is shown in Fig. 3. The proposed network consists of 7 convolution layers, 2 max-pooling layers, 2 fully connected layers, and 1 softmax layer. Each convolution operation is followed by Rectified Linear Unit (ReLU) to avoid negative values in the feature maps. Also, feature maps are zero-padded to keep the spatial dimensions.

The proposed network is inspired by the VGG- 16 network [19]. The VGG network was runner up in the image classification challenge. The original VGG-16 consists of five blocks with 16 weight layers in total, thus the name. VGG-16 is the famous architecture which proposed the use of smaller kernel size 3×3. The authors claimed that the receptive field of two 3×3 kernels is effectively equal to the receptive field of 5×5 kernels. Whereas the receptive field of three 3×3 kernels stacked over each other has a receptive field equal to that of 7×7 kernels. Such a schema reduces the number of parameters needed by 30%.

The first two blocks (4 convolution layers, 2 max-pooling layers) of the proposed network are similar to the VGG. This helps to share the pre-trained weights from already trained VGG networks from imageNet dataset. First, two blocks use a set of 3×3 kernels stack over each other followed by the max pooling. Each block down-samples the input by half. The number of kernels being used is 64, 128, and 64 in each block.

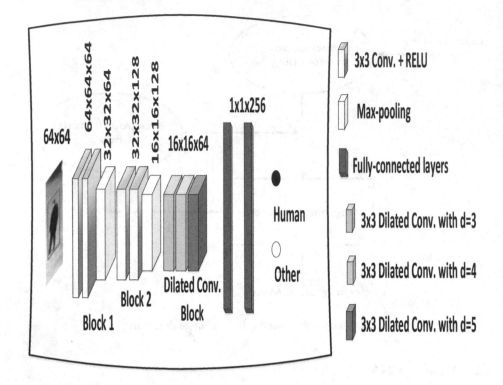

Fig. 3. Dilated CNN for human verifier

The third block of the proposed network applies dilated convolution operation. Dilated convolution operation works by inserting zeros between the kernel weights. This increases the receptive field of the kernel without increasing the number of parameters as shown in Fig. 4. Dilation rate (d) controls the receptive field of a convolution kernel. A dilation rate $d = 1$ is equivalent to the standard convolution operation. Similarly, $d = 2$, 3, 4 and 5 would result in 5×5, 7×7, 9×9, and 11×11 convolution kernel. There are two fully connected layers followed by a softmax layer. The network verifies the region of interest as human or other. If an intruder is verified, the algorithm sends intrusion alerts.

The dual approach to training the proposed network had been implemented. The proposed network has been trained using a pre-trained VGG model. First, two blocks used the weights that were already trained on the imageNet dataset. While the third block (dilated block) were unfrozen and trained on the particular video. Such schema helped to learn the specific features related to the foreground object of the i-LIDS dataset [11].

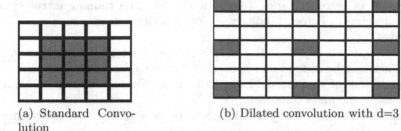

(a) Standard Convo-   (b) Dilated convolution with d=3
lution

Fig. 4. The two types of convolution operations employed in the proposed algorithm.

Fig. 5. Examples of training images for the dilated CNN for human verifier.

3 Experimental Analysis

3.1 Dataset Description

The proposed algorithm was tested on Imagery Library for Intelligent Detection
Systems (i-LIDS) dataset for sterile zone monitoring [20]. Table 1 shows a detail
description of datasets with challenges. Similarly, positive and negative samples
for training a human verifier is shown in Fig. 5. The challenges put forth by
i-LIDS dataset are summarized as:

1. The distance of intruders from the camera varies from near to far. The
   intruder may appear in the sequence from far which is a challenging situation.

2. The speed of intruder varies from slow to fast. The running intruder may be challenging to detect. Similarly, a slow walking intruder may cause false negatives.
3. Static foreground object. If the intruder stays static for a long time in the scene, it might be merged into background causing false negatives.
4. Different time of day. It could be challenging due to illumination changes particularly the night time.
5. Camouflage foreground object. IR camera poses a strong camouflage effect.

Table 1. Dataset description.

Video name	Duration	Time	Scenario
1	0:30	Day	Normal walk
2	0:30	Day	Running
3	0:30	Day	Crawling
4	0:30	Day	Slow walk
5	0:30	Day	Walking fast
6	0:30	Night	Walking away
7	0:30	Night	Walking away slowly
8	0:30	Night	Far from camera
9	0:30	Night	Camouflage intruder
10	0:30	Night	Camouflage intruder

3.2 Parameter Setting

Table 2 shows the parameters setting used along with the definition. All the video sequences were tested using the same parameter setting. The optimal values were chosen through extensive experiments in the literature. Also, optimal parameters were kept for GMM and its improvements. Similarly, SuBSENSE [8], PAWCS [9], and WeSamBE [10] were used with the original setting. The dilated CNN based human verifier was implemented in Keras [19].

Table 2. Parameter setting.

Parameter Name	Symbol	Value
Number of Gaussian	K	3
Pixel labeling threshold	λ	2.5
First learning rate	α	0.001
Second learning rate	β	$\alpha/10$
Structuring element for opening	SE1	3×3
Structuring element for closing	SE2	5×5

3.3 Quantitative Analysis

Table 3 shows the quantitative analysis of the proposed algorithm and the state of the art methods. The famous performance metrics such as recall R, precision P, and F-measure F were used.

$$R = \frac{TP}{(TP + FN)} \tag{8}$$

$$P = \frac{TP}{(TP + FP)} \tag{9}$$

$$F = \frac{2 \times P \times R}{(P + R)} \tag{10}$$

where TP = true positive, FP = false positive, TN = true negative and FN = false negative is defined as follows:

- TP: Intruder is correctly labeled as intruder.
- FP: Noise is incorrectly labeled as intruder.
- FN: Intruder is incorrectly labeled as noise.
- TN: Noise is correctly labeled as noise.

If intruder (true positive) is detected at least for 75% of the video sequence, it is considered successful, as defined by the i-LIDS dataset for video surveillance benchmark. For example, the i-LIDS dataset consists of 10 videos, and each video constitutes 10% of the overall F-measure. For instance, SuBSENSE detects and tracks an intruder in 8 video sequences of the i-LIDS dataset. Therefore, it has F-measure equals to 80%. PAWCS and WeSamBE were able to detect and track an intruder in 6 and 3 sequences of the i-LIDS dataset with false positives respectively. The proposed algorithm was able to segment intruder in all the video sequences of i-LIDS. Therefore, it has F-measure equals to 100%.

Table 3. Quantitative comparison on i-LIDS dataset using Recall R, Precision P, and F-measure F.

Algorithm	R	P	F
Proposed	1.00	1.00	1.00
SuBSENSE [8]	0.80	0.80	0.80
PAWCS [9]	0.60	0.60	0.60
WeSamBE [10]	0.30	0.30	0.30

3.4 Qualitative Analysis

Figure 6 shows the final results of the proposed algorithm. The video sequences show all the videos of the i-LIDS dataset as outlined in Table 1. The first row shows day time sequences while the second row shows night time sequences. The proposed algorithm detects and tracks intruders in all the video sequences.

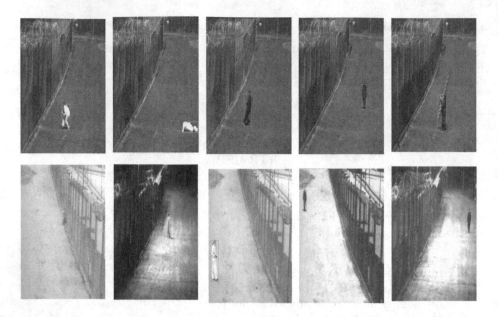

Fig. 6. The final detection results on the i-LIDS dataset. The first row shows the day time sequences. Second row shows night time sequences. The videos are ordered according the Table 1. For instance, first video is the first image in first row and first column.

4   Conclusion

This paper proposes dual-stage intrusion detection algorithms for intelligent surveillance systems. First, the input frames are passed through GMM based probabilistic change detector to segment intruder from the background. The intruder is verified using dilated convolutional neural networks. The proposed algorithm outperforms comparative algorithms on the i-LIDS dataset of sterile zone monitoring.

References

1. Shahbaz, A., Kurnianggoro, L., Wahyono, Jo, K.H.: Recent advances in the field of foreground detection: an overview. In: Król, D., Nguyen, N., Shirai, K. (eds) Advanced Topics in Intelligent Information and Database Systems (ACIIDS 2017). SCI, vol. 710, pp. 261–269. Springer, Cham (2017). https://doi.org/10.1007/978-3-319-56660-3_23
2. Shahbaz, A., Hariyono, J., Jo, K.H.: Evaluation of background subtraction algorithms for video surveillance. In: 2015 21st Korea-Japan Joint Workshop on Frontiers of Computer Vision (FCV), pp. 1–4, January 2015
3. Bouwmans, T., El Baf, F., Vachon, B.: Statistical background modeling for foreground detection: a survey. In: Handbook of Pattern Recognition and Computer Vision, pp. 181–199. World Scientific Publishing, January 2010

4. Shahbaz, A., Jo, K.: Probabilistic foreground detector for sterile zone monitoring. In: 2015 12th International Conference on Ubiquitous Robots and Ambient Intelligence (URAI), pp. 199–201, October 2015. https://doi.org/10.1109/URAI.2015.7358868

5. Kurnianggoro, L., Shahbaz, A., Jo, K.: Dense optical flow in stabilized scenes for moving object detection from a moving camera. In: 2016 16th International Conference on Control, Automation and Systems (ICCAS), pp. 704–708, October 2016. https://doi.org/10.1109/ICCAS.2016.7832395

6. Shahbaz, A., Hernández, C.D., Filonenko, A., Hariyono, J., Jo, K.: Probabilistic foreground detector with camouflage detection for sterile zone monitoring. In: 2016 IEEE 25th International Symposium on Industrial Electronics (ISIE), pp. 997–1001, June 2016. https://doi.org/10.1109/ISIE.2016.7745027

7. KaewTraKulPong, P., Bowden, R.: An improved adaptive background mixture model for real-time tracking with shadow detection. In: Remagnino, P., Jones, G.A., Paragios, N., Regazzoni, C.S. (eds.) Video-Based Surveillance Systems, pp. 135–144. Springer, Boston (2002). https://doi.org/10.1007/978-1-4615-0913-4_11

8. St-Charles, P.L., Bilodeau, G.A., Bergevin, R.: SuBSENSE: a universal change detection method with local adaptive sensitivity. IEEE Trans. Image Process. **24**(1), 359–373 (2015)

9. St-Charles, P., Bilodeau, G., Bergevin, R.: Universal background subtraction using word consensus models. IEEE Trans. Image Process. **25**(10), 4768–4781 (2016)

10. Jiang, S., Lu, X.: WeSamBE: a weight-sample-based method for background subtraction. IEEE Trans. Circuits Syst. Video Technol. **28**(9), 2105–2115 (2018)

11. Wang, R., Bunyak, F., Seetharaman, G., Palaniappan, K.: Static and moving object detection using flux tensor with split Gaussian models. In: 2014 IEEE Conference on Computer Vision and Pattern Recognition Workshops, pp. 420–424, June 2014

12. Bianco, S., Ciocca, G., Schettini, R.: Combination of video change detection algorithms by genetic programming. IEEE Trans Evol. Comput. **21**(6), 914–928 (2017)

13. Braham, M., Droogenbroeck, M.V.: Deep background subtraction with scene-specific convolutional neural networks. In: 2016 International Conference on Systems, Signals and Image Processing (IWSSIP), pp. 1–4, May 2016

14. Babaee, M., Dinh, D.T., Rigoll, G.: A deep convolutional neural network for video sequence background subtraction. Pattern Recogn. **76**(C), 635–649 (2018)

15. Wang, Y., Luo, Z., Jodoin, P.M.: Interactive deep learning method for segmenting moving objects. Pattern Recogn. Lett. **96**(C), 66–75 (2017)

16. Braham, M., Piérard, S., Van Droogenbroeck, M.: Semantic background subtraction. In: IEEE International Conference on Image Processing (ICIP), Beijing, China, pp. 4552–4556, September 2017. https://doi.org/10.1109/ICIP.2017.8297144. http://hdl.handle.net/2268/213419

17. Wang, Y., Jodoin, P.M., Porikli, F., Konrad, J., Benezeth, Y., Ishwar, P.: CDnet 2014: an expanded change detection benchmark dataset. In: 2014 IEEE Conference on Computer Vision and Pattern Recognition Workshops, pp. 393–400, June 2014

18. Chollet, F., et al.: Keras (2015). https://github.com/fchollet/keras

19. Simonyan, K., Zisserman, A.: Very deep convolutional networks for large-scale image recognition. CoRR. abs/1409.1556 (2014)

20. H. O. S. D. Branch: Imagery library for intelligent detection systems (i-LIDS). In: The Institution of Engineering and Technology Conference on Crime and Security, pp. 445–448, June 2006

Occlusion-Aware Skeleton Trajectory Representation for Abnormal Behavior Detection

Onur Temuroglu[1(✉)], Yasutomo Kawanishi[1], Daisuke Deguchi[1],
Takatsugu Hirayama[1], Ichiro Ide[1], Hiroshi Murase[1], Mayuu Iwasaki[2],
and Atsushi Tsukada[2]

[1] Nagoya University, Nagoya, Japan
onurt@murase.is.i.nagoya-u.ac.jp
[2] Sumitomo Electric Industries, Ltd., Osaka, Japan

Abstract. Surveillance cameras are expected to play a large role in the development of ITS technologies. They can be used to detect abnormally behaving individuals which can then be reported to drivers nearby. There are multiple works that tackle the problem of abnormal behavior detection. However, most of these works make use of appearance features which have redundant information and are susceptible to noise. While there are also works that make use of pose skeleton representation, they do not consider well how to handle cases with occlusions, which can occur due to the simple reason of pedestrian orientation preventing some joints from appearing in the frame clearly. In this paper, we propose a skeleton trajectory representation that enables handling of occlusions. We also propose a framework for pedestrian abnormal behavior detection that uses the proposed representation and detect relatively hard-to-notice anomalies such as drunk walking. The experiments we conducted show that our method outperforms other representation methods.

Keywords: Pose skeleton · Anomaly detection · Surveillance cameras

1 Introduction

Pedestrian-vehicle accidents occur frequently, and deaths in these accidents are not uncommon. Drivers not reacting fast enough to the behavior of pedestrians is one of the reasons for these accidents, making the task of understanding pedestrian behavior important. Drunk pedestrians especially pose a danger to traffic due to their abnormal walking patterns and decreased ability to react to surrounding environment. By detecting abnormally behaving pedestrians and warning drivers to their presence, we consider that it is possible to reduce accidents. While in-vehicle cameras can be used for this purpose, blind spots will always exist due to their positioning. As such, surveillance cameras are expected to play an active role in detecting abnormally behaving pedestrians that might pose a danger to drivers nearby.

© Springer Nature Singapore Pte Ltd. 2020
W. Ohyama and S. K. Jung (Eds.): IW-FCV 2020, CCIS 1212, pp. 108–121, 2020.
https://doi.org/10.1007/978-981-15-4818-5_9

There are multiple works done on anomaly detection from a surveillance camera footage. However, most of these works focus on a different goal and make use of the pixel-based features directly [4,5,13]. These features are high-dimensional, and as such have large amounts of completely irrelevant information that could reduce the efficiency of models, or become harmful by acting as noise, masking relevant information [14]. These high-dimensional pixel-based features also open the way for variance that does not directly relate to behavior, such as different clothing or background, to become a problem.

To overcome the problems that might be caused by noise and variance, this paper proposes occlusion-aware 2D pose skeleton trajectory representation to detect abnormal behavior of a pedestrian in a surveillance camera footage. Pedestrian behavior is comprised of the actions pedestrians take, while the actions themselves can be deduced from the body skeleton trajectories of the pedestrians. Due to this, while pose skeletons are smaller in data size, they pack the same relevant information as appearance features and are easier to work with as they can be structured into a set of keypoint locations consistently, even revealing direction information.

While state-of-the-art pose estimation methods [2,3,8,12] can achieve highly accurate results, surveillance camera images often include pedestrians that are occluded mainly due to their orientation and sometimes due to external elements, leading to missing keypoint information. An example of this can be seen in Fig. 1. By implementing a distance metric that takes into consideration the effect of missing keypoint information, we should be able to achieve high accuracy behavior classification even for occluded data.

After acquiring the pose skeletons, we combine them into a sequence and use an AutoEncoder [6] network to encode and decode it. We classify the sequence into normal or abnormal by calculating the difference between the input and output. As AutoEncoder networks are not able to reconstruct data that vastly differ from those they were trained on, a large difference between input and output indicates an anomaly in the scope of the training data [11]. By using this method we can detect any kind of abnormal behavior without ever needing to define them, as we can just define the normal behavior instead. The contributions of this paper are as follows:

- We propose a skeleton trajectory representation that takes occluded keypoints into consideration and a distance metric for the said representation to achieve accurate classifications.
- We propose a framework for detecting abnormally behaving pedestrians from surveillance camera images, using the proposed skeleton trajectory representation. By doing so, we also eliminate the effects of variance such as clothing or background. Thanks to the processes we apply, our framework can detect abnormal behaviors even with relatively little posture change.
- We evaluate our method against other conventional methods using data taken in a real-like environment and show that our method achieves the highest accuracy in classifying normal and abnormal behaviors.

(a) Original image   (b) Pose estimation result

Fig. 1. Example of an occluded pose estimation result. Note that the right hand and the eyes are not detected at all due to the pedestrian's orientation. The blue dot indicates the right shoulder. (Color figure online)

The rest of this paper is organized as follows. In Sect. 2, we give summaries of related work. In Sect. 3, we describe our complete method in detail. In Sect. 4, we evaluate our method against other methods. In Sect. 5, we conclude our paper with a discussion on results and future work.

2   Related Work

Anomaly detection has always been a popular task in computer vision fields. There are multiple previous works challenging the anomaly detection problem for surveillance purposes, with different task settings and methodologies. Before deep learning methods became popular, Piciarelli et al. [9] used One-Class SVM to detect anomalous behavior by analyzing trajectories. There are also more recent works involving different deep learning methods. Hasan et al. [4] used AutoEncoder networks to extract features and detect abnormal events. Sultani et al. [13] employed a 3D convolutional network combined with fully connected layers to make the decision of whether a sequence is abnormal or not. Hinami et al. [5] used a generic convolutional network with environment specific classi-fiers to classify the type of abnormal action. However, all of these methods use appearance features directly, which as we mentioned, are susceptible to noise and variance such as different clothing and backgrounds. Bera et al. [1] used pedes-trian tracking to learn the trajectories of the crowd and classifies trajectories deviating from the crowd trend as anomalies.

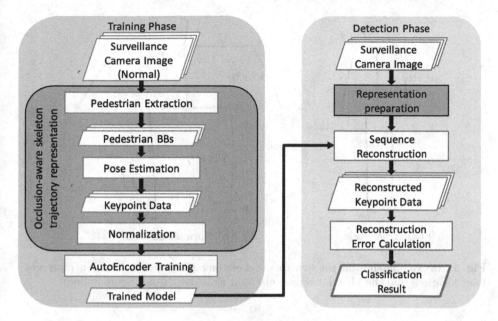

Fig. 2. Overall process flow of the proposed framework for abnormal behavior detection.

There are also some works using pose skeleton information for anomaly detection. An example of this is the work by Morais et al. [7], which proposes an RNN based method using pose skeletons. However, their method does not take into consideration the often occurring cases of occluded pose estimation results, which our paper addresses.

3   Abnormal Behavior Detection Making Use of Skeleton Representations

In this section, we describe our method for abnormal behavior detection in detail. This section mainly consists of two parts: Representing the skeleton information using the occlusion-aware skeleton trajectory representation and the details of implementation for our complete framework. Figure 2 shows the overall process flow for our framework.

3.1   Occlusion-Aware Skeleton Trajectory Representation

In our research, we define human skeleton as a set of 2D points $\{(x^j, y^j)\}_{j=1}^{J}$, where each element represents one of J body joints we use as shown in Fig. 3. We use the term keypoints for these body joint points. Often, there are cases where at least one of these keypoints are occluded and are not estimated properly. However, as the networks that use skeletons to classify behavior take fixed

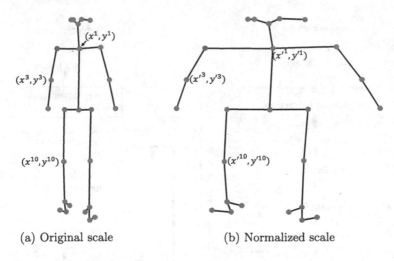

(a) Original scale   (b) Normalized scale

Fig. 3. An example showing the structure of skeleton representation. The dots represent joint locations and the blue dot represents right shoulder. (Color figure online)

shapes as input, these missing keypoints must also be represented in a way. If not represented properly, these missing keypoints will have an effect on both training and classification steps, leading to inaccurate results. In this paper, we use a homogeneous coordinate system-like representation with an additional dimension for occlusion flags. By making this distinction between detected and missing keypoints, we achieve a less noisy training set and open the way for a better loss function, explained in Sect. 3.2.

We first need to apply pose estimation on an N-frame long pedestrian sequence we acquire using YOLO [10], as detailed in Sect. 3.2. For pose estimation we use OpenPose [2]. For each frame, OpenPose generates a heatmap of each keypoint and part affinity fields, which it then uses to estimate the coordinates of keypoints together with a confidence value for each keypoint. A joint is considered missing or occluded if the values for it are zero. Using OpenPose, we obtain a skeleton trajectory $\mathcal{P} = \{P_1, ..., P_n, ..., P_N\}$, where each skeleton is represented as $P_n = \{(x_n^1, y_n^1, c_n^1), ..., (x_n^j, y_n^j, c_n^j), ..., (x_n^J, y_n^J, c_n^J)\}$. Here, x_n^j, y_n^j are 2D coordinates of the jth keypoint in the nth frame, and $c_n^j \in [0, 1]$ is the confidence level of the jth keypoint in the nth frame. We then normalize these values using Eqs. (1) and (2) and obtain a normalized skeleton P_n':

$$x_n'^j = \begin{cases} \dfrac{x_n^j - \min\limits_i(x_n^i)}{\max\limits_i(x_n^i) - \min\limits_i(x_n^i)} & \text{if } c_n^j > 0 \\ 0 & \text{otherwise} \end{cases}$$

$$y_n'^j = \begin{cases} \dfrac{y_n^j - \min\limits_i(y_n^i)}{\max\limits_i(y_n^i) - \min\limits_i(y_n^i)} & \text{if } c_n^j > 0 \\ 0 & \text{otherwise} \end{cases} \tag{1}$$

$$c_n^{ij} = \begin{cases} 1, & c_n^j > 0 \\ 0, & \text{otherwise} \end{cases} \tag{2}$$

Eq. (2) is used here to make the difference between missing keypoints and detected keypoints more apparent. This normalization is applied to each element of $\mathcal{P}$ to obtain $\mathcal{P}'$.

3.2 Implementation Details

In this section we explain the implementation and general process flow of the proposed framework, divided into multiple subsections.

Pedestrian Detection. 2D pose estimation in images is a popular research topic with multiple implementations readily available. However, even when using a state-of-the-art technology, there are cases where it might estimate pedestrian poses incorrectly, especially in cases where a pedestrian is distant from the camera.

To overcome this problem, we extract regions with pedestrians which allows us to focus only on them for pose estimation. To do this, we apply pedestrian detection and N-frame tracking on the target footage, which outputs a pedestrian bounding box sequence $\mathcal{D} = \{d_1, ..., d_n, ..., d_N\}$ for each pedestrian, and then apply pose estimation on each detected pedestrian in each frame. Here, the result of each pedestrian detection consists of four values $d_n = \{x_n, y_n, w_n, h_n\}$ where x_n, y_n denotes the center point of detection in a frame, w_n the width, and h_n the height of the pedestrian. To ensure even the distant pedestrians, which are the major cases of low accuracy detections and offsets, are completely covered by the bounding box, we double the height and width to obtain bounding boxes with a size of $2h_o \times 2w_o$ for each detection. The end result is that we are able to extract more accurate pose skeleton information, allowing us to detect even abnormal behaviors that show relatively little change in posture such as drunk walking.

Conversion of Detections into Skeleton Representations. We input the pedestrian bounding box sequence $\mathcal{D}$ and convert the sequence into skeleton trajectory representation with the method described in Sect. 3.1, acquiring $\mathcal{P}'$.

Training the AutoEncoder Network. AutoEncoders are popular networks for feature extraction. They work by learning to represent the data they are trained on in lower dimensions through compression and decompression of the data. As such, in theory, they are not able to represent data that are not similar to the data they were trained on, and will have problems reconstructing them. This characteristic of AutoEncoders is exploited for anomaly detection. By only training on normal data, we are able to separate normal and abnormal behaviors based on their reconstruction results.

We use the representation $\mathcal{P}'$ we generated in Sect. 3.1 as the input for our AutoEncoder. The proposed AutoEncoder is a very simple network, comprised of only a few dense layers. This is because the pose skeletons are compact while having relevant information. The network consists of an encoder network E and a decoder network D which are used sequentially to acquire the reconstruction $\hat{\mathcal{P}}' = D(E(\mathcal{P}'))$. As we map the x, y values for missing keypoints to 0 and the network tries to reconstruct them, we use the custom loss function shown in Eq. (3) to optimize the parameters of the network

$$L(\hat{\mathcal{P}}', \mathcal{P}') = \frac{1}{2NJ} \sum_{n=1}^{N} \sum_{j=1}^{J} c_n'^j ((\hat{x}_n'^j - x_n'^j)^2 + (\hat{y}_n'^j - y_n'^j)^2), \tag{3}$$

where $(\hat{x}_n'^j, \hat{y}_n'^j)$ are the reconstruction result of the jth keypoint of the nth skeleton. Note that we introduce all the parameters used in Eq. (3) in Sect. 3.1.

Abnormal Behavior Detection. During test time, we use the loss function as it is to calculate the reconstruction difference between our normalized test input $\mathcal{P}^*$ and its respective output $\hat{\mathcal{P}}^*$, and classify the input as abnormal if the difference is above a certain threshold τ as shown in Eq. (4). Here, τ is determined empirically as explained in Sect. 4.4.

$$C(\mathcal{P}^*) = \begin{cases} \text{normal} & \text{if } L(\hat{\mathcal{P}}^*, \mathcal{P}^*) \leq \tau \\ \text{abnormal} & \text{otherwise} \end{cases} \tag{4}$$

4   Experiment

In this section, we describe the experiment we prepared to evaluate the proposed method in detail.

4.1   Drunk Walking Dataset

The data we used in our experiment were taken by ourselves and consists of multiple people walking in a normal fashion for the normal pattern, and acting out drunkenness while walking for the abnormal pattern. With the relatively little posture changes in the dataset, it is useful for showing the effectiveness of the proposed method in classifying abnormal behaviors with little posture changes. It contains 112 video clips of people walking in aforementioned patterns, taken at 10 frames per second. Out of these video clips, 56 are normal clips and 56 are abnormal clips. Figure 4 shows example sequences from the dataset. We process this data into 7,223 normal sequences and 10,629 abnormal sequences with a length of 30 frames each. The discrepancy in sequence counts is due to an abnormal clip being longer than a normal clip on average. Out of the 7,223 normal sequences, we use 4,124 for training, 1,147 for validation, and 1,952 for testing. For the abnormal sequences, we randomly pick 1,000 sequences out of 10,629 sequences for testing. Note that we use the same exact sequences for preparing each of the comparison methods in Sect. 4.2.

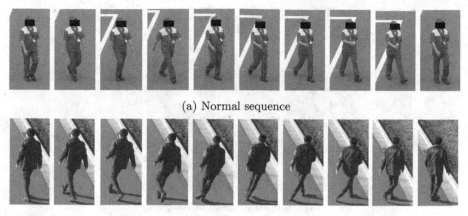

(a) Normal sequence

(b) Abnormal sequence

Fig. 4. Sample sequences from the dataset. The facial region is masked for the sake of anonymization in this paper.

4.2   Comparison Methods

In addition to the proposed method, we prepare multiple representations of our drunk walking dataset for use as comparison methods in our experiment, detailed as follows:

Comparative 1 (Keypoints without occlusion flags): This method is closest to our representation, featuring 2D coordinates of J keypoints for N frames where the nth frame is $P_n^e = \{(x_n^1, y_n^1), ..., (x_n^j, y_n^j), ..., (x_n^J, y_n^J)\}$.

Comparative 2 (Heatmaps): A heatmap represents an image based output that shows the possible area for each keypoint at the same size as the input image, with higher pixel value being more probable. In this experiment we prepare sequences composed of images with a size of 96×96 pixels where each pixel has a value between 0 and 1.

Comparative 3 (Cropped pedestrian images): For this method, we crop the greyscale results of the pedestrian detection in a square shape and scale the images to the same size of 96×96 pixels. We then normalize the values of pixels between 0 and 1.

Fig. 5 visualizes the three variations.

(a) Cropped pedestrian image

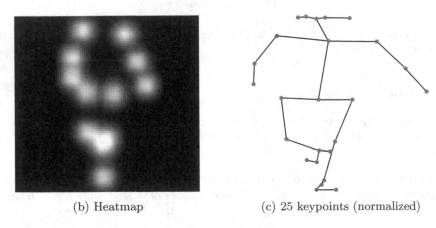

(b) Heatmap   (c) 25 keypoints (normalized)

Fig. 5. Different variations of data used for experiments. The blue dot indicates the right shoulder. (Color figure online)

4.3 Network Parameters

We prepare multiple AutoEncoder based networks for the variations we prepared. For heatmaps and cropped pedestrian image sequence, we use a Convolutional AutoEncoder network where the sequence of frames are given as channels while we use a standard AutoEncoder network comprised of dense layers for the other variations. However, we adjust the parameter count in accordance to the keypoint counts for each. For the AutoEncoder, we compose it with four encoding and four decoding layers, while reducing the number to three for the Convolutional AutoEncoder, as complex and powerful networks shrink the reconstruction gap between normal and abnormal patterns. We use sigmoid as the activation function on the last layer for all networks, and ReLU for all middle layers. Also, we use mean squared error as the loss function for all variations except for the proposed one.

Table 1. Results of methods by epoch count.

Epoch	Comparative 1 (Keypoints no flags)	Comparative 2 (Heatmap)	Comparative 3 (Image)	Proposed
20	0.838	0.889	0.577	**0.927**
100	0.856	0.855	0.551	**0.914**

4.4 Experimental Setting

For the pedestrian detection and pose estimation methods, we applied YOLO [10] and OpenPose [2], respectively, and used all available keypoints ($J = 25$).

We opted to use balanced accuracy for the accuracy metric as shown in Eq. (5).

$$\text{Balanced Accuracy} = \frac{1}{2}\left(\frac{\text{TP}}{\text{TP} + \text{FN}} + \frac{\text{TN}}{\text{TN} + \text{FP}}\right) \tag{5}$$

Here, TP, TN, FP, and FN represent the number of true positive, true negative, false positive, and false negative results, respectively. Using balanced accuracy instead of standard accuracy allows us to evaluate the performance more accurately when using unbalanced data.

We decided on the threshold by acquiring the reconstruction difference for all test data and calculating the balanced accuracy on 100 different thresholds. Here these thresholds are chosen as intervals between the mean reconstruction difference of normal data, and the abnormal data. We used the threshold with best results out of them for each of the methods. We trained the networks for 20 epochs and 100 epochs. The reason we evaluated at a low epoch count is because the aim is not to accurately reconstruct, but to have a large difference of reconstruction accuracy in normal patterns and abnormal patterns.

4.5 Results

The results are summarized in Table 1. We can see that methods that make use of pose skeleton representation vastly outperform the method using cropped pedestrian images. We can also see that the proposed method of pose skeleton representation and custom loss function outperforms the comparison methods. Figure 6 shows the reconstruction difference distribution of the data for the proposed method, and the relation of the thresholds with the balanced accuracy.

4.6 Performance on Data with Different Levels of Missing Joints

We evaluated the accuracy of methods by grouping the experimental data into various levels of missing keypoint information. For the grouping, we use 25 keypoint data with a length of 30 frames for abnormal sequences and split them into three groups to evaluate them separately. We use all 10,629 abnormal sequences and separate them into three datasets as Easy (0–22), Moderate (23–86), and

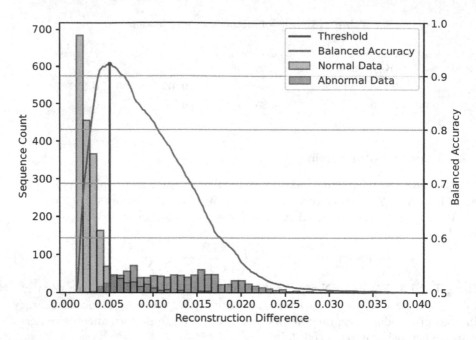

Fig. 6. Distribution of reconstruction difference of the data for the proposed method and the relation of threshold selection to the balanced accuracy.

Table 2. Accuracy of methods on grouped abnormal data.

Dataset	Comparative 1(Keypoints no flags)	Comparative 2(Heatmap)	Proposed
Easy (0–22)	0.710	0.911	**0.986**
Moderate (23–86)	0.958	0.988	**0.996**
Hard (87+)	0.850	0.865	**0.894**

Hard (87+) according to the number of joints missing out of 750 total joints in a sequence. This gives us 3,435, 3,611, and 3,583 sequences for Easy, Moderate, and Hard sequences, respectively. The graph showing sequence counts by missing keypoints is shown in Fig. 7.

In this experiment, we evaluated three methods, namely the methods that use heatmaps, skeletons with no occlusion flags, and skeletons with occlusion flags (proposed). Table 2 shows the accuracy of classification for each method on the grouped abnormal data. We can see that the representation without occlusion flags has the lowest accuracy in all categories. This is because of the noise that occur in the training data, as a result of the representation. The network is trained on this noisy data, and adapted for it, which is why it has trouble trying to classify data in the easy category. We can see this effect diminishes for the moderate category, as it is what the network adapted to. The hard category has a lower accuracy compared to moderate, due to emerging patterns that are too extreme to be classified correctly by the network.

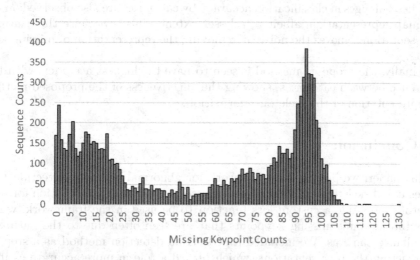

Fig. 7. Histograms of sequence counts by missing keypoints.

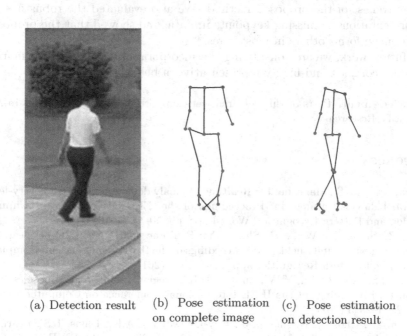

(a) Detection result   (b) Pose estimation   (c) Pose estimation
                        on complete image   on detection result

Fig. 8. Comparison between using OpenPose on a complete image and on a pedestrian detection result. The pose estimation target pedestrian cropped from a larger image is shown in (a). Result of using OpenPose on the complete image is shown in (b) and the result of using OpenPose on the detection result is shown in (c). The blue dot indicates the right shoulder. (Color figure online)

These changes in classification accuracy by categories are also observed on the heatmap representation, albeit to a lesser extent. This is because the heatmap representation removes the noise by removing the representation of missing keypoints.

Finally, the proposed method is seen to have the highest accuracy, with less difference between categories, showing the effectiveness of the proposed method in representation of the skeleton information.

5   Conclusion

In this paper, we proposed a framework for abnormal behavior detection that makes use of skeleton representation. We also proposed a representation for pose skeletons alongside a custom loss function to be used in the framework, which takes into account missing keypoints that are seen often due to the nature of surveillance cameras. We included a pedestrian detection method as a step for constructing the representations, which played a role in more accurate estimations. An example of this can be seen in Fig. 8.

We compared our method with multiple representation methods and showed the effectiveness of the proposed method. We also evaluated the robustness of the representations to missing keypoints in data, and showed that the proposed method outperforms others in most cases.

As future work, we are considering the incorporation of motion information as they are compact and highly representative of behavior.

Acknowledgment. Parts of this research were supported by MEXT, Grants-in-Aid for Scientific Research.

References

1. Bera, A., Kim, S., Manocha, D.: Realtime anomaly detection using trajectory-level crowd behavior learning. In: Proceedings of the IEEE Conference on Computer Vision and Pattern Recognition Workshops, pp. 50–57 (2016)
2. Cao, Z., Simon, T., Wei, S.E., Sheikh, Y.: Realtime multi-person 2D pose estimation using part affinity fields. In: Proceedings of the IEEE Conference on Computer Vision and Pattern Recognition, pp. 7291–7299 (2017)
3. Fang, H.S., Xie, S., Tai, Y.W., Lu, C.: RMPE: regional multi-person pose estimation. In: Proceedings of the IEEE International Conference on Computer Vision, pp. 2334–2343 (2017)
4. Hasan, M., Choi, J., Neumann, J., Roy-Chowdhury, A.K., Davis, L.S.: Learning temporal regularity in video sequences. In: Proceedings of the IEEE Conference on Computer Vision and Pattern Recognition, pp. 733–742 (2016)
5. Hinami, R., Mei, T., Satoh, S.: Joint detection and recounting of abnormal events by learning deep generic knowledge. In: Proceedings of the IEEE International Conference on Computer Vision, pp. 3619–3627 (2017)
6. Hinton, G.E., Salakhutdinov, R.R.: Reducing the dimensionality of data with neural networks. Science **313**(5786), 504–507 (2006)

7. Morais, R., Le, V., Tran, T., Saha, B., Mansour, M., Venkatesh, S.: Learning regularity in skeleton trajectories for anomaly detection in videos. In: Proceedings of the IEEE Conference on Computer Vision and Pattern Recognition, pp. 11996–12004 (2019)
8. Papandreou, G., Zhu, T., Chen, L.-C., Gidaris, S., Tompson, J., Murphy, K.: PersonLab: person pose estimation and instance segmentation with a bottom-up, part-based, geometric embedding model. In: Ferrari, V., Hebert, M., Sminchisescu, C., Weiss, Y. (eds.) Computer Vision – ECCV 2018. LNCS, vol. 11218, pp. 282–299. Springer, Cham (2018). https://doi.org/10.1007/978-3-030-01264-9_17
9. Piciarelli, C., Micheloni, C., Foresti, G.L.: Trajectory-based anomalous event detection. IEEE Trans. Circuits Syst. Video Technol. **18**(11), 1544–1554 (2008)
10. Redmon, J., Divvala, S., Girshick, R., Farhadi, A.: You only look once: unified, real-time object detection. In: Proceedings of the IEEE Conference on Computer Vision and Pattern Recognition, pp. 779–788 (2016)
11. Sakurada, M. Yairi, T.: Anomaly detection using autoencoders with nonlinear dimensionality reduction. In: Proceedings of the MLSDA 2nd Workshop on Machine Learning for Sensory Data Analysis, 4 p. (2014)
12. Sekii, T.: Pose proposal networks. In: Ferrari, V., Hebert, M., Sminchisescu, C., Weiss, Y. (eds.) ECCV 2018. LNCS, vol. 11217, pp. 350–366. Springer, Cham (2018). https://doi.org/10.1007/978-3-030-01261-8_21
13. Sultani, W., Chen, C., Shah, M.: Real-world anomaly detection in surveillance videos. In: Proceedings of the IEEE Conference on Computer Vision and Pattern Recognition, pp. 6479–6488 (2018)
14. Zimek, A., Schubert, E., Kriegel, H.P.: A survey on unsupervised outlier detection in high-dimensional numerical data. Stat. Anal. Data Min. ASA Data Sci. J. **5**(5), 363–387 (2012)

A Deep-Learning Based Worker's Pose Estimation

Prabesh Paudel[✉] and Kyoung-Ho Choi

Mokpo National University, Mokpo, Cheonggye-Myeon, South Korea
{prabesh123,khchoi}@mokpo.ac.kr

Abstract. Work in a factory is physically demanding. It requires workers to perform tasks in different awkward positions. Thus, long work shifts might have prolonged effects on workers' physical health. To minimize the risks, we introduce an automatic workers' pose estimation system, which will calculate a worker's body angle and indicate which angles are safe or not safe for performing tasks in various work places. By combining CMU OpenPose with body assessment tools, such as Rapid Entire Body Assessment (REBA) and Rapid Upper Limb Assessment (RULA), the proposed system automatically determines a worker's risk pose. This method, intended to replace a manual analysis of work posture, will help build safer environments for workers.

Keywords: Workers' pose estimation · Smart pose observation · Accident minimization · Ergonomics · Body angle calculation

1 Introduction

In this paper, we claim that pose estimation in ergonomics needs to be addressed with digital camera observation rather than manual observation. With the number of ageing populations increasing in the world, many countries are forced to find compatible solutions to increase work efficiency in factories. Many workers leave the industry early due to ill health and musculoskeletal disorders [1]. In Hong Kong, the Pilot Medical Examination Scheme (PMES) for construction workers revealed that 41% of registered workers have musculoskeletal pain [2]. In ergonomics, to address this problem, technical manpower is used to analyze a worker's working poses and the types of risk that are created in their work environments. These manual methods may be inaccurate and inefficient due to subjective bias [3]. Limitations are common due to frequent changes in work environments. It is difficult to record a worker's accurate working poses manually.

Since manual observation is done for accident minimization in different work places, we need to change that perspective. Here, we focus mainly on three manual observation techniques in ergonomics accident minimization which are:

- OWAS (Ovako Working Analysis System)
- RULA (Rapid Limb Upper Assessment)
- REBA (Rapid Entire Body Assessment)

© Springer Nature Singapore Pte Ltd. 2020
W. Ohyama and S. K. Jung (Eds.): IW-FCV 2020, CCIS 1212, pp. 122–135, 2020.
https://doi.org/10.1007/978-981-15-4818-5_10

Although the above mentioned methods are popular manual observation methods, they have some limitations. Certain angles of a worker's body pose are not clearly defined and difficult to inspect manually. The OWAS method, for example, does not give information about posture duration, does not distinguish between arms (whether it is left or right), and does not give information about elbow position. Similarly, the other two methods also do not provide valid angles for upper limbs and body bending while working. RULA is a survey method developed for use in ergonomics investigations of work places where work-related upper limb disorders are reported [4]. Likewise, REBA is a postural analysis tool sensitive to musculoskeletal risks in a variety of tasks and assessments of working postures found in health care and other service industries [5]. We propose a method in this paper which will help to increase the efficiency of the above mentioned methods using digital technology.

Ergonomics efficiency is a necessity these days in factories. Many companies do not want to lose their experienced workers due to illness or physical pain. The application of ergonomic principles can help to increase machine performance and productivity, but mostly to help human operators to be comfortable and secure [6]. This can help a significant number of workers adopting bad work postures. Several studies show that the above mentioned working positions need some new techniques to lower the work risk. Thus, we propose an automatic worker's pose estimation system as well as a neck and wrist angle calculation study in an attempt to find an efficient way to minimize factory workers' accidents. Our main focus is on minimizing accidents by calculating a worker's pose estimation and body angles to minimize pain and increase efficiency in work environments.

Figure 1 shows our proposed work frame for creating smart worker's accident reduction. It shows how video frames are used in CMU OpenPose to locate key joints and how RULA and REBA scores are calculated. After the scores and angles are calculated, it checks for the risk angles of work posture. After that, it generates a warning sign if the posture is at risk, so we can stop and correct a worker's posture.

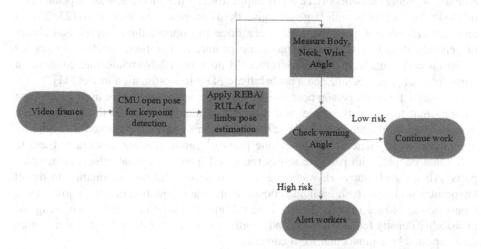

Fig. 1. Block diagram of the proposed system for smart pose estimation.

2 Related Work

Recently, many studies are being done in ergonomics to reduce human fatalities. Research focused on minimizing human work load via manual inspection such as work related musculoskeletal disorders at construction sites [7]. Most of these problems were caused due to prolonged work in awkward positions, overhead lifting, squatting, and stooping [8, 9]. Accordingly, many work environment assessment rules have been proposed for hazard monitoring and control. Representative research on awkward posture assessment rules include the RULA, an ergonomic assessment tool focusing on upper limbs [4]. OWAS is for identifying and evaluating work postures [10]. The ISO 11226:2000 is for determining the acceptable angles and holding times of working postures [11], and the EN 1005-4 is defined as a guidance when designing machinery component parts in assessing machine-related postures and body movements, i.e. during assembly, installation, operation, maintenance, and reparation [12].

Due to the fast development of technology for data acquisition, manual observation is being replaced. Recently, a 3D model was proposed to imitate and animate manual construction tasks in virtual environments based on RULA [13]. Their work also includes analysis of body joint angles based on traditional ergonomic assessment rules to identify postural ergonomic hazards. Some also applied the same method to establish a virtual 3D workplace [14].

Beside manual work posture estimation, many studies have focused on estimating single person and multi person poses. In terms of single person pose estimation, it is mainly focused on finding the joints and adjacent joints. The traditional approach is to articulate human pose estimation for a combination of body parts [15–17]. These are spatial models for articulated poses based on tree-structured graphical models, which parametrically encode the spatial relationship between adjacent parts following a kinetic chain, or non-tree models [18–21]. Tompon et al. applied a deep architecture with a graphical model whose parameters are learned jointly with the network [22]. Pfister et al. used convulsion neural networks (CNNs) to implicitly capture global spatial dependencies by designing networks with large receptive fields proposed by Weit et al. [23, 24]. In terms of ergonomics, some work has been done to improve the accuracy and ability of generalization in vision-based ergonomic posture recognition, which estimates 3D skeletons and joints from 2D video frames. Multi-stage CNN architecture combines a convolutional pose machine and a probabilistic 3D joints estimation model [31].

Similarly for multi person pose estimation, most approaches have used a top down strategy that first detects people, and then independently estimates the pose of each detected region of each person [25–29]. Pischulin et al. [30] proposed a bottom-up model that jointly detects and labels the parts of candidates and associates them to individual people, with pairwise scores regressed from the spatial offsets of detected parts. Also, significant work was done in multi person 2D pose estimation to detect keypoint association, both for human position and the orientation of human joints [32]. Construction hazard remedy is also done taking 2D skeleton as reference using the probability density feature of angle and length ratio extracted from 2D skeleton motion data captured by a monocular RGB camera.

3   Worker Pose Estimation System

3.1   Architecture of the Proposed System

Figure 2 illustrates the overall pipeline of our method. The system takes a video as input and CMU OpenPose is used as a baseline algorithm for keypoints detection. After the keypoints are located, we combine them with REBA and RULA to calculate a risk score. With REBA and RULA, we calculate all possible angles required to detect the faulty or risky posture. After this calculation, we apply the 2D plane coordinate method to calculate possible angle elevation between shoulder and head keypoints. This allows us to figure out how much elevation the worker is doing while working. For this calculation, we divide the upper body, called the sagittal part, into the limbs and head. This makes a plane angle concept, so it is easier to calculate angles. Similarly for wrist angle calculation, we need to consider the weight a worker is lifting and what surface the worker's body is elevating. It is the trickiest part because we need to consider different surface angles to evaluate possible risk angles. After this process, the evaluation of risk angles is done which finally shows warning signs. If a worker's keypoints are not clearly located or bending angles are abnormal, it notifies with warning signs. We consider CMU OpenPose as a baseline of our study to calculate the REBA and RULA scores.

The goal of our system is to digitize the worker's posture observation. To address the problem of manual observation system, we propose a smart method which combines the CMU OpenPose and manual observation method. With OpenPose we sent our video data to locate the body joints. After the joints are located, we can consider the sagittal part (upper half) of body for angular observation. We measure the angle between the shoulder and neck with a 2D angular evaluation vector. After angles between the shoulder and head and wrist are calculated, we pass those angles in the risk checking section. This section checks the possible angles with ground truth data to determine whether to precede working or notify the worker about the possible risk. Hence, this reduces the total time consuming in manual observations and makes the work of posture evaluation lot easier and faster.

4   Neck and Wrist Angle Calculations

In order to minimize the risk for neck and wrist injuries, we need to focus on calculating the appropriate angle of a worker's neck position and wrist movements. For this purpose, we have to divide the body into two parts (a) upper body and (b) lower body. The upper body includes the limbs, neck, and wrist. We called it the sagittal plane. In this paper, we consider the shoulder and head keypoints to calculate the bending of the neck. This is explained as a vector equation below. Similarly for wrist angle, we need to consider different hand gestures and positions considering the weight workers are lifting and the surface they are elevating.

This is essential because feature points from OpenPose do not include information about the neck and wrist angle. Using OpenPose as a baseline tool for body pose estimation, we can locate the key body joints (left and right L&R) as shoulder (L&R), elbow (L&R), spine, wrist (L&R), hip (L&R), knee (L&R), ankle (L&R). From the raw data, we locate seventeen joints that are helpful for our study in calculating the angles between

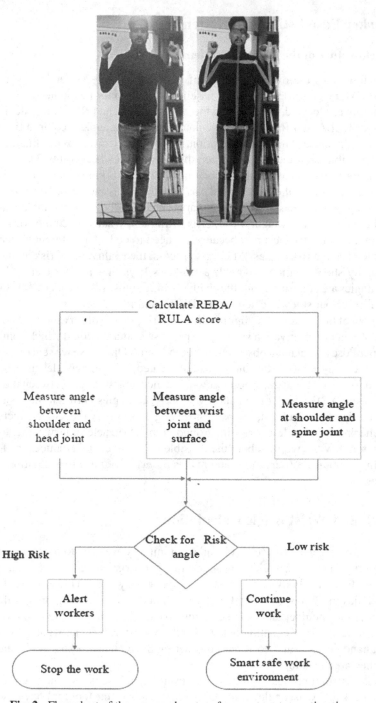

Fig. 2. Flow chart of the proposed system for smart posture estimation.

the shoulder and head for neck movements and wrist angles from elbow movement from 2D video data sets.

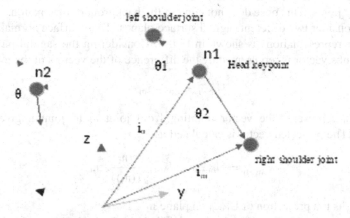

Fig. 3. Projection of shoulder angles in vector on the sagittal plane (upper body).

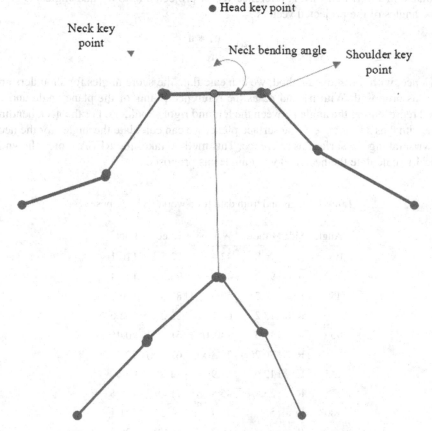

Fig. 4. Skeleton figure body model resembling angle joints.

We used a webcam for video data recording and locating joints as per defined by OpenPose. We have articulated widely adopted poses that are representative of human posture. It is because the degree of freedom of movement of the human body is mainly measured by joints. This pose does not contain the background information.

Let us consider two different sagittal surface planes. Their surface normal is n_1 and n_2 as vector representation, as shown in Fig. 3. Considering the sagittal plane of the body, the limbs vector is represented by the difference of the vectors of the joints:

$$U_{m-n} = i_n - i_m \tag{1}$$

where U_{m-n} represents the vector pointing from joint m to joint n given by 3D coordinates. The projected vector is calculated as:

$$U_{m-n}^{n_i} = U_{m-n} - U_{m-n} \cdot \frac{n_i}{((n_i))^2} \cdot n_i \tag{2}$$

where $U_{m-n}^{n_i}$ is the projection of U_{m-n} on plane n_i.

For angle calculation, we consider the left half of the body. The right side can be calculated in a mirrored way. A reference vector projected onto n_2, and angle θ is given by the angles of the projected vectors:

$$\cos \theta = \frac{n_1 * n_2}{|n_1||n_2|} \tag{3}$$

Hence, with the above method, we can calculate the score angles for shoulders and wrists as proposed. With n1 and n2 as the reference points of the plane angle and $\theta 1$ and $\theta 2$ representing the angle between the left and right shoulders. For the neck bending angle with θ as a reference to the surface plane, we can calculate the angles for the neck and wrist taking the surface as reference. This method takes the REBA scores shown in Table 1 to calculate the neck and wrist angles as proposed.

Table 1. A ground truth data for a worker's body pose

Angle	Side	Elbow	Wrist	Knee	Foot
0°	L	96.8	42.4	72.5	116.1
	R	98.2	49.1	99.5	121.4
45°	L	11.7	59.5	87.5	116.1
	R	13.2	60.1	82.2	102.6
90°	L	71.5	140.1(x)	61.7(x)	70.4(x)
	R	76.2(x)	29.3(x)	69.6(x)	72.3(x)
135°	L	12.6	47.9	74.5	96.5
	R	23.1	45.8	114.9	128.6
180°	L	5.9	58.4	96.2	121.1
	R	6.9	65.7	104.8	125.8

5 Experimental Results

5.1 Discussion and Analysis

Here we show a ground truth data of a worker's pose at different angles and explain our results. The (x) sign in Table 1 shows when joint are not clearly located. The starting position is taken with reference as body at 0° angle or −180°. The angles of different body parts are measures as reference of REBA scores with the CMU Open Pose as reference.

The measure angles from REBA scores in Table 1 show the different angles of body key joints as shown in Fig. 5. We measure the angles of the left and right elbow, wrist, knee, and foot. Hence different measured angle values are shown in Table 1. When some key joints are not clearly identified by the program, it shows some x notation that means from 2D USB web camera it is not possible to calculate all joint values, so for this remedy we can use a multi angle camera to measure all body joints clearly.

Fig. 5. Sample images of bad postures with keypoints located

Hence, with all of the upper limbs scores that we evaluated with the CMU OpenPose estimation program finally we can calculate the angles we proposed to limit work place hazards for workers. With the angles, we can distinguish whether it is a high or low risk angle. Then the system program indicates whether to stop working or continue work. Bad posture is identified with a warning sign. We are optimistic this method will be a milestone in identifying the bad work posture of factory workers.

In Tables 2 and 3 above, we show the measurement of REBA scores of the body at different angle positions. We can monitor how the angle variation helps in generating different scores and, with reference to same scores, we categorize the risk level of the body and actions taken. With the level of risk from low to high, we can predict the risk of musculoskeletal disorder (MSD). From the Tables 1 and 2, we can now easily determine which risk level is high and low. Also, it helps in dividing the body into segments to evaluate movement and scoring them according to risk level. Hence, it can be a user friendly tool to calculate REBA scores with less effort in a minimal time frame.

Table 2. Measurement of angles for each body joint

Starting position angle	Left elbow	Right elbow	Left wrist	Right wrist	Left knee	Right knee	Left foot	Right foot
0°	93.2	49.6	6.6	8.1	54.8	4.0	5.0	0.8
45°	74.7	77.3	4.2	5.9	11.0	46.1	2.8	3.0
90°	89.9	80.4	139.9	143.0	10.0	0.0	8.4	0.7
135°	63.4	58.8	94.0	108.7	9.3	0.7	6.9	0
150°	56.0	58.4	116.4	122.8	6.6	0.7	1.6	0.7
180°	70.4	71.2	110.8	119.0	9.2	0	7.6	0.7

Table 3. REBA action level and MSD risk evaluation

Score	Level of MSD Risk
1	Negligible Risk
2–3	Low Risk, no change needed
4–5	Medium Risk, Change may be needed
6+	High Risk, Further investigation and change needed soon

The main focus of our research is to automate a worker's pose estimation. With reference from CMU OpenPose, we want to make this easier, but there are some limitations in which CMU OpenPose does not define some body angles. The main features of OpenPose are on keypoints detection. They provide real time multi person 2D and 3D keypoints detection. This keypoints detection is helpful in our research, so we use CMU OpenPose as a baseline tool to measure the body bending angles and wrist angles.

In our research, we use body estimation for 2D real time person video. With reference to manual observation methods widely used in industrial areas known as REBA and RULA, we want to make this process easier to estimate. These methods provide visual indications of risk levels and where action is needed to lower risk. REBA provides an easy observational postural analysis tool for whole body activities for high risk. RULA is mainly developed to measure musculoskeletal risk caused by sedentary tasks where upper body demand is high. Both produce risk level scores on a given scale to indicate whether the risk is negligible through to very high. Hence, all of these methods are used in our research to increase the accuracy of pose estimation and make it smart observatory. With digital observatory, it will be a plus point in lowering a worker's risk in the work place.

Video was recorded via webcam for the simulation of the proposed system. For evaluation, we used CMU OpenPose combined with REBA and RULA tools. With these methods, we evaluate the pose where it shows a warning sign. We evaluate which position is appropriate for workers to perform. This evaluation is further used in calculating the movement angle of neck and wrist positions, which is helpful in calculating the angles of positions that are hazardous for work. Here we take the measurement of movements for the left half of the body, since the other half can be self-mirrored. We provide some body angles in Table 1 and 2 as a ground truth, and measured data with some snapshots of the experiment showing a warning sign when a worker's pose is prone to future accidents in Fig. 4 and 5.

In this study, we are trying to focus on the possible outcome to make the manual observation of worker's pose estimation digital. As mentioned above, we can calculate the plane angle taking reference from the shoulder and head joint locations. Similarly for wrist angles, we need to consider if we are carrying a load, since the condition is different with and without weight in the hand. For this study, we took reference videos of some poses that workers do daily in their work environments. With that data set, we calculated the working body pose angles and also located the joints to know which parts of the body are clearly located. As seen in Table 1 and 2, there are some drawbacks we need to improve to increase our accuracy. We collected our data on a 2D webcam, so some parts of body were not detected at some body angles. Based on the CMU OpenPose and REBA and RULA tools, we developed an automatic worker's pose detection system. In Fig. 5 and 6, we can see how we combined all three methods in one frame to calculate our desired pose estimation. Figure 6 shows frames of the image data for angle evaluation and after evaluation with warning notations on Fig. 5 to identify workers' bad poses. However, we had some complications finding the keypoints when they were not visible to the webcam. The camera output shows random angle for keypoints when they are not clearly located. Hence, for future work, we have to execute this problem and work with a bigger data set that includes all work related poses and try to solve that problem. Also, a remedy for prolonged work hour posture will be our main focus in near future.

6 Limitations and Ongoing Work on the Proposed System

So far in our article, we have been able to locate keypoints for joints, calculate the RULA scores which can predict bending limits, and propose an angle calculation method for joints in pose estimation. Beside this, there are certain limitations we are working on such as how to find the focal point for the head so as to locate it when the neck is bending since workers move their heads frequently. We need to focus on the accuracy of angles, human detection rates, body bending risk angles, and REBA scores. So far, we are using our system for single images. Work for groups of moving workers is ongoing. Similarly, we are working to ease the wrist angle calculation complications regarding how much weight is lifted by different workers. At this moment, experimental results are presented for our collected data that is primitive and can only be useful to show an introductory system. Thus, we are working on collecting real workers' data.

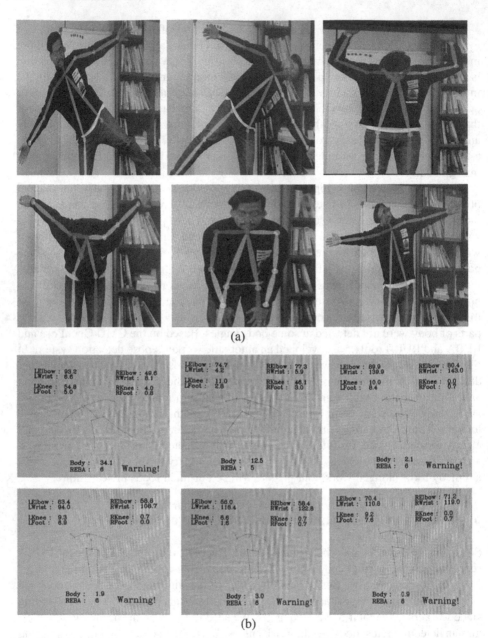

Fig. 6. Worker's pose estimation (a) With keypoints located (b) With and without warning signs in skeleton figures while estimating with the CMU OpenPose and REBA methods.

7 Conclusion

This paper has presented a smart method for detecting a worker's pose combining a manual method, REBA, and CMU OpenPose. With CMU OpenPose as our reference, digital REBA scores calculation makes observation smart. As CMU OpenPose gives us a clear location of joints and keypoints, we present an angle calculation method based on the notations of those keypoints. Real time person 2D pose estimation was helpful in our research in visually understanding human joint locations and helpful in calculating REBA scores.

This study proposed a new smart method for calculating RULA and REBA from 2D poses, making it easier to measure work posture and stop work place hazards caused due to bad work posture. We want to make the manual observation more smart and efficient with high accuracy so that work place hazards can be reduced to lower levels. Hence, we provide a smart framework with pose hazard that can be detected by combining all three methods discussed above. In result, we can see how good pose and bad pose are differentiated. We can clearly see that whenever there is a bad pose our system generates a warning signal. With this, we can reduce work place hazards immediately.

For further work, we will be focusing on collecting more work related posture data to solve those problems with deep neural networks. We will work to update our system for different conditions, for example, when there is a bad pose which is not detected by OpenPose and when there are obstacles that might block the vision of the camera that is installed to monitor a worker's posture observations.

Acknowledgement. This research was supported by Basic Science Research Program through the National research Foundation of Korea (NRF) funded by the Ministry of Education (2018R1D1A1B07047936).

References

1. Arndt, C., Robinson, S., Tarp, F.: Parameter estimation for a computable general equilibrium model: a maximum entropy approach. Econ. Model. **19**(3), 375–398 (2002)
2. Straker, L., Campbell, A., Coleman, J., Ciccarelli, M., Dankaerts, W.: In vivo laboratory validation of the physiometer: a measurement system for long-term recording of posture and movements in the workplace. Ergonomics **53**(5), 672–684 (2010). https://doi.org/10.1080/00140131003671975
3. McAtamney, L., et al.: RULA: a survey method for the investigation of world-related upper limb disorders. Appl. Ergon. **24**, 91–99 (1993)
4. Hignett, S., McAtamney, L.: REBA: a survey method for the investigation of work-related upper limb disorders. Appl. Ergon. (2000)
5. Zaheer, A. et al.: Ergonomics: a work place realities in Pakistan. Int. Posture J. Sci. Technol. **2**(1), (2012)
6. Dieën, J.H.V., Hoozemans, M.J.M., Toussaint, H.M.: Stoop or squat: a review of biomechanical studies on lifting technique. Clin. Biomech. **14**(10), 685–696 (1999)
7. Umer, W., Li, H., Szeto, G.P.Y., Wong, A.Y.L.: Identification of biomechanical risk factors for the development of lower-back disorders during manual rebar tying. J. Constr. Eng. Manage. **143**(1), 04016080 (2016)

8. Jiayu, C., Jun, Q., Changbum, A.: Construction worker's awkward posture recognition through supervised motion tensor decomposition. Autom. Constr. **77**, 67–81 (2017)

9. Osmo, K., Kansi, P., Kuorinka, I.: Correcting working postures in industry: a practical method for analysis. Appl. Ergon. **8**(4), 199–201 (1977)

10. Delleman, N., Boocock, M., Kapitaniak, B., Schaefer, P., Schaub, K.: ISO/FDIS 11226: evaluation of static working postures. In: Proceedings of the Human Factors and Ergonomics Society Annual Meeting vol. 44, no. 35, pp. 442–443 (2000)

11. Delleman, N.J., Dul, J.: International standards on working postures and movements ISO 11226 and EN 1005-4. Ergonomics **50**(11), 1809–1819 (2007)

12. Xinming, L., Han, S., Gül, M., Al-Hussein, M., El-Rich, M.: 3D visualization-based ergonomic risk assessment and work modification framework and its validation for a lifting task. J. Constr. Eng. Manag. **144**(1), 04017093 (2017)

13. Golabchi, A., Han, S., Seo, J., Han, S., Lee, S., Al-Hussein, M.: An automated biomechanical simulation approach to ergonomic job analysis for workplace design. J. Constr. Eng. Manage. **141**(8), 04015020 (2015)

14. Felzenszwalb, P.F., Huttenlocher, D.P.: Pictorial structures for object recognition. Int. J. Comput. Vis. **61**, 55–79 (2005). https://doi.org/10.1023/B:VISI.0000042934.15159.49

15. Ramanan, D., Forsyth, D.A., Zisserman, A.: Strike a pose: tracking people by finding stylized poses. In: CVPR (2005)

16. Andriluka, M., Roth, S., Schiele, B.: Monocular 3D pose estimation and tracking by detection. In: CVPR (2010)

17. Wang, Y., Mori, G.: Multiple tree models for occlusion and spatial constraints in human pose estimation. In: Forsyth, D., Torr, P., Zisserman, A. (eds.) ECCV 2008. LNCS, vol. 5304, pp. 710–724. Springer, Heidelberg (2008). https://doi.org/10.1007/978-3-540-88690-7_53

18. Sigal, L., Black, M.J.: Measure locally, reason globally: occlusion-sensitive articulated pose estimation. In: CVPR (2006)

19. Lan, X., Huttenlocher, D.P.: Beyond trees: common-factor models for 2D human pose recovery. In: ICCV (2005)

20. Karlinsky, L., Ullman, S.: Using linking features in learning non-parametric part models. In: Fitzgibbon, A., Lazebnik, S., Perona, P., Sato, Y., Schmid, C. (eds.) ECCV 2012. LNCS, vol. 7574, pp. 326–339. Springer, Heidelberg (2012). https://doi.org/10.1007/978-3-642-33712-3_24

21. Tompson, J.J., Jain, A., LeCun, Y., Bregler, C.: Joint training of a convolutional network and a graphical model for human pose estimation. In: NIPS (2014)

22. Pfister, T., Charles, J., Zisserman, A.: Flowing convnets for human pose estimation in videos. In: ICCV (2015)

23. Wei, S.-E., Ramakrishna, V., Kanade, T., Sheikh, Y.: Convolutional pose machines. In: CVPR (2016)

24. He, K., Gkioxari, G., Doll'ar, P., Girshick, R.: Mask R-CNN. In: ICCV (2017)

25. Fang, H.-S., Xie, S., Tai, Y.-W., Lu, C.: RMPE: regional multiperson pose estimation. In: ICCV (2017)

26. Papandreou, G., et al: Towards accurate multi-person pose estimation in the wild. In: CVPR (2017)

27. Chen, Y., Wang, Z., Peng, Y., Zhang, Z., Yu, G., Sun, J.: Cascaded pyramid network for multi-person pose estimation. In: CVPR (2018)

28. Xiao, B., Wu, H., Wei, Y.: Simple Baselines for Human Pose Estimation and Tracking. In: Ferrari, V., Hebert, M., Sminchisescu, C., Weiss, Y. (eds.) ECCV 2018. LNCS, vol. 11210, pp. 472–487. Springer, Cham (2018). https://doi.org/10.1007/978-3-030-01231-1_29

29. Pishchulin, L., et al: Deepcut: joint subset partition and labeling for multi person pose estimation. In: CVPR (2016)

30. Zhang, H., Yan, X., Li, H.: Ergonomic posture recognition using 3D view-invariant features from single ordinary camera. Autom. Constr. **94**, 1–10 (2018)
31. Cao, Z., et al.: Realtime multi-person 2D pose estimation using part affinity fields. In: Proceedings of the IEEE Conference on Computer Vision and Pattern Recognition (2017)
32. Yan, X., et al.: Development of ergonomic posture recognition technique based on 2D ordinary camera for construction hazard prevention through view-invariant features in 2D skeleton motion. Adv. Eng. Inf. **34**, 152–163 (2017)

Identifying People Using Body Sway
in Case of Self-occlusion

Takuya Kamitani(✉), Yuta Yamaguchi, Masashi Nishiyama, and Yoshio Iwai

Tottori University, Tottori 680-8550, Japan
D18T2102M@edu.tottori-u.ac.jp

Abstract. We propose a method of identifying people in case of self-occlusion by using body sway measured at the head using a top-view camera. To accurately represent the identities of people as reflected in body sway, it is important to acquire accurate appearances in images. However, such images frequently contain defects, especially self-occlusion, that degrade the performance of one of the prevalent methods for identifying people because it uses whole-body regions to identify people. To solve the problem of self-occlusion in this context, our method computes silhouette images of regions at the head by applying a segmentation technique. To reflect people's identities using body sway, we spatially divide the head region into local blocks and temporally measure movements in them. The results of experiments show that the proposed method can improve the performance of the prevalent method of identification from 17.3% to 57.9%.

Keywords: Body sway · Self-occlusion · Identification

1   Introduction

The widespread use of surveillance cameras is expected to help further develop biometric authentication systems [14,21]. To identify people accurately from images captured through such cameras, behavioral characteristics [7,9,13] have been considered in research on biometrics as they can be used to identify people based on their movements. Features of the gait [7,13] represent identities as reflected in periodic movements of such parts of the body as the limbs, and have been used as representative behavioral characteristics for identifying people with high accuracy. However, gait features do not adequately represent identities encapsulated in body movements in certain cases, e.g., when people are stationary, because periodic movements of the body parts no longer occur. Therefore, body sway [9] has been recommended for use in identifying people when they are not moving. Body sway is defined as continuous, slight, and unconscious movements of the body to maintain pose even when a person is otherwise not moving. People can be identified using these slight movements. Note that we consider an upright pose to be a typical example of the pose of a person who had been walking but has now stopped. Body sway can be used to identify people who

© Springer Nature Singapore Pte Ltd. 2020
W. Ohyama and S. K. Jung (Eds.): IW-FCV 2020, CCIS 1212, pp. 136–149, 2020.
https://doi.org/10.1007/978-981-15-4818-5_11

maintain an upright pose, say, in front of a security gate or an automatic door. People who work in factories, for one, appear very similar because they wear a uniform. The aim in such cases is to accurately identify people using body sway when their appearances are similar.

To the above end, we need to extract appropriate features contained in body sway in both the spatial and the temporal domains. The identity in the spatial domain lies in the shape of the body and that in the temporal domain in the movement of the entire body. In the following, we consider how to obtain identities using body sway in the spatial and temporal domains by using images acquired from surveillance cameras. In this scenario, we observe the shape of the body in spatial domain as a person's appearance, and the movement of the entire body in the temporal domain as sequential changes in their appearance. To appropriately represent identity as reflected by body sway, a person's accurate appearance needs to be acquired in images from the camera. However, defects in this appearance are common when occlusion occurs, and depend on the relationship between the position of the camera and that of the person being photographed. This problem needs to be solved.

We examine why occlusion occurs when we measure body sway. There are two main types of occlusion. The first type occurs when an individual stands in front of another. In this case, part of the appearance of the person far from the camera is hidden by the one close to it. This phenomenon is called mutual occlusion, and occurs when in case of a large number of people. The use of a top-view camera reduces the occurrence of mutual occlusion. The second type of occlusion is one where part of a person's own body obstructs the sight of him/her. This phenomenon is called self-occlusion, and occurs even when the top-view camera is used. Therefore, we need to consider how to reduce the influence of self-occlusion for identifying people using body sway.

The region around the head is the most robust against the influence of self-occlusion when using a top-view camera. Some prevalent methods use regions of the head acquired using a top-view camera to count the number of people in a given image [1, 16, 20] or to track people's walking routes [11, 15]. However, regions around the head have not been used to aim to identify people. Another such method [9] does not use the region around the head, although it is designed to identify people using body sway. This method causes the accuracy of the identification to decrease dynamically in case of self-occlusion because it uses whole-body regions to obtained features used to identify people.

To this end, we propose a method of representing identities as reflected in body sway by using the region around the head acquired using a top-view camera to accurately identify people in case of self-occlusion. Our method computes silhouette images around the head regions by applying a segmentation technique. To represent identities contained in body sway, we spatially divide the head regions into local blocks and temporally measure movements in these blocks. In this way, we can appropriately represent identities reflected in body sway in the spatial and temporal domains. We formed a dataset of images of body sways of 50 participants with self-occlusion. The results of experiments to verify

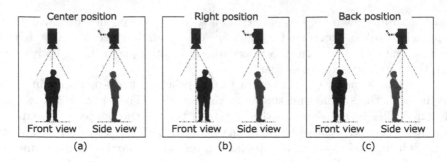

Fig. 1. The standing positions of a person used to investigate the influence of self-occlusion.

the proposed method show that it can improve the accuracy of identification of prevalent methods, which use images of whole-body regions, from 17.3% to 57.9% by using only images of regions around the head. The remainder of this paper is organized as follows: Sect. 2 explains the influence of self-occlusion, and Sect. 3 describes our method of extracting features for identification contained in the body sway using images of regions of the head, Sect. 4 details identification performance when using body sway, and Sect. 5 presents the conclusions of this study.

2   The Influence of Self-occlusion

The appearances of an individual acquired from a top-view camera depend on his/her standing position when self-occlusion occurs. In a preliminary experiment, we compared the appearances of an individual in different standing positions. The position of the top-view camera was fixed, as shown in Fig. 1. We defined the point where the optical axis of the camera was orthogonal to the floor as the center. Figure 1(a) shows the condition when the person standing at the center was observed, and Figs. 1(b) and (c) show conditions of observation of people standing to the right and behind the center, respectively.

Figure 2 shows examples of the appearance of the entire bodies of two people acquired in three standing positions, where the upper row shows individual 1 and the lower row shows individual 2. In comparison with Figs. 2(a), (b), and (c), we see that the appearances of the entire body acquired from each standing position were different. We also describe the head regions used in this paper. Figure 3 shows examples of head regions acquired under the same observation conditions as in Fig. 2. The green pixels in the images represent the head regions. A comparison of Figs. 3(a), (b), and (c) shows that the head regions acquired from each standing position were similar. We also examined regions of the shoulders, which changed in each standing position due to self-occlusion as shown in Fig. 3. Regions of the left and right shoulders were symmetrically at the center as shown in Fig. 3 (a). However, in Fig. 3(b), the parts of regions of the right shoulder acquired at the center are hidden by the head regions, and parts of regions

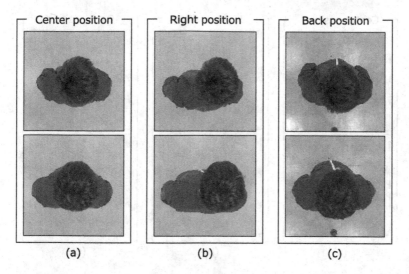

┌─ Center position ─┐ ┌─ Right position ─┐ ┌─ Back position ─┐

(a)   (b)   (c)

Fig. 2. Examples of the appearance of entire body acquired from two people standing in three different positions.

of the left shoulder hidden by the head regions at the center are acquired. The same tendency can be observed in Fig. 3(c). Therefore, the head regions are more robust against the influence of self-occlusion than any other region of the body. We thus use them for identifying people based on body in case of self-occlusion.

3 Our Method

3.1 Overview

We propose a method to extracting spatio-temporal features from images using region of the head to identify people based on body sway. Figure 4 provides an overview of our method. We acquire a set of images of a person by using a top-view camera while he/she maintains an upright pose. To reduce the influence of self-occlusion, we compute silhouette images of the head regions from this set by applying a segmentation technique. To extract features for identification, we spatially divide the head regions into local blocks and temporally measure movements in each local block. The details of our method are described below.

3.2 Estimating Head Regions from a Set of Images of a Person

The head regions can be estimated accurately by statistically learning using a large number of training images featuring variations in the appearance of people. Various segmentation techniques are available based on statistical approaches [3–5,10,18,19]. Segmentation methods that use deep learning techniques [2,12,17] have been popular in recent years as they are highly accurate. We prepared a

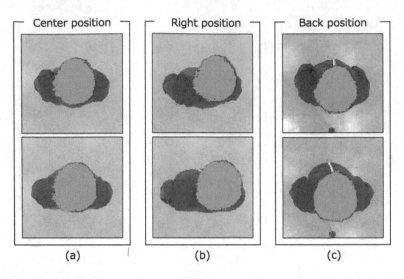

Fig. 3. Examples of head regions acquired from two people in three different standing positions. The green pixels represent the head regions. (Color figure online)

large number of pairs of images of people with the head regions annotated to train a network model for segmentation. Figure 5(a) shows examples of the annotation labels of the head regions, and Fig. 5(b) shows examples of the images of people that were used. The trained network model output candidate head regions.

The candidate head regions estimated by deep learning techniques contained noise. Some pixels of the head regions were incorrectly identified as pixels belonging to other regions of the body, and some belonging to other regions were incorrectly identified as belonging to the head region. Figure 6(a) shows examples of candidate head regions containing noise. To reduce it, we selected the largest regions from the candidate head regions in a single image and corrected all pixels in them. We reduced noise around a boundary between the head region and background regions by using a median filter. Figure 6(b) shows examples of silhouette images of the head regions after noise had been reduced.

3.3 Extracting a Spatio-Temporal Feature from Silhouette Images of Head Regions

The proposed method to extract spatio-temporal features from silhouette images of the head regions extends our previous method [9]. The head slightly moves as a person maintains an upright pose, where this movement occurs around a center acquired at a reference time. To obtain this reference time, we select the silhouette image of a person most similar to each silhouette image of the same person, and set a time acquired it as the reference time. To represent identity in the spatial domain, we radially divide each silhouette image into local blocks using the central position of the head at the reference time. To represent identity

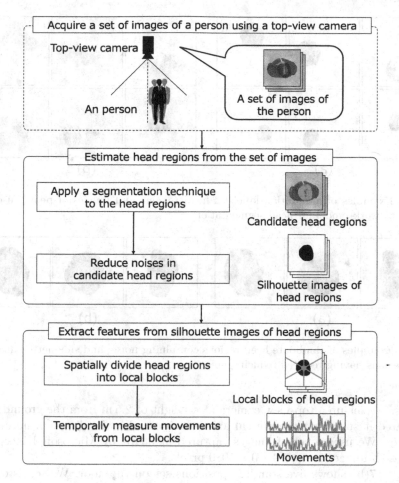

Fig. 4. Overview of our method.

in the temporal domain, we compute movements over time from the local blocks. To extract features for identification, we estimate the power spectral density (PSD) [23] of each movement.

4 Experiments

4.1 Dataset

To evaluate the validity of our method, we collected sets of images of the body sways of 50 participants (average age, 22.7 ± 3 years; 42 males and eight females) using a top-view camera as they stood in different positions. Each participant maintained an upright pose (Romberg posture) with the limbs aligned. We asked all participants to wear the same dark-blue nylon outerwear similar to the uniform worn by factory workers. Figure 7(a) shows the examples of poses and

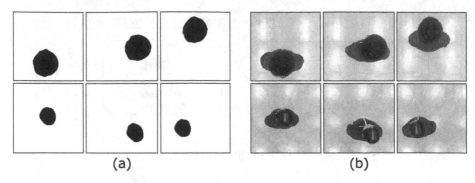

Fig. 5. Examples of annotation labels of head regions and images of people used to train a network model for head segmentation.

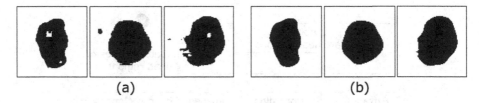

Fig. 6. Examples of candidate head regions containing noise, and silhouette images of these regions having reduced reducing noise.

clothes. We set-up a top-view camera at a height of 2.5 m from the ground, and calibrated it such that the optical axis coincided with the direction normal to the floor. We used a set of images captured at 30 fps by Microsoft Kinect V2, where each image size was 1920 × 1080 pixels.

Figure 7(b) shows five standing positions set on the floor. We set as center the point where the optical axis of the top-view camera was orthogonal to the floor. We set the remaining four standing positions as points that were shifted to the front, back, left, and right from the center by 0.15 m, respectively. Circle markers were set on the floor to indicate each standing position. We asked all participants to stand so that the center of his/her feet corresponded to the circle marker as shown in Fig. 7(c). Figure 7(d) shows the setup for acquiring a set of images of the body sway when a participant stood in the front. We asked each participant to look at a target point 3 m away to fix the direction of the head. We set the target point in front of the participant in each standing position. The time needed to acquire a set of images was 60 s for each standing position. We observed each participant two times in five standing positions. They were allowed to sit and rest between observations. The order of standing positions was random. We cropped the 1920 × 1080-pixels images of all participants to 1080 × 1080 pixels, and resized them to 256 × 256 pixels.

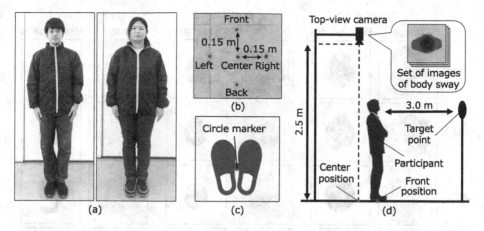

Fig. 7. The conditions under which each participant was observed. (a) shows their poses and clothes, and (b) shows their standing positions set on the floor. (c) shows the circle marker to align the position of the feet of the participants, and (d) shows the setup used to acquire a set of images of the body sway.

4.2   Assessing Accuracy of Estimating Head Regions

We evaluated the accuracy of estimating head regions from images of people using a top-view camera. We applied U-net [17], which was used in research [11], to estimate the head regions. We set eight down-sampling layers and eight up-sampling layers in the U-net architecture. To train the U-net, we randomly selected 25 participants from the dataset described in Sect. 4.1. Data for the remaining 25 participants were used to test the performance of the proposed method. We repeated the random selection five times, and used 45,000 pairs of images and annotation labels of head regions to train the U-net. The sizes of both the images and the annotation labels were set to 256 × 256 pixels, and the number of epochs of training was set to 200. To evaluate the accuracy of the proposed method to estimate head regions, we used the F-measure, which is the harmonic mean of precision and recall. A value of 1 indicates the best result that of 0 the worst.

The proposed method recorded an accuracy of 0.96 ± 0.03 in terms of estimating the head regions. Figure 8 shows examples of head regions estimated for images of three participants in five standing positions using U-net. It is clear that the head regions in Figs. 8(a) and (b) were estimated with high accuracy in all positions. The appearances of the head regions in Fig. 8(c) were different in each position. Although a part of the head regions was incorrectly estimated, the mean value of the F-measure was close to 1. Thus, the results were accurate.

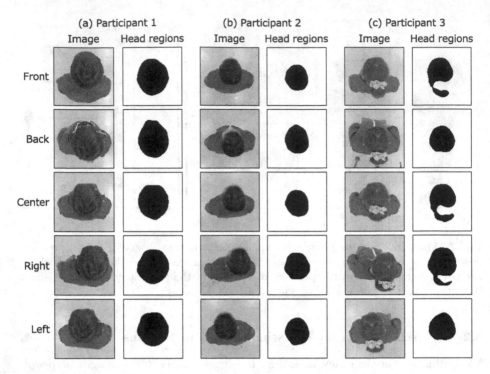

Fig. 8. Examples of head regions estimated from images of three participants in five standing positions using U-net.

4.3 Evaluation of Identification Performance

We assessed whether our method can be used to identify people from images of the head regions in case of self-occlusion. We compared the head regions obtained using it with other regions of the body to this end. The experimental conditions were as follows.

> **Head:** We used head regions estimated by our method. Figure 9(a) shows examples of them.
> **Whole body:** We used whole-body regions as used in a prevalent method [9]. Figure 9(b) shows examples of them.
> **Shoulder:** We used shoulder regions excluding the head regions from entire-body regions. Figure 9(c) shows examples of them.

We estimated the whole-body regions and shoulder regions by applying the method described in Sect. 3.2. We extracted features to identify people from silhouette images of each body part by applying the method described in Sect. 3.3. We set the number of blocks to spatially divide regions of each body part to 25. We selected a set of silhouette images at the center as query, and a set at a position other than the center as target. We also evaluated the performance of the

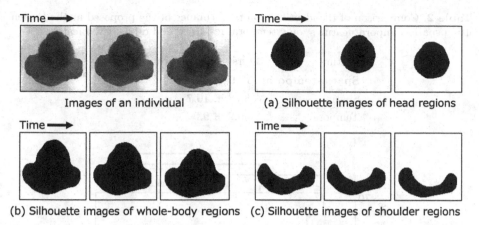

Images of an individual

(a) Silhouette images of head regions

(b) Silhouette images of whole-body regions   (c) Silhouette images of shoulder regions

Fig. 9. Examples of the silhouette images of each body part.

Table 1. Comparison of identification performance using regions of each body part.

Region	First matching rate (%)
Head	**57.9 ± 11.1**
Whole body	17.3 ± 6.8
Shoulder	9.8 ± 5.3

proposed method when switching the query with the target. We used the nearest-neighbor algorithm to identify people from the images and the first matching rate to assess performance. The proposed applied a metric learning technique, the large-margin nearest-neighbor (LMNN) method [22]. We randomly selected 25 participants not from the target and the query 4.1, and used them for LMNN. Data for the remaining 25 participants were used for identification. We repeated the random selection five times.

Table 1 shows the identification performance of the proposed method when it used regions of each body part. Using the head regions as in our method yielded better performance than whole-body regions and shoulder regions. The worst performance was obtained when using shoulder regions (that excluded the head regions). Therefore, the head regions were more robust to self-occlusion than whole-body regions and shoulder regions when using a top-view camera to identify people.

4.4 Performance Comparison When Using Spatial Features and Temporal Features

To determine whether the spatio-temporal features extracted by our method were valid, we compared its performance when using spatio-temporal features with the results obtained when using only spatial features and only temporal

Table 2. Comparison of the identification performance of the proposed method when using spatio-temporal features, only temporal features, and only spatial features.

Feature	First matching rate (%)
Spatio-temporal	**57.9 ± 11.1**
Spatial	33.8 ± 10.7
Temporal	40.2 ± 9.9

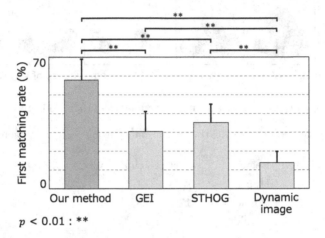

$p < 0.01 : **$

Fig. 10. Comparison of the identification performance of our method, which uses spatio-temporal features, with prevalent methods.

features. We extracted each set of features from the same head regions. The experimental conditions were as follows.

Spatio-temporal features: We extracted the spatio-temporal features from the set of silhouette images of the head regions using our method.

Spatial features: To extract features in the spatial domain from the head regions, we selected a single silhouette image from the set of silhouette images, and used it at the reference time as described in Sect. 3.3.

Temporal features: To extract features in the temporal domain from the head regions, we computed the central position of the head regions in a silhouette image and measured the central positions of the entire set of silhouette images. We used the temporal changes in the central positions as features for identification.

The experimental conditions except for the features used were the same as described in Sect. 4.3.

Table 2 shows the performance of the proposed method when using spatio-temporal features, only temporal features, and only spatial features. It is clear that it performance in terms of identification was superior when using only temporal features than when using only spatial features. It is also evident that the spatio-temporal features extracted by the proposed method yielded the best performance. Thus, extracting features from both the spatial and the temporal domains is the best means of accurately reflecting features of body sway in the head regions.

4.5   Comparison of Proposed Method with Prevalent Methods

We compared the performance of the proposed method with that of prevalent methods in terms of identification. The GEI [7] and STHOG [8] methods are widely used to authenticate gait, and were chosen along with the dynamic image method [6], which is used in action recognition, for comparison with the proposed method. To extract the GEI, we computed the average image from the silhouette images for 60 s. To extract the STHOG, we set the number of spatio-temporal blocks to $6 \times 6 \times 6 = 216$, and computed the gradients. To extract the dynamic image, we applied rank SVM to the silhouette images of the head regions. The experimental conditions, except for the spatio-temporal features used, were the same as described in Sect. 4.3.

Figure 10 compares the identification performance of all methods. It is clear that our method outperformed all other methods. The results of the Wilcoxon signed-rank test and the Bonferroni correction verify this. A significant difference was observed between our method and GEI. The same tendencies were observed for the STHOG, and dynamic images.

5   Conclusions

In this paper, we proposed a method to identify people using their body sway in the spatial and temporal domains by using head regions acquired from a top-view camera in case of self-occlusion. To estimate head regions from the set of images of a person, we applied a method of segmentation using deep learning technique and reduced noise in the candidate head regions chosen. To represent identity-related information reflected in the body sway, we spatially divided the head regions into local blocks and temporally measured movements in these blocks. To evaluate our method, we formed a dataset containing images of people, with a focus on their body sways in the presence of self-occlusion. The results of experiments showed that the proposed method, using head regions, outperforms a prevalent method, which uses the whole-body region.

In future work, we intend to represent identities reflected in the body sways of people in spite of occlusion due to headwear, such as a hat or helmet. Furthermore, we plan to reduce the time needed to observe the body sway.

Acknowledgments. This work was partially supported by JSPS KAKENHI under grant number JP17K00238 and MIC SCOPE under grant number 172308003.

References

1. Agusta, B.A.Y., Mittrapiyanuruk, P., Kaewtrakulpong, P.: Field seeding algorithm for people counting using kinect depth image. Indian J. Sci. Technol. **9**, 48 (2016)
2. Badrinarayanan, V., Kendall, A., Cipolla, R.: SegNet: a deep convolutional encoder-decoder architecture for image segmentation. IEEE Trans. Pattern Anal. Mach. Intell. **39**(12), 2481–2495 (2017)
3. Boykov, Y., Veksler, O., Zabih, R.: Fast approximate energy minimization via graph cuts. IEEE Trans. Pattern Anal. Mach. Intell. **23**, 122–1239 (2001)
4. Brox, T., Bourdev, L., Maji, S., Malik, J.: Object segmentation by alignment of poselet activations to image contours. In: Proceedings of the IEEE Conference on Computer Vision and Pattern Recognition, pp. 2225–2232 (2011)
5. Felzenszwalb, P.F., Huttenlocher, D.P.: Efficient graph-based image segmentation. Int. J. Comput. Vis. **59**(2), 167–181 (2004)
6. Fernando, B., Gavves, E., Oramas, J., Ghodrati, A., Tuytelaars, T.: Rank pooling for action recognition. IEEE Trans. Pattern Anal. Mach. Intell. **39**(4), 773–787 (2016)
7. Han, J., Bhanu, B.: Individual recognition using gait energy image. IEEE Trans. Pattern Anal. Mach. Intell. **28**(2), 316–322 (2006)
8. Hua, C., Makihara, Y., Yagi, Y.: Pedestrian detection by using a spatio-temporal histogram of oriented gradients. IEICE Trans. Inf. Syst. **96**(6), 1376–1386 (2013)
9. Kamitani, T., Yoshimura, H., Nishiyama, M., Iwai, Y.: Temporal and spatial analysis of local body sway movements for the identification of people. IEICE Trans. Inf. Syst. **102**(1), 165–174 (2019)
10. Krähenbühl, P., Koltun, V.: Efficient inference in fully connected CRFs with Gaussian edge potentials. In: Advances in Neural Information Processing Systems, pp. 109–117 (2011)
11. Liciotti, D., Paolanti, M., Pietrini, R., Frontoni, E., Zingaretti, P.: Convolutional networks for semantic heads segmentation using top-view depth data in crowded environment. In: Proceedings of 24th International Conference on Pattern Recognition, pp. 1384–1389 (2018)
12. Long, J., Shelhamer, E., Darrell, T.: Fully convolutional networks for semantic segmentation. In: Proceedings of the IEEE Conference on Computer Vision and Pattern Recognition, pp. 3431–3440 (2015)
13. Makihara, Y., Sagawa, R., Mukaigawa, Y., Echigo, T., Yagi, Y.: Gait recognition using a view transformation model in the frequency domain. In: Leonardis, A., Bischof, H., Pinz, A. (eds.) ECCV 2006. LNCS, vol. 3953, pp. 151–163. Springer, Heidelberg (2006). https://doi.org/10.1007/11744078_12
14. Min, R., Choi, J., Medioni, G., Dugelay, J.L.: Real-time 3D face identification from a depth camera. In: Proceedings of the 21st International Conference on Pattern Recognition, pp. 1739–1742 (2012)
15. Mukherjee, S., Saha, B., Jamal, I., Leclerc, R., Ray, N.: A novel framework for automatic passenger counting. In: Proceedings of 18th IEEE International Conference on Image Processing, pp. 2969–2972 (2011)
16. Munir, S., et al.: Real-time fine grained occupancy estimation using depth sensors on arm embedded platforms. In: Proceedings of 2017 IEEE Real-Time and Embedded Technology and Applications Symposium, pp. 295–306 (2017)
17. Ronneberger, O., Fischer, P., Brox, T.: U-net: convolutional networks for biomedical image segmentation. In: Navab, N., Hornegger, J., Wells, W.M., Frangi, A.F. (eds.) MICCAI 2015. LNCS, vol. 9351, pp. 234–241. Springer, Cham (2015). https://doi.org/10.1007/978-3-319-24574-4_28

18. Shotton, J., Winn, J., Rother, C., Criminisi, A.: Textonboost for image understanding: multi-class object recognition and segmentation by jointly modeling texture, layout, and context. Int. J. Comput. Vis. **81**(1), 2–23 (2009)

19. Tighe, J., Niethammer, M., Lazebnik, S.: Scene parsing with object instances and occlusion ordering. In: Proceedings of the IEEE Conference on Computer Vision and Pattern Recognition (2014)

20. Vera, P., Monjaraz, S., Salas, J.: Counting pedestrians with a zenithal arrangement of depth cameras. Mach. Vis. Appl. **27**(2), 303–315 (2015). https://doi.org/10.1007/s00138-015-0739-1

21. Wang, X.: Intelligent multi-camera video surveillance: a review. Pattern Recognit. Lett. **34**(1), 3–19 (2013)

22. Weinberger, K.Q., Saul, L.K.: Distance metric learning for large margin nearest neighbor classification. J. Mach. Learn. Res. **10**, 207–244 (2009)

23. Welch, P.: The use of fast fourier transform for the estimation of power spectra: a method based on time averaging over short, modified periodograms. IEEE Trans. Audio Electroacoust. **15**(2), 70–73 (1967)

Action Recognition in Sports Video Considering Location Information

Rina Ichige[✉] and Yoshimitsu Aoki

Keio University, 3-14-1, Hiyoshi, Kohoku-ku, Yokohama 223-8522, Japan
richige@aoki-medialab.jp

Abstract. The purpose of this study is to develop a tactics analysis system using image recognition for rugby. With the Rugby World Cup in 2019 and the Tokyo Olympics in 2020, demand for sports video analysis is increasing. Rugby has more complicated play such as dense play than other sports, and the ball is hidden between players, making it difficult to track. By developing a high-precision analysis technology for rugby with few research cases, we thought that it could be used for other sports and industrial fields other than sports. In this research, we propose a method that adds spatial information to time-series information as a new feature. Using the coordinates obtained by projectively transforming the match video onto the bird's-eye view image, play classification was performed using the player position, the ball position, and the dense area position as feature amounts. Also, in order to further improve the detection accuracy of the boundaries between plays, attention was paid to the positional relationship of each player on the field.

Keywords: Dense play · Heatmap features · Subdivision of play area

1 Introduction

In recent years, the demand for video analysis utilizing ICT (Information and Communication Technology) as content for strengthening teams and tactics and watching sports has been increasing in the sports world. In particular, companies that have had little relevance in the sports field have begun to actively participate in the event, especially since the 2019 Rugby World Cup Japan Games in Japan and the 2020 Tokyo Olympics have hosted global sports festivals.

For team sports such as soccer and basketball, action recognition for the actions of players during a game has already been performed. On the other hand, there are few studies on rugby at present. The reason is the rugby's playing characteristics. First, the number of players participating in the game is 15 per team, which is larger than volleyball (6), baseball (9), soccer (11), and football (11). In addition, since the movements and postures of the players vary widely, it is necessary to pay attention to the movements of each player, such as the speed and direction in which they run. In addition, players such as "Scrum", "Lineout" etc. are often hidden behind shadows due to contact play or dense play, which makes tracking difficult. Play continues until a goal is scored, the ball goes out of the touch line, or an offense occurs, during which time offense and defense changes occur frequently.

© Springer Nature Singapore Pte Ltd. 2020
W. Ohyama and S. K. Jung (Eds.): IW-FCV 2020, CCIS 1212, pp. 150–164, 2020.
https://doi.org/10.1007/978-981-15-4818-5_12

Therefore, by developing a highly accurate analysis technology for rugby with complex game characteristics, it was thought that it would be possible to use it for other sports and use it as content for watching games on TV.

In addition, due to the lack of widespread analysis technology, rugby play is currently tagged manually by analysts after watching the match video (40 min in the first half). We thought that if we could automatically extract the necessary play scenes, we would reduce the burden on analysts and directly use the time for tagging for on-site coaching of players, which would strengthen the team.

2 Previous Work

Conventionally, a play classification method utilizes an LSTM (Long Short-Term Memory) [1] for handling sequence data. As shown in Fig. 1, a still image cut out from a video is converted into a feature amount by a CNN (Convolutional Neural Network) [2] for each frame, and is input to an LSTM with 512 nodes in a fully connected layer. This is to calculate the probability distribution of the labeled play by averaging the outputs of the nodes of the number of classes in all the connected layers [3]. This method has the advantage that everything from video design to feature classification to play classification can be performed automatically by machine learning, but since all the play is detected by inputting the frame images all at once. The accuracy of each play is not high.

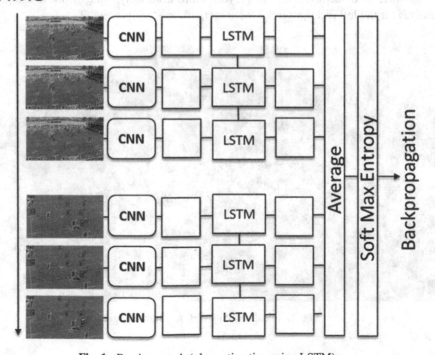

Fig. 1. Previous work (play estimation using LSTM)

3 Proposed Method

This time, we focused on the characteristics of rugby, where players and balls are easily hidden in dense areas, clarified the relationship between players and players and between players and balls, and focused on the role of each player by subdividing the play area. At this point, we conducted research with a view to watching TV broadcast content by automatic detection and real-time detection of play scenes required for analysis. In this study, since the player's play recognition is the main axis, we analyzed the game video in which the player position, ball position, and dense area position were taught in advance. For the feature extraction, three methods were considered: the handcraft feature, the heatmap feature, and the use of the subdivision region.

3.1 Shooting Method

As a method of detecting a player's position, it is conceivable to take a picture by switching the multi-view camera, but this time we will use the video taken by the fixed camera in terms of installation cost.

In the conventional method, since an image obtained by pan shooting with only one camera is input, there is a problem that fluctuations in camera work when the image is taken affect the movement of players. there were.

Therefore, this time, we fixed the camera and considered a shooting method that shows the whole field. In this method, if a player can be detected, the position of the player with respect to the field is fixed, so that the positional relationship can be accurately set as a feature amount.

In order to detect even distant players more accurately, images taken using two cameras for the left and right fields were merged, as shown in Fig. 2.

Fig. 2. Fixed shooting (left and right merge)

3.2 Conversion to Overhead Image

In order to design features that are not affected by camera work, the projection trans-formation matrix (1) [4–6] was estimated for each frame from the movement of the corresponding points (4 points) (x, y) on the white line, and converted to an overhead image Player/ball positions (x', y') (Fig. 3) were used. As a result, the distance between the players does not depend on the distance between the object and the camera, and the positional relationship between the players is uniformly maintained.

$$\begin{pmatrix} x' \\ y' \\ 1 \end{pmatrix} = \begin{pmatrix} a_1 & b_1 & c_1 \\ a_2 & b_2 & c_2 \\ a_0 & b_0 & c_0 \end{pmatrix} \begin{pmatrix} x \\ y \\ 1 \end{pmatrix} \qquad (1)$$

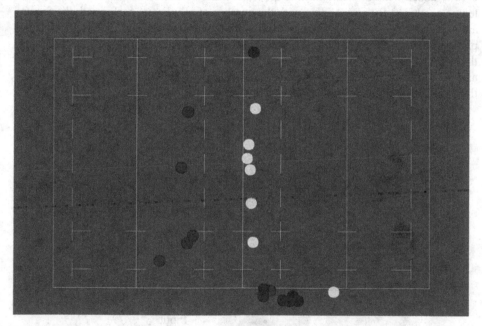

Fig. 3. Conversion to overhead image

3.3 Handcraft Features

In this method, handcraft features (static features and dynamic features) were designed and input for each frame instead of an image as shown in Fig. 4. The feature that did not automatically extract features using CNN as in the conventional method of Fig. 1 is that there are few precedents in rugby research, and at this time a large number of videos with the player and ball positions taught are prepared. Was difficult. If high-dimensional data such as an image is used as an input for a small amount of learning data, learning may be affected by unnecessary information included in the image, and over-learning may occur.

The average of the player positions and the variance of the player positions were used for the static features. The average player position was determined for all players in that frame without distinguishing between teams. Then, the variance of the player positions was calculated from the average position obtained by the following equation.

$$s_x^2 = \frac{1}{n} \sum_{i=1}^{n} (x_i - \bar{x})^2 \tag{2}$$

$$s_y^2 = \frac{1}{n} \sum_{i=1}^{n} (y_i - \bar{y})^2 \tag{3}$$

The average of the player velocities between certain frames was used as the dynamic feature value. This time, since it is used as a feature value for classification of play regardless of the team, the sum of the speeds issued for each player with the same ID is fully added without distinguishing the team, and it is detected in that frame that both teams combined By normalizing with the number of all players performed, the feature amount in the sense of the average of the movement amount and direction of all the players between 1 frames was obtained. For example, in dense play such as "Lineout", the speed of the player is small in the dense area, so the magnitude of the speed is small, and in "Turnover", the change of offense and defense occurs between the teams, so it is the moment when the overall speed vector is reversed Conceivable.

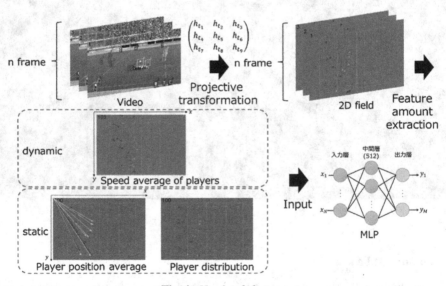

Fig. 4. Handcraft features

3.4 Heatmap Features

The handcraft feature is a high-dimensional image called a low-dimensional matrix containing numerical values for each time series. On the other hand, the heatmap feature quantity has a feature that only necessary information is extracted while maintaining the format of an image as shown in Fig. 5. Since the size of the rugby field varies depending on the shooting location, the input frame is first normalized. Like the handcraft feature, the feature includes a static feature and a dynamic feature.

A zero matrix (black image) having the same size as the normalized bird's-eye view image (Y, X) is prepared for 6 channels (4 static feature values + 2 dynamic feature values) × the number of frames.

For the coordinates at which the position is detected, a pixel value of 1 is inserted instead of 0 in the static feature amount. A Gaussian filter is applied to this image. This operation is performed for all four channels $ch_0 \sim ch_3$ (the player position p_{ayx} of the team 1, the player position p_{byx} of the team 2, the ball position b_{yx}, and the dense area position c_{yx}).6

In the case of the dynamic feature amount, the velocity vector (ch_4, ch_5) corresponding to the movement compared with the past frame (y_{prev}, x_{prev}) is inserted.

$$ch_0 = \begin{pmatrix} p_{a00} & \cdots & p_{a0X} \\ \vdots & \ddots & \vdots \\ p_{aY0} & \cdots & p_{aYX} \end{pmatrix} \tag{4}$$

$$ch_1 = \begin{pmatrix} p_{b00} & \cdots & p_{b0X} \\ \vdots & \ddots & \vdots \\ p_{bY0} & \cdots & p_{bYX} \end{pmatrix} \tag{5}$$

$$ch_2 = \begin{pmatrix} b_{00} & \cdots & b_{0X} \\ \vdots & \ddots & \vdots \\ b_{Y0} & \cdots & b_{YX} \end{pmatrix} \tag{6}$$

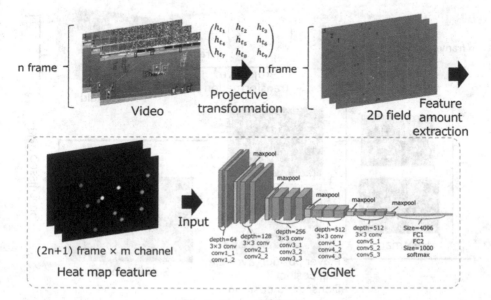

Fig. 5. Heatmap features

$$ch_3 = \begin{pmatrix} c_{00} & \cdots & c_{0X} \\ \vdots & \ddots & \vdots \\ c_{Y0} & \cdots & c_{YX} \end{pmatrix} \tag{7}$$

$$\begin{pmatrix} ch_4 \\ ch_5 \end{pmatrix} = \left(\begin{pmatrix} y_{00} & \cdots & y_{0X} \\ \vdots & \ddots & \vdots \\ y_{Y0} & \cdots & y_{YX} \\ x_{00} & \cdots & x_{0X} \\ \vdots & \ddots & \vdots \\ x_{Y0} & \cdots & x_{YX} \end{pmatrix} \right) - \left(\begin{pmatrix} y_{prev00} & \cdots & y_{prev0X} \\ \vdots & \ddots & \vdots \\ y_{prevY0} & \cdots & y_{prevYX} \\ x_{prev00} & \cdots & x_{prev0X} \\ \vdots & \ddots & \vdots \\ x_{prevY0} & \cdots & x_{prevYX} \end{pmatrix} \right) \tag{8}$$

3.5 Use of Heatmap Features and Subdivision Areas

In EPV (expected possession value) [7], the expected value of the score is calculated by the dispersion of players on the basketball court. In RPR (Reachable polygonal region) [8], the dominant region of each player is calculated using approximate bisectors drawn for each pair of players. Referring to these conventional studies, consider where the players, balls, and dense areas belong to the subdivided areas as shown in Fig. 6. In the heatmap feature, the variance of players, the ball position, and the position of the dense area in the entire field were applied on the heatmap. For example, in the case of "Lineout", a dense area is assigned to an area near the line, so that it is possible to distinguish it from "Scrum", which is the same dense play. In Fig. 6, the location of the average player position/ball position/dense area position is labeled in the subdivided play area, and added as a new channel to heatmap feature amounts (4) to (8).

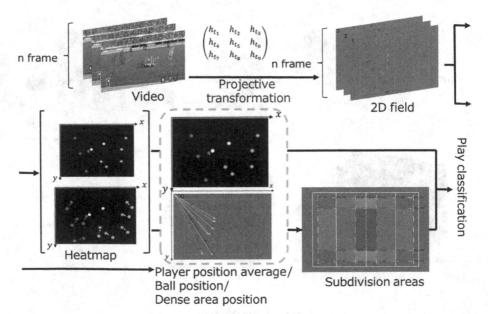

Fig. 6. Use of heatmap features and subdivision areas

4   Experiment

4.1   Dataset Details

As shown in Table 1, the data set used in this experiment is a set of eight fixed images (30 fps, Fig. 2) obtained by merging two fixed cameras into a left-right image. Used as a minute video.

Play labels were given for six classes as shown in Table 2. In fact, 7 classes are labeled, including the other play "Other Play". However, as shown in Table 2, the proportion of "Other Play" included in the data set is large, For the purpose of improving the accuracy of play classification in this study, this time we used labels for 6 classes excluding "Other Play" in order to consider the difference in accuracy due to the method.

Table 1. Dataset

Movie	1	2	3	4	5	6	7	8
Frame (7 label)	21177	19779	1919	21536	22239	44968	37121	40129
Frame (6 label)	1790	1589	1350	770	764	2073	1313	2048

Table 2. Label

Label	0	1	2	3	4	5
Play	Scrum	Lineout	Kick off	Kick counter	Turnover	Penalty

4.2   Evaluation Index

In Table 3, Accuracy, Precision, Recall, and F-measure were used as evaluation indices in Table 3.

$$Accuracy = \frac{TP + TN}{TP + FP + FN + TN} \tag{9}$$

$$Precision = \frac{TP}{TP + FP} \tag{10}$$

$$Recall = \frac{TP}{TP + FN} \tag{11}$$

$$F\text{-}measure = \frac{2 \cdot Recall \cdot Precision}{Recall + Precision} \tag{12}$$

Table 3. Evaluation index

		GT	
		P	N
Predict	P	TP	FP
	N	FN	TN

5 Discussion

"Handcraft" method using handcraft feature amount, "heatmap" method using only heatmap feature amount, and "heatmap" indicating where the average player position, ball position, and dense area position belong to the subdivided play area in Fig. 6 compare each method as "player", "ball", "crowd", and unify all of them as all. GT is above, prediction results are below, light blue is "Scrum", orange is "Lineout", gray is "Kick off", yellow is "Kick counter", blue is "Turnover", green is "Penalty".

In this article, we consider video 6, the labels included "Scrum" 7.5%, "Lineout" 14%, "Kick off" 31%, "Kick counter" 18%, "Turnover" 18%, and "Penalty" 12%. GT and predicted values are shown in Figs. 7, 8, 9, 10, 11 and 12.

Fig. 7. GT and predict (handcraft) (Color figure online)

Fig. 8. GT and predict (heatmap) (Color figure online)

Fig. 9. GT and predict (player) (Color figure online)

Fig. 10. GT and predict (ball) (Color figure online)

Fig. 11. GT and predict (crowd) (Color figure online)

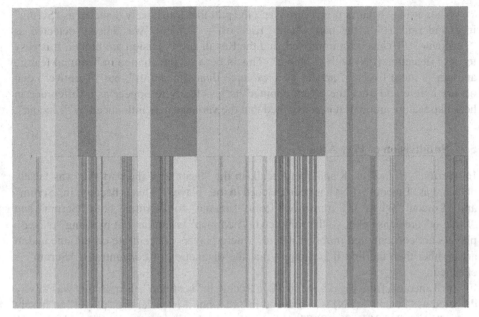

Fig. 12. GT and predict (all) (Color figure online)

5.1 Handcraft Features and Heatmap Features

From Figs. 7 and 8, when "heatmap" is used in "Scrum", the "Kick off", "Kick counter", "Turnover", "Penalty" and false detection (FN) in "handcraft" have been improved, but "Lineout" has been falsely detected. (FN). This is thought to be due to the fact that the frequency of switching between plays in GT is high, and the part that was difficult to appear with the scalar amount of handcraft is easy to distinguish "Scrum" as a play with small dispersion in "heatmap".

When using "heatmap" in "Lineout", the part that was falsely detected (FN) as "Kick off", "Kick counter", and "Penalty" in "handcraft" has been improved, but it is easier to falsely detect (FN) as "Scrum". This is thought to be because, as with "Scrum", the "heatmap" makes it easy to distinguish small play from play that is not, but dense play with small variance is unlikely to appear as a difference in feature amount.

Regarding "Kick off", when using "heatmap", the part (FN) that was incorrectly detected as "Scrum" and "Turnover" in "handcraft" has been improved, and the recall has been increased, but the "Kick counter" has been mistakenly detected as "Kick off" (FP) and it has become easier to falsely detect (FP) I have.

Also, using "heatmap" for the "Kick counter", the part that was falsely detected as "Penalty" in "handcraft" (FN), the part where "Scrum", "Lineout", "Kick off" was falsely detected as "Kick counter" (FP) has been improved, and Recall, Precision is higher. This is probably because the variance clearly appears as a heatmap feature and is easily distinguished from a play ("Scrum", "Lineout") with a small variance, but the "Kick off" cannot be distinguished from the "Kick counter" performed at the end of the field.

When using "heatmap" in "Turnover", the part that was falsely detected as "Scrum" in "handcraft" (FN), the part where "Kick off", "Penalty" was falsely detected as "Turnover" (FP) has been improved, and the Recall and Precision are higher, It is easy to false detection (FN) with "Lineout". This is because the change in heatmap feature amount is more likely to appear as a variance than "handcraft", but "Turnover" that occurs before and after the "Kick counter" is less likely to appear as a difference in heatmap feature amount. It is considered that the variance in is influenced by "Lineout".

5.2 Subdivision of Play Area

In "Scrum", from Figs. 8 and 9 in Recall, in the "heatmap", the part that was falsely detected as "Lineout" (FN) has been reduced in the "player". This is because in "Scrum" and "Lineout" where GT transitions from "Lineout" to "Scrum", both "Scrum" and "Lineout" are dense play, so the variance in "heatmap" is similar, but by using "player", players are concentrated in the "Lineout" where players concentrate on the line and in areas other than the line It is thought that the distinction of concentrated "Scrum" is clarified.

In "Lineout", from Figs. 8, 9 and 12 in Recall, in "heatmap", the part that was falsely detected as "Penalty" (FN) was reduced in "all", but it is easier for "player" to falsely detect "Scrum" and "Kick off". This is considered to be because most of "Penalty" in GT occurs before and after "Lineout", but by using "crowd", it becomes clear to distinguish between "Lineout" where dense areas are detected at the line and "Penalty" where dense areas are not detected. Also, in the "player", the "Lineout" that occurs before and after "Scrum" in GT is similar in the area where players concentrate, and the "Lineout" that occurs before and after "Scrum" is both players concentrated on the line, making it difficult to distinguish.

In "Kick off", from Figs. 8, 9, 10 in Recall, in the "heatmap", the part that was falsely detected (FN) as "Kick counter" and "Turnover" is reduced in the "player", but it is easier to falsely detect as "Lineout" (FN) in "crowd". This happens in GT before and after "Kick off" for both "Kick counter" and "Turnover", but "Kick off" where the area where players concentrate by "player" is on the line and "Kick counter" where the area where players concentrate is other than line It is thought that the distinction of "Turnover", whose formation changes instantaneously, becomes clearer. Also, in GT, most of "Lineout" occurs before and after "Kick off", but it is affected by "Lineout" at the boundary between "Kick off" and "Lineout", and it is difficult to distinguish because dense areas are detected at the line side Conceivable.

In the "Kick counter", from Figs. 8, 10 and 12 in Recall, the part that was falsely detected as "Kick off" and "Penalty" (FN) in "heatmap" decreased in "all", but increased in "ball". This is a "Kick counter", "Penalty" occurs before and after "Kick off" in GT, but "Kick off", where the area where players concentrate by the "player" is on the line, and "Kick counter", where the area where players concentrate is other than the line, This is probably because the distinction between "Penalty", where the concentration area is not limited, is clarified. In addition, it is considered that the frequency of transition in a short frame interval from kick to kick to "Penalty" in GT is high, and the ball position is affected by the play before and after, making it difficult to distinguish.

In "Turnover", from Figs. 8, 10 and 11 in Recall, in "heatmap", the false detection of "Scrum", "Lineout", "Kick off", "Penalty" (FN) is reduced in the "crowd", but in the "ball", "Scrum", "Kick off", "Kick counter", "Penalty" is more likely to be falsely detected. This is due to the fact that most of "Scrum" and "Turnover" in GT immediately before "Lineout" most of "Penalty", but crowded area is detected in places other than line by "crowd", "Scrum", dense area is detected in line It is thought that the distinction between "Lineout" and "Turnover" where the dense area is not detected is clarified, and it is clear that the distinction between "Penalty" and "Turnover" will be clear depending on whether the dense area is detected in the play of the boundary depending on whether it occurs before or after the "Lineout" Can be "Kick off" and "Kick counter", which occur at short frame intervals before and after "Turnover" in GT, have similar ball positions, are difficult to distinguish, and frequently transition at short play intervals of "Penalty" → "Lineout" → "Turnover". It is considered that because a ball is not detected in a certain "Lineout", it is difficult to detect the ball position in the front and rear "Penalty" and "Turnover", and it is difficult to distinguish the ball position.

In "Penalty", from Figs. 8, 10 and 12 in Recall, "Scrum" in "heatmap", the part that was falsely detected as "Kick off" (FN) is reduced in "all", but "Scrum", It is easy to mistakenly detect as "Turnover". This is probably because the distinction between "Scrum" and "Penalty" based on the presence or absence of a crowded area in the crowd and the distinction between "Kick off" and "Penalty" based on whether or not the ball detection position by the ball is on the line are clear. In addition, since the ball position is not detected in the portion where the transition is short at "Penalty" → "Lineout" → "Turnover" and the "Lineout" → "Scrum" in GT, the ball position is difficult to detect in the front and rear "Penalty" and "Turnover", making it difficult to distinguish it is considered to be the body.

6 Conclusion

In this research, for six rugby plays, the variance of players in the "heatmap" feature value was clarified, and then the attribute of the subdivided area was added to the feature value for the average position of the players and the location of the dense area, and the dense play was performed. ("Scrum", "Lineout") and the other play and the play on the line ("Lineout", "Kick off") were determined, and the accuracy of the play was improved. With regard to the ball position, if we could accurately predict the players and the parts hidden behind the crowded area, we thought that it would be possible to add a new feature value and detect the offense and defense alternation as seen in "Turnover" more accurately.

References

1. Hochreiter, S., Schmidhuber, J.: LSTM can solve hard long time lag problems. In: Advances in Neural Information Processing Systems, pp. 473–479 (1997)
2. Simonyan, K., Zisserman, A.: Very deep convolutional networks for large-scale image recognition. arXiv1409.1556 (2014)

3. Ouchi, K.: Development of a rugby video analysis system. J. Inst. Electron. Inf. Commun. Eng. B **100**(12), 941–951 (2017)
4. Von Gioi, R.G., Jakubowicz, J., Morel, J.M., Randall, G.: LSD: A fast line segment detector with a false detection control. IEEE Trans. Pattern Anal. Mach. Intell. **32**(4), 722–732 (2008)
5. Hartley, R., Zisserman, A.: Multiple View Geometry in Computer Vision. Cambridge University Press, Cambridge (2003)
6. Beaton, A.E., Tukey, J.W.: The fitting of power series, meaning polynomials, illustrated on band-spectroscopic data. Technometrics **16**(2), 147–185 (1974)
7. Cervone, D., D'Amour, A., Bornn, L., Goldsberry, K.: A multiresolution stochastic process model for predicting basketball possession outcomes. J. Am. Stat. Assoc. **111**(514), 585–599 (2016)
8. Gudmundsson, Joachim, Wolle, Thomas: Football analysis using spatio-temporal tools. Comput. Environ. Urban Syst. **47**, 16–27 (2014)

Object Detection and Tracking

Adaptive Feature Selection Siamese Networks for Visual Tracking

Mustansar Fiaz[1], Md. Maklachur Rahman[1], Arif Mahmood[2],
Sehar Shahzad Farooq[1], Ki Yeol Baek[1], and Soon Ki Jung[1](✉)

[1] School of Computer Science and Engineering, Kyungpook National University,
Daegu, Republic of Korea
{mustansar,skjung}@knu.ac.kr
[2] Department of Computer Science, Information Technology University,
Lahore, Pakistan
arif.mahmood@itu.edu.pk

Abstract. Recently, template based discriminative trackers, especially
Siamese network based trackers have shown great potential in terms
of balanced accuracy and tracking speed. However, it is still difficult
for Siamese models to adapt the target variations from offline learning. In this paper, we introduced an Adaptive Feature Selection Siamese
(AFS-Siam) network to learn the most discriminative feature information
for better tracking. Features from different layers contain complementary information for discrimination. Proposed adaptive feature selection
module selects the most useful feature information from different convolutional layers while suppresses the irrelevant ones. Proposed tracking
algorithm not only alleviates the over-fitting problem but also increases
the discriminative ability. The proposed tracking framework is trained
end-to-end. And extensive experimental results over OTB50, OTB100,
TC-128, and VOT2017 demonstrate that our tracking algorithm exhibits
favorable performance compared to other state-of-the-art methods.

Keywords: Siamese networks · Convolutional Neural Networks ·
Visual Object Tracking · Attentional networks

1 Introduction

Visual Object Tracking (VOT) is the process of determining the location of
a target object in a video sequence. VOT is a famous sub-field of computer
vision and considered as one of the basic building blocks in various vision applications including human-computer interaction, autonomous vehicles, robotics,
intelligent surveillance, and scene understanding. VOT is a challenging problem
due to limited information provided in the initial frame of a video. Usually, the
bounding box of target object is provided in first frame of video and objective
of VOT is to track the object of interest in the subsequent frames in a sequence.
Despite the popularity of VOT in the recent years, it is still an open and challenging problem due to various issues such as occlusions, fast motion, deformation,
motion blue, in planer-rotation, out-planer rotation, and scale variations.

© Springer Nature Singapore Pte Ltd. 2020
W. Ohyama and S. K. Jung (Eds.): IW-FCV 2020, CCIS 1212, pp. 167–179, 2020.
https://doi.org/10.1007/978-981-15-4818-5_13

In general, visual tracking approaches are classified as discriminative and generative tracking methods. In generative tracking approach, appearance representation is constructed with minimum reconstruction error for the target and the model finds the most similar candidates in the next frames [22,32,37]. On the other hand, discriminative tracking approaches have solved the tracking problem as classification or regression problem [1,27,41]. The discriminative approaches aim to discriminate the target from the background. Discriminative methods require an offline and online training to update the model which require a large number of training samples. Correlation Filter based Trackers (CFTs) are extremely efficient by enlarging the training samples using circular samples. Convolutional Neural Networks (CNN) has shown great progress in many vision applications including object detection [16], face verification [34], and semantic segmentation [33]. An empirical study [12,13] revealed that deep CNN features exploited into CFTs have shown outstanding performance compared to hand-crafted features including color-names, Histogram of Oriented Gradients (HOG), color histogram, and Scale-Invariant Feature Transform (SIFT). However, it is an exhaustive job to train the deep trackers due to data-hungry characteristics of deep learning. To handle this issue, deep trackers such as [6,9,28] utilize pre-trained models to extract the deep features but do not fully understand the specific target appearance. To fully exploit the target appearance and improve tracking performance, deep trackers including [11,30,43] are trained end-to-end. However, these trackers encounter over-fitting problem due to model update to adapt new target appearances. Moreover, online learning requires extra computational cost for feature extraction, inference and model update operations.

Recently, Siamese-based trackers [2,10,17,18] are getting enormous popularity owing to balance the tracking accuracy and speed. Siamese based trackers are categorized as similarity learning problem. A similarity measure function is trained offline on a large benchmark to compute a similarity between the input images. Although, Siamese trackers have shown great performance but do not learn the target specific features for discrimination resulting in degraded performance in certain scenarios. Moreover, all the convolutional features do not equally contribute for discrimination. Therefore, it is required to select the most discriminative features. To address aforementioned limitations, we introduced a novel adaptive feature selection module to select the meaningful discriminative features to improve the tracking performance.

In this work, we propose an Adaptive Feature Selection Siamese (AFS-Siam) network to select important features which are useful for discrimination. Li et al. [24] proposed a Selective Kernel Network (SKNet) to select the receptive field for image classification. SKNet consists of three components including split, fusion and select. First, SKNet splits the features with different dilated rate and then fusion operation computes the selective weights for those features. Finally, select component combines the selected information with selected weights. Inspired by SKNet, we integrated an adaptive feature selection mechanism within Siamese network for efficient feature selection. The proposed AFS-Siam computes weights for features as attentional weights from different layers and combines the features which are most informative. Datasets including OTB50, OTB100 [42], temple color-128 [25], and VOT2017 [21] were selected to validate the performance of the proposed tracker. Experimental results revealed that the proposed algorithm performed better compared to other compared methods.

We summarize our contributions in current work as:

– We propose an adaptive feature selection mechanism into Siamese network to compute weights for the features from different layers. The final more informative and discriminative features are selected based on feature weights. The network holds the end-to-end property.
– To measure the effectiveness of our proposed tracker against recent trackers, we performed an extensive comparison on the datasets such as OTB50, OTB100, VOT2017 and Temple color-128.

We organize rest of the paper as follows. The related work is presented in Sect. 2 while proposed method is explained in Sect. 3. Experiments and evaluations are described in Sect. 4. Finally, Sect. 5 presents conclusion of the paper.

2 Related Work

This section presents the most related work to tracking algorithm such as Siamese based and attentional based trackers. Interested readers can find a detailed study in [12,13,23].

2.1 Siamese Based Trackers

Siamese network consists of the two parallel convolutional neural networks where both networks share the same parameters to reduce the parameters overhead. These types of tracking are formulated as similarity learning problems. Based on the similarity learning, SiameseFC [2] computes a similarity map as a response for a pair of images. The model is composed of two parallel embedded convolutional layers and is trained end-to-end over a huge benchmark. GOTURN [19] is composed of two-stream network and solves the tracking problems as bounding box regression. SiamTri [10] introduces a triplet loss that helps to perform tracker in the real-time speed with a similar accuracy of the baseline SiamFC tracker. CFNet [36] uses the low-level feature-based correlation filters for speeding up the tracker regardless of dropping the accuracy. Tao et al. [35] introduced an optical flow within Siamese networks to acquire better accuracy with high computational cost. In order to suppress the background information, Guo et al. [17] proposed DSiam and performed online learning to capture target appearance variations. Siamese based trackers may face over-fitting problem due to joint feature representation and discriminative learning. Moreover, Siamese trackers do not fully exploit the target features to select discriminative features for improved tracking.

2.2 Attention-Based Trackers

Inspired by the human visual system [29], numerous trackers propose visual attention mechanism within the Siamese network to boost the tracking performance in terms of accuracy. Recently, attention mechanism gained a huge popularity in wide range of computer vision applications such as image classification [38], and segmentation [15]. Wang et al. [40] integrated three kinds of attentions including residual attention, channel attention, and general attention within Siamese networks. SA-Siam [18] incorporated channel attention in the semantic branch of the target pipeline to enhance the robustness. Pu et al. [31] proposed regularization base training to produce attentional maps through back and forth operations. Cui et al. [5] utilized multi-directional recurrent neural networks to yield saliency maps and drew attention to possible targets. In our proposed work, instead of using multiple attentions, we integrated an adaptive feature selection mechanism for different convolutional layers to compute reliable discriminative features for improved accuracy.

3 Proposed Tracking Framework

In this section, we present our proposed tracking algorithm in detail. The proposed tracking framework is shown in Fig. 1. We proposed an Adaptive Feature Selection Siamese (AFS-Siam) tracker which selects more informative features while suppressing less useful features. The intention behind this work is to adapt target appearances by exploiting discriminative semantic features from different layers in a similarity learning problem.

3.1 Fully Convolutional Siamese Network

We used SiameseFC [2] as our baseline tracker. SiameseFC learns a similarity measure function from embedded CNN models between a pair of images during end-to-end training. SiameseFC is composed of two parallel branches knows as exemplar and search branches. Each branch consists of embedded CNN model. A cross-correlation operation is performed to compute a similarity map between template and search region as shown in Fig. 2. During tracking, template Z from initial frame is provided at exemplar branch. While search patch X is provided at search branch to compute a similarity measure function $g(Z, X)$ for the subsequent frames as:

$$g(Z, X) = \theta(Z) * \theta(X) + b, \tag{1}$$

where $\theta(\cdot)$ represents embedded space, $*$ denotes cross-correlation, and b indicates offset. The SiameseFC utilizes only semantic features from the last convolutional layer which are insensitive to intra-class discrimination. Moreover, SiameseFC treats all the features equally which also degrades the tracking performance. In order to handle SiameseFC issues, we utilized features from different layers. Furthermore, we selected more informative features compared to less informative features by integrating an adaptive feature selection module in Siamese tracking framework.

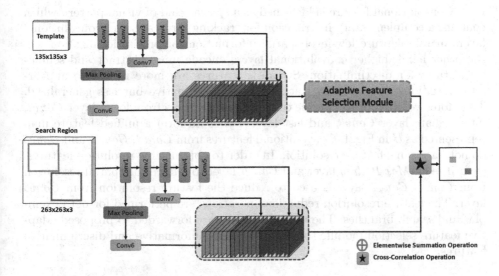

Fig. 1. The pipeline of proposed AFS-Siam tracker. Features from *Conv7*, *Conv6*, and *Conv5* are concatenated to form a unified features as U. Unified features are forwarded to an adaptive feature selection module to select more informative features for template branch. A cross-correlation operation is performed between template and search branches to compute a response map.

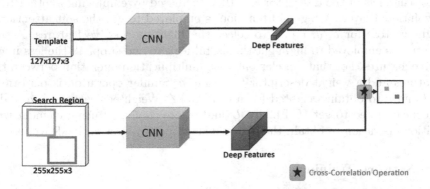

Fig. 2. SiameseFC tracking framework. Target and search patches are forwarded to embedded CNN models to compute deep features. A cross-correlation operation is performed to obtain a similarity response map between the input image patches.

3.2   Adaptive Feature Selection Siamese Tracker

Each Convolutional feature is identified as a special kind of visual pattern which contains a complementary information for tracking targets. Lower convolutional layers mainly capture low-level spatial information for precise localization. On the other hand, higher convolutional layers encode more abstract and semantic features for discrimination. Semantic features are more robust to appearance variations, thus make a tracker more discriminative but less generalized. Therefore, we attempt to fuse the convolutional features from lower layer $Conv1$, intermediate layer $Conv3$, and last layer $Conv5$ to form a unified feature map represented as U in Fig. 1. Convolutional features from $Conv1$, $Conv3$, and $Conv5$ do not have same feature resolution. In order to obtain same resolution features, we utilized a *Max Polling* layer and $Conv6$ layer to reduce the spatial resolution from $Conv1$. $Conv7$ layer is used to reduce the feature resolution from $Conv3$ layer. The feature resolution reduction operations are performed for both exemplar and search branches. The unified features are forwarded to proposed adaptive feature selection module to obtain the more informative and discriminative features.

Adaptive Feature Selection Module. The network architecture of proposed adaptive feature selection module is shown in Fig. 3. Motivated by Selective Kernel Network (SKNet) [24], we integrated a special kind of kernel selection procedure for Siamese tracking. First, adaptive feature selection module splits the U into a, d, and e, and then combines those features by element-wise addition operation to form D features map as shown in Fig. 3. Features are fused by employing global pooling operation and fully connected layers. A global pooling operation is performed over D to obtain a $1 \times 1 \times c$ dimension descriptors, given c the number of channels. A fully connected layers is used to decrease the number of channels of the descriptor and then increased by employing another fully convolutional layer. A Sigmoid function is employed to get the soft attentional weight vectors for a, d, and e to select the high informative features. A soft attention is employed to highlight the useful feature and suppress the less informative features. For that, an element-wise multiplication operation between the a features and a weight descriptor to obtain $á$. Similar operation is performed for d and e to obtain weighted features $d́$ and $é$. Weighted features $á$, $d́$ and $é$ are concatenated to get $Ú$. Finally, U and $Ú$ are combined using element-wise addition operation to obtain the highly discriminative informative features.

3.3   Network Training

We used the AlexNet as backbone network with an additional *Max Pooling*, $Conv6$, and $Conv7$ layers. We utilized GOT10K [20] dataset to train our network. During the training, we set template and search sizes same as of SiameseFC $127 \times 127 \times 3$ and $255 \times 255 \times 3$ respectively. We fix momentum and weight decay to 0.9 and $5e-4$ respectively. The learning rate starts at 10^{-2} and reduces till 10^{-5}. During testing, template and search sizes set to $135 \times 135 \times 3$ and $263 \times 263 \times 3$

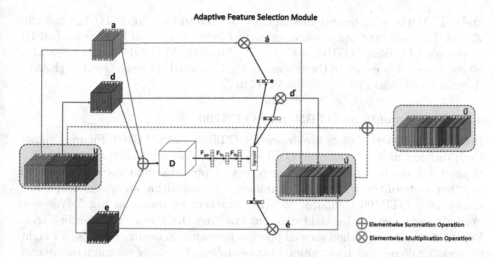

Fig. 3. The pipeline of the proposed AFS module. Unified features U are separated into a, d, and e. Features from a, d, and e are combined by element-wise addition operation. A global pooling, fully connected layers, and Sigmoid functions are applied over D to get feature weight vectors. Weighted features are combined to select the more informative features.

respectively. We build a pyramid over three scales $(0.963, 1, 1.0375)$ and set the penalties to 0.9745 to get optimal scale of object. The network parameters ϑ were trained end-to-end using Stochastic Gradient Descent (SGD) method for 50 epochs to minimize the following loss function:

$$\underset{\vartheta}{\text{argmin}} \frac{1}{M} \sum_{m=1}^{M} L(g(Z_m, X_m), Y_m), \tag{2}$$

where M represents the total number of training samples and $L(.)$ indicates the logistic loss function and is computed as:

$$L(g_m, y_m) = \frac{1}{|\delta|} \sum_{(i,j) \in \delta} log(1 + exp(-g_m(i, j).y_m(i, j)), \tag{3}$$

where $y_m(i, j) \in \{+1, -1\}$ defines the ground truth label, $g_m(i, j)$ denotes the similarity value corresponding to the (i, j)th position on the score map, while set of position for the search window is represented by δ on the score map.

4 Experiments

4.1 Comparison with State-of-the-Art Trackers

We performed an extensive experimental evaluation over OTB50, OTB100, TempleColor128 (TC-128), and VOT2017 datasets. OTB50 contains 50 sequences and OTB100 is an extended version contains 100 videos, while TC-128 has 128 videos. Precision and success are computed using One Pass Evaluation (OPE) to evaluate OTB50, OTB100 and TC128 datasets. VOT2017 dataset contains 60 sequences. We evaluate the tracker using Expected Average Overlap (EAO), Accuracy (A), and Failure (F) for VOT2017.

4.2 Experiments on OTB50 and OTB100

Precision and success plots are drawn for OTB50 and OTB100. Figure 4 shows the precision and success over OTB50 dataset. We observe that our tracker showed outstanding performance in terms of precision and success compared to other state-of-the-art trackers. Similarly, our algorithm showed good performance over OTB100 compared to other trackers as shown in Fig. 5. We also evaluated our method for eight different tracking challenges as shown in Fig. 6. We notice that our method showed best performance in terms of success for eight different challenges such as motion blur, occlusion, in-planer rotation, out-planer rotation, fast motion, deformation, out of view, and scale variations. A qualitative analysis is performed over six sequences and we notice that our tracker does not leave the object as shown in Fig. 7.

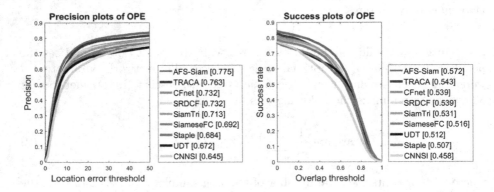

Fig. 4. Performance comparison of proposed tracker with other trackers over OTB50.

4.3 Experiments on TC128

We elevate our tracking algorithm over TC128 dataset. We observed that our method demonstrated better performance in terms of both precision and success as shown in Table 1.

4.4 Experiments on VOT2017

We present comparative performance on VOT2017 in Table 2. We notice that our tracker surpassed the other trackers in terms of accuracy overlap and EAO. However, CSRDCF showed better results in terms of failure. We also observe that SiamDCF and CSRDCF showed same EAO score as ours.

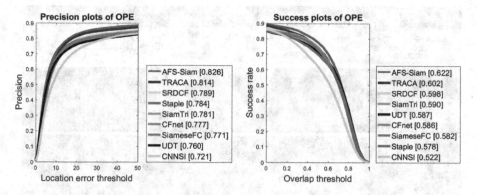

Fig. 5. Performance comparison of proposed tracker with various trackers over OTB100.

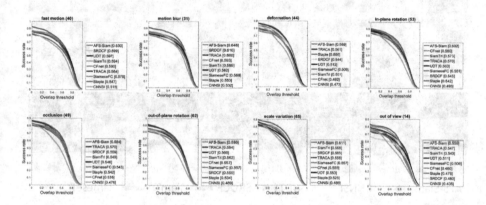

Fig. 6. Performance comparison for eight different tracking challenges over OTB100.

Table 1. Comparison of the proposed method with various state-of-the-art methods over TC128 using precision, success, and speed in FPS.

Trackers	Precision	Success	FPS
SCT [4]	62.7	46.6	40
CNNSI [14]	63.8	45.6	<1
UDT [39]	71.7	50.7	70
CFNet [36]	60.7	45.6	43
SiameseFC [2]	68.8	50.3	86
AFS-Siam	**74.6**	**55.2**	66

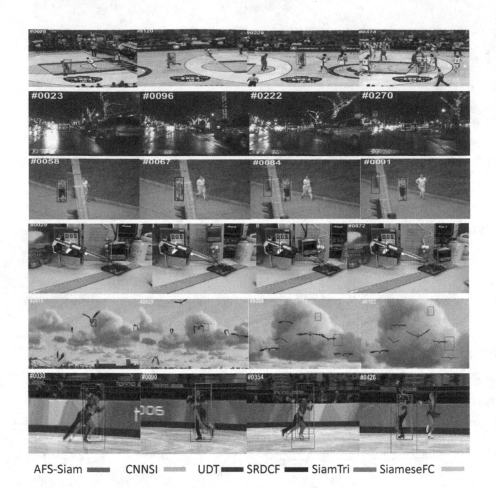

AFS-Siam ▬▬   CNNSI ▭▭   UDT▬▬ SRDCF ▬▬   SiamTri ▬▬ SiameseFC ▭▭

Fig. 7. Qualitative analysis over sequences including *Basketball, Box, CarDar, Bird, Jogging-1, and Skating2-2.*

Table 2. Performance comparison for different trackers over VOT2017.

Trackers	Overlap	Failure	EAO	FPS
CSRDCF [26]	0.48	**23.57**	**0.25**	13
SRDCF [7]	0.48	64.11	0.11	6
DSST [8]	0.39	95.56	0.08	24
SiamDCF [3]	0.50	29.40	**0.25**	60
UCT [44]	0.48	30.11	0.23	41
SiameseFC [2]	0.50	34.06	0.19	86
AFS-Siam	**0.53**	29.25	**0.25**	66

5 Conclusion

In this study, we integrated an adaptive feature selection module within the template branch of Siamese network for improved tracking. Proposed adaptive feature selection module selects the most meaningful feature information from different convolutional layers. Features from different layers are combined and a weight vector is generated. Weighted features from different layers are combined to get adaptive discriminative features. Adaptive feature selection module gives the most useful feature information while reduces the impact of less informative features. Comparison study over four datasets revealed that our algorithm showed better performance. Furthermore, it exhibited outstanding performance for various tracking challenges.

Acknowledgment. This research was supported by Development project of leading technology for future vehicle of the business of Daegu metropolitan city (No. 20171105).

References

1. Avidan, S.: Support vector tracking. IEEE Trans. Pattern Anal. Mach. Intell. **26**(8), 1064–1072 (2004)
2. Bertinetto, L., Valmadre, J., Henriques, J.F., Vedaldi, A., Torr, P.H.S.: Fully-convolutional Siamese networks for object tracking. In: Hua, G., Jégou, H. (eds.) ECCV 2016. LNCS, vol. 9914, pp. 850–865. Springer, Cham (2016). https://doi.org/10.1007/978-3-319-48881-3_56
3. Chen, S., Qiu, D., Huo, Q.: Siamese networks with discriminant correlation filters and channel attention. In: 2018 14th International Conference on Computational Intelligence and Security (CIS), pp. 110–114. IEEE (2018)
4. Choi, J., Jin Chang, H., Jeong, J., Demiris, Y., Young Choi, J.: Visual tracking using attention-modulated disintegration and integration. In: Proceedings of the IEEE Conference on Computer Vision and Pattern Recognition, pp. 4321–4330 (2016)
5. Cui, Z., Xiao, S., Feng, J., Yan, S.: Recurrently target-attending tracking. In: IEEE CVPR, pp. 1449–1458 (2016)
6. Danelljan, M., Hager, G., Shahbaz Khan, F., Felsberg, M.: Convolutional features for correlation filter based visual tracking. In: Proceedings of the IEEE International Conference on Computer Vision Workshops, pp. 58–66 (2015)
7. Danelljan, M., Hager, G., Shahbaz Khan, F., Felsberg, M.: Learning spatially regularized correlation filters for visual tracking. In: Proceedings of the IEEE international Conference on Computer Vision, pp. 4310–4318 (2015)
8. Danelljan, M., Häger, G., Khan, F.S., Felsberg, M.: Discriminative scale space tracking. IEEE Trans. Pattern Anal. Mach. Intell. **39**(8), 1561–1575 (2016)
9. Danelljan, M., Bhat, G., Shahbaz Khan, F., Felsberg, M.: ECO: efficient convolution operators for tracking. In: Proceedings of the IEEE Conference on Computer Vision and Pattern Recognition, pp. 6638–6646 (2017)
10. Dong, X., Shen, J.: Triplet loss in Siamese network for object tracking. In: Ferrari, V., Hebert, M., Sminchisescu, C., Weiss, Y. (eds.) ECCV 2018. LNCS, vol. 11217, pp. 472–488. Springer, Cham (2018). https://doi.org/10.1007/978-3-030-01261-8_28

11. Fan, H., Ling, H.: SANet: structure-aware network for visual tracking. In: Proceedings of the IEEE Conference on Computer Vision and Pattern Recognition Workshops, pp. 42–49 (2017)
12. Fiaz, M., Mahmood, A., Jung, S.K.: Tracking noisy targets: a review of recent object tracking approaches. arXiv preprint arXiv:180203098 (2018)
13. Fiaz, M., Mahmood, A., Javed, S., Jung, S.K.: Handcrafted and deep trackers: recent visual object tracking approaches and trends. ACM Comput. Surv. (CSUR) 52(2), 43 (2019)
14. Fiaz, M., Mahmood, A., Jung, S.K.: Convolutional neural network with structural input for visual object tracking. In: Proceedings of the 34th ACM/SIGAPP Symposium on Applied Computing, pp. 1345–1352. ACM (2019)
15. Fu, J., et al.: Dual attention network for scene segmentation. In: Proceedings of the IEEE Conference on Computer Vision and Pattern Recognition, pp. 3146–3154 (2019)
16. Girshick, R., Donahue, J., Darrell, T., Malik, J.: Rich feature hierarchies for accurate object detection and semantic segmentation. In: Proceedings of the IEEE Conference on Computer Vision and Pattern Recognition, pp. 580–587 (2014)
17. Guo, Q., Feng, W., Zhou, C., Huang, R., Wan, L., Wang, S.: Learning dynamic Siamese network for visual object tracking. In: IEEE CVPR, pp. 1763–1771 (2017)
18. He, A., Luo, C., Tian, X., Zeng, W.: A twofold Siamese network for real-time object tracking. In: IEEE CVPR, pp. 4834–4843 (2018)
19. Held, D., Thrun, S., Savarese, S.: Learning to track at 100 FPS with deep regression networks. In: Leibe, B., Matas, J., Sebe, N., Welling, M. (eds.) ECCV 2016. LNCS, vol. 9905, pp. 749–765. Springer, Cham (2016). https://doi.org/10.1007/978-3-319-46448-0_45
20. Huang, L., Zhao, X., Huang, K.: GOT-10k: a large high-diversity benchmark for generic object tracking in the wild. arXiv preprint arXiv:181011981 (2018)
21. Kristan, M., Leonardis, A., Matas, J., Felsberg, M., et al.: The visual object tracking VOT2017 challenge results. In: Proceedings of the IEEE International Conference on Computer Vision, pp. 1949–1972 (2017)
22. Kwak, S., Nam, W., Han, B., Han, J.H.: Learning occlusion with likelihoods for visual tracking. In: 2011 IEEE International Conference on Computer Vision (ICCV), pp. 1551–1558. IEEE (2011)
23. Li, P., Wang, D., Wang, L., Lu, H.: Deep visual tracking: review and experimental comparison. Pattern Recogn. 76, 323–338 (2018)
24. Li, X., Wang, W., Hu, X., Yang, J.: Selective kernel networks. In: Proceedings of the IEEE Conference on Computer Vision and Pattern Recognition, pp. 510–519 (2019)
25. Liang, P., Blasch, E., Ling, H.: Encoding color information for visual tracking: algorithms and benchmark. IEEE Trans. Image Process. 24(12), 5630–5644 (2015)
26. Lukezic, A., Vojir, T., Cehovin, Z.L., Matas, J., Kristan, M.: Discriminative correlation filter with channel and spatial reliability. In: Proceedings of the IEEE Conference on Computer Vision and Pattern Recognition, pp. 6309–6318 (2017)
27. Ma, B., Hu, H., Shen, J., Liu, Y., Shao, L.: Generalized pooling for robust object tracking. IEEE Trans. Image Process. 25(9), 4199–4208 (2016)
28. Ma, C., Huang, J.B., Yang, X., Yang, M.H.: Hierarchical convolutional features for visual tracking. In: IEEE CVPR, pp. 3074–3082 (2015)
29. Mnih, V., Heess, N., Graves, A., et al.: Recurrent models of visual attention. In: Advances in Neural Information Processing Systems, pp. 2204–2212 (2014)

30. Nam, H., Han, B.: Learning multi-domain convolutional neural networks for visual tracking. In: Proceedings of the IEEE Conference on Computer Vision and Pattern Recognition, pp. 4293–4302 (2016)

31. Pu, S., Song, Y., Ma, C., Zhang, H., Yang, M.H.: Deep attentive tracking via reciprocative learning. In: Advances in Neural Information Processing Systems, pp. 1931–1941 (2018)

32. Sevilla-Lara, L., Learned-Miller, E.: Distribution fields for tracking. In: 2012 IEEE Conference on Computer Vision and Pattern Recognition (CVPR), pp. 1910–1917. IEEE (2012)

33. Shaban, M., Mahmood, A., Al-maadeed, S., Rajpoot, N.: Multi-person head segmentation in low resolution crowd scenes using convolutional encoder-decoder framework. In: Chen, L., Ben Amor, B., Ghorbel, F. (eds.) RFMI 2017. CCIS, vol. 842, pp. 82–92. Springer, Cham (2019). https://doi.org/10.1007/978-3-030-19816-9_7

34. Taigman, Y., Yang, M., Ranzato, M., Wolf, L.: DeepFace: closing the gap to human-level performance in face verification. In: Proceedings of the IEEE conference on Computer Vision and Pattern Recognition, pp. 1701–1708 (2014)

35. Tao, R., Gavves, E., Smeulders, A.W.: Siamese instance search for tracking. In: Proceedings of the IEEE Conference on Computer Vision and Pattern Recognition, pp. 1420–1429 (2016)

36. Valmadre, J., Bertinetto, L., Henriques, J., Vedaldi, A., Torr, P.H.: End-to-end representation learning for correlation filter based tracking. In: Proceedings of the IEEE Conference on Computer Vision and Pattern Recognition, pp. 2805–2813 (2017)

37. Wang, D., Lu, H., Xiao, Z., Yang, M.H.: Inverse sparse tracker with a locally weighted distance metric. IEEE Trans. Image Process. 24(9), 2646–2657 (2015)

38. Wang, F.: Residual attention network for image classification. In: Proceedings of the IEEE Conference on Computer Vision and Pattern Recognition, pp. 3156–3164 (2017)

39. Wang, N., Song, Y., Ma, C., Zhou, W., Liu, W., Li, H.: Unsupervised deep tracking. In: The IEEE Conference on Computer Vision and Pattern Recognition (CVPR) (2019)

40. Wang, Q., Teng, Z., Xing, J., Gao, J., Hu, W., Maybank, S.: Learning attentions: residual attentional Siamese network for high performance online visual tracking. In: Proceedings of the IEEE Conference on Computer Vision and Pattern Recognition, pp. 4854–4863 (2018)

41. Wen, L., Cai, Z., Lei, Z., Yi, D., Li, S.Z.: Online spatio-temporal structural context learning for visual tracking. In: Fitzgibbon, A., Lazebnik, S., Perona, P., Sato, Y., Schmid, C. (eds.) ECCV 2012. LNCS, vol. 7575, pp. 716–729. Springer, Heidelberg (2012). https://doi.org/10.1007/978-3-642-33765-9_51

42. Wu, Y., Lim, J., Yang, M.H.: Object tracking benchmark. IEEE Trans. Pattern Anal. Mach. Intell. 37(9), 1834–1848 (2015)

43. Yun, S., Choi, J., Yoo, Y., Yun, K., Young Choi, J.: Action-decision networks for visual tracking with deep reinforcement learning. In: Proceedings of the IEEE Conference on Computer Vision and Pattern Recognition, pp. 2711–2720 (2017)

44. Zhu, Z., Huang, G., Zou, W., Du, D., Huang, C.: UCT: learning unified convolutional networks for real-time visual tracking. In: Proceedings of the IEEE International Conference on Computer Vision, pp. 1973–1982 (2017)

Faster R-CNN with Attention Feature Map for Robust Object Detection

Youl-Kyeong Lee and Kang-Hyun Jo$^{(\boxtimes)}$

University of Ulsan, Ulsan, Korea
`yklee@islab.ulsan.ac.kr`, `acejo@ulsan.ac.kr`

Abstract. This paper describes the improved object detection method from Faster R-CNN using an attention feature map in RPN. The research work adopts Faster R-CNN is used as the input feature map of the RPN using the last block in the backbone network, but the proposed method takes the created feature maps from the combination of dilated convolution and attention feature map for RPN networks. Attention feature map takes the high probability to object and emphasize the location of object. With the new feature map, the proposed bounding box and class determine the final output for object detection. As backbone network, ResNet50, ResNet101 and ResNet152 have trained on ImageNet. On PASCAL VOC 2007, our proposed method achieves 79.83% mAP that is 73.2% mAP.

Keywords: Faster R-CNN · Dilated convolution · Object detection · Attention feature map

1 Introduction

The research work in deep convolutional neural networks has been drastically flourished into many fields of applications. In the object detection and classification, object plays an important role in scene understanding. Recently, region-based convolutional neural network, R-CNN [1], Fast R-CNN [2], and Faster R-CNN [3] are proposed by the region based object detection algorithms in deep learning. Despite the fact that these works are getting better performance about accuracy and inference time, it still many room to improve for better performance applications.

Region based CNN is an expansive computation cost with selective search [4] for proposed region. To overcome the efficient computation, Fast R-CNN supposes single-stage to update all network layers. Feature extraction using very deep networks [5,6], economically reduces the huge computation and the single stage takes updating the weight of all network's layers at the same time. Towards the real-time work, Faster R-CNN proposes the region proposals network (RPN). In the region proposal network, it is a sharing computation with the weight of Fast R-CNN.

© Springer Nature Singapore Pte Ltd. 2020
W. Ohyama and S. K. Jung (Eds.): IW-FCV 2020, CCIS 1212, pp. 180–191, 2020.
https://doi.org/10.1007/978-981-15-4818-5_14

In the development of object detection with deep convolutional neural network, changing network structure and training strategies have the room for improvement. As changing the architecture of design network, two-stage model [3,4], feature modification and concatenation [6] in the model take advantage to affect all weights of network.

The research in this paper proposes the modified region proposal network to improve the accuracy of object detection. As input feature map for rpn, it comes from the last layer of ResNet50, ResNet101, and ResNet152 [5], respectively. Given the input feature map, it creates the feature map that is concatenated with three kinds of dilated convolutions and 1×1 convolution. The new feature map passes to few processes in the rpn to adjust the bounding box regression and prediction of object existence. With two fully connected layers, it expects to spot the proposed location of object. After RoI pooling, detector decides the location and size of object. This work goes as follows:

- Using pre-trained model as backbone network: ResNet50, ResNet101, ResNet152
- Cover the wide receptive field with dilated convolution
- Using attention mechanism, to emphasize the location of object

Objects are chosen general objects in the real world. PASCAL VOC 2007 and 2012 [8] have 20 classes (Person, Animal, Vehicle, and Indoor) and background. In the following section, the proposed method explains in Sect. 3 and shows the experiment result in Sect. 4. Last Section is the conclusion of this paper (Fig. 1).

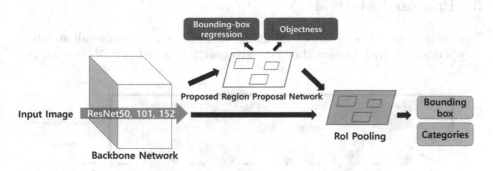

Fig. 1. Overall proposed architecture. Pre-trained models with ImageNet [12] are ResNet50, ResNet101 and ResNet152.

2 Related Works

Previous traditional techniques consider with color (RGB, HSV, Lab, etc), size, texture similarities and so on. HOG [9], SIFT [10], and SURF [11] have a detector that is based on a shape of object with an orientation histogram. These works need the complex and several stages to detect the object. R-CNN [1] has been proposed as a region-based method using deep learning. First, the region proposal algorithm attempts to find the initial candidate area in the image. Selective search [4] that is one of the region proposal algorithm, generates a set of similarities for RGB color, texture, size, and fill. The generated set determines the similarity with surrounding areas to generate new set of similarity. This work continues until one area is available. Secondly, when the initial candidate region is determined, it classifies the region by applying CNN to each region. Since R-CNN has applied individual CNNs to the proposed area, it takes an expensive computation and time from initial candidate area determination to classification. Fast R-CNN [2] is a proposed method to overcome the shortcomings of applying CNN to individual domains. As the input value for the object region prediction, proposed method in Fast R-CNN uses the feature map of the last block using VGG16, ResNet, etc. The inputs are then located through the RoI Pooling, the region of interest pooling, and the fully connected layer to find the location, size and type of the object. Finally, Faster R-CNN [3] uses RPN, region proposal network, to solve bottlenecks in the region proposal method of Fast R-CNN. The region proposal network uses a single input image and generates rectangular object proposals and objectness scores as outputs. For the bounding box regression, 9 anchor boxes can be specified in any combination of three different ratios and three sizes. In the sliding window, it computes the bounding box proposal from the anchor boxes by applying it to each pixel point. RoI pooling is used to find the classification and correct bounding box position.

3   Proposed Method

This section describes the proposed model in detail. First, the overall architecture is designed with presented object detection, Faster R-CNN [3]. Second, the

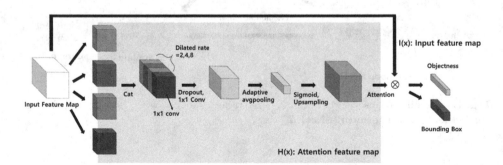

Fig. 2. This is an example of dilated spatial attention feature map. There are three kinds of dilation rate (d = 2,4,8) and 1 × 1 convolution. After that the concatenated feature map applies the dropout, adaptive avg pooling, max pooling, sigmoid and upsampling. After upsampling the feature map, the input feature map takes the attention mechanism.

attention feature map generation will be described. To emphasize the region of object in the image, dilated convolutional operation helps to extract the location of object. The dilated convolution can see a wider area than the conventional computational area and extract the characteristics of computational efficiency. The attention feature map can have a high probability of emphasizing the area where the object will be.

3.1 Extraction for Attention Feature Map

In Fig. 2, the attention feature map is created as the input feature map to be used in region proposal network. For example, using the last layer of feature map in ResNet50, feature maps are created with three dilation rates and 1×1 convolution feature map that are concatenated and used in the RPN (Fig. 3).

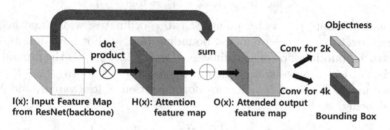

Fig. 3. This is a detail expression for attention process. Input feature map, $I(x)$, generated attention feature map, $H(x)$ and attended output feature map, $O(x)$.

The concatenated feature map goes to dropout for avoiding the overfitting model. There are adaptive avg pooling and max pooling. The adaptive avg pooling can resize 2×2. It helps to generate the same size of output that is no matter the different input feature size. With max pooling, it generates the $1 \times 1 \times 1024$ matrix into the sigmoid function to convert a probability. Next it creates an approximate object mask through upsampling. When given x represents the position of the pixel, the input feature map, $I(x)$ and attention feature map, $H(x)$ have a dot product for an object mask, and apply to sum up the input, I(x) like equation (1).

$$O(x) = (1 + H(x)) \times I(x) \tag{1}$$

$O(x)$, output feature of RPN focus on the object location. With the output, the objectness obtains two values for checking the existence of object in the bounding box.

3.2 Multi Task Loss

This work adopts loss function method in from Faster R-CNN [3] for multi-task. To train the RPN, each anchor determines the existence of a class and bounding box coordinates. The output is returned as a fully connected vector that is a probability to determine the presence of an object and bounding box regression. Loss function contains L_{cls} and L_{loc} in (2):

$$L(\{p_i\}, \{t_i\}) = \frac{1}{N_{cls}} \sum_i L_{cls}(p_i, p_i^*)(p, u) + \lambda \frac{1}{N_{reg}} \sum_i p_i^* L_{reg}(t_i, t_i^*) \quad (2)$$

in which $L_{cls}(p_i, p_i^*) = -\log(p_i - p_i^*)$, p_i shows a probability of objectness at anchor box. p_i^* is a ground truth label that if $p_i^* = 1$, object is in anchor box, $p_i^* = 0$, object is not in anchor box. In bounding box regression, the parameters come from R-CNN [1] as follows:

$$\begin{aligned}
t_x &= (x - x_a)/w_a, & t_y &= (y - y_a)/h_a, \\
t_w &= \log(w/w_a), & t_h &= \log(h/h_a), \\
t_x^* &= (x^x - x_a)/w_a, & t_y^* &= (y^* - y_a)/h_a, \\
t_w^* &= \log(w^*/w_a), & t_h^* &= \log(h^*/h_a)
\end{aligned} \quad (3)$$

x, y, w, and h denote the center point for two coordinates, width and height of bounding box. x, x_a, x^* are predicted bounding box, anchor bounding box, and ground truth bounding box of coordinates. $t^* = (t_x^*, t_y^*, t_w^*, t_h^*)$ is the ground truth value when object is a positive in anchor. $L_{reg}(t_i, t_i^*) = \text{smooth}_{L_1}(t_i - t_i^*)$ is (4) as defined in [2]. N_{cls} and N_{reg} are for normalization of loss values, and $\lambda = 10$ is for balancing.

$$\text{smooth}_{L_1}(x) = \begin{cases} 0.5x^2 & \text{if } |x| < 1 \\ |x| - 0.5 & \text{otherwise,} \end{cases} \quad (4)$$

3.3   Training

In the feature map extraction, ResNet50, ResNet101 and ResNet152 are the backbone network. In the case of region proposal network, each convolutional layer has a relu operation and batch normalization. The dropout is 0.5. For network optimization, model is trained end-to-end using stochastic gradient descent (SGD) and back-propagation on the PASCAL dataset. RPN training is divided into mini-batch, with a learning rate of 0.001 for 7k steps, 0.0001 for the next 17.5k, and 0.00001 for the rest of them. The number of anchor size is four, 64, 128, 256, and 512. 64×64 anchor conducts the small size of object in the training. Training process randomly selects 256 anchors from a trained image and applies a loss function. One sample contains many positive and negative anchors, and the ratio is 1:1 if there are less than 128 positive anchors, this sample is excluded with negative anchors. SGD has a momentum of 0.9 and a weight decay of 0.0005. The research is carried out at PyTorch.

4   Experiment

4.1   Experimental Setup

In the proposed model, the initial values of all layers of the backbone structure use pre-trained models, ResNet50, ResNet101, and ResNet152, which are

Table 1. Table 1 shows the distribution of datasets for voc 2007 and 2012, coco2017. The dataset splits into three, train, validation, and test.

	voc2007	voc2012	coco2017
ALL	9,963	22,531	245,496
TEST	4,952	10,991	40,775
TEST2015	–	–	81,434
VAL	2,510	5,823	40,504
TRAIN	2,501	5,717	82,783
OBJECT	24,640	27,450	2.5 M

trained with ImageNet [12]. The datasets used in this paper are PASCAL VOC 2007, VOC 2012 and COCO2017. The VOC 2007 and 2012 datasets contain for 21 classes, including objects in 20 kinds and backgrounds. The COCO2017 is a Common Objects in Context that is a large-scale object detection, segmentation, and captioning dataset. It has 80 objects and contains images, bounding boxes and labels for the 2017 version. The Table 1 shows the number of images and object ground truth as follows. Table 2 shows the results with the various training parameters. In the original paper [3], Faster R-CNN shows the original experiment results are 69.9% mAP for VGG16's backbone network and voc2007 dataset, 73.2% mAP for voc2007 and 2012, and 78.8% mAP for additional coco dataset. Original ResNet50, 101, 152 models are trained on the voc2007 dataset in Table 2. For each model, mAP(%) results of 70.22, 75.66 and 78.57 are shown. The results are used to compare with the proposed models. The proposed model shows the results according to anchor size, backbone and dilated rate. The experimental results are generated using ResNet101, and 152 models, and shows 74.91, 76.69% mAP when dilated rate = 6, 12, 18. The following results are 61.65, 71.15, 74.08% mAP with anchor size = 64, 128, 256, 512 considering small objects, which is 2.5~3.8% lower than previous results. When extracting features from RPN, the performance decreases with the large value of dilated rates. The reason is that it is a difficult to extract the feature. Because it looks around the wide receptive field which is relatively unnecessary in the existing feature map. The final results conduct the change in dilated rate. In the case of backbone network in ResNet152 to achieve 79.56% mAP for dilated rate = 3, 6, 9, 79.83% mAP for dilated rate = 2, 4, 8, and 79.12% mAP for dilated rate = 1, 2, 3. In the combination of dilated feature maps, dilated rate = 2, 4, 8 is 0.27% and 0.71% better than dilated rate = 3, 6, 9 and 1, 2, 3, respectively. There are different results from voc2007 dataset. The voc2012 dataset is the double number of dataset than voc2007. One of reason that the performance is a different for approximately 13% mAP. The size of the input feature map is reduced to 1/16 of the original image, and the dilated rate is considered the wide receptive field. However the feature extraction of dilated rate = 2, 4, 8 is 3.14% mAP higher than that of dilated rate = 6, 12, 18. In the case of coco dataset, the proposed models conduct with two dilated rate. The evaluation of coco2017 are shown in Table 3. The results

Table 2. According to backbone network, anchor sizes, and dilated rate, result on Pascal VOC2007 test set with proposed RPN method.

method	anchor_size	backbone	dataset	dilated rate	mAP(%)
Faster R-CNN	128, 256, 512	VGG16	voc2007	–	69.9
Faster R-CNN	128, 256, 512	VGG16	voc2007 + 2012	–	73.2
Faster R-CNN	128, 256, 512	VGG16	voc2007 + 2012+COCO	-	78.8
Faster R-CNN	128, 256, 512	ResNet50	voc2007	–	70.22
Faster R-CNN	128, 256, 512	ResNet101	voc2007	–	75.66
Faster R-CNN	128, 256, 512	ResNet152	voc2007	–	78.57
Proposed RPN	128, 256, 512	ResNet101	voc2007	6, 12, 18	74.91
Proposed RPN	128, 256, 512	ResNet152	voc2007	6, 12, 18	76.69
Proposed RPN	64, 128, 256, 512	ResNet50	voc2007	6, 12, 18	61.65
Proposed RPN	64, 128, 256, 512	Resnet101	voc2007	6, 12, 18	71.15
Proposed RPN	64, 128, 256, 512	ResNet152	voc2007	6, 12, 18	74.08
Proposed RPN	64, 128, 256, 512	ResNet50	voc2007	3, 6, 9	70.18
Proposed RPN	64, 128, 256, 512	Resnet101	voc2007	3, 6, 9	76.09
Proposed RPN	64, 128, 256, 512	ResNet152	voc2007	3, 6, 9	79.56
Proposed RPN	64, 128, 256, 512	ResNet50	voc2007	2, 4, 8	70.74
Proposed RPN	64, 128, 256, 512	Resnet101	voc2007	2, 4, 8	77.81
Proposed RPN	64, 128, 256, 512	ResNet152	voc2007	2, 4, 8	**79.83**
Proposed RPN	64, 128, 256, 512	Resnet101	voc2007	1, 2, 3	77.28
Proposed RPN	64, 128, 256, 512	ResNet152	voc2007	1, 2, 3	79.12
Proposed RPN	64, 128, 256, 512	ResNet152	voc2012	3, 6, 9	66.18
Proposed RPN	64, 128, 256, 512	ResNet152	voc2012	2, 4, 8	64.76
Proposed RPN	64, 128, 256, 512	ResNet152	voc2012	1, 2, 3	66.90

Table 3. According to the ResNet152 with different dilated rate, result on MS COCO2017 test set. The result depends on AP@IoU rates and scales of detection object.

method	dilated rate	AP@[0.5:0.95]	AP@[0.5]	AP@[0.75]	AP S	AP M	AP L
Faster R-CNN	–	21.2	41.5	–	–	–	–
resnet152	2, 4, 8	28.4	47.6	29.7	9.8	31.9	44.7
resnet152	3, 6, 9	28.3	47.3	30.2	9.7	31.6	44.6

are generated by training the proposed model for ResNet152. AP @ [0.5: 0.95] is the result of calculating the average AP for ten IOU values with IOU threshold values between 0.5 and 0.95. AP S is the result for objects in the image that are smaller than 32^2 pixels, where M is $32^2 < area < 96^2$ and L is $area > 96^2$. In the proposed model, the original Faster R-CNN is 41.5% for AP @ [0.5] and 21.2% for AP @ [0.5: 0.95]. The proposed models (dilated rate = 2, 4, 83, 6, 9) show a difference of 6.1 and 5.8% and 7.2 and 7.1% from original model, respectively. While the small scale of object is a challenge to detect in the proposed model. That is why the only additional small anchor size is not a solution to detect the small object in the image (Figs. 4 and 5).

Fig. 4. Experimental results on the PASCAL VOC2007 test set using the proposed method. The result is working on the voc 2007 trainval (79.83% mAP). The bounding box drawing uses the IOU of 0.7.

Fig. 5. Experimental results on the coco2017 test set using the proposed method. The result is generating on the coco 2017 train (28.4% mAP at AP@0.5:0.95 and 47.6 at AP@0.5).

Fig. 5. (*continued*)

Fig. 5. (*continued*)

5   Conclusion

In this paper, proposed region proposal network suggests an feature combination and attention mechanism to detect the object location in rpn. The existing rpn network takes a fully connected layer of objectness and bounding box regression using a single convolutional operation. In this work, the region proposal in rpn with Attention feature map and the wide area of the receptive field using dilated convolution shows an approximately 1% mAP improvement in object detection. However, the complexity of dataset and scale of object in the image are still critical challenge in this task. In the future, the next work will propose a method to develop a model with lighter model size and improved performance by improving the current model.

Acknowledgments. This work was supported by the National Research Foundation of Korea (NRF) grant funded by the Korea government (MSIP, Ministry of Science, ICT & Future Planning) (No. 2019R1F1A1061659).

References

1. Girshick, R., Donahue, J., Darrell, T., Malik, J.: Rich feature hierarchies for accurate object detection and semantic segmentation. In: 2014 IEEE Conference on Computer Vision and Pattern Recognition, Columbus, OH, pp. 580–587 (2014)
2. Girshick, R.: Fast R-CNN. In: 2015 IEEE International Conference on Computer Vision (ICCV), Santiago, pp. 1440–1448 (2015)
3. Ren, S., He, K., Girshick, R., Sun, J.: Faster R-CNN: towards real-time object detection with region proposal networks. In: Neural Information Processing Systems (NIPS) (2015)

4. Uijlings, J.R., van de Sande, K.E., Gevers, T., Smeulders, A.W., et al.: Selective search for object recognition. Int. J. Comput. Vis. **104**, 154–171 (2013). https://doi.org/10.1007/s11263-013-0620-5

5. He, K., Zhang, X., Ren, S., Sun, J.: Deep residual learning for image recognition. In: 2016 IEEE Conference on Computer Vision and Pattern Recognition (CVPR), Las Vegas, NV, pp. 770–778 (2016)

6. Huang, G., Liu, Z., Maaten, L.V.D., Weinberger, K.Q.: Densely connected convolutional networks. In: 2017 IEEE Conference on Computer Vision and Pattern Recognition (CVPR), Honolulu, HI, pp. 2261–2269 (2017)

7. Everingham, M., Van Gool, L., Williams, C.K.I., et al.: The PASCAL visual object classes (VOC) challenge. Int. J. Comput. Vis. **88**, 303–338 (2010). https://doi.org/10.1007/s11263-009-0275-4

8. Dalal, N., Triggs, B.: Histograms of oriented gradients for human detection. In: 2005 IEEE Computer Society Conference on Computer Vision and Pattern Recognition (CVPR 2005), San Diego, CA, USA, vol. 1, pp. 886–893 (2005)

9. Lowe, D.G.: Distinctive image features from scale-invariant keypoints. Int. J. Comput. Vis. **60**, 91–110 (2004). https://doi.org/10.1023/B:VISI.0000029664.99615.94

10. Bay, H., Tuytelaars, T., Van Gool, L.: SURF: speeded up robust features. In: Leonardis, A., Bischof, H., Pinz, A. (eds.) ECCV 2006. LNCS, vol. 3951, pp. 404–417. Springer, Heidelberg (2006). https://doi.org/10.1007/11744023_32

11. Russakovsky, O., et al.: ImageNet large scale visual recognition challenge. Int. J. Comput. Vis. **115**(3), 211–252 (2015). https://doi.org/10.1007/s11263-015-0816-y

12. Chen, L., Papandreou, G., Kokkinos, I., Murphy, K., Yuille, A.L.: DeepLab: semantic image segmentation with deep convolutional nets, atrous convolution, and fully connected CRFs. In: IEEE Transactions on Pattern Analysis and Machine Intelligence, vol. 40, no. 4, pp. 834–848, 1 April 2018. Oct 2017

Indoor Visual Re-localization Based on Confidence Score Using Omni-Directional Camera

Toshihiro Takahashi[✉], Hisato Fukuda, Yoshinori Kobayashi,
and Yoshinori Kuno

Graduate School of Science and Engineering, Saitama University, Saitama, Japan
toshihiro.takahashi.6i@hci.ics.saitama-u.ac.jp

Abstract. In this paper, we propose a novel re-localization method with deep learning using monocular image. A data augmentation method with semi-omni-directional image is introduced. Our method aims re-localization to be robust for changes in the surrounding situation. It is achieved by applying the uncertainty measurement obtained from Bayesian Neural Network. We confirm the effectiveness of our proposed method through the experiments.

Keywords: Indoor localization · Deep learning · Omni-directional camera

1 Introduction

In recent years, due to the declining birthrate and aging population, lack of workers becomes social problem, especially for hospitals, nursing homes, hotels and other facilities. Therefore, it is desired to reduce manpower by replacing the work that can be automated. Most of these facilities require the task of transporting equipments or luggages. At present, most of these operations are performed manually, and the use of autonomous robots in those tasks may help the situation. In order for a mobile robot to travel autonomously in a given environment, a self-localization function is necessary. The largely implemented method of self-localization is the local estimation applying a stochastic process such as particle filter. This method employs the motion model defined by the movement from previous to the current position and the environmental model defined by the structural information obtained from external sensors. The method compares these models to the environmental map, which is created in advance and possesses structural information, to estimate self-location. This method implements Markov model, which exploits previous information to estimate present information, so once the self-location is lost, it can no longer produce reliable estimates. Due to this property, in order for a mobile robot to recover its estimation, re-localization with a certain degree of accuracy is required. A re-localization method only requires the current external sensor information and

© Springer Nature Singapore Pte Ltd. 2020
W. Ohyama and S. K. Jung (Eds.): IW-FCV 2020, CCIS 1212, pp. 192–205, 2020.
https://doi.org/10.1007/978-981-15-4818-5_15

does not implement Markov model. In some conditions, when a robot travels in a facility relying only on the local estimation, its self-location is easily lost. A typical example of it is a corridor environment. In a corridor, the only structural information, a robot obtains, is wall. While walls do not possess sufficient structural features to be distinguished, the local estimation method, which utilizes structural information, tends to fail.

In recent years, the research of re-localization method, which performs by feeding image data to a neural network, has been studied. By inputting image data, a network can learn not only the structural information, but also textural information. Since this method is not dependent on the structural information, it is expected to be robust in the corridor environment. By combining this method to the local estimation method, we assume a more stable navigation can be achieved. Therefore, this paper focuses on the re-localization method utilizing deep learning. Outdoor re-localization is the mainstream of this field, however we propose a method that performs indoor re-localization. One of the problems of performing indoor re-localization is its narrow field of view. In the outdoor environment, objects such as walls, rarely shields a robot's field of view. Therefore, an ordinary web camera is sufficient for collecting features for self-localization. On the other hand, if an ordinary web camera is applied in the indoor environment, a little deviation from the expected path is capable of shielding much of a robot's field of view. To solve this problem, our proposing method employs an omni-directional camera, which obtains 360° view. Another problem of the corridor environment is the existence of dynamic objects such as pedestrians and equipments. It is highly conceivable that a corridor sustains a great deal of dynamic objects, so the re-localization method should be robust to these indelible noises. It is difficult to include all expected environmental conditions in the training dataset. So, regardless of the gap in the test dataset to the training dataset, the proposed method should perform accurate self-localization.

To solve these problems, at first, our method converts the semi-omni-directional image into a panoramic image. And by dividing the panoramic image at the fixed angles, we perform data augmentation. By defining the final estimation as the average estimation from augmented images, we assume that the re-localization accuracy and robustness improve. Furthermore, we apply uncertainty measurement obtained from Bayesian Neural Network to calculate the confidence of estimation from each augmented image. The confidence is applied to weight each estimation, and by calculating the weighted average, more robust self-localization is achieved. The validity of the proposed method is carried out by the experiments.

2   Related Work

As a related research of re-localization, Martinez-Mozos et al. [1] proposed a method applying topological map. This method extracts low level structural features with a laser sensor from the environment and labels each low level features with the affiliated high level features such as T-junction, wall and corridor. These features are applied to classify the topological node of self-location. A topological map is not compatible with metric measurement, so it only estimates rough self-location. For this reason, it is difficult to acquire sufficient accuracy to recover to the local estimation. Thrun et al. [2] proposed a method utilizing the textural information observed on the ceiling. This method takes pictures of the ceiling at different locations and synthesizes a gray-scale mosaic environmental map. The self-location is estimated by matching the mosaic environmental map and the low level features of the ceiling's brightness pattern. To implement this method, the ceiling in the environment needs to abound in textural pattern. However, in general, ceilings of corridors do not possess abundant textural pattern. For this reason, we consider the implementation of this method is not effective.

Kendall et al. [3] proposed a re-localization method applying deep learning. This method collects image data from the environment and labels each image with self-location information. The dataset consists of images and self-location labels, and the method employs CNN (Convolutional Neural Network), which is proficient in picture recognition tasks. The CNN estimates self-location as a regression problem. The paper argues that this method is robust, since the network processes not only structural features but also textural features for the self-localization. The network model is based on GoogLeNet [5] and is named PoseNet. Kendall et al. [4] further developed [3] by employing Bayesian Neural Network, which estimates the probability distribution of the network's output. The network model is named Bayesian PoseNet, and this method improved the accuracy from [3]. The paper also proposed the calculation of self-localization uncertainty.

Umeda et al. [6] proposed a re-localization method with deep learning using semi-omni-directional image. This method implements omni-directional camera and operates by classifying the grid of self-location from an environmental grid map. This method applies equirectangular projection to convert semi-omni-directional image into a panoramic image. After the panoramic conversion, the method performs data augmentation by changing the field of angle from the original panoramic image several times. [6] conducted experiments on a outdoor dataset, and their method does not consider dynamic objects. However in this paper, we conduct experiments on indoor datasets and consider dynamic objects.

3   Proposed Method

3.1   System Overview

The proposed method applies PoseNet [3] and Bayesian PoseNet [4]. Original PoseNet processes web camera images, however the proposed method processes semi-omni-directional images. By implementing semi-omni-directional images, sufficient features for re-localization are obtained, regardless of the narrow field of view. After the application of equirectangular projection to convert the semi-omni-directional image into a panoramic image, data augmentation is performed to produce six images by dividing the panoramic image at every 60°. By performing re-localization with the augmented images and calculating the average, the final estimation is defined (the Averaging Method). The data augmentation method produces six images facing at different directions, so by calculating the average estimation, it is expected that the contribution ratio of an image with a big estimation error to the final estimation dissipates. Based on the uncertainty measurements generated by Bayesian PoseNet, the estimation confidences of the six augmented images are calculated. By weighting each estimation with confidence and calculating the weighted average, final estimation is defined (the Confidence Weighting Method). The more different the environment in the test dataset from the training dataset is, the lower the confidence tends to be. The lower the confidence is, the bigger the estimation error tends to be. Therefore, by setting small weight to an image with low confidence, the improvement in the robustness is expected (Fig. 1).

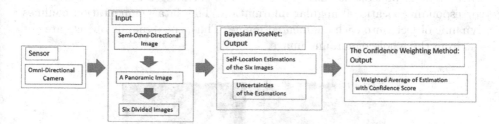

Fig. 1. System overview.

3.2   PoseNet and Bayesian PoseNet

With input image I, PoseNet [3] defines its loss function $Loss(I)$ as the sum of squared norm of error between the estimated positional coordinates $p(x, y, z)$ and quaternion $q(x, y, z, w)$ and the true value $\hat{p}$, $\hat{q}$. To calibrate the vector length between positional coordinates and quaternion, a hyper parameter β is defined (1). Compared to separately feed positional and angular losses to the network, [3] argues that feeding both at the same time improves the accuracy.

$$Loss(I) = \| \hat{p} - p \|^2 + \beta \| \hat{q} - q \|^2 \tag{1}$$

Bayesian PoseNet [4] is modeled by applying Bayesian Neural Network to PoseNet. Bayesian Network applies dropout to the fully connected layers at the time of inference. It produces several outputs from a single input and is able to estimate the probability distribution of the input inference. Bayesian PoseNet adopts this property, and estimates the self-location uncertainty from dispersion of the probability distribution. The uncertainty is defined by the trace of covariance matrix obtained from the distribution.

3.3   Data Augmentation with Semi-Omni-Directional Image

When collecting indoor dataset with web camera, due to the shields such as walls, often the field of view becomes narrow. Therefore, with a slight angular movement of a robot, features that are valid for estimation become lost (Fig. 2(a)). The use of omni-directional camera widens the field of view and solves this problem (Fig. 2(b)). However, a semi-omni-directional image contains distorted structural information, thus objects and their placements are difficult to be recognized. By applying equirectangular projection to convert into a panoramic image (Fig. 3), we calibrated the distortion. We conducted the accuracy comparison of re-localization between the application of semi-omni-directional and panoramic images, and the application of panoramic images showed accuracy improvement. We performed data augmentation by dividing the panoramic image at every 60° with the field of view at 120° (Fig. 4). These six images are labeled with the corresponding locational angular information. The data augmentation confines dynamic objects into each augmented image. Thus, the dynamic objects are cut out from the whole panoramic image.

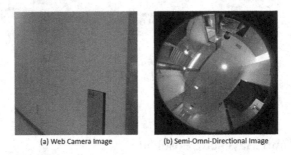

(a) Web Camera Image   (b) Semi-Omni-Directional Image

Fig. 2. Web camera and semi-omni-directional image. (a) Shows a web camera image. It contains insufficient features. (b) Shows an semi-omni-directional image. The view is acquired for 360°. However, structural features are severely distorted.

Fig. 3. Panoramic image. The structural distortion is calibrated, and objects are recognizable.

Fig. 4. Six divided images. This data augmentation method calibrates the contribution ratio of each augmented image to the final estimation. The dynamic objects are confined in each augmented image.

3.4 Localization Method

The Averaging Method. In the Averaging Method, self-localization is performed on each augmented image, and the average of estimations determines the final estimation. Calculating the average value alleviates the influence of an image with low accuracy.

The Confidence Weighting Method. In the Confidence Weighting Method, the probability distributions are estimated for each augmented image, and the covariance matrice's traces are calculated separately for both positional coordinates and quaternions. The values of the traces are defined as the estimation's uncertainty $U(\mathbf{Up}, \mathbf{Uq})$, and the normalized inverse of uncertainty is defined as confidence $C(\mathbf{Cp}, \mathbf{Cq})$. The final estimation $Pose(\tilde{p}, \tilde{q})$ is determined by calculating the weighted average of the positional and angular estimations and confidences from the augmented images. Since low confidence is defined for an image with high uncertainty, the contribution rate of an image with high uncertainty to the final estimation lowers. For the image which contains dynamic objects and greatly differs from the training dataset, the uncertainty is expected to be high. While the image which has high uncertainties is weighted with low confidence, the performance of the proposed method is assumed to be robust. (2) and (3) respectively show the equations for the confidence and the weighted average of self-location. The vectors $\mathbf{Up}^{-1}$, $\mathbf{Uq}^{-1}$ hold the inverse values from each element of $\mathbf{Up}$, $\mathbf{Uq}$. i implies the number of augmented images produced from a panoramic image.

$$C(\mathbf{Cp}, \mathbf{Cq}) = (\frac{\mathbf{Up}^{-1}}{\sum_i (Up_i^{-1})}, \frac{\mathbf{Uq}^{-1}}{\sum_i (Uq_i^{-1})}) \tag{2}$$

$$Pose(\tilde{p}, \tilde{q}) = (\sum_i p_i Cp_i, \sum_i q_i Cq_i) \tag{3}$$

4 Experiment

4.1 Dataset

Test datasets are generated using a robot which performs SLAM (Simultaneous Localization and Mapping) with a laser sensor. Self-location information

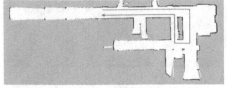
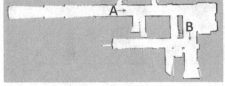

(a) 2D Structural Map and Data Collection Path   (b) Data Collection Sites

Fig. 5. 2D structural map of the environment, the data collection path and sites. (a) The dataset is collected in the designated path. (b) The dataset is collected at the designated sites. The camera stays at the same pose facing the indicated direction, while the number of pedestrians changes.

is acquired by SLAM, and the datasets are generated by labeling each image obtained from the camera with self-location information. The datasets are collected in our university's corridor to simulate an ordinary facility's corridor. The datasets are collected in the space of 15 m × 5 m, and the omni-directional camera is mounted at the height of 0.85 m parallel to the ground. The 2D map of the environment is shown in Fig. 5(a).

The training dataset is collected in daytime with no dynamic objects in sight. Keeping the training dataset unique, the robustness of each method to a different environment can be tested. The training dataset is collected in the middle of corridor, following the indicated path in Fig. 5(a). Training dataset samples are shown in Fig. 6.

Fig. 6. Training dataset. Sample images from training dataset. The dataset is collected during daytime and contains no dynamic objects.

4.2   Experimental Setting

To evaluate the accuracy and robustness of the proposed re-localization methods, we conducted two experiments.

The first experiment verifies the validity of the Averaging Method and the Confidence Weighting Method. The estimation accuracy with a whole panoramic image is compared with each proposed method.

The second experiment is conducted to verify the robustness of the Confidence Weighting Method. The estimation accuracy is compared with the dataset which contains 0 to 3 pedestrians in sight. The experiment is evaluated by comparing the accuracy between the Averaging Method and the Confidence Weighting Method.

The training dataset contains 909 images, and with the data augmentation, the number of images expands to 5454. The pixel of a panoramic image is 224 × 672 and for augmented images 224 × 224. For the training and testing, Gigabyte BRIX Gaming VR BNi7HG6-1060 Ultra Compact PC Intel Core i7-7700HQ is used. The parameter β from the loss function (1) is set to 500, learning method is SGD, learning rate is 0.00001 and the number of epochs is 1500.

4.3   Experimental Result

First Experiment. We conducted an evaluation experiment with the method inputting a whole panoramic image, the Averaging Method and the Confidence Weighting Method. The test dataset is collected in the path indicated in Fig. 5(a) and includes one pedestrian in sight. Samples of dataset are shown in Fig. 7. Figures 8 and 9 show the estimated positional and angular error of the test dataset in the order of time scale at collection. Table 1 compares the accuracy of each method.

Fig. 7. Sample images from the dataset. Lighting condition and collection path is very similar to the training dataset. It contains one pedestrian as a dynamic object.

Table 1. Accuracy comparison. The table compares each method's average positional and angular error.

	Average error	Standard deviation
Estimation with a panoramic image	0.94 m, 10.71°	0.84 m, 19.15°
The averaging method	**0.68 m, 3.17°**	0.29 m, 1.45°
The confidence weighting method	**0.69 m, 3.15°**	0.30 m, 1.22°

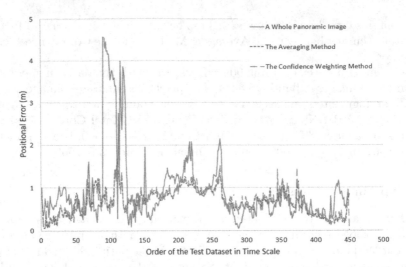

Fig. 8. Positional estimation comparison. Positional estimation error with three different methods is shown. The test dataset is estimated in the order of time scale at collection, which follows the path designated in Fig. 5(a).

Some outliers are observed in Figs. 8 and 9 with the method inputting a whole panoramic image. We consider that these outliers occurred due to the existence of a pedestrian and the gap in the definition of the middle of corridor. Figure 9 also shows samples from the area where outliers are observed. From Figs. 8, 9 and Table 1, it is observed that the Averaging Method and the Confidence Weighting Method did not produce outliers, and the accuracy improved. The reason for the invariance in the accuracy of both methods is considered that the test dataset resembles much to the training dataset. From this experiment, the validity of both proposed methods is verified.

Second Experiment. To evaluate the robustness of the Averaging Method and the Confidence Weighting Method, the test dataset is collected at sites A and B, with the robot facing the direction indicated in Fig. 5(b). At both sites, pedestrians are observed, and the number of the pedestrians changes from 0 to 3. Each condition's dataset starts with the frame including a complete number of pedestrians and ends when lacking even a part of the pedestrians (Fig. 11). Figures 12 and 13 show the estimated angular and positional error of the test dataset in the order of the time scale at collection. Figures 12 and 13 are collected at sites A and B respectively under different conditions. Table 2 shows the accuracy evaluation between these two methods. Figure 10 shows an example data of confidence measurement. The confidence of angular estimation and angular estimation error are shown for each augmented image.

From Figs. 12, 13 and Table 2, between the proposed methods, the accuracy difference in positional estimation is hardly observed. However, in terms of the angular estimation, as the number of pedestrians increases, the Confidence

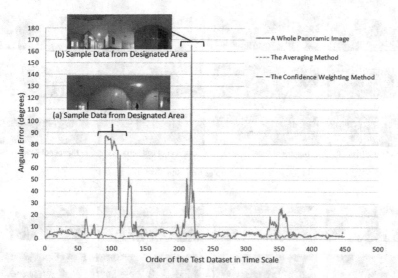

Fig. 9. Angular estimation comparison. Angular estimation error with three different methods is shown. The test dataset is estimated in the order of time scale at collection, which follows the path designated in Fig. 5(a). (a) and (b) also show sample images from outliers.

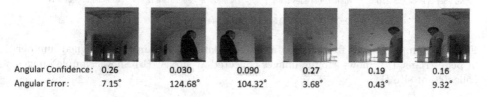

Fig. 10. The figure shows an example of how the confidence is measured. The highest two confidences are shown in red, and the lowest two in blue. (Color figure online)

Weighting Method sustains its accuracy, while the Averaging Method declines in accuracy and produces outliers. From Fig. 10, we observe that high confidence is defined for the images without dynamic objects and with abundant textural features. From this experiment, in terms of the angular estimation, the robustness of the Confidence Weighting Method is verified.

5   Discussion

We will discuss the reason why with the Confidence Weighting Method, only the angular estimation accuracy improved. We examined the cause by calculating the correlation between the uncertainty of estimation and the estimation error. The examination is conducted on the dataset collected at site A (Figs. 5(b), 11(a)). The correlation coefficient between the uncertainty of positional estimation and the positional estimation error is calculated to be -0.23, so the correlation is

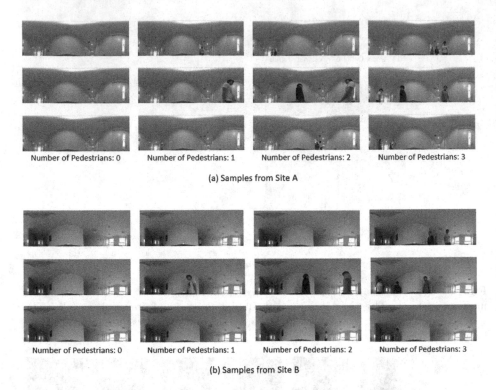

(a) Samples from Site A

(b) Samples from Site B

Fig. 11. Sample images from the dataset. The dataset contains the assigned number of pedestrians. (a) Shows sample images collected at site A. (b) Shows sample images collected at site B.

weak. On the other hand, with the angular estimation, the correlation is calculated to be 0.80, so a strong correlation is observed. Without the correlation between the uncertainty and estimation accuracy, the Confidence Weighting Method does not function properly. We consider the strong correlation is the reason for the angular estimation improvement.

We assume the proper uncertainty measurement of angular estimation is attributed to the correspondence of angular information between picture coordinate and global coordinate. The equirectangular projection converts an omnidirectional image in accord with the angular information of the global coordinate, however the distortion of the depth perception is not calibrated. We assume these factors have influenced the reliable and unreliable uncertainty measurement of the angular and positional estimation.

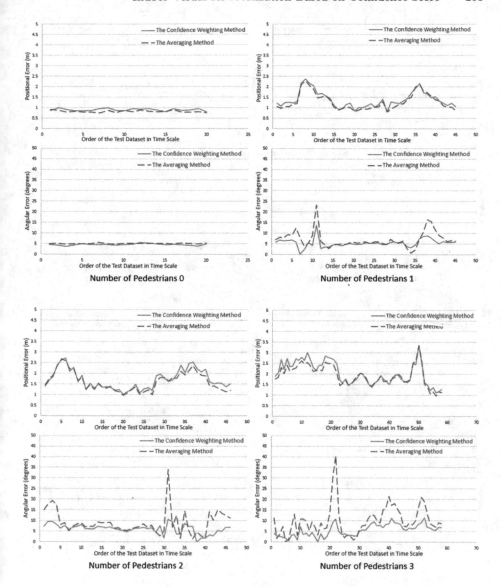

Fig. 12. Estimation at site A. Each graph shows assigned condition's positional or angular error. Comparison is made between the Confidence Weighting Method and the Averaging Method.

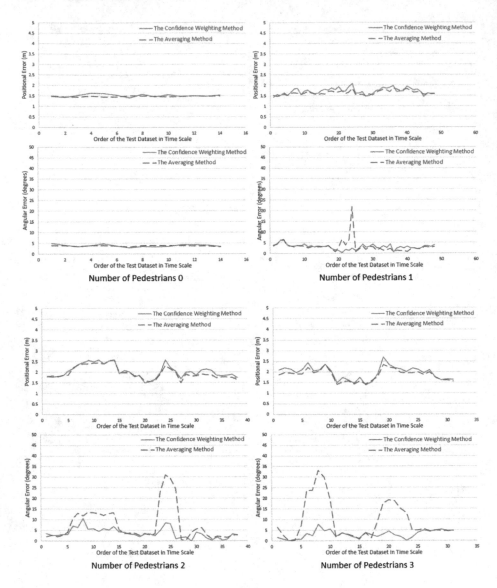

Fig. 13. Estimation at Site B. Each graph shows assigned condition's positional or angular error. Comparison is made between the Confidence Weighting Method and the Averaging Method.

6   Conclusion

In this paper, we proposed a novel indoor re-localization method with deep learning using omni-directional camera, and the validity of the proposed method is proven by the experiments. Firstly, we have shown that in the indoor environment, web camera images often miss important features for localization. To

Table 2. Accuracy comparison at site A and B. The table compares each method's average positional and angular error.

Number of pedestrians	0	1	2	3
Site A: the averaging method	0.90 m, 5.07°	1.40 m, 7.11°	1.59 m, 9.04°	1.94 m, 10.09°
Site A: the averaging method (Bayesian PoseNet)	0.87 m, 5.07°	1.32 m, 7.05°	1.66 m, 9.03°	1.99 m, 10.00°
Site A: the confidence weighting method	1.00 m, 4.58°	1.48 m, **5.47°**	1.72 m, **6.12°**	2.00 m, **5.53°**
Site B: the averaging method	1.48 m, 3.73°	1.64 m, 3.27°	1.97 m, 7.75°	1.85 m, 9.46°
Site B: the averaging method (Bayesian PoseNet)	1.48 m, 3.72°	1.62 m, 3.23°	1.97 m, 7.52°	1.84 m, 9.28°
Site B: the confidence weighting method	1.51 m, 3.884°	1.71 m, **3.10°**	2.04 m, **3.75°**	1.95 m, **3.08°**

solve this problem, we proposed the application of omni-directional camera. Secondly, we proposed a data augmentation method, which converts a semi-omni-directional image into a panoramic image and generates multiple images by dividing it at certain angles. Finally, we proposed a method which calculates the confidence of estimation for each augmented image by applying Bayesian Neural Network, and it improved the robustness in the angular estimation. In future work, firstly, we aim to build a system which switches from the local estimation method to the proposed method, in case of a localization failure. Secondly, we aim to lower the depth of network to improve the processing speed. With the application of confidence measurement, the influence of accuracy declination from each augmented image can be considered subtle. For this reason, lowering the depth of network may sustain its accuracy, while improving its processing speed.

References

1. Martinez-Mozos, O., et al.: Supervised semantic labeling of places using information extracted from sensor data. Robot. Auton. Syst. **55**(5), 391–402 (2007)
2. Thrun, S., et al.: MINERVA: a second-generation museum tour-guide robot. In: IEEE Transactions on Robotics and Automation (1999)
3. Kendall, A., et al.: PoseNet: a convolutional network for real-time 6-DoF camera relocalization. In: Proceedings of the IEEE International Conference on Computer Vision, pp. 2938–2946 (2015)
4. Kendall, A., et al.: Modelling uncertainty in deep learning for camera relocalization. In: Proceedings of the International Conference on Robotics and Automation, pp. 4762–4769 (2016)
5. Szegedy, C., et al.: Going deeper with convolutions. In: Proceedings of the IEEE Conference on Computer Vision and Pattern Recognition, pp. 1–9 (2015)
6. Umeda, M., et al.: Spherical panoramic image-based localization by deep learning. Soc. Instrum. Control Eng. **54**(5), 483–493 (2018)

Analysis of Information Flow in Hidden Layers of the Trained Neural Network by Canonical Correlation Analysis

Keijiro Kanda, Muthusubash Kavitha, Junichi Miyao, and Takio Kurita[✉]

Department of Information Engineering, Hiroshima University,
1-4-1 Kagamiyama, Higashi-Hiroshima 739-8527, Japan
{keijirokanda,kavitha,miyao,tkurita}@hiroshima-u.ac.jp

Abstract. Convolutional neural network (CNN) have been extensively applied for a variety of tasks. However, the internal processes of hidden units in solving problems are mostly unknown. In this study, we presented the use of canonical correlation analysis (CCA) to understand the information flow of the hidden layers in CNN. The proposed method analyzed and compared the information flow by measuring the correlations between a given feature vector and the activation pattern at each layer of the CNN. We quantified and analyzed specific information flows using the CCA to examine how the architecture works in the two experiments. In the first experiment, we analyzed the information flow of the U-net and auto-encoder architectures to remove the distorted light source information, and showed that the U-net works more efficiently for this task. In the second experiment, we analyzed the information flow of the architecture used for multitask learning, in which the classification of shifted characters in images and the estimation of the shift amount are performed simultaneously, and showed that it performed properly according to the task.

Keywords: Hidden layer · Information flow · Canonical correlation · White balance · Multi-task learning

1 Introduction

Deep convolutional neural network (CNN) are currently being used in various applications. It is because the significant contributions of CNN can be suitable to handle almost all kinds of problems such as object recognition, speech recognition, image retrieval, natural language processing and so on. However, it is difficult to understand the internal mechanism of the model, which is often hidden in one of the downsides of the deep neural network.

Various analysis techniques have been proposed to understand the performance and processing techniques of CNN. In the feature visualization technique proposed by Zeiler et al. [13], weight coefficients or convolution filters in a trained

© Springer Nature Singapore Pte Ltd. 2020
W. Ohyama and S. K. Jung (Eds.): IW-FCV 2020, CCIS 1212, pp. 206–220, 2020.
https://doi.org/10.1007/978-981-15-4818-5_16

network are visually represented as the shape of the objects. It is very use-ful for understanding intuitively about the characteristics of the responses of the network. A number of dimension-reduction techniques have been proposed for feature space visualization, including principal component analysis (PCA) [14], Fisher's linear discriminant analysis (FLDA) [15], and t-stochastic neigh-bor embedding (t-SNE) [16]. However, the aforementioned methods can visualize only the individual feature space and do not consider to compare them for visual predictions. In addition, all the above-aforementioned techniques were not appro-priate to demonstrate the changes of a certain amount of information of input image as it flows through the network.

In order to understand and analyze the flow of information in the hidden layer, we proposed to analyze the information flow and measure the activity in each layer of the network using canonical correlation analysis (CCA) [11]. The CCA is a technique for analyzing the interrelationship between the two sets of variables. Hidaka et al. [12] compared the feature values of the adjacent layers using CCA and showed better visualization results than the traditional methods. Likewise, by utilizing the strength of the specific information contained in each layer, it is possible to compare the internal workflow across the network. Using a simple architecture in the proposed two experiments, we evaluated the information flow by measuring the correlation between a given feature vector and the activation pattern of each hidden layer of CNN using CCA. The analysis of the middle-tier activity showed that efficient learning was performed to achieve the best performance for each task.

2   Method

2.1   Canonical Correlation Analysis

Canonical Correlation Analysis (CCA) [11] is a multivariate analysis of corre-lation for extracting information consisted of two multidimensional variables. It measures the strength of association between canonical variables.

Let p-dimensional vectors and q-dimensional vectors represented as $x = [x_1, \ldots, x_p]^T$ and $y = [y_1, \ldots, y_q]^T$, respectively. Given sets of N samples $X = \{x_1, \ldots, x_N\}$ and $Y = \{y_1, \ldots, y_N\}$, the CCA gives linear transforma-tions, which are

$$s_i = A^T(x_i - \bar{x}) \tag{1}$$
$$t_i = B^T(y_i - \bar{y}) \tag{2}$$

where x_i and y_i are observed from the same i-th instance, and $\bar{x}$ and $\bar{y}$ are the mean vector of $x \in X$ and $y \in Y$, respectively.

The Eqs. (1) and (2) maximize the correlation coefficients between sets of new features $S = \{s_1, \ldots, s_N\}$ and $T = \{t_1, \ldots, t_N\}$. The coefficient matrices A and B are computed using the following eigen equations,

$$\Sigma_{XY}\Sigma_Y^{-1}\Sigma_{YX}A = \Sigma_X A\Lambda^2 \quad (A^T\Sigma_X A = I_{d^*}) \tag{3}$$
$$\Sigma_{YX}\Sigma_X^{-1}\Sigma_{XY}B = \Sigma_Y B\Lambda^2 \quad (B^T\Sigma_Y B = I_{d^*}) \tag{4}$$

where Λ^2 is a diagonal matrix and diagonal components are the eigenvalues. A dimension of canonical principal components (CPC) of s and t is denoted as $d^* \leq \min(p,q)$. The matrices Σ_X, Σ_Y, Σ_{XY} and Σ_{YX} are represented as

$$\Sigma_X = \sum_{i=1}^{N}(\boldsymbol{x}_i - \bar{\boldsymbol{x}})(\boldsymbol{x}_i - \bar{\boldsymbol{x}})^T \tag{5}$$

$$\Sigma_Y = \sum_{i=1}^{N}(\boldsymbol{y}_i - \bar{\boldsymbol{y}})(\boldsymbol{y}_i - \bar{\boldsymbol{y}})^T \tag{6}$$

$$\Sigma_{XY} = \sum_{i=1}^{N}(\boldsymbol{x}_i - \bar{\boldsymbol{x}})(\boldsymbol{y}_i - \bar{\boldsymbol{y}})^T = (\Sigma_{YX})^T \tag{7}$$

2.2   CCA for Information Flow Analysis

It is possible to understand the various types of flow of information and the activity possessed by the hidden layers of the CNN with the help of CCA analysis [12]. The advantage of using deep learning model is that it automatically learns the features from the data which is suitable for the target task while hiding the internal processes. However, understanding a certain amount of information that is included in the hidden layer activities of CNN can help users to train the model intuitively.

For example, in the first experiment, the purpose of using CCA is to analyze the activity of the hidden layer in order to understand the internal processing of a simple U-net for a white balance task. It is demonstrated using simple CNN as shown in Fig. 1. For the white balancing task, it is necessary to remove the illuminant color information from the original input image. So the illuminant color information is used as the external information and correlations between the illuminant color information and the activations of each hidden layers are calculated by using CCA. Generally, the layers of CNN are intended to remove some specific information about the input data. Therefore, the layer which is responsible for greatly removing the information can be easily recognized by using CCA from the degree of correlation which is measured between the activity of each layer and the specific information. If the amount of information gradually decreases with almost similar correlation coefficients from input to the output then it can be determined that the whole network is involved in removing the information. Whereas, if the information is extremely reduced at a layer with some specific activity, then the convolutional layer which is previous to that layer with high correlation coefficient is highly involved in removing the information. In this study, we used CCA for determining the correlation coefficients between each activity of the layer and the specific illuminant information of the input image. The degree of removal of illuminant information is observed through the degree of correlation coefficient values by the representations of activities.

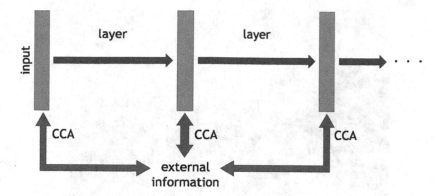

Fig. 1. Analysis of information flow in simple CNN

3 Experiments and Results

3.1 White Balancing by CNN

We proposed to solve the analysis of information flow in the hidden layers of U-net architecture using CCA through the task of white balancing. White balancing is the correction of photos that are affected by biased light sources as if they were taken under white and is considered as an important task in the field of image engineering as shown in Fig. 2. Various methods have been proposed for the correction of white balancing [2–6,9,10]. In this study, we evaluated the flow of information of CNN using CCA through the task of removing light source information for white balancing.

Our proposed task included two main steps, (i) to use simple U-net architecture for white balancing and validate to prove its better performance over auto-encoder and (ii) use CCA for analyzing the information flow of hidden layers for better understanding the internal mechanism to achieve the task.

The U-net architecture shown in Fig. 3 is used for white balancing. The activity number three and four represents before and after concatenation, respectively. U-net [1] is a typical convolutional neural network architecture consists of repeated utilization of convolutions. It is developed specifically for the precise segmentation of medical images. The architecture includes paths between down-sampling and up-sampling to retrieves local information and context information, respectively to produce global information, which is important for valid segmentation. We feed the input image patches of size 128×128 with some illuminant color information into the network and output the white-balanced image patches as the same size as the input.

The down-convolution path includes two layers of 3×3 convolutional layers with 2 pixels stride. Each of the convolutions is followed by a ReLU. At each down-convolution step, the number of feature channels is increased from 3, 16 and 32. The up-convolution path consists of two convolutional steps with 2 pixels stride. However, the up-convolution step used in this paper is different from the

Fig. 2. Image for left half composited with red illuminant and right half is white balanced (Color figure online)

down-convolution step. The ReLU is applied in the first up-convolution step, and not used in the second up-convolution step. The feature channels of the first down-convolution and first up-convolution steps are concatenated as shown in the figure.

The mean squared errors (MSE) is used to evaluate the goodness of the trained model for white balancing task. It is estimated between the predicted output and the ground truth by using

$$e_{MSE} = \frac{1}{MN} \sum_{m=0}^{M-1} \sum_{n=0}^{N-1} (\boldsymbol{p}_{D(m,n)} - \hat{\boldsymbol{p}}_{D(m,n)})^2 \tag{8}$$

where $\boldsymbol{p}_D$ and $\hat{\boldsymbol{p}}_D$ are pixel values of predicted and ground truth images, respectively.

We used SUN [7] dataset to evaluate the performance of our proposed architecture for color correction. The dataset contains more than 900 variety of scene categories such as indoor, urban, nature, etc. It is mainly used for scene recognition. However, most of the images in this dataset do not contain illuminant information. Thus we prepare synthetic data to add the illuminant information in the images for the evaluation of our proposed method.

We assumed that the images are uniformly influenced by only one light source and produced illuminated images from the original image based on this assumption. The color of the light source used for the preparation of the data is randomly generated on each image, whereas its illuminant value is not perfectly random. The value is selected based on the range of values corresponding to the natural scenes and their frequencies. To generate random values of distributions for suitable illuminant colors, we used NUS 8-Camera Dataset [8]. This dataset contains

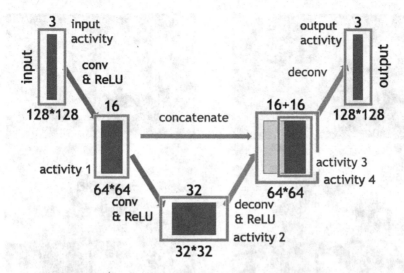

Fig. 3. U-net architecture and representation of activities

1736 images and color information corresponding to each illuminant. The distribution of the light source information is assumed to be equivalent to that of the light source information affecting the natural image. The illumination image is generated using the light source information of this dataset. The color values for preparing the synthetic dataset to get illumination is represented by

$$p_{filt} = p_{orig} \circ p_{coef} \qquad (9)$$

where $p_{filt} = (r_{filt}, g_{filt}, b_{filt})^T$ is a pixel value of the illuminated image obtained by Hadamard's product of a simple original image pixel value $p_{orig} = (r_{orig}, g_{orig}, b_{orig})^T$ with the coefficient of illuminants $p_{coef} = (r_{coef}, g_{coef}, b_{coef})^T$. The coefficient values are generated for each image using a random distribution of normalized light source information.

The examples of the original images from SUN dataset (hereafter original images are referred as ground truth) and their artificially illuminated images for the evaluation of the performance of the trained network are shown in Fig. 4. We use 128×128 random patches of ground truth images and illuminated images to feed to the trained network as input.

In order to confirm the effectiveness of the simple U-Net architecture, we compare it with simple autoencoder as shown in Fig. 5. We select 13000 and 3000 images for training and testing samples, respectively. The performance comparison is executed based on the average value of MSE using test dataset.

For training the network architecture of both, we applied Adam Optimizer with a learning rate of 0.0001. The weight decay and batch size are set to 0.0001 and 100, respectively. The total number of epochs are set to 1000. We experiment with a different random number of seeds ten times on training and testing. Hence we consider an average MSE value for our comparison.

Fig. 4. Ground truth images (left) and manually illuminated images (right)

The comparisons of the MSE value of both is presented in Table 1. The results indicated that our proposed method is superior to autoencoder. Figure 6 shows the predicted white balanced images obtained by both.

Table 1. Comparisons of white balancing method

Method	MSE Value
Auto encoder	0.00397
Proposed	**0.00343**

We evaluated the information flow for the task of white balancing in terms of observing the internal processes of the architecture. For observing the internal activity we used the simple U-net and the autoencoder. To compare the differences between these two architectures, we particularly focused on calculating the activity of the paths connecting downsampling and upsampling as shown in Fig. 7. We fed 13000 input images to train the two learned architectures and examined the correlation coefficients of CCA between activities in each layer and the illuminant information. The dimensionality of activities in each layer is reduced to 100.

The list of correlation coefficients of CCA is presented in Table 2. The concatenating step of activity four is not included in the autoencoder. The coefficient value of the U-Net is smaller than that of autoencoder, indicates a large amount of illuminant information is removed. The coefficient values of each activity of

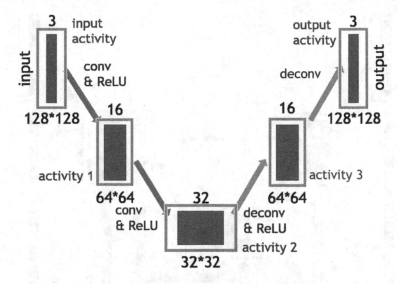

Fig. 5. Auto-encoder architecture and representation of activities

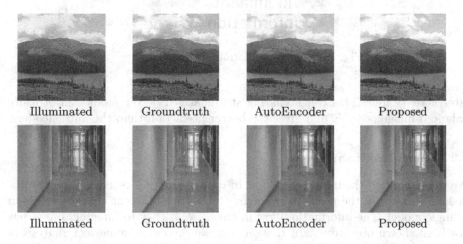

Fig. 6. Comparison of proposed methods in predicting white balanced images with statistics-based and learning-based methods for SUN dataset

U-net and auto-encoder is demonstrated as shown in Fig. 8(a) and (b). In both the networks, the coefficient value rapidly decreases with the increase of output activity number. It clearly verifies that the up-convolution step helps to remove the illuminant information. The coefficients of all middle layers of the U-Net are larger than those values compared to the autoencoder. However, after the concatenating step, the coefficient value of the U-Net is drastically decreasing. Hence the concatenate step helps to convey location information to global information and hence the local dominant illuminant are gathered in the middle layers

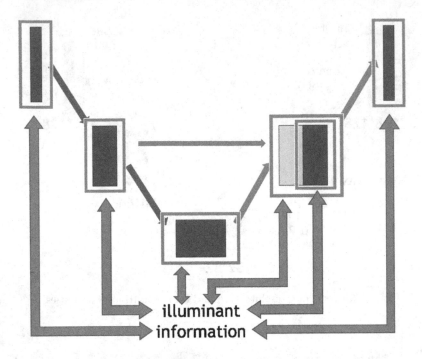

Fig. 7. Analysis of information flow in U-net

after activity four. This concatenating step makes a better prediction of white balanced image possible and gives the better prediction than the autoencoder.

3.2   Multi-task Learning

We then analyzed the information flow in multitasking tasks using CCA. Multitasking learning is the problem of solving tasks with different characteristics in a single model. The information flow in this case, is easy to imagine, but it has not been shown objectively. In this section, we present a numerical analysis of information flow in multitask learning using our method.

The task to be processed is to simultaneously estimate the character label and shift information from the character image to which the shift information is added as shown in Fig. 9. Our proposed task consists of two steps. (i) The model we used shows that simple multitasking problems are solved and (ii) the hidden layer information flow obtained using CCA shows that the problem is solved efficiently.

The architecture used for multitask learning is shown in Fig. 10. The architecture consists of three elements. A feature extraction part for extracting necessary information from an input image, and a label estimation part and a shift estimation part for obtaining respective output values from the features obtained there.

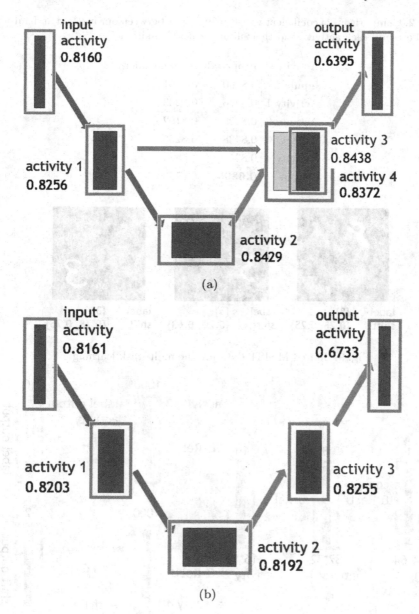

Fig. 8. Coefficient values of activities of architectures (a) U-net and (b) auto-encoder

The extraction section consists of two 3 × 3 convolutional layers with 2 pixels stride, and each estimation section consists of two connecting layers. ReLU is used as an activation function immediately after layers other than those used to obtain output values.

Table 2. Comparisons of coefficient values using CCA between our method and autoencoder based on each activity and their illuminant information.

Activities	Proposed	Auto encoder
Input	0.8160	0.8161
Activity 1	0.8256	0.8203
Activity 2	0.8429	0.8192
Activity 3	0.8438	0.8255
Activity 4	0.8372	–
Output	**0.6395**	0.6733

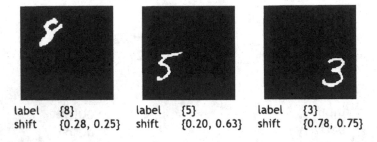

label	{8}	label	{5}	label	{3}
shift	{0.28, 0.25}	shift	{0.20, 0.63}	shift	{0.78, 0.75}

Fig. 9. Shifted MNIST data for the multi-task learning

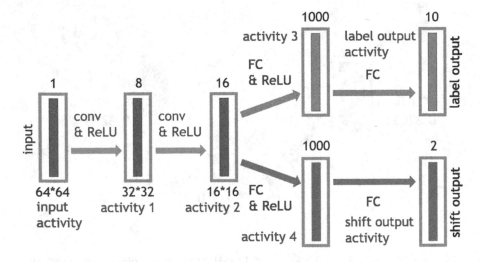

Fig. 10. Multi-task learning architecture and representation of activities

We used the MNIST [17] dataset for this experiment. The original MNIST had 28×28 images with handwritten digits centered, but we edited them and added shift information as shown in Fig. 9. First, the image was padded to a size of 64×64 to create an area for shifting. The added space is black as the original background. Next, each image is randomly shifted using a uniform random number. Therefore, even after the conversion, some images have numbers in the center. The possible values of the random numbers are in a range where the numbers are not hidden so that information about the label is not lost. The ground truth form of the shift is a two-dimensional continuous value obtained by normalizing the distance shifted in the x-axis direction and the y-axis direction, respectively, with the lower limit being 0 and the upper limit being 1. The sample size of the dataset is 60,000 for learning and 10,000 for testing.

To compare the output data with the ground truth, we used softmax cross entropy (SCE) for the label and mean square error (MSE) for the shift. The error for learning is the sum of the two.

For training the network architecture of both, we applied Momentum SGD Optimizer with a learning rate of 0.001. The weight decay and batch size are set to 0.001 and 256, respectively. The total number of epochs are set to 300.

Table 3 shows the accuracy of label classification and errors in shift estimation. The results show that the architecture was successfully learned for the task.

Table 3. Results of the multi-task learning

	Values
Label accuracy	0.8136
Shift loss	0.0002

Next, we evaluated the information flow of the architecture to solve multitasking problems. We input 60,000 train images into the learned architecture, and examined the correlation coefficient between the obtained activity and the label and shift information. At this time, the number of dimensions exceeding 100 was reduced to 100 using PCA.

Table 4 and Fig. 11 shows the correlation coefficient of each activity obtained. As we expected, the information contained in the output values indicates that more is required and less is not, but the information flow throughout the architecture is a very interesting result.

In the feature extraction part, both correlation coefficients hardly change. This indicates that these layers perform extraction without changing each information amount. In each estimation unit, the correlation of target information increases after passing through the front layer, and the correlation of non-target information decreases after passing through the rear layer. This indicates that the two layers involved play different roles. In other words, the front layer collects as much information as possible that contains the desired information, and the rear layer discards unnecessary information from it.

Table 4. Coefficient values using CCA for the multi-task learning

Activities	Label information	Shift information
Input	0.4867	0.9352
Activity 1	0.4730	0.9243
Activity 2	0.4857	0.9384
Activity 3	0.8254	0.9211
Label output	0.7493	0.1320
Activity 4	0.5336	0.9988
Shift output	0.0172	0.9988

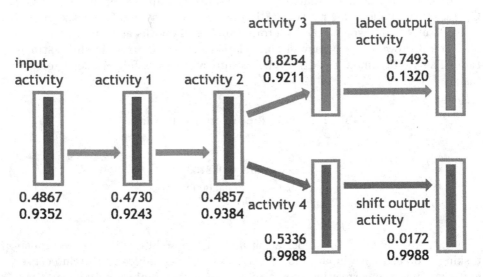

Fig. 11. Coefficient values of activities of architectures. Green value is the correlation coefficient for the label information, and red is for the shift information. (Color figure online)

4 Conclusion

In order to understand the internal processes of the architecture to achieve the task, we propose to evaluate the learned CNN information flow and activity analysis using CCA. The CCA used in this study was applied to determine the correlation between each activity in the convolution layer and the specific information contained in the input image. In the first experiment, the internal activity of a simple U-net model was compared with an automatic encoder in removing the light source information. Although the upconvolution steps of both networks help to remove the light source information, the coefficient values of the middle layer activity of the U-net are greater than those of the autocoder, thus providing good results for white balance images. In the second experiment, we analyzed the behavior of a model that simultaneously estimates label and shift information of an image. The inner layers of the model can be divided into three parts, each of which has a role to play for task resolution. Therefore, it is recommended that the process of analyzing the internal mechanisms using the CCA be useful for identifying intermediate layers that contribute significantly to setting potential parameters for accomplishing tasks.

Acknowledgments. This work was partly supported by JSPS KAKENHI Grant Number 16K00239.

References

1. Ronneberger, O., Fischer, P., Brox, T.: U-Net: convolutional networks for biomedical image segmentation. In: Navab, N., Hornegger, J., Wells, W.M., Frangi, A.F. (eds.) MICCAI 2015. LNCS, vol. 9351, pp. 234–241. Springer, Cham (2015). https://doi.org/10.1007/978-3-319-24574-4_28
2. Hunt, R.: The Reproduction of Colour. Wiley, New York (2004)
3. Lam, E.: Combining gray world and retinex theory for automatic white balance in digital photography. In: ISCE, pp. 134–139 (2005)
4. Land, E.H., McCann, J.J.: Lightness and retinex theory. J. Opt. Soc. Am. **61**(1), 1–11 (1971)
5. Nikitenko, D., Wirth, M., Trudel, K.: Applicability of white-balancing algorithms to restoring faded colour slides: an empirical evaluation. J. Multimedia **3**(5), 9–18 (2008)
6. Bianco, S., Cusano, C., Schettini, R.: Color constancy using CNNs. In: CVPR Workshops, pp. 81–89 (2015)
7. Xiao, J., Hays, J., Ehinger, K.A., Oliva, A., Torralba, A.: SUN database: large-scale scene recognition from abbey to zoo. In: CVPR (2010)
8. Cheng, D., Prasad, D.K., Brown, M.S.: Illuminant estimation for color constancy: why spatial-domain methods work and the role of the color distribution. J. Opt. Soc. Am. A **31**(5), 1049–1058 (2014)
9. Lam, H.-K., Au, O.C., Wong, C.-W.: Automatic white balancing using luminance component and standard deviation of RGB components. In: ICASSP, pp. 493–496 (2004)
10. Rizzi, A., Gatta, C., Marini, D.: A new algorithm for unsupervised global and local color correction. Pattern Recogn. Lett. **24**(11), 1663–1677 (2003)
11. Hotelling, H.: Relations between two sets of variates. Biometrica **28**(3–4), 321–377 (1936)
12. Hidaka, A., Kurita, T.: Consecutive dimensionality reduction by canonical correlation analysis for visualization of convolutional neural networks. In: Proceedings of the ISCIE International Symposium on Stochastic Systems Theory and its Applications, pp. 160–167 (2017)
13. Zeiler, M.D., Fergus, R.: Visualizing and understanding convolutional networks. In: Fleet, D., Pajdla, T., Schiele, B., Tuytelaars, T. (eds.) ECCV 2014. LNCS, vol. 8689, pp. 818–833. Springer, Cham (2014). https://doi.org/10.1007/978-3-319-10590-1_53
14. Pearson, K.: On lines and planes of closest fit to systems of points in space. Philos. Mag. **2**(11), 559–572 (1901)

15. Fisher, R.A.: The use of multiple measurements in taxonomic problems. Ann. Eugen. **7**(2), 179–188 (1936)
16. van der Maaten, L., Hinton, G.E.: Visualizing data using t-SNE. J. Mach. Learn. Res. **9**(Nov), 2579–2605 (2008)
17. LeCun, Y., Bottou, L., Bengio, Y., Haffner, P.: Gradient-based learning applied to document recognition. Proc. IEEE **86**(11), 2278–2324 (1998)

Inspection and Diagnosis

Study of GANs Using a Few Images for Sealer Inspection Systems

Dongwook Seo[1], Yejin Ha[2], Seungbo Ha[3], Kang-Hyun Jo[1],
and Hyun-Deok Kang[2,3(✉)]

[1] School of Electrical Engineering, Uinversity of Ulsan,
Ulsan 44610, Republic of Korea
seodongwook99@gmail.com, acejo2208@gmail.com
[2] Seohong Tech Co., Ulsan 44919, Republic of Korea
yejinha24@gmail.com, seohongtech@gmail.com
[3] School of Electrical and Computer Engineering, UNIST,
Ulsan 44919, Republic of Korea
{mj0829,khd0425}@unist.ac.kr
http://islab.ulsan.ac.kr, http://feetness.co.kr

Abstract. This paper describes a comparative study of the performance of Generative Adversarial Networks (GANs) through the quality of the generated images by using a few samples. In the deep learning-based systems, the amount and quality of data are important. However, in industrial sites, data acquisition is difficult or limited for some reasons such as security and industrial specificity, etc. Therefore, it is necessary to increase small-scale data to large-scale data for the training model. GANs is one of the representative image generation models using deep learning. Three GANs such as DCGAN, BEGAN, and SinGAN are used to compare the quality of the generated image samples. The comparison is carried out based on the score with different measuring methods.

Keywords: Generative Adversarial Networks · Sealer · Vision inspection systems

1 Introduction

The machine vision acquires images using cameras, optical systems, lights, etc. to inspect products and detect defects during manufacturing processes [3]. The automated machine vision system surpasses human abilities and realizes high optical resolution, consistency, and high accuracy. However, traditional machine vision systems show limitations to various environmental conditions at industrial sites. Especially, they are very sensitive to illumination variation and difficult to adapt to different inspected items. Also, they have possibilities of image distortion from changes in both of the angle and the position. It is very inefficient to modify the systems due to each of the environmental changes for maintaining successful inspection systems. A deep learning model combines the self-learning

© Springer Nature Singapore Pte Ltd. 2020
W. Ohyama and S. K. Jung (Eds.): IW-FCV 2020, CCIS 1212, pp. 223–235, 2020.
https://doi.org/10.1007/978-981-15-4818-5_17

ability of humans and the data processing speed of computing systems and overcomes the limitations of traditional visual inspection systems [3]. For the machine vision inspection system using deep learning, data acquisition is difficult due to the specificity of the data, security issues, and environmental limitations.

The accuracy and validity of deep learning models are significantly affected by the quality and quantity of input data [8,27]. Learning with limited data cause over-fitting or fails to train. According to Goodfellow et al. [8], at least 5 thousand training data are needed for each category to reach acceptable performance, and more than 10 million training samples are required to reach or surpass human abilities. For this reason, the importance of large datasets has grown fast and, therefore, various attempts such as data augmentation, data generation, data labeling, etc. have been tried to increase data [27]. Currently, datasets based on daily lives (ImageNet [5], Visual Object Classes (VOC) [6], Common Object in Context (COCO) [20], etc.) are available for deep learning researches, but it is hard to acquire data from the industrial process [7].

A sealing image is one example of hardly accessible data. A sealant is used to attach heterogeneous materials in manufacturing processes, and a machine vision system inspects whether the sealant is applied properly. Thousands of high-quality sealing images are required for deep learning-based machine vision inspections, but data is not acquired easily because the images are obtained from specific processes at the industrial site, and the security issues are related to the products.

Generating artificial data has been tried by learning the properties of the given training data, and the GANs is a representative image generative model based on deep learning [32]. Since 2014, the GANs is first introduced by Goodfellow et al. [9], it has been modified and improved for various image manipulation tasks including realistic image synthesis [34,35], image editing [12,19,22,31], image-to-image translations [14,17,26,38], etc.

Although GANs also show higher performance with a larger number of input data just like any deep-learning models [4,24,36], some versions of GANs shown outstanding performances with very limited data [11,25,29,33]. These researches mainly focus on modifying networks.

Increasing the amount of industrial data using GANs would help us developing machine vision inspection systems. In this article, artificial sealing images are generated using three GANs - DCGAN (Deep Convolutional GAN) [26], SinGAN [29], and BEGAN (Boundary Equilibrium GAN) [2] and the input data is a small number of sealing images. We will evaluate those models by FID (Fréchet Inception Distance) and SIFID (Single Image FID) [13,29]. This research will provide a guide to use GANs to supplement datasets not only for industrial sites but also for many cases with a lack of training data.

2   Methods

It is not easy to obtain images from industrial sites with different light conditions and camera positions. Therefore, the goal is developing a deep learning model to augment learning data with a stable performance using GANs. In this research, three GANs - DCGAN, BEGAN, and SinGAN - are used to generate sealing images from a few input images, and compared in an aspect of the quality of the generated images. Modifications of Inception Score (IS) [28] are used to evaluate the performance of the generated images using each network of three GANs. The Fréchet Inception Distance (FID) [13] is calculated for evaluating images from DCGAN and BEGAN, and SIFID [29] is used for images from SinGAN.

2.1   Generative Adversarial Networks

DCGAN. The DCGAN (Deep Convolutional GAN) first succeeded in constructing images using CNN. Moreover, its process is stable. Consequently, many recent researchers compare their model based on it [1,16]. The DCGAN achieved its goal by adopting some changes to CNN architectures: no pooling layer, no fully-connected layer and applying batch normalization which is newly demonstrated in those days. These techniques helped a stable procedure. The discriminator distinguished real and fake images by a classifier on the convolutional features, while the generator up-sampled images by transpose convolutional layers (Fig. 1).

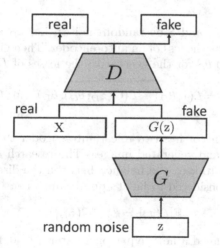

Fig. 1. DCGAN generator [26]. A uniform distribution z is projected into a spatial convolutional representation with many feature maps, resulting in a higher dimension 64×64 pixel image through four fractionally-strided convolution layers.

BEGAN. It is a variation of EBGAN (Energy-based GAN) [37] which first built a discriminator with an auto-encoder. The two models ultimately try to match auto-encoder loss distributions of real and fake. BEGAN (Boundary Equilibrium GAN) is different from its predecessor in that it measures the gap between the two-loss distributions using the Wasserstein distance (Fig. 2).

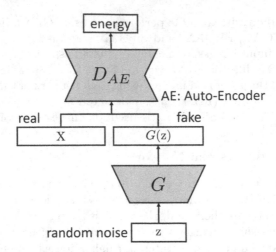

Fig. 2. BEGAN's architecture for the generator and discriminator [2]. The 3×3 convolutions with exponential linear units (ELUs) are applied to each layer. The convolution filters increase linearly with each down-sampling. At the boundary between the encoder and the decoder, the tensors of the processed data are mapped through fully-connected layers.

Let x be real images and z be random noises. Let z_D and z_G are random samples from z. Let $\mathcal{L}$ be the loss of an auto-encoder. Then given a parameter θ_D for a discriminator and θ_G for the generator, the losses of D and G are defined as

$$\begin{cases} \mathcal{L}_D = \mathcal{L}(x; \theta_D) - \mathcal{L}(G(z_D; \theta_G); \theta_D) & \text{for } \theta_D \\ \mathcal{L}_G = -\mathcal{L}_D & \text{for } \theta_G \end{cases} \tag{1}$$

Note that the discriminator has two roles: auto-encoder the real data and distinguish between real and generated images. The research also suggests a new formula of equilibrium to keep the balance between the discriminator and generator. D and G are considered to be at equilibrium when

$$\mathbb{E}[\mathcal{L}(x)] = \mathbb{E}[\mathcal{L}(G(z))] \tag{2}$$

The researchers defined a new hyper-parameter $\gamma \in [0, 1]$ to relax the equilibrium and called it the diversity ratio. The parameter allows us to adjust the two tasks of the discriminator.

$$\gamma = \frac{\mathbb{E}[\mathcal{L}(x)]}{\mathbb{E}[\mathcal{L}(G(z))]} \tag{3}$$

Consequently, the overall objective of BEGAN is:

$$\begin{cases} \mathcal{L}_D = \mathcal{L}(x) - k_t \cdot \mathcal{L}(G(z_D)) & \text{for } \theta_D \\ \mathcal{L}_G = \mathcal{L}(G(z_G)) & \text{for } \theta_G \\ k_{t+1} = k_t + \lambda_k(\gamma \mathcal{L}(x) - \mathcal{L}(G(z_G))) & \text{for each training step } t \end{cases} \tag{4}$$

where λ_k is a learning rate for k.

The BEGAN has an advantage of its simpler architecture relative to former GANs. It avoids conventional GANs tricks such as batch normalization or trans-pose convolution. Also, we do not have to train D and G alternately. Furthermore, it converges fast and stably using its convergence measure:

$$\mathcal{M}_{global} = \mathcal{L}(x) + |\gamma\mathcal{L}(x) - \mathcal{L}(G(z_G))| \tag{5}$$

SinGAN. This method uses the internal statistics of a single training image to learn an unconditional generative model. To do this, it captures global properties such as the arrangement and shape of objects in the image, as well as fine details and texture information.

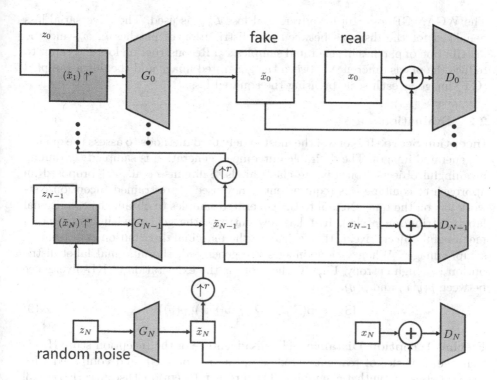

Fig. 3. SinGAN's multi-scale pipeline. Architecture consists of a pyramid of GANs, where both training and inference are done in a coarse-to-fine fashion.

As shown in Fig. 3, this model has a pyramid structure, where x_0 is a training image, down-sampling by a factor $r^n (r > 1)$ as step by step. At each scale, the generator combines noise and the resulting image from the previous step, and the discriminator at the current step is trained to distinguish the down-sampled real image. The generator sequentially constructs images from the coarsest scale to the finest scale and the noise is added at every scale. At the coarsest scale, the generation is purely generative, i.e. G_N maps spatial white Gaussian noise z_N to an image sample $\tilde{x}_N$,

$$\tilde{x}_N = G_N(z_N). \tag{6}$$

Each generator G_n at the finder scales ($n < N$) adds details that are not generated by the previous scales. So, in addition to spatial noise z_n, each generator G_n accepts an up-sampled version of an image at the coarser scale,

$$\tilde{x}_n = G_n(z_n, (\tilde{x}_{n+1}) \uparrow^r), \quad n < N. \tag{7}$$

Learning is similar to learn traditional GANs. Training loss for nth GAN consists of adversarial term and a reconstruction term,

$$\min_{G_n} \max_{D_n} \mathcal{L}_{adv}(G_n, D_n) + \alpha \mathcal{L}_{rec}(G_n). \tag{8}$$

The WGAN-GP loss [10] for adversarial loss $\mathcal{L}_{adv}$ is used. The adversarial loss penalized for the distance between the distribution of patches in x_n and the distribution of patches in generated samples $\tilde{x}_n$. Reconstruction loss $\mathcal{L}_{rec}$ aims to reduce the pixels difference between the generated image and the down-sampled (GT) image at each scale by using the squared loss.

2.2 Evaluation

Inception Score. It is one of the most widely used methods to assess the quality of generated images. The desirable outcome of generation is sampled containing meaningful objects from diverse class labels. Salimans et al. [28] proposed an approach to combine this requirement. They used a pre-trained Inception Network [30] on the ImageNet [5] to the generated samples to obtain the conditional label distribution $p(y|x)$. If it has low entropy, the generated images contain meaningful objects. Next, they calculate the marginal distribution $p(y)$ from all sample images. When various images are generated, the marginal label distribution has high entropy. Finally, the score is the expectation of KL-divergence between $p(y|x)$ and $p(y)$.

$$\text{IS} = \exp(\mathbb{E}_{x \sim p_q} D_{KL}(p(y|x)\|p(y))) \tag{9}$$

Fréchet Inception Distance. The disadvantage of the Inception score (IS) is that the statistics of real generated samples are not used, and compared with the statistics of synthetic samples. The Fréchet Inception Distance (FID) [13] proposed to improve on the IS. It is a metric for evaluating GANs measures the deviation between deep features of the generated images and that of the real samples. The FID score is then calculated using the following equation:

$$\text{FID}^2 = \|\mu_r - \mu_g\|^2 + Tr(\Sigma_r + \Sigma_g - 2(\Sigma_r \Sigma_g)^{1/2}), \tag{10}$$

where μ_r and μ_g refer to the feature-wise mean of the real and generated images. The Σ_r and Σ_g are the covariance matrix for the real and generated feature vectors. $X_r \sim \mathcal{N}(\mu_r, \Sigma_r)$ and $X_g \sim \mathcal{N}(\mu_g, \Sigma_g)$ are the 2048-dimensional activation of the Inception Network pool3 layer for real and generated samples respectively.

Single Image Fréchet Inception Distance. Shaham et al. [29] proposed the Single Image FID (SIFID) metric. Instead of using the activation vector after the last pooling layer in the Inception Network, they use the internal distribution of deep features at the output of the convolutional layer just before the second pooling layer. SIFID is the FID between the statistics of those features in the real image and the generated sample.

3   Results and Discussion

We use 40 real sealing images obtained from an automotive manufacturing plant to generate artificial sealing images using three GANs – DCGAN, BEGAN, and SinGAN.

Fig. 4. Representative images of the real sealing images. A sealing gun (a green arrow) is moved from left to right direction, and the sealant (a blue arrow) is loaded on the surface. Each image size is 658 × 490. (Color figure online)

Figure 4 shows 6 representative images of the real sealing images. A sealing gun (green arrow) is moved from left to right, and the sealant (blue arrow) is loaded on the surface with a shape of continuously linked circles. Since a camera is attached to above of the sealing gun, various types of sealing images are obtained by the angles between the sealant loaded material and the sealing gun. While the gun is moving, the shapes of sealant in images are maintained, but the illumination of images is affected by the angles of sealing gun, light changes, the angle changes of input light, etc.

Figure 5 shows the result of generated image using DCGAN. For the DCGAN, we resize the generated images into the 229 × 229. In Fig. 5, some of the sealant shows vague boundaries, and most of the backgrounds are not clear. In this case, the performance of classification with generated images can be debased, and it

Fig. 5. Samples of the generated images using DCGAN.

could lead to the low performance of the inspection system using deep-learning. On the other hand, the generated images using DCGAN reflect the patterns of the input images and maintain the diversity of the real images. Among 16 images in Fig. 5, 9 images show the sealant is loaded from the left-up to the right-down, and the other 7 images present the sealant is laid in a horizontal direction from left to right.

In Fig. 6, the result of BEGAN is likely to be mode collapse. It is one of the problems with GANs that has not been solved yet. For example, when input image distributions show 0 to 9, generated images also required to have the same distribution as the input images. However, the mode collapse generates only one of the easiest numbers, such as 1, from the training data due to the model sinks into only one mode. Although various input images are used, the results seem to produce almost on an image. When mode collapse occurs, the variety of generated images is not enough, but the quality of a single image itself can be quite good.

For SinGAN, we set the minimal dimension at the coarsest scale to 25px and chose the number of scales N s.t. the scaling factor r is as close as possible to 4/3. We resize the training image to maximal dimension 250px. The generated images are not resized from the real images. We resize the training image to maximal dimension 250px. The generated images are not resized from the real

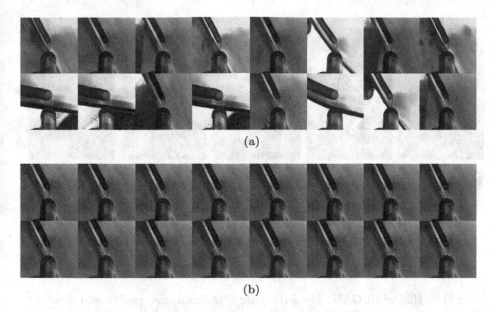

(a)

(b)

Fig. 6. The samples for BEGAN. (a) Randomly selected input images. (b) Generated images using BEGAN.

images. Figure 7 shows a sample of the generated image using SinGAN. SinGAN generates one artificial image from only one input image, and the three right columns are random samples and the left-most column shows input images in Fig. 7. SinGAN can be trained to capture the internal distribution of patches within an image and then generate a variety of high-quality samples that deliver the same visual content as the image [29]. Thus, when images are generated using SinGAN from three different input images, high-quality images are obtained by image distribution of input images.

For quantifying the performances of each GANs with the limited images, the qualities of the generated images are evaluated. The FID and SIFID are used for comparing the performances of three GANs. To compute the FID and SIFID scores, we use the Inception model of pre-trained on ImageNet.

Table 1. Fréchet Inception Distance (FID). Smaller is better.

Methods	Epoch/Iteration	Noise	Best FID	Image size
DCGAN	300 (epoch)	Gaussian	52.27	658×490
BEGAN	100,000 (iter)	Uniform	169.97	128×128

Table 1 shows the FID scores of DCGAN and BEGAN. The lower value of the FID score means the better image quality, and the FID score of DCGAN is

Input images   **Random Samples**

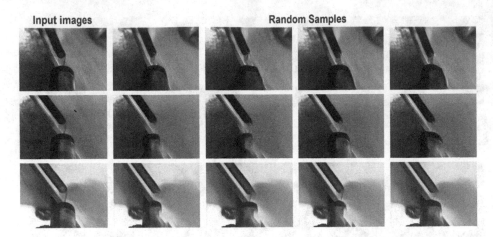

Fig. 7. Samples of the generated images using SinGAN.

lower than that of BEGAN. The FID score contains image quality and diversity. Generated images by DCGAN have lower quality than real images, but reflect the diversity of real images, and show relatively low FID score. On the other hand, obtained images by BEGAN show a similar image quality to real images with a sufficient number of iterations but lose the diversity due to the mode collapse. As a result, it is assumed that they show higher FID score even with the high quality images.

The SinGAN is a network that generates images using the internal distribution of the input images. With its pyramid structure, the inputs in each level are affected by the previous level. Inference at N scale means generation from noise, and inference at $N-1$ scale means down-sampling of the input image and putting it as the input of the $N-1$ generator. An image with a shape and array similar to the input image is created at scale N. Consequently, the larger scale leads to the better quality of the images. As shown in Table 2, the average SIFID is lower for generation from scale $N-1$ than for generation from scale N. It means the image quality of $N-1$ is better than that of N, although the difference is small.

Table 2. Single Image FID (SIFID) for SinGAN.

Scale	SIFID
N	0.1750302
N − 1	0.1750298

In fact, this method has several drawbacks to compare GANs for generating sealing images with very limited input images. Firstly, one uniformed system is not used to evaluate three GANs, and the direct comparison of them is not possible. DCGAN and BEGAN are compared with FID scores, and SinGAN is evaluated with SIFID. Also, the evaluation methods possess limitations. An evaluation method for GANs has been controversial. A verified system for evaluating generated images dose not exist yet. In this situation, modified inception scores are the most commonly used evaluating methods, but they need to be used with more than 5 thousand images from ImageNet. However, generating images with very limited industrial data is meaningful in academically and industrially. Moreover, the direct comparison of FID scores between DCGAN and BEGAN provides the significant information of the image quality and diversity for generating images using GANs to develop the machine vision inspection system.

While maintaining high-quality images, providing diversity to artificial sealing image using illumination changes can be tried as further work. In case of sealing images, variations among obtained images are very small. However, illumination condition can be changes, and especially, illumination changes make significant impact to images. Using the Lambertian properties [18] which give same amount of light to an observer at any angle, a surface brightness can be controlled by altering a surface slope. This can be applied to an input of a generation network for the sealing image generation by illumination changes. Then, image quality will be maintained and a robust model will be obtained against the mode collapse [23].

4 Conclusion

This paper present a comparative study of the performance of GANs for small-scale data. In qualitative results, SinGAN and BEGAN results are better than DCGAN. In the case of BEGAN, however, only one type of sample is generated due to mode collapse. In order to solve this problem, we expect to add more optical conditions such as Lambertian's law in the future to generate more diverse samples using the input of the generator. In quantitative evaluation, DCGAN, the basic form of GANs, is the best. In the case of SinGAN, a new image can be generated from a single image, but it can be found that it is not easy to apply in the industrial sites. It is not easy to evaluate because there is no standardized method of evaluating the results of GANs. A quantitative evaluation method for GANs is needed for further research. We use only three kinds of GANs for comparing the result by the effects of limited data. It is not enough to compare the effects of GANs. Our future work will be compared to the results by adding more GANs methods such as Transferring-Gans [33], DeLiGAN [11], StyleGAN [15], LSGAN [21], WGAN-GP [10], BigGAN [4], etc.

Acknowledgement. This work was supported by the Technology development Program (S2760246) funded by the Ministry of SMEs and Startups (MSS, Korea).

References

1. Arjovsky, M., Chintala, S., Bottou, L.: Wasserstein GAN (2017). arXiv:1701.07875
2. Berthelot, D., Schumm, T., Metz, L.: BEGAN: Boundary Equilibrium Generative Adversarial Networks (2017). arXiv:1703.10717
3. Beyerer, J., Puente León, F., Frese, C.: Machine Vision: Automated Visual Inspection: Theory, Practice and Applications. Springer, Heidelberg (2016). https://doi.org/10.1007/978-3-662-47794-6
4. Brock, A., Donahue, J., Simonyan, K.: Large Scale GAN Training for High Fidelity Natural Image Synthesis (2018). arXiv:1809.11096
5. Deng, J., Dong, W., Socher, R., Li, L.J., Li, K., Fei-Fei, L.: ImageNet: a large-scale hierarchical image database. In: IEEE Conference on Computer Vision and Pattern Recognition (CVPR), pp. 248–255, June 2009
6. Everingham, M., Eslami, S.M.A., Van Gool, L., Williams, C.K.I., Winn, J., Zisserman, A.: The pascal visual object classes challenge: a retrospective. Int. J. Comput. Vision (IJCV) **111**(1), 98–136 (2015)
7. Gauen, K., et al.: Comparison of visual datasets for machine learning. In: IEEE International Conference on Information Reuse and Integration (IRI), pp. 346–355, August 2017
8. Goodfellow, I., Bengio, Y., Courville, A.: Deep Learning. MIT Press, Cambridge (2016)
9. Goodfellow, I., et al.: Generative adversarial nets. In: Advances in Neural Information Processing Systems (NIPS), pp. 2672–2680 (2014)
10. Gulrajani, I., Ahmed, F., Arjovsky, M., Dumoulin, V., Courville, A.C.: Improved training of Wasserstein GANs. In: Advances in Neural Information Processing Systems (NIPS), pp. 5767–5777 (2017)
11. Gurumurthy, S., Sarvadevabhatla, R.K., Babu, R.V.: DeLiGAN: generative adversarial networks for diverse and limited data. In: IEEE Conference on Computer Vision and Pattern Recognition (CVPR), pp. 4941–4949, July 2017
12. He, K., Sun, J.: Statistics of patch offsets for image completion. In: Fitzgibbon, A., Lazebnik, S., Perona, P., Sato, Y., Schmid, C. (eds.) ECCV 2012, Part II. LNCS, pp. 16–29. Springer, Heidelberg (2012). https://doi.org/10.1007/978-3-642-33709-3_2
13. Heusel, M., Ramsauer, H., Unterthiner, T., Nessler, B., Hochreiter, S.: GANs trained by a two time-scale update rule converge to a local Nash equilibrium. In: Advances in Neural Information Processing Systems (NIPS), pp. 6626–6637 (2017)
14. Isola, P., Zhu, J., Zhou, T., Efros, A.A.: Image-to-image translation with conditional adversarial networks. In: IEEE Conference on Computer Vision and Pattern Recognition (CVPR), pp. 5967–5976, July 2017
15. Karras, T., Laine, S., Aila, T.: A style-based generator architecture for generative adversarial networks. In: IEEE/CVF Conference on Computer Vision and Pattern Recognition (CVPR), pp. 4396–4405, June 2019
16. Karras, T., Aila, T., Laine, S., Lehtinen, J.: Progressive Growing of GANs for Improved Quality, Stability, and Variation (2017). arXiv:1710.10196
17. Karras, T., Laine, S., Aila, T.: A Style-Based Generator Architecture for Generative Adversarial Networks (2018). arXiv:1812.04948
18. Koppal, S.J.: Lambertian Reflectance, pp. 441–443. Springer, Boston (2014). https://doi.org/10.1007/978-0-387-31439-6

19. Lempitsky, V., Vedaldi, A., Ulyanov, D.: Deep image prior. In: IEEE/CVF Conference on Computer Vision and Pattern Recognition (CVPR), pp. 9446–9454, June 2018
20. Lin, T.Y., et al.: Microsoft coco: common objects in context (2014). arXiv:14 05.0312
21. Mao, X., Li, Q., Xie, H., Lau, R.Y.K., Wang, Z., Smolley, S.P.: Least squares generative adversarial networks. In: IEEE International Conference on Computer Vision (ICCV), pp. 2813–2821, October 2017
22. Mechrez, R., Shechtman, E., Zelnik-Manor, L.: Saliency driven image manipulation. In: IEEE Winter Conference on Applications of Computer Vision (WACV), pp. 1368–1376, March 2018
23. Metz, L., Poole, B., Pfau, D., Sohl-Dickstein, J.: Unrolled Generative Adversarial Networks (2016). arXiv:1611.02163
24. Miyato, T., Kataoka, T., Koyama, M., Yoshida, Y.: Spectral Normalization for Generative Adversarial Networks (2018). arXiv:1802.05957
25. Osokin, A., Chessel, A., Salas, R.E.C., Vaggi, F.: GANs for Biological Image Synthesis (2017). arXiv:1708.04692
26. Radford, A., Metz, L., Chintala, S.: Unsupervised Representation Learning with Deep Convolutional Generative Adversarial Networks (2015). arXiv:1511.06434
27. Roh, Y., Heo, G., Whang, S.E.: A Survey on Data Collection for Machine Learning: a Big Data - AI Integration Perspective (2018). arXiv:1811.03402
28. Salimans, T., et al.: Improved techniques for training GANs. In: Lee, D.D., Sugiyama, M., Luxburg, U.V., Guyon, I., Garnett, R. (eds.) Advances in Neural Information Processing Systems 29, pp. 2234–2242 (2016)
29. Shaham, T.R., Dekel, T., Michaeli, T.: SinGAN: learning a generative model from a single natural image. In: IEEE International Conference on Computer Vision (ICCV), pp. 4570–4580 (2019)
30. Szegedy, C., et al.: Going deeper with convolutions. In: IEEE Conference on Computer Vision and Pattern Recognition (CVPR), pp. 1–9, June 2015
31. Cho, T.S., Butman, M., Avidan, S., Freeman, W.T.: The patch transform and its applications to image editing. In: IEEE Conference on Computer Vision and Pattern Recognition (CVPR), pp. 1–8, June 2008
32. Turhan, C.G., Bilge, H.S.: Recent trends in deep generative models: a review. In: International Conference on Computer Science and Engineering (UBMK), pp. 574–579, September 2018
33. Wang, Y., Wu, C., Herranz, L., van de Weijer, J., Gonzalez-Garcia, A., Raducanu, B.: Transferring GANs: generating images from limited data. In: European Conference on Computer Vision (ECCV), pp. 220–236 (2018)
34. Zhang, H., et al.: StackGAN: text to photo-realistic image synthesis with stacked generative adversarial networks. In: IEEE International Conference on Computer Vision (ICCV), pp. 5908–5916, October 2017
35. Zhang, H., et al.: StackGAN++: realistic image synthesis with stacked generative adversarial networks. IEEE Trans. Pattern Anal. Mach. Intell. 41(8), 1947–1962 (2019)
36. Zhang, H., Goodfellow, I., Metaxas, D., Odena, A.: Self-Attention Generative Adversarial Networks (2018). arXiv:1805.08318
37. Zhao, J., Mathieu, M., LeCun, Y.: Energy-based Generative Adversarial Network (2016). arXiv:1609.03126
38. Zhu, J., Park, T., Isola, P., Efros, A.A.: Unpaired image-to-image translation using cycle-consistent adversarial networks. In: IEEE International Conference on Computer Vision (ICCV), pp. 2242–2251, October 2017

Consistency Ensured Bi-directional GAN for Anomaly Detection

Kyosuke Komoto[✉], Hiroaki Aizawa, and Kunihito Kato

Gifu University, 1-1, Yanagido, Gifu 501-1193, Japan
komoto@cv.info.gifu-u.ac.jp

Abstract. Anomaly detection is a challenging and fundamental issue in computer vision tasks. In recent years, GAN (Generative Adversarial Networks) based anomaly detection methods have achieved remarkable results. But the instability of training of GAN could be considered that decreases the anomaly detection score. In particular, Bi-directional GAN has the following two causes that make the training difficult: the lack of consistency of the mutual mapping between the image space and the latent space, and the difficulty in conditioning by the latent variables of the image. Here we propose a novel GAN-based anomaly detection model. In our model, we introduce the consistency loss for ensuring mutual mappings. Further, we propose introducing the projection discriminator as an alternative of concatenating discriminator in order to perform efficient conditioning in the Bi-directional GAN model. In experiments, we evaluate the effectiveness of our model in a simple dataset and real-world setting dataset and confirmed that our model outperforms the conventional anomaly detection methods.

Keywords: Anomaly detection · Generative Adversarial Networks · Projection discriminator

1 Introduction

Anomaly detection is one of the most important issues in many situations and hence has been studied in a broad range of fields including industry, fraud detection and medical applications [1]. However, in actual anomaly detection situations, adequate anomalous data samples are often difficult to obtain since they rarely tend to appear as compared to normal samples of which a lot exist. Moreover, innumerable anomalous patterns make it impossible to define and engineer anomalous features. Because of these kinds of reasons, using a supervised machine learning method is extremely limited for anomaly detection. Therefore, anomaly detection in real-world settings needs to model the distribution of normal data for anomaly detection in an unsupervised manner without abnormal data.

Generative Adversarial Networks (GAN) [2] is one of the generative models consisting of two neural networks: the generator and the discriminator. The generator learns to generate realistic images for fooling the discriminator, whereas the discriminator tries to discriminate between real images and generated images. The generator trained with an adversarial manner allows us to generate images that appear like real images. In

© Springer Nature Singapore Pte Ltd. 2020
W. Ohyama and S. K. Jung (Eds.): IW-FCV 2020, CCIS 1212, pp. 236–247, 2020.
https://doi.org/10.1007/978-981-15-4818-5_18

other words, GAN has succeeded in modeling complex and high-dimensional data such as images [3]. Some anomaly detection methods using GAN have been proposed that model normal data distribution using this characteristic of GAN [4]. However, GAN is widely known to be difficult to train and unstable [5]. According to this reason, instability could decrease the accuracy of the GAN-based anomaly detection method. In this work, we introduced a restriction in order to ensure consistency in the image space and the latent space in Bi-directional GAN (Bi-GAN) based anomaly detection method [6]. Further, we propose using the projection discriminator [7] in Bi-GAN model for combining an image and a latent vector. Therefore, it has made it possible to stabilize the training of Bi-GAN, which has resulted in highly accurate anomaly detection. In the experiment, we show the effectiveness of our model by using two types of datasets.

2 Related Work

GAN-Based Anomaly Detection. GAN is one of the generative models which is leaned in an adversarial manner. The Generator G is trained for the purpose of acquiring the data distribution. On the other hand, The Discriminator D estimates the probability that sample data is the training data $x \sim p_{data}$ or random noise vecto $z \sim p_z$. Then, GAN has succeeded to acquire the data distribution that expresses training data. The training objective of GAN is expressed:

$$\min_G \max_D V(D, G) = \mathbb{E}_{x \sim p_{data}}\big[\log D(x)\big] + \mathbb{E}_{z \sim p_z}[\log(1 - D(G(z)))] \tag{1}$$

Schlegl et al. proposed AnoGAN [8] that is the first method exploiting GAN's capacity to modeling complex and high-dimensional data. In this method, GAN is trained only normal data, and then mapping from the latent space to the image space is learned. Anomaly detection is performed using the assumption that normal images used for the training of GAN have a corresponding latent variable but an abnormal image does not have a corresponding latent variable. In the inference phase, AnoGAN requires the process of searching a latent variable corresponding to a target image, but GAN learned the mapping from the latent space to the image space and its inverse mapping is undefinable. Therefore, Schlegl et al. approximate the inverse mapping using the generator and the discriminator with the stochastic gradient descent manner. Its approximation is conducted by minimizing following equations for $\gamma = 1, 2, ..., \Gamma$ steps.

$$L_r(z_\gamma) = \big\| x - G(z_\gamma) \big\|_1 \tag{2}$$

$$L_D(z_\gamma) = \| f(x) - f(G(z)) \|_1 \tag{3}$$

Equation 2 is called Residual Loss and it minimizes the difference in image space. On the other hand, Eq. 3 is the feature-matching loss [9] in consideration of the Discriminator and minimizes the difference in the feature space. Function f denotes the output of the intermediate layer of the discriminator. Hence, the approximation minimizes

$$L(z_\gamma) = (1 - \lambda) \cdot L_R(z_\gamma) + \lambda \cdot L_D(z_\gamma), \tag{4}$$

where λ is weighting parameters between the Residual Loss and the feature-matching loss. Finally, the anomaly score is defined as:

$$A_{AnoGAN}(x) = (1 - \lambda) \cdot L_R(x) + \lambda \cdot L_D(x). \tag{5}$$

However, AnoGAN enables highly accurate abnormality detection, but the approximation requires optimization using multiple times of backpropagation in every single target image inference. Thus, inference in AnoGAN is tremendously time-consuming and is impractical. To solve this problem, some methods are proposed. Schlegl et al. also proposed to train an Encoder that maps image space to latent space using the generator and the discriminator trained with GAN [10].

Bi-directional GAN-Based Anomaly Detection. Zenati et al. proposed Efficient GAN-Based Anomaly Detection (EGBAD) [6] which is based on Bi-directional GAN (Bi-GAN) [11] intending to solve the time-consuming problem. Bi-GAN learns the mapping of the latent space to the image space the same as vanilla GAN, and learns the mapping from the image space to the latent space simultaneously by training an encoder in the adversarial training. Bi-GAN consists of 3 sub-networks: the Encoder E, the Generator G and the Discriminator D. Bi-GAN training objective is expressed as:

$$\min_{G,E} \max_{D} V(D, G, E) = \mathbb{E}_{x \sim p_{data(x)}}[\mathbb{E}_{z \sim p_{E(z|x)}}[\log(x, E(x))]]$$
$$+ \mathbb{E}_{z \sim p_{data(z)}}[\mathbb{E}_{x \sim p_{G(x|z)}}[\log(1 - D(G(z), z))]] \tag{6}$$

By training Bi-GAN using only normal data, we obtained the Generator and the Encoder that can perform the mutual mapping between image space and latent space according to the distribution of normal data. The Anomaly score is similar to AnoGAN and is computed by residual loss and the discrimination loss. The residual loss is:

$$L_R(x) = \|x - G(E(x))\|_1. \tag{7}$$

The discrimination loss is defined in 2 ways. The first is the feature-matching loss and defined as:

$$L_{Df}(x) = \|f(x, E(x)) - f(G(E(x)), E(x)\|_1. \tag{8}$$

The second uses cross-entropy loss, which is the probability that the Discriminator identifies the image as a real image and is defined as:

$$L_{D\sigma}(x) = \sigma(D(x, E(x)), 1), \tag{9}$$

where σ denotes the cross-entropy loss function.

The Anomaly score in EGBAD is defined as:

$$A_{EGBAD}(x) = (1 - \lambda) \cdot L_R(x) + \lambda \cdot L_D(x). \tag{10}$$

Owing to the simultaneous training of the Encoder, the time required in inference is greatly decreased.

Our model is based on Bi-GAN architecture. However, in contrast to original Bi-GAN architecture, our model has an additional Encoder and Generator module. These modules allow us to ensure the consistency of mutual mapping between image space and latent space. In addition to this, our model has the Projection Discriminator which enables us to efficient integration of an image and a latent variable. Figure 1 shows the comparison of AnoGAN, EGBAD and our model.

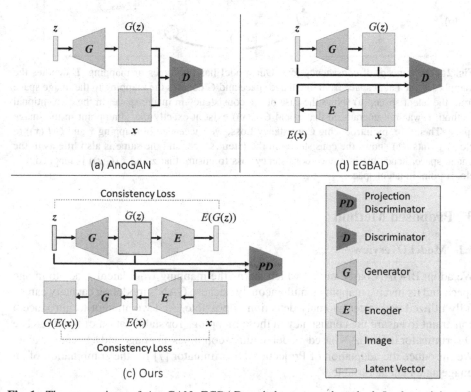

Fig. 1. The comparison of AnoGAN, EGBAD and the proposed method. In the training of AnoGAN, the Encoder that maps from images to latent variables is not trained. EGBAD and our model train the Encoder at the same time as adversarial learning. Moreover, our model has another Encoder and Generator in order to ensure the consistency of mappings.

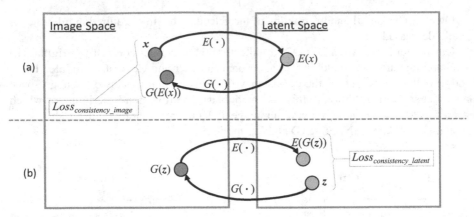

Fig. 2. The concept of consistency loss. Our model has two types of mapping: E denotes the mapping to the latent space from the image space and G denotes the mapping to the image space from the latent space. (a) shows the case of the consistency in image space. In the conventional method, it was not guaranteed that x and $G(E(x))$ exist at exactly the same point in the image space. Therefore, by introducing Consistency Loss, we succeeded in mapping x and $G(E(x))$ to closer points. (b) shows the consistency in the latent space, and the same is also true as in the image space, hence we introduce consistency loss to ensure that z and $E(G(z))$ is mapped to a closer point in latent space.

3   Proposed Method

3.1   Model Overview

We adopt Bi-GAN based model which learns the mapping from latent space to image space and its inverse mapping simultaneously because GAN's modeling capacity can be fully utilized and faster anomaly detection is possible. And we attempt to introduce a constraint to ensure the consistency in these mappings for stabilization of training. The Discriminator in Bi-GAN based model requires combines an image and a latent variable. We introduce the adaptation of Projection Discriminator [7] for the combination of an image and a latent variable.

3.2   Consistency of Mappings Between Image Space and Latent Space

Our model has Bi-GAN based architecture which learns mappings from the image space and the latent space and its inverse mapping simultaneously. However, if the network model has a large capacity, learning by Adversarial training does not guarantee the consistency of the mapping [12]. In other words, if an image maps from image space to latent space and back again, there is no guarantee that the acquired image will be the same as the first image. Especially in GAN-based anomaly detection methods utilizing reconstruction error to compute the anomaly score, it is considered that this is a factor that greatly reduces the accuracy in abnormality detection using Bi-GAN. And the same situation could happen when a latent variable map from latent space to image space and back again. Thereby, here we introduce the Consistency Loss. Our consistency loss has 2 types of consistency in image space and consistency in latent space and is defined as:

$$Loss_{consistency\_image} = \mathbb{E}_{x \sim P_x} \|x - G(E(x))\|_1,$$ (11)

$$Loss_{consistency\_latnet} = \mathbb{E}_{z \sim P_z} \|z - E(G(z))\|_1.$$ (12)

Figure 2 shows the conceptual image of our consistency loss. In our model, the Encoder and the Generator minimize the consistency loss and the adversarial loss simultaneously, which enables the model to learn mutual mappings between the image space and the latent space in consideration of the consistency.

3.3 Conditioning of Image with Latent Variables in Bi-GAN Architecture

Miyato et al. propose projection discriminator [7] for conditioning class labels to images for conditional image generation tasks. Introducing projection discriminator can be enabled to generate more precise images compared to the traditional method that conditions class labels to images by concatenating [13] and the method of inferring class labels at the output layer of discriminator [14]. Teterwak et al. succeeded in conditioning semantic information in an image expansion task by introducing a projection discriminator [15]. Thus, from these studies, it is assumed that the projection discriminator is effective for conditioning images. As regards Bi-GAN, the discriminator adopts simple channel-wise concatenate for conditioning images. In our studies, we introduce a

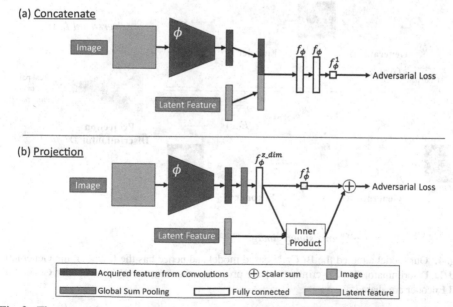

Fig. 3. The comparison of sample concatenate and projection. (a) shows traditional concatenate method which concatenates acquired feature maps and a latent variable in channel-wise. (b) shows the procedure for integrating feature maps and a latent variable by projection manner in our model.

projection discriminator for the integration of images and latent variables. We try to stabilize the training of Bi-GAN, to improve the quality of generated images and hence improve the accuracy of anomaly detection task. In our model, the output $D(x, z)$ of the Discriminator when integrating the image x and the latent variable z using the projection is shown as follows:

$$D(x, z) = f_\phi^1(f_\phi^{z\_dim}(\text{GSP}(\phi(x)))) + < f_\phi^{z\_dim}(\text{GSP}(\phi(x))), z >, \quad (13)$$

Where ϕ is convolution operations in the Discriminator and $\phi(x)$ is feature maps acquired from the Discriminator with input image x. f_ϕ^n denotes a fully connected layer with n dimensions and z_dim is the dimension of a latent variable. $< \cdot >$ is the inner product of two vectors and GSP($\cdot$) denotes Global Sum Pooling [16]. Figure 3 shows the comparison of simple concatenate and projection. Some traditional research using projection discriminator adopts an embedding layer but we do not adopt it, because latent variables to condition images are continuous values in our model.

3.4 Model Training

Algorithm 1 shows the training procedure for our model and Fig. 4 shows the overview of our model.

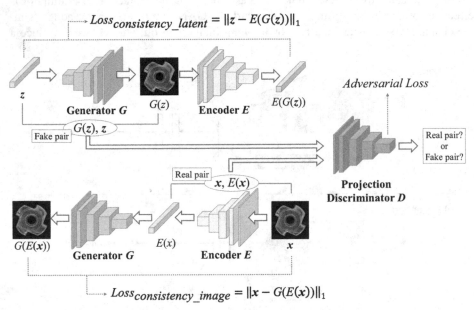

Fig. 4. Our model adopted the Bi-GAN based model and hence has the Encoder, the Generator and the Discriminator. The Discriminator has a projection mechanism. Weights of each Generator and Encoder are shared.

Our model is trained in an adversarial manner. The basic training procedure follows Bi-GAN. Additionally, the Encoder and the Generator in our model are trained by minimizing consistency loss. In our experiments, we set $\alpha = 0.9$ which weighs consistency loss and adversarial loss.

Algorithm 1 Training procedure of the proposed model

Input:
   Encoder E, Generator G, Discriminator D with parameters $\theta_E, \theta_G, \theta_D$
   batch size M, weighting parameters α
   Initialize parameters $\theta_E, \theta_G, \theta_D$.

Repeat:
   · Sample minibatch of M images from data distribution p_x
   $$x^{(1)} \cdots x^{(M)} \sim p_x$$
   · Sample minibatch of M noise samples from noise prior p_z
   $$z^{(1)} \cdots z^{(M)} \sim p_z$$
   · Generate images and latent vectors with the Encoder and the Generator
   $$\tilde{z}^{(i)} \leftarrow E(x^{(i)}), \quad i = 1, \ldots, M$$
   $$\tilde{x}^{(i)} \leftarrow G(z^{(i)}), \quad i = 1, \ldots, M$$
   $$\hat{x}^{(i)} \leftarrow G(\tilde{z}^{(i)}), \quad i = 1, \ldots, M$$
   $$\hat{z}^{(i)} \leftarrow E(\tilde{x}^{(i)}), \quad i = 1, \ldots, M$$
   · Compute gradient for the Encoder and the Generator
   $$L_{consistency} \leftarrow \frac{1}{M} \sum_{i=1}^{M} \left\| x^{(i)} - \hat{x}^{(i)} \right\|_1 + \frac{1}{M} \sum_{i=1}^{M} \left\| z^{(i)} - \hat{z}^{(i)} \right\|_1$$
   $$L_{adversarial} \leftarrow -\frac{1}{M} \sum_{i=1}^{M} \log(D(x^{(i)}, \tilde{z}^{(i)})) - \frac{1}{M} \sum_{i=1}^{M} \log(1 - D(\tilde{x}^{(i)}, z^{(i)}))$$
   $$L_{Encoder} \leftarrow \alpha L_{consistency} + (1-\alpha) L_{adversarial}$$
   $$L_{Generator} \leftarrow \alpha L_{consistency} + (1-\alpha) L_{adversarial}$$
   · Compute gradient for the Discriminator
   $$L_D \leftarrow -\frac{1}{M} \sum_{i=1}^{M} \log(D(\tilde{x}^{(i)}, z^{(i)})) - \frac{1}{M} \sum_{i=1}^{M} \log(1 - D(x^{(i)}, \tilde{z}^{(i)}))$$
   · Update weights of the Encoder, the Generator and the Discriminator
   $$\theta_E \leftarrow \theta_E - \nabla_E L_E$$
   $$\theta_G \leftarrow \theta_G - \nabla_G L_G$$
   $$\theta_D \leftarrow \theta_D - \nabla_D L_D$$

Until convergence

3.5 Anomaly Score

Our model computes the anomaly score using trained Generator, Encoder and Discriminator. Anomaly score is defined by residual loss L_R and feature-matching loss L_D which considers intermediate output f of the Discriminator.

$$L_R(x) = \| x - G(E(x)) \|_1 \tag{14}$$

$$L_D(x) = \| f(x) - f(G(x, E(x))) \|_1 \qquad (15)$$

Finally, the anomaly score in our model is defined as:

$$A(x) = (1 - \lambda) \cdot L_R(x) + \lambda \cdot L_D(x). \qquad (16)$$

As regards abnormal image x, $L_R(x)$ becomes larger because the Encoder is not able to acquire corresponding latent variables. For this reason, the Generator cannot reconstruct the image, and the reconstructed image differs from the original input image. Similarly, $L_D(x)$ increases for abnormal images in comparison using the feature-matching. Accordingly, $A(x)$ is expected to be large for abnormal images.

4 Experiments

We use 2 types of the dataset to evaluate our model: simple dataset MNIST and real-world setting dataset MVTec Anomaly Detection Dataset [17]. To compare traditional anomaly detection methods, we conducted the experiments using AutoEncoder [18], AnoGAN [8], EGBAD [6] and our model. All models are evaluated using the area under the receiver operating characteristic curve (AUROC).

In our model, the Encoder, the Generator and the Discriminator are optimized with Adam optimizer [19] with an initial learning rate $lr = 1\mathrm{e}{-4}$, and momentums $\beta1 = 0.9$, $\beta2 = 0.999$ and are applied Batch Normalization [20] for all convolution layers. Spectral Normalization [21] is applied to convolutional layers of the Discriminator to prevent anomaly detection accuracy from decreasing due to learning instability.

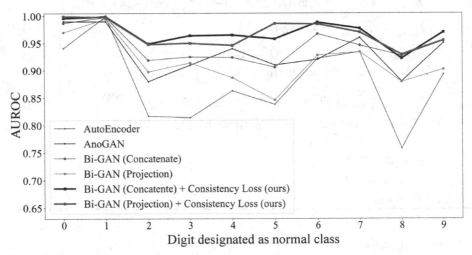

Fig. 5. The result of experiments using MNIST dataset. Each column indicates the digit that is designated as normal digits. The score of AnoGAN is obtained from [22].

4.1 MNIST Dataset

The MNIST dataset contains handwritten digit images 0 to 9. We made 10 different datasets from MNIST dataset by designating one digit as a normal class and other digits as an abnormal class. We used only normal data for training in all models and tested them with both normal and abnormal images. Figure 5 shows the result of the experiments. In experiments using MNIST, all of the methods work well. However, our models that introduce both concatenate and projection outperform other methods.

4.2 MVTec Anomaly Detection Dataset

In order to evaluate anomaly detection in real-world settings dataset, we used the Metal Nut dataset in MVTec Anomaly Detection Dataset [17]. Metal Nut dataset has normal images for training and both normal and abnormal images for testing. Table 1 shows the result of anomaly detection experiments. Our model using projection results in a better score than the model using concatenate and this implies that adopting projection discriminator is effective for anomaly detection in real-world setting datasets.

Table 1. The result of anomaly detection experiments using the Metal Nut dataset. In this table, the score of AnoGAN is obtained from [17].

Model	AUROC
AutoEncoder	0.63
AnoGAN	0.76
Bi-directional GAN (Concatenate) (EGBAD)	0.78
Bi-directional GAN (Projection)	0.77
Bi-directional GAN (Concatenate) + Consistency Loss (ours)	0.79
Bi-directional GAN (Projection) + Consistency Loss (ours)	**0.84**

Figure 6 shows test images x and their reconstructed images $G(E(x))$ of our model using projection discriminator. Regarding normal images, the Encoder is able to acquire latent variables corresponding to images. Therefore, the Generator is possible to reconstruct original test images from the latent variables. However, regarding abnormal images, the Generator cannot reconstruct original test images because the Encoder fails to acquire latent variables corresponding to images.

Normal Samples   Abnormal Samples

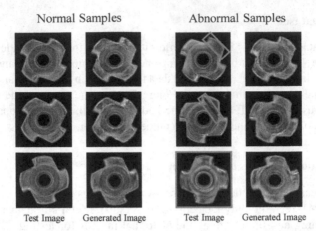

Test Image   Generated Image   Test Image   Generated Image

Fig. 6. Visualization of test images and generated images of normal samples and abnormal samples with anomalies highlighted in red rectangles. However our model succeeded to generate normal images, our model fails to generate abnormal samples. (Color figure online)

5 Conclusion

We proposed a novel anomaly detection model based on Bi-directional GAN. We have the following two main contributions. First, we focused on the fact that mutual mapping between the image space and the latent space was not guaranteed in the anomaly detection method using Bi-GAN. Hence to solve this important problem, we introduce consistency loss. Second, we introduce the projection discriminator for Bi-directional GAN model to integrate images and the corresponding latent variables, which allows improvement of the quality of reconstruction and anomaly detection with high accuracy. In the experiment, we compared our model to conventional anomaly detection methods: AutoEncoder, AnoGAN and EGBAD by using MNIST dataset and the Metal Nut dataset. We confirmed that our model is able to detect anomalies and outperform conventional methods.

Acknowledgments. This work has received funding from Human resource development and research project on production technology for aerospace industry: Subsidy from Gifu Prefecture.

References

1. Chalapathy, R., Chawla, S.: Deep learning for anomaly detection: a survey. arXiv preprint arXiv:1901.03407 (2019)
2. Goodfellow, I., et al.: Generative adversarial nets. In: Advances in Neural Information Processing Systems, pp. 2672–2680 (2016)
3. Radford, A., Metz, L., Chintala, S.: Unsupervised Representation Learning with Deep Convolutional Generative Adversarial Networks. In: International Conference on Learning Representations, Workshop (2016)
4. Di Mattia, F., Galeone, P., De Simoni, M., Ghelfi, E.: A survey on GANs for anomaly detection. arXiv preprint arXiv:1906.11632 (2019)

5. Wiatrak, M., Albrecht, Stefano, V.: Stabilizing generative adversarial network training: a survey. arXiv preprint arXiv:1910.00927 (2019)
6. Zenati, H., Foo, C.S., Lecouat, B., Manek, G., Chandrasekhar, V.R.: Efficient GAN-based anomaly detection. In: International Conference on Learning Representations, Workshop (2018)
7. Miyato, T., Koyama, M.: cGANs with projection discriminator. In: International Conference on Learning Representations (2018)
8. Schlegl, T., Seeböck, P., Waldstein, S.M., Schmidt-Erfurth, U., Langs, G.: Unsupervised anomaly detection with generative adversarial networks to guide marker discovery. In: Niethammer, M., et al. (eds.) IPMI 2017. LNCS, vol. 10265, pp. 146–157. Springer, Cham (2017). https://doi.org/10.1007/978-3-319-59050-9_12
9. Salimans, T., Goodfellow, I., Zaremba, W., Cheung, V., Radford, A., Chen, X.: Improved techniques for training GANs. In: Advances in Neural Information Processing Systems, pp. 2234–2242 (2016)
10. Schlegl, T., Seeböck, P., Waldstein, S.M., Langs, G., Schmidt-Erfurth, U.: f-AnoGAN: fast unsupervised anomaly detection with Generative Adversarial Networks. Med. Image Anal. **54**, 30–44 (2019)
11. Donahue, J., Krähenbühl, P., Darrell, T.: Adversarial feature learning. In: International Conference on Learning Representations (2017)
12. Zhu, J.Y., Park, T., Isola, P., Efros, A.A.: Unpaired image-to-image translation using cycle-consistent adversarial networks. In: Proceedings of the IEEE International Conference on Computer Vision, pp. 2223–2232 (2017)
13. Mirza, M., Osindero, S.: Conditional generative adversarial nets. arXiv preprint arXiv:1411. 1784 (2014)
14. Odena, A., Olah, C., Shlens, J.: Conditional image synthesis with auxiliary classifier GANs. In: Proceedings of the 34th International Conference on Machine Learning, vol. 70, pp. 2642–2651 (2017)
15. Teterwak, P., et al.: Boundless: Generative Adversarial Networks for image extension. In Proceedings of the IEEE International Conference on Computer Vision, pp. 10521–10530 (2019)
16. Aich, S., Stavness, I.: Global sum pooling: a generalization trick for object counting with small datasets of large images. In: Proceedings of the IEEE Conference on Computer Vision and Pattern Recognition Workshops, pp. 73–82 (2019)
17. Bergmann, P., Fauser, M., Sattlegger, D., Steger, C.: MVTec AD–A comprehensive real-world dataset for unsupervised anomaly detection. In: Proceedings of the IEEE Conference on Computer Vision and Pattern Recognition, pp. 9592–9600 (2019)
18. Hinton, G.E., Salakhutdinov, R.R.: Reducing the dimensionality of data with neural networks. Science **313**(5786), 504–507 (2006)
19. Kingma, D.P., Ba, J.: Adam: a method for stochastic optimization. In: International Conference on Learning Representations (2015)
20. Ioffe, S., Szegedy, C.: Batch normalization: accelerating deep network training by reducing internal covariate shift. In: Proceedings of the 32nd International Conference on Machine Learning, vol. 37, pp. 448–456 (2015)
21. Miyato, T., Kataoka, T., Koyama, M., Yoshida, Y.: Spectral normalization for Generative Adversarial Networks. In: International Conference on Learning Representations (2018)
22. Huang, C., Cao, J., Ye, F., Li, M., Zhang, Y., Lu, C.: Inverse-transform autoencoder for anomaly detection. arXiv preprint arXiv:1911.10676 (2019)

Unsupervised Adversarial Learning for Dynamic Background Modeling

Maryam Sultana[1], Arif Mahmood[2], Thierry Bouwmans[3], and Soon Ki Jung[1(✉)]

[1] School of Computer Science and Engineering, Kyungpook National University, Daegu, South Korea
maryam@vr.knu.ac.kr, skjung@knu.ac.kr
[2] Department of Computer Science, Information Technology University (ITU), Lahore, Pakistan
arif.mahmood@itu.edu.pk
[3] Laboratoire MIA, Universite deLaRochelle, LaRochelle, France
thierry.bouwmans@univ-lr.fr

Abstract. Dynamic Background Modeling (DBM) is a crucial task in many computer vision based applications such as human activity analysis, traffic monitoring, surveillance, and security. DBM is extremely challenging in scenarios like illumination changes, camouflage, intermittent object motion or shadows. In this study, we proposed an end-to-end framework based on Generative Adversarial Network, which can generate dynamic background information for the task of DBM in an unsupervised manner. Our proposed model can handle the problem of DBM in the presence of the challenges mentioned above by generating data similar to the desired information. The primary aim of our proposed model during training is to learn all the dynamic changes in a scene-specific background information. While, during testing, inverse mapping of data to latent space representation in our model generates dynamic backgrounds similar to test data. The comparative analysis of our proposed model upon experimental evaluations on SBM.net and SBI benchmark datasets has outperformed eight existing methods for DBM in many challenging scenarios.

Keywords: Background initialization · Generative Adversarial Networks · Unsupervised learning

1 Introduction

The Background initialization, background modeling or background subtraction with a fixed camera pose have been the most active research topics over the last two decades in the field of computer vision for many applications like industrial machine vision [4,25], human activity analysis [32], video surveillance [27,36], security [19] and traffic monitoring [2]. This fundamental operation of isolating

W. Ohyama and S. K. Jung (Eds.): IW-FCV 2020, CCIS 1212, pp. 248–261, 2020.
https://doi.org/10.1007/978-981-15-4818-5_19

moving pixels called 'foreground' from static or moving regions called 'background' is formally known as Dynamic Background Modeling (DBM). The task of DBM is interrelated means with prior knowledge of background information, it is convenient to achieve foreground segmentation and vice versa. However, DBM could be extremely challenging in complex scenes like illumination changes, camouflage, camera jitters and intermittent object motion.

Conventional methods for DBM are mainly Robust Principle Component Analysis (RPCA) [9,13,14,16,37] based methods. These approaches work on the principle of decomposing the input data matrix into two entities, low-rank and sparse components ($X = B + F$). In this formulation the low-rank matrix B corresponds to background initialization while the sparse component F is foreground segmentation. Until now a tremendous amount of study has been conducted on RPCA based methods [4,28] to handle different challenging conditions in DBM. Alot of success is also achieved to handle complex challenging scenarios for DBM by RPCA based methods but on the cost of being partially online and high computational complexity. On the contrary deep learning based methods have also shown significantly high performance to handle DBM in the presence of various challenging conditions [18,21,24,26,33]. These methods directly learn features with the help of Convolutional Neural Network (CNN) to model high-dimensional input data to a class label. However, recently deep learning based models in an adversarial fashion have been introduced in the area of DBM by considering this task as a segmentation problem rather than a classification one based on supervised learning [3,35]. Although GAN based methods for DBM have shown high performance but unsupervised DBM is currently an open challenging problem.

Therefore, in this study, we aim to propose an end-to-end framework generating dynamic background information for the task of DBM in an unsupervised manner. To address the problem of DBM in the presence of challenges like illumination changes, camouflage, bootstrapping, we present a model based on Generative Adversarial Network (GAN) [11]. The primary aim of our proposed model is background initialization by GAN, we call it 'BI-GAN'. The training of BI-GAN is similar to unsupervised adversarial learning mechanism; nonetheless, during testing, the crucial task is how to determine that the generated data from the trained GAN model is similar to the desired information? Therefore, our proposed BI-GAN has two constraints, ensuring that the generated dynamic background is similar to the test data. Restricting the generator network of BI-GAN to a particular number of back-propagation steps and analyzing the role of discriminator network as a decision maker, we achieve dynamic background initialization. The motivation and contribution of this study is summarized as follows:

- In this study, we proposed a scene-specific end-to-end framework for DBM in an unsupervised manner.
- We incorporated the role of discriminator network during testing process as a decision making entity in the GAN framework for efficient dynamic background initialization.

- Our experimental evaluation on SBM.net and SBI benchmark datasets provide the comparative analysis of our proposed BI-GAN with eight existing methods to handle DBM in the presence of various challenging conditions.

The rest of the paper is organized as follows: Sect. 2 discusses the details of state-of-the-art-methods handling DBM. In Sect. 3 we provide a brief explanation of our proposed BI-GAN. Section 4 is about details on the implementation of the BI-GAN, Sect. 5 is about experimental evaluations of BI-GAN on SBM.net benchmark dataset, and at the end, we concluded our study in Sect. 6.

2   Related Work

DBM is diverse in context to its applications in the field of computer vision therefore, a lot of research study has been conducted on this topic over the last two decades.

Classical Methods to handle DBM in challenging scenarios are either subspace learning based or RPCA based [6,7,20]. For instance Wright *et al.* [29] proposed the first idea of RPCA method, which can handle various outliers in the input data matrix and later Candes *et al.* [8] applied RPCA for DBM which showed high performance. After that many studies have been conducted by acquiring basic RPCA framework and updating it with spatio-temporal constraints [15,16]. Despite significant high performance of the subspace learning and RPCA based methods, high computational complexity and data processing in batch formulation makes them unsuitable for real-time applications.

To overcome the batch constraint of RPCA-based methods Xu *et al.* [30] presented a method called *Grassmannian Online Subspace Updates with Structured-sparsity* (GOSUS). Although this method performs well for background estimation problems, global optimality remains a challenging issue in this approach. Zhao *et al.* [34] presented a method called *Bayesian Robust Tensor Factorization for Incomplete Multiway Data* (BRTF). This method is a generative model for robust tensor factorization in the presence of missing data and outliers. Guo *et al.* [12] presented a method called *Robust Foreground Detection Using Smoothness and Arbitrariness Constraints* (RFSA). In this method, the authors considered the smoothness and arbitrariness of a static background, thus formulating the problem in a unified framework from a probabilistic perspective.

Deep Learning Methods currently are very popular to handle DBM challenging scenarios [1,5,18] by using CNN models. For instance [1] explored DBM as a classification problem to achieve foreground segmentation by computing probability of foreground for each pixel on a pre-trained CNN. Nonetheless, more recently, GANs have been introduced in the area of DBM by addressing the problem of foreground segmentation with prior knowledge of background [35]. Bakkay *et al.* [3] proposed a solution for DBM by using conditional GANs in which generator network learns a mapping from input data along with its background information and ground-truth foreground segmentation mask. On the contrary, deep learning based methods have shown high performance but supervised learning with the huge amount of manually annotated ground-truth information makes it quite challenging in context of training CNN models.

3   Proposed Methodology

This section discusses the details of the proposed methodology. In this study, BI-GAN aims to perform background initialization based on two loss functions using the back-propagation technique for the purpose of DBM. BI-GAN has two stages: (1) Unsupervised training of the BI-GAN with an adversarial loss to learn dynamic changes in background information. (2) Testing of the BI-GAN to achieve dynamic background initialization based on two different loss functions. The objective of BI-GAN is to generate similar information as test data, which leads to background initialization. Following sections contains the details of training and testing of BI-GAN.

3.1   BI-GAN Training

The well-known Generative adversarial networks or GANs [11] are class of generative models based on a competition between a discriminator network D and a generator network G. The generator network G corresponds to a probability distribution $p_{model}(x)$. The sample from this distribution is obtained by applying the generator network G with a random noise z, sampled from p_z and drawn from the uniform distribution. Thus this formulation corresponds to $x = G(z)$ which is the mapping of random noise sample z to a $2d$ image representation, which should be similar to input training data x. However, the objective of the discriminator network is to distinguish that whether input given to it belongs to real training x or fake data $G(z)$ generated by the generator network. Thus the goal of the training process is to recover the actual distribution p_{data} that generated the original data.

For the training of BI-GAN we have exploited Non-Saturating GAN in our framework rather than minimax GAN because non-saturating GANs are applicable to problems that cannot be fitted by Jensen-Shannon divergence minimization [10].

Non-saturating GANS: In the original formulation of GAN presented by Goodfellow *et al.* [11], the discriminator's output is a probability that whether the input given to it is drawn from real training samples or fake data generated by the generator. Mathematically the cost function for the discriminator is specified as the negative log-likelihood of the binary classification task for discriminator network to decide that samples are real or fake:

$$S^{(D)}(D, G) = - \mathbb{E}_{x \sim p_{data}}[log(D(x))] - \mathbb{E}_{z \sim p_z(z)}[log(1 - D(G(z)))]. \tag{1}$$

Nonetheless, the postulatory analysis given by Goodfellow *et al.* as mentioned in [11] refers GANs to work on the principle of the zero-sum game, also known as "minimax GANs" as shown in Eq. (2). The term 'minimax' corresponds to the idea that a GAN should minimize the probability of a generator to generate fake data and maximize the probability of discriminator to identify fake samples correctly. Although, practically, it is recommended [10] to implement an alternative approach for cost function that generated samples should own a high probability of being real samples, by minimizing an alternative objective (3) for generator network.

$$S^{(G)}(G) = \mathbb{E}_{z \sim p_z(z)} \, log[1 - D(G(z))]. \tag{2}$$

$$S^{(G)}(G) = -\mathbb{E}_{z \sim p_z(z)} \, log \, D(G(z)). \tag{3}$$

The alternative objective mentioned in Eq. (3) is referred as non-saturating, because of the non-saturating behavior of the gradients during the training process [10]. As mentioned in [11], whenever discriminator network D can successfully minimize $S^{(D)}$ optimally, maximizing $S^{(D)}$ with respect to the generator network is, in fact, equivalent to minimizing the Jensen-Shannon divergence. This observation leads to establish the fact that there is a unique Nash equilibrium in function space which corresponds to $p_{data} = p_{model}$ [11]. Thus during the training process, the generator network tries to generate realistic fake samples; however, the discriminator network tries to identify fake and real samples. After training of non-saturating GAN model, the next stage is to test the model by generating desired information based on the back-propagation technique for background initialization. The following section discusses the testing of BI-GAN in detail.

3.2   BI-GAN Testing

As explained in the previous section that during the training of non-saturating GAN, the aim of the generator network G is to learn the mapping from $1d$ random noise samples z drawn from uniform distribution to a $2d$ image representation i.e $G(z) = z \mapsto x$. Nonetheless inverse mapping of random noise samples to original data i.e $\Psi(x) = x \mapsto z$ in GAN can not be achieved directly. The importance of inverse mapping of test data is, we need desired information to be generated by the generator network G which has similar statistics as test data. In order to achieve inverse mapping, back-propagation is exploited by using loss functions, on discriminator network so that our generator network can generate similar information as test data [31]. The details of the loss functions are as follows:

Background Initialization Losses: For given test data x^i our aim is to find a random noise sample z in the latent space representation which was used in training to generate $G(z)$ having similar statistics as x^i. In order to find that specific noise sample z, we randomly initialize the generator network G with z^0 to generate a $2d$ image sample $G(z^0)$ as shown in Fig. 1. It is not necessarily the case that the first generated image sample $G(z^0)$ is exactly similar as test data, this leads to an idea that our generator should generate several samples which matches best with test data. For this purpose we minimize a norm based distance $N(z^\theta, x^i)$ between the generated image and test image in an iterative fashion. The noise vector z is adapted to the given test image such that the generated image matches best to test image.

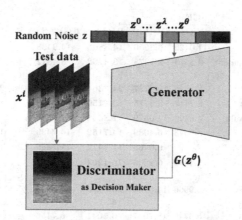

Fig. 1. BI-GAN framework generating background information by discriminator network as a decision maker during testing.

The second loss function we exploited is on our discriminator network for the generation of samples similar as the test data is to use it as a decision maker [31]. Since the purpose of discriminator network is to penalizes unrealistic images generated by generator therefore using discriminator as a decision making entity forces the generator network to generate similar information as test data as shown in Fig. 1. As discriminator network's purpose here is now similar to training, so we use adversarial loss function:

$$D(z^\theta) = log(1 - D(G(z^\theta))). \tag{4}$$

The final loss term can be represented as the sum of discriminator loss with norm based distance measure which is as follows:

$$\Psi(z^\theta, x^i) = (1 - \kappa)D(z^\theta) + \kappa N(z^\theta, x^i). \tag{5}$$

where κ is a relative weight factor to balance the two loss terms.

4   Implementation of BI-GAN

Our proposed BI-GAN is inspired by [22] where generator network G generates a $64 \times 64 \times 3$ image by taking a random noise vector z of 100 dimension from uniform distribution fixed between $[-1, 1]$. The discriminator network D takes an input of dimension $64 \times 64 \times 3$ and downsample it using five convolutional layers with an output layer, of two class softmax. The training of BI-GAN is done with augmented data by using translation and rotation and Adam optimization [17] with a learning rate of 0.0002. The back-propagation steps is set as $\theta = 3000$.

Table 1. BI-GAN AGE scores estimated on SBM.net dataset and compared with five existing methods for background initialization. The best AGE scores for each video sequence is shown in blue, and the best average AGE score for each category is shown in red.

Category	Videos	AGE ↓					
		BI-GAN	DCP [26]	RFSA [12]	GRASTA [13]	BRTF [34]	GOSUS [30]
Background motion	Canoe	11.0422	6.3250	14.8805	14.9438	14.8798	14.9677
	Advertisement board	4.5574	2.3378	3.4762	3.4812	3.4640	3.4733
	Fall	8.8745	19.0737	24.3364	24.6026	24.4283	24.5935
	Fountain 01	8.7117	9.6775	5.7150	5.7539	5.7383	5.7750
	Fountain 02	4.0120	14.0579	7.3288	7.0811	7.3307	7.0867
	Overpass	8.9543	6.4089	14.7162	14.7489	14.7183	14.7614
	Average AGE	7.6920	9.6468	11.7422	11.7686	11.7599	12.1183
Illumination changes	Camera parameter	7.4353	6.2206	75.1204	6.1471	6.1126	6.1389
	Dataset3 camera1	5.9966	14.5708	23.3046	22.0816	22.5116	22.0816
	Dataset3 camera2	5.5740	18.7047	6.5041	5.7156	5.8965	5.7156
	I_IL_01	11.2693	7.4329	8.3048	23.6585	23.5775	23.6585
	I_IL_02	9.9795	19.3833	8.4842	7.5423	7.4007	7.5423
	Cubicle	3.8472	11.4636	26.1490	19.4842	31.2116	19.4842
	Average AGE	7.3503	12.9627	24.6445	14.1049	16.1184	14.1035
Average AGE of categories		7.5211	11.3047	18.1933	12.9367	13.9391	13.1109

5   Experiments

We have evaluated our proposed BI-GAN on two datasets for background initialization, one is benchmark dataset SBM.net[1] and other is scene background initialization (SBI) dataset[2]. We have divided the 70% of total data in training and 30% data in testing for both datasets. The results of BI-GAN for DBM are compared with eight existing methods including DCP [26], GRASTA [13], RFSA [12], BRTF [34], GOSUS [30], MOG2 [38], KNN [39] and BE-AAPSA [23]. For background initialization of BI-GAN on both datasets following metrics are used for the evaluation of the proposed model in comparison with existing methods:

(a) Average Gray Error (AGE),
(b) Percentage of Clustered Error Pixels (pCEPs),
(c) Peak Signal-to-Noise Ratio (PSNR),
(d) Multiscale Structural Similarity Index (MSSSIM),
(e) Percentage of Error Pixels (pEPs) and
(f) Color image Quality Measure (CQM).

---

[1] http://scenebackgroundmodeling.net/.
[2] http://sbmi2015.na.icar.cnr.it/SBIdataset.html.

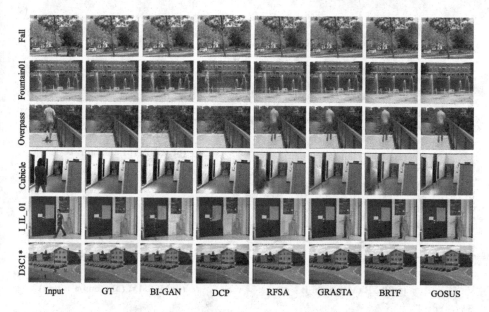

Fig. 2. Qualitative performance comparison of BI-GAN along with ground-truth and five existing methods on SBM.net dataset.

The metrics presented above are given by SBM.net and SBI datasets evaluation criteria for standard and fair assessment of results estimated via DBM algorithms.

5.1 Evaluation of BI-GAN on SBM.net Dataset

We have evaluated our proposed BI-GAN for background initialization on two challenging categories in SBM.net dataset as shown in the Table 1. The categories 'Background Motion' and 'Illumination Changes' is extremely challenging in complex scenes as most of the algorithms works on the assumption that background should be static and foreground should be dynamic. This scenario where background as well as foreground is dynamic pose a great challenge to algorithms with motion constraints only satisfying foreground segmentation thus causing performance degradation for background initialization. Category wise discussion is as follows.

Background Motion category in SBM.net dataset contains six challenging video sequences for the purpose of background estimation as shown in Table 1. All the six video sequences pose plenty of challenges to five existing methods, for instance, it can be seen in the Fig. 2 (row 3, video sequence: Overpass) that except BI-GAN and DCP and the other two compared methods have shown foreground ghosting effects in their background estimation results, thus suffering from performance degradation. Furthermore, quantitative results presented in the Table 1 shows that for category background motion BI-GAN has achieved

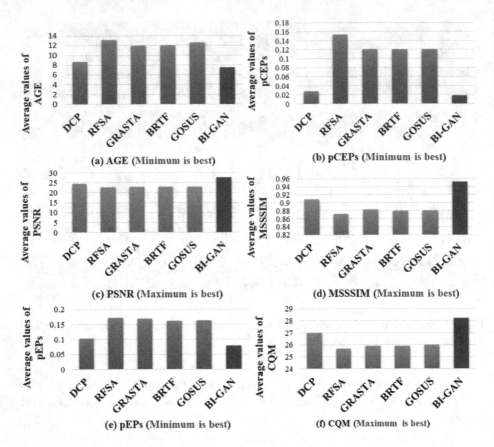

Fig. 3. Average performance comparison of BI-GAN with eight existing methods on six metrics provided by SBM.net dataset.

best average AGE score 7.6920 because discriminator network as a decision maker can identify the best matching information with test data.

Illumination Changes category in SBM.net dataset also contains six challenging video sequences for the purpose of background estimation, as shown in Table 1. Among all six video sequences, four of them have illumination changes in indoor scenes, and two of them contain illumination changes in outdoor scenes. Table 1 clearly shows that upon average, all compared methods are suffering from performance degradation and also visual comparison in Fig. 2 again shows ghosting effects of foreground information. However, our proposed BI-GAN has achieved minimum AGE score as compared to all existing methods in this category too for accurate background estimation.

Average Results obtained on both categories and evaluated by six metrics provided by the SBM.net dataset, we have presented the results in Fig. 3. The minimum AGE score is achieved by our proposed BI-GAN as compared to all the methods presented in Fig. 3 and also for other five metrics such as pCEPS,

PSNR, MSSSIM, pEPs and CQM our BI-GAN have achieved best scores as compared to all five existing methods.

Table 2. The metric scores on six video sequences of SBI dataset by our proposed BI-GAN.

Sequence	AGE ↓	pEPs ↓	pCEPS ↓	MSSSIM ↑	PSNR ↑	CQM ↑
*Candela_m*1.10	4.9075	0.9033	0.0488	0.9800	31.3445	30.5143
CAVIAR1	8.5872	7.0801	0.8057	0.9529	26.2490	25.6144
CAVIAR2	12.7988	13.6963	2.0020	0.9809	24.8151	24.0820
CaVignal	4.5303	2.1484	0.0977	0.9877	30.8977	30.4240
HallAndMonitor	3.9255	0.1709	0.0000	0.9899	34.1297	33.3695
HumanBody2	7.1523	4.1748	0.2930	0.9744	28.7653	27.2292
Average	6.9836	4.6956	0.5412	0.9776	29.3668	28.5389

Table 3. The quantitative comparison of proposed BI-GAN using six metric scores (on average) of SBI dataset with five existing approaches. The best score for each method is shown in red while the second best score is shown in blue color.

Methods	AGE ↓	pEPs ↓	pCEPS ↓	MSSSIM ↑	PSNR ↑	CQM ↑
Mean	14.1944	22.5150	18.4428	0.8737	25.6980	43.5839
Color median	10.3744	13.4008	10.5571	0.8533	28.0044	42.4746
MOG2 [38]	14.3579	4.0847	2.8080	0.8935	25.9576	38.1916
KNN [39]	20.6968	7.5118	4.5180	0.7595	18.4701	26.3836
BE-AAPSA [23]	11.4846	12.5518	10.0605	0.9247	27.8024	41.8124
BI-GAN	6.9836	4.6956	0.5412	0.9776	29.3668	28.5389

5.2 Evaluation of BI-GAN on SBI Dataset

We have evaluated our proposed BI-GAN on six video sequences of scene background initialization (SBI) dataset [6] including *Candela_m*1.10, CAVIAR1, CAVIAR2, CaVignal, HallAndMonitor and HumanBody2. Table 2 shows the results of all six metrics on each video sequence while Table 3 shows the quantitative results comparison with five existing methods. On average our proposed BI-GAN has achieved best score for AGE (6.9836) score while Color Median approach has achieved second best score (10.3744). For the metric percentage of error pixels (pEPs) MOG2 method has achieved best score (4.0847) while KNN method has achieved second best score (7.5118). Nonetheless our proposed BI-GAN has also obtain better score (7.8369) with a minimal difference. In the case of percentage of clustered error pixels (pCEPS) and multi scale structural similarity index (MSSSIM) again our proposed BI-GAN has achieved best scores (0.7772) and (0.9672) respectively. On the other hand MOG2 and BE-AAPSA

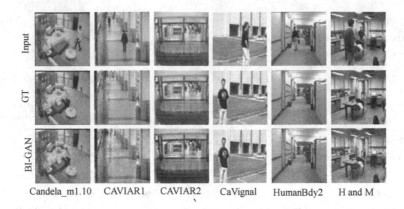

Candela_m1.10 CAVIAR1 CAVIAR2 CaVignal HumanBdy2 H and M

Fig. 4. Qualitative performance comparison of BI-GAN along with ground-truth for background initialization on SBI dataset.

has achieved second best scores (2.8080 and 0.9247) for these metrics. For the last metric which is color quality measure (CQM) Temporal mean has achieved best score (43.5839) and Color Median approach has achieved second best score (42.4746) while our proposed BI-GAN has shown performance degradation. The reason behind this fact is sometimes the generated images from our model contains foreground objects along with background information which effects CQM of background information. The qualitative results of SBI in comparison with ground-truth is presented in Fig. 4.

5.3 Failure Cases

Although BI-GAN achieved the best performance in most of the experiments for background initialization however, it has some failure cases. For instance, the visual results presented in Fig. 5, category 'illumination changes' from SBM.net dataset our proposed BI-GAN have shown performance degradation. The reason behind this fact is sometimes because of high empirical value of back-propagation steps our proposed BI-GAN generate information containing foreground rather than true background.

Input   BI-GAN   GT

Fig. 5. Qualitative performance comparison of BI-GAN along with ground-truth for background initialization on SBM.net dataset.

6   Conclusion

In this study, we proposed an end-to-end framework based on Generative Adversarial Network or GAN, which can generate dynamic background information for the task of DBM in an unsupervised manner. Our proposed model BI-GAN addresses the problem of DBM in the presence of challenges like illumination changes, camouflage, and dynamic background. The training of BI-GAN is conventional unsupervised adversarial learning mechanism; however, during testing, the task of our model is to generate data similar to the desired information by two constraints. The comparative evaluation of BI-GAN on SBM.net and SBI benchmark datasets provides the evidence that our proposed method has significantly high performance for accurate DBM.

Acknowledgements. This research was supported by Development project of leading technology for future vehicle of the business of Daegu metropolitan city (No. 20171105).

Also this study was supported by the BK21 Plus project (SW Human Resource Development Program for Supporting Smart Life) funded by the Ministry of Education, School of Computer Science and Engineering, Kyungpook National University, Korea (21A20131600005).

References

1. Babaee, M., Dinh, D.T., Rigoll, G.: A deep convolutional neural network for video sequence background subtraction. Pattern Recogn. **76**, 635–649 (2018)
2. Baber, C., Morar, N.S., McCabe, F.: Ecological interface design, the proximity compatibility principle, and automation reliability in road traffic management. IEEE Trans. Hum.-Mach. Syst. **49**, 241–249 (2019)
3. Bakkay, M., Rashwan, H., Salmane, H., Khoudour, L., Puigtt, D., Ruichek, Y.: BSCGAN: deep background subtraction with conditional generative adversarial networks. In: 2018 25th IEEE International Conference on Image Processing (ICIP), pp. 4018–4022. IEEE (2018)
4. Bouwmans, T., Garcia-Garcia, B.: Background subtraction in real applications: challenges, current models and future directions. arXiv preprint arXiv:1901.03577 (2019)
5. Bouwmans, T., Javed, S., Sultana, M., Jung, S.K.: Deep neural network concepts for background subtraction: a systematic review and comparative evaluation. arXiv preprint arXiv:1811.05255 (2018)
6. Bouwmans, T., Maddalena, L., Petrosino, A.: Scene background initialization: a taxonomy. Pattern Recogn. Lett. **96**, 3–11 (2017)
7. Bouwmans, T., Zahzah, E.H.: Robust PCA via principal component pursuit: a review for a comparative evaluation in video surveillance. Comput. Vis. Image Underst. **122**, 22–34 (2014)
8. Candès, E.J., Li, X., Ma, Y., Wright, J.: Robust principal component analysis? J. ACM (JACM) **58**(3), 11 (2011)
9. Cao, X., Yang, L., Guo, X.: Total variation regularized RPCA for irregularly moving object detection under dynamic background. IEEE Trans. Cybern. **46**(4), 1014–1027 (2016)

10. Fedus, W., Rosca, M., Lakshminarayanan, B., Dai, A.M., Mohamed, S., Goodfellow, I.J.: Many paths to equilibrium: GANs do not need to decrease a divergence at every step. CoRR abs/1710.08446 (2018)

11. Goodfellow, I., et al.: Generative adversarial nets. In: Advances in Neural Information Processing Systems, pp. 2672–2680 (2014)

12. Guo, X., Wang, X., Yang, L., Cao, X., Ma, Y.: Robust foreground detection using smoothness and arbitrariness constraints. In: Fleet, D., Pajdla, T., Schiele, B., Tuytelaars, T. (eds.) ECCV 2014. LNCS, vol. 8695, pp. 535–550. Springer, Cham (2014). https://doi.org/10.1007/978-3-319-10584-0_35

13. He, J., Balzano, L., Szlam, A.: Incremental gradient on the Grassmannian for online foreground and background separation in subsampled video. In: 2012 IEEE Conference on Computer Vision and Pattern Recognition (CVPR), pp. 1568–1575. IEEE (2012)

14. Javed, S., Bouwmans, T., Sultana, M., Jung, S.K.: Moving object detection on RGB-D videos using graph regularized spatiotemporal RPCA. In: Battiato, S., Farinella, G.M., Leo, M., Gallo, G. (eds.) ICIAP 2017. LNCS, vol. 10590, pp. 230–241. Springer, Cham (2017). https://doi.org/10.1007/978-3-319-70742-6_22

15. Javed, S., Mahmood, A., Bouwmans, T., Jung, S.K.: Background–foreground modeling based on spatiotemporal sparse subspace clustering. IEEE Trans. Image Process. **26**(12), 5840–5854 (2017)

16. Javed, S., Mahmood, A., Bouwmans, T., Jung, S.K.: Spatiotemporal low-rank modeling for complex scene background initialization. IEEE Trans. Circuits Syst. Video Technol. **28**(6), 1315–1329 (2018)

17. Kingma, D.P., Ba, J.: Adam: a method for stochastic optimization. arXiv preprint arXiv:1412.6980 (2014)

18. Laugraud, B., Piérard, S., Droogenbroeck, M.V.: LaBGen-P-semantic: a first step for leveraging semantic segmentation in background generation. J. Imaging **4**, 86 (2018)

19. Mabrouk, A.B., Zagrouba, E.: Abnormal behavior recognition for intelligent video surveillance systems: a review. Expert Syst. Appl. **91**, 480–491 (2018)

20. Maddalena, L., Petrosino, A.: Towards benchmarking scene background initialization. In: Murino, V., Puppo, E., Sona, D., Cristani, M., Sansone, C. (eds.) ICIAP 2015. LNCS, vol. 9281, pp. 469–476. Springer, Cham (2015). https://doi.org/10.1007/978-3-319-23222-5_57

21. Patil, P., Murala, S.: FgGAN: a cascaded unpaired learning for background estimation and foreground segmentation. In: 2019 IEEE Winter Conference on Applications of Computer Vision (WACV), pp. 1770–1778 (2019)

22. Radford, A., Metz, L., Chintala, S.: Unsupervised representation learning with deep convolutional generative adversarial networks. arXiv preprint arXiv:1511.06434 (2015)

23. Ramirez-Alonso, G., Ramirez-Quintana, J.A., Chacon-Murguia, M.I.: Temporal weighted learning model for background estimation with an automatic reinitialization stage and adaptive parameters update. Pattern Recogn. Lett. **96**, 34–44 (2017)

24. Sakkos, D., Ho, E.S.L., Shum, H.P.H.: Illumination-aware multi-task gans for foreground segmentation. IEEE Access **7**, 10976–10986 (2019)

25. Sharma, L., Lohan, N.: Performance analysis of moving object detection using BGS techniques in visual surveillance. Int. J. Spatio-Temporal Data Sci. **1**(1), 22–53 (2019)

26. Sultana, M., Mahmood, A., Javed, S., Jung, S.K.: Unsupervised deep context prediction for background estimation and foreground segmentation. Mach. Vis. Appl. **30**, 375–395 (2018). https://doi.org/10.1007/s00138-018-0993-0
27. Sultani, W., Chen, C., Shah, M.: Real-world anomaly detection in surveillance videos. In: Proceedings of the IEEE Conference on Computer Vision and Pattern Recognition, pp. 6479–6488 (2018)
28. Vaswani, N., Bouwmans, T., Javed, S., Narayanamurthy, P.: Robust subspace learning: robust PCA, robust subspace tracking, and robust subspace recovery. IEEE Signal Process. Mag. **35**(4), 32–55 (2018)
29. Wright, J., Ganesh, A., Rao, S., Peng, Y., Ma, Y.: Robust principal component analysis: exact recovery of corrupted low-rank matrices via convex optimization. In: Advances in Neural Information Processing Systems, pp. 2080–2088 (2009)
30. Xu, J., Ithapu, V., Mukherjee, L., Rehg, J., Singh, V.: GOSUS: Grassmannian online subspace updates with structured-sparsity. In: ICCV (2013)
31. Yeh, R.A., Chen, C., Lim, T.Y., Schwing, A.G., Hasegawa-Johnson, M., Do, M.N.: Semantic image inpainting with deep generative models. In: Proceedings of the IEEE Conference on Computer Vision and Pattern Recognition, pp. 5485–5493 (2017)
32. Yeung, S., Russakovsky, O., Jin, N., Andriluka, M., Mori, G., Fei-Fei, L.: Every moment counts: dense detailed labeling of actions in complex videos. Int. J. Comput. Vision **126**(2–4), 375–389 (2018)
33. Zhao, C., Cham, T.L., Ren, X., Cai, J., Zhu, H.: Background subtraction based on deep pixel distribution learning. In: 2018 IEEE International Conference on Multimedia and Expo (ICME), pp. 1–6. IEEE (2018)
34. Zhao, Q., Zhou, G., Zhang, L., Cichocki, A., Amari, S.I.: Bayesian robust tensor factorization for incomplete multiway data. IEEE Trans. Neural Netw. Learn. Syst. **27**(4), 736–748 (2016)
35. Zheng, W., Wang, K., Wang, F.: Background subtraction algorithm based on Bayesian generative adversarial networks. Acta Automatica Sinica **44**, 878–890 (2018)
36. Zhou, J.T., Du, J., Zhu, H., Peng, X., Liu, Y., Goh, R.S.M.: AnomalyNet: an anomaly detection network for video surveillance. IEEE Trans. Inf. Forensics Secur. **14**, 2537–2550 (2019)
37. Zhou, X., Yang, C., Yu, W.: Moving object detection by detecting contiguous outliers in the low-rank representation. IEEE T-PAMI **35**(3), 597–610 (2013)
38. Zivkovic, Z.: Improved adaptive Gaussian mixture model for background subtraction. In: Proceedings of the 17th International Conference on Pattern Recognition, ICPR 2004, vol. 2, pp. 28–31. IEEE (2004)
39. Zivkovic, Z., Van Der Heijden, F.: Efficient adaptive density estimation per image pixel for the task of background subtraction. Pattern Recogn. Lett. **27**(7), 773–780 (2006)

Transfer Learning by Cascaded Network to Identify and Classify Lung Nodules for Cancer Detection

Shah B. Shrey[1,2], Lukman Hakim[2], Muthusubash Kavitha[2],
Hae Won Kim[3], and Takio Kurita[2(✉)]

[1] Birla Institute of Technology and Science, Pilani, India
[2] Department of Information Engineering, Hiroshima University,
Higashihiroshima, Japan
tkurita@hiroshima-u.ac.jp
[3] Department of Nuclear Medicine, Keimyung University Dongsan Medical Center,
Daegu, Korea

Abstract. Lung cancer is one of the most deadly diseases in the world.
Detecting such tumors at an early stage can be a tedious task. Existing deep learning architecture for lung nodule identification used complex architecture with large number of parameters. This study developed a cascaded architecture which can accurately segment and classify
the benign or malignant lung nodules on computed tomography (CT)
images. The main contribution of this study is to introduce a segmentation network where the first stage trained on a public data set can help
to recognize the images which included a nodule from any data set by
means of transfer learning. And the segmentation of a nodule improves
the second stage to classify the nodules into benign and malignant. The
proposed architecture outperformed the conventional methods with an
area under curve value of 95.67%. The experimental results showed that
the classification accuracy of 97.96% of our proposed architecture outperformed other simple and complex architectures in classifying lung
nodules for lung cancer detection.

Keywords: Image segmentation · Classification · Cascade network ·
Lung nodule · Deep learning · CT images

1 Introduction

Lung cancer is one of the deadliest cancers in existence. The mortality rate due
to lung cancer is higher than to colorectal, breast, and prostate cancers combined
[1]. Anyone can get lung cancer and approximately 60% to 65% of all new lung
cancer diagnoses are among people who have never smoked or are former smokers
[1–5]. Only 19% of all people diagnosed with lung cancer will survive 5 years or
more, but if it's caught before it spreads, the chance for 5-year survival improves
dramatically [1]. The difficulty in diagnosing the lung cancer arises from the

© Springer Nature Singapore Pte Ltd. 2020
W. Ohyama and S. K. Jung (Eds.): IW-FCV 2020, CCIS 1212, pp. 262–273, 2020.
https://doi.org/10.1007/978-981-15-4818-5_20

fact that it never shows the symptoms in the earlier stages. The fact that early diagnosis can significantly improve the survival rates of the patients makes it a challenging yet important task.

Computed tomography (CT) imaging is one of the most effective and has been widely used for the detection of lung cancers. However, non invasive methods of early stage cancer detection is important [6]. On average the radiologists subjective measurement of lung nodules takes around 2–3.5 min per slice of CT scan and also there can be variations in their judgements [7]. Therefore, an unbiased automatic model which can quickly diagnosing the nodules for lung cancer is an important task. A lot of computer aided techniques have been attempted in the past [8–10] but it is shown clearly that deep learning techniques [11–14] have a significant advantage over the others [15,16]. However, the lack of annotated data makes it challenging to train a deep neural networks due to their dependence on the number of data set. This study proposed to use a U-Net architecture to segment the lung nodules from the CT scan images and thus screen the CT scan slices that are suspicious of having nodules. The model employed the idea of transfer learning by training on publicly available data set and then testing on a private data set. The subsequent part of the paper compared various methods to classify the resulting CT scan images containing nodules into cancerous and non-cancerous. The performance of the proposed encoder followed by fully connected network is compared with the simple fully connected and encode-decoder followed by fully connected network in classifying the lung nodules for lung cancer detection, along with some of the other pre-existing models such as Resnet50, VGG and Densenet.

2   Materials and Methods

We used the existing LUNA data set to train the model for lung nodule segmentation [17]. The data set included 888 CT images. The LIDC/IDRI database also contains annotations which were collected during a two-phase annotation process using four experienced radiologists. Each radiologist marked lesions as

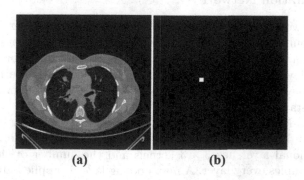

(a)   (b)

Fig. 1. (a) Original CT image, (b) generated ground truth mask.

they identified as non-nodule, nodule <3 mm, and nodules ≥3 mm. The reference standard of our challenge consists of all nodules ≥3 mm accepted by at least 3 out of 4 radiologists. Annotations that are not included in the reference standard (non-nodules, nodules <3 mm, and nodules annotated by only 1 or 2 radiologists) are referred as irrelevant findings. The ground truth mask for each of the cancerous nodules was generated by using the nodule centre and the diameter value of the image pixels indicated in the annotation file. The annotation file is stored as a csv file that contains one finding per line. Each line holds the SeriesInstanceUID of the scan, the world coordinate pixels x, y and z position of each finding and the corresponding diameter in mm. The annotation file contains 1186 nodules. The corresponding nodule centre and diameter value for the image pixels were turned into white and the remaining pixels were turned into black as shown in Fig. 1.

The testing was done on a private data set where the ground truth for segmentation was absent but the label for each patient whether benign or malignant was used. The data set consisted of 102 benign and 102 malignant patients with CT images. The private data set acquired from Keimyung University Dongsan Medical Center, South Korea. Each subject has CT volume and PET volume data set. The CT resolution was 512 × 512 pixels at 0.98 mm × 0.98 mm, with a slice thickness and a inter-slice distance of 3 mm. The PET resolution was 128 × 128 pixels at 2.4 mm × 2.4 mm, with slice thickness and interslice distance of 33 mm.

3   Cascaded Architecture

This study proposed to suggest a cascaded network to segment and classify benign or malignant nodules for the identification of lung cancer. The segmentation network used to recognize the suspected nodules on CT images which are then classified by using classification network into benign or malignant nodules. The proposed cascaded architecture is shown in Fig. 2.

3.1   Segmentation Network

We proposed two-stage lung cancer identification network using CT lung data sets. We used public data set of lung CT slices to train the segmentation network. The lung region slices and their corresponding ground truth for nodules were generated as it was described earlier in the annotation file. We have included the slices between starting and ending slices along with five more slices before and after the starting and ending slice of the ground truth.

A typical U-Net type model [18] was proposed as shown in Fig. 3. For the encoder, we used five convolutional layers, each layer with a ReLU activation. Each convolutional layer has 3 × 3 kernels and the number of channels starts from 64 and doubles every layer. A max pooling layer is applied after every convolution layer that reduces the size of the channel by half. The purpose of using pooling layers is to progressively reduce the spatial size of the representation to

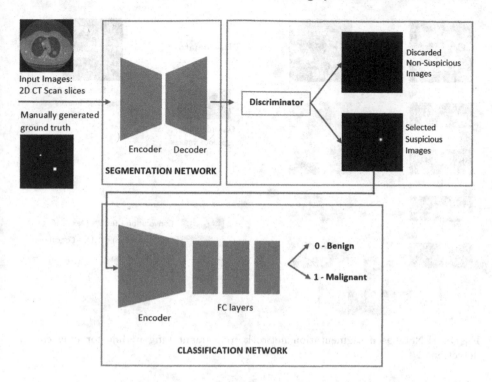

Fig. 2. Proposed cascaded architecture for the identification of lung cancer.

reduce the amount of parameters and computation in the network, and hence to also control over fitting. The Max Pooling Layer operates independently on every depth slice of the input and resizes it spatially, using the MAX operation. A 50% drop out is applied on last two convolutions after applying ReLU activation. ReLU activation function is a piece-wise linear function which prunes the negative part to 0 and retains the positive part. It is much faster as compared to other activation functions due to it's simple max operation. For the decoder, we used four upsampling convolutions layers, each layer followed by ReLU. The output of a upsampling convolution is concatenated with an output of the corresponding part of the decoder. The softmax with the binary cross entropy loss function is calculated for accounting the error value. The receiver operating characteristic curve (ROC) along with the loss variation based on the test data set is presented in Fig. 4.

The segmentation network consists of 2 stages, the first stage is network trained with public dataset to predict the output image pixels y_i from a given input image pixels x_i. So, we can define the loss function on segmentation network L_1 as:

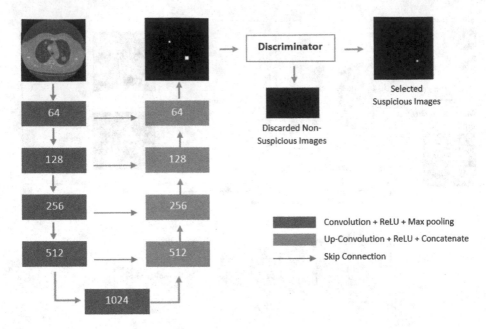

Fig. 3. U-Net based segmentation network to segment lung nodule for lung cancer detection

$$L_1 = \sum_i^M \{t_i log(y_i) + (1 - t_i)log(1 - y_i)\} \tag{1}$$

where $(x_i, t_i)|i = 1, ..., M$, x_i is a ith input data from the training public dataset X, and t_i is a ith from data target or label T of public dataset. The number of training samples and labels is denoted by M and N, respectively.

The second stage is trained network used to predict the nodule segmentation from the private data set. The trained weight of the segmentation network is utilized as a screening network to find the presence of lung nodules on the private lung CT data set.

In the segmentation architecture we used discriminator, that decides whether the segmented image consisted a nodule or not. The objective criterion used in the discriminator was if the maximum value of the pixel values >0.35 then the resultant image contains suspicious nodules, otherwise discarded.

3.2   Classification Network

The images which were suspected to have nodules by the previous stage segmentation network were further used in the classification network for classifying nodules. The images did not include nodules were omitted for training.

The segmented nodule images with their corresponding original CT images and labels indicating whether the nodules are benign or malignant were used as

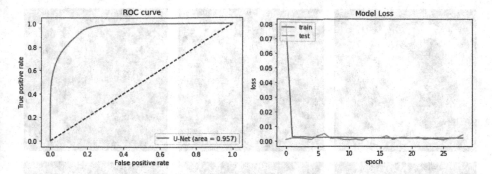

Fig. 4. Performance plot of the lung nodule segmentation. The left and right figures shows the ROC curve and loss variations, respectively for the segmentation network.

input into the coder network for classification. For this task, we define input $\bar{x}_i$ for classification network as:

$$\bar{x}_i = \{\hat{x}_i, \hat{y}_i\} \tag{2}$$

where $(\hat{x}_i \in \hat{X})$ is original image from private dataset and $(\hat{y}_i \in \hat{Y})$ is image with suspicious nodule. The classification network architecture is trained to predict the class labels $\bar{y}_i$ from a given input $\bar{x}_i$. If $(\hat{t}_i \in \hat{T})$ is labels for private dataset, we can define the loss function on classification network L_2 as:

$$L_2 = \sum_i^M \{\hat{t}_i log(\bar{y}_i) + (1 - \hat{t}_i)log(1 - \bar{y}_i)\} \tag{3}$$

The ratio of the benign and malignant nodules is 1:5. Therefore, to increase the number of benign nodules we used thrice the oversampling technique to rectify the data imbalance problem. The encoder with the fully connected layer is developed to classify the nodules for the lung cancer. The proposed classification network is shown in Fig. 6. For the encoder, we used three convolutional layers, each layer with a ReLU activation. Each convolutional layer has 3×3 kernels and the number of channels starts from 8 and doubles every layer. A max pooling layer is applied after every convolution layer that reduces the size of the channel by half. A 50% drop out is applied on last convolution after ReLU activation. Dropout changed the concept of learning all the weights together to learning a fraction of the weights in the network in each training iteration. Dropout is highly effective in reducing over-fitting of the network. It prevents the network from being too reliant on one or a small group of neurons, and can force the network to be more accurate even in the absence of certain information. The output is then flattened and fed into a fully connected layer with 128 nodes. It is transferred to a two node fully connected layer which is used to predict the class of the nodule in one-hot fashion. The loss and accuracy variation of our proposed classification network based on the test data set is shown in Fig. 7.

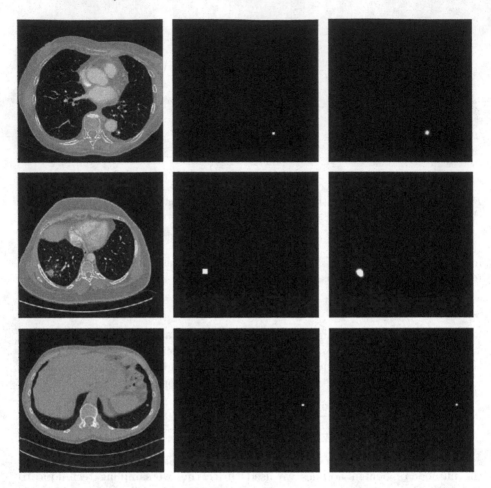

Fig. 5. Segmented results of lung nodules. The left image shows the original CT. The middle image is the ground truth. The right image shows the predicted lung nodule for lung cancer using our segmentation network.

4   Experimental Settings

4.1   Experiment

The U-Net model for segmentation network used train, validation and test data set. Out of 888 CT images, the data set used for train, validation and test is 80%, 5% and 15%, respectively. For segmentation network, we used batches of 16 images and their corresponding ground truth. Adam optimizer with a learning rate of 1e−4 is used. The encoder network for classification used train, validation and test data set. For classification, the data set used for train, validation and test is 60%, 15% and 25%, respectively. We used Adam as an optimizer and

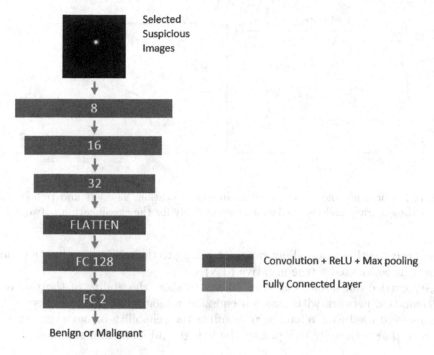

Fig. 6. Encoder based classification network to classify the lung nodules for lung cancer detection

set the learning rate of 1e−4. All networks were implemented using Keras and Tensorflow backend with 4GB memory.

4.2   Evaluation

We evaluated our proposed segmentation network based on U-Net with discriminator and classification network based on encoder with fully connected for the segmentation and classification of two classes of lung nodules on private CT data set. The efficiency of the architecture in predicting the two classes of lung nodules is compared to the ground truth. We compared the performance of our proposed classification network based on encoder with fully connected network with simple fully connected network and encoder and decoder followed by the fully connected layer, along with other pre-existing models like Resnet50, VGG and DenseNet. In the fully connected network the image is flatten and directly fed into the fully connected network layers. The encoder and decoder followed by the fully connected layer network is similar with the segmentation network architecture. All classification networks were trained with a similar hyper-parameter values. The quantitative networks performance was measured using the average value of precision, recall, F1 score and accuracy. If the predicted class region belongs to the valid ground truth region, then it is considered a true positive (TP), otherwise, it is considered as a false positive (FP). If the predicted class

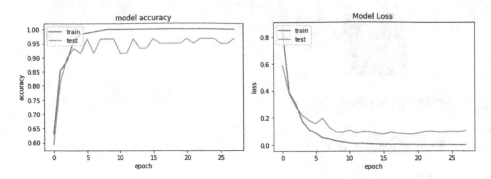

Fig. 7. Performance plot of the lung nodule classification. The left and right figures shows the accuracy and loss variations, respectively for the classification network.

region is correctly identified but does not belong to the valid groundtruth region; then, it is considered a true negative (TN).

We carried out additional experiments to show the ability of the proposed segmentation network with positron emission tomography (PET) images. PET images were used as a reference to confirm the reliability of our segmentation network that accurately recognizing the benign and malignant nodules.

5   Results

The visualization of few representative examples of segmentation of nodules for lung cancer is presented in Fig. 5. In addition, the proposed segmentation network shows highest performance in recognizing the lung nodules is confirmed with the reference PET image which is shown in Fig. 8. The comparison of the performance of our proposed encoder with fully connected network outperforms the simple fully connected network and encoder and decoder followed by the fully connected layer.

Our proposed classification network shows highest precision, recall and F1 score of 98.0%, and accuracy of 97.9%, which is much higher than the coupled encoder and decoder network as shown in Table 1. Furthermore the performance of our proposed classification network is higher than the simple fully connected network. It is because the simple fully connected network is not capable of extracting precise features for classification. In addition, our proposed model outperformed the state-of-the-arts such as Resnet50, VGG and Densenet with a huge difference of accuracy as shown in Table 2. This can be attributed to the fact that our segmentation model was superior and boosted the performance of our classification model over the existing models. Furthermore, other existing methods for lung cancer classification performed using deep learning model produced 80.0% [19] and 94.50% [20] accuracy. Whereas, our proposed cascaded architecture for lung cancer identification achieved high accuracy of 97.9%, indicated the effectiveness of the proposed framework in lung nodule location for cancer.

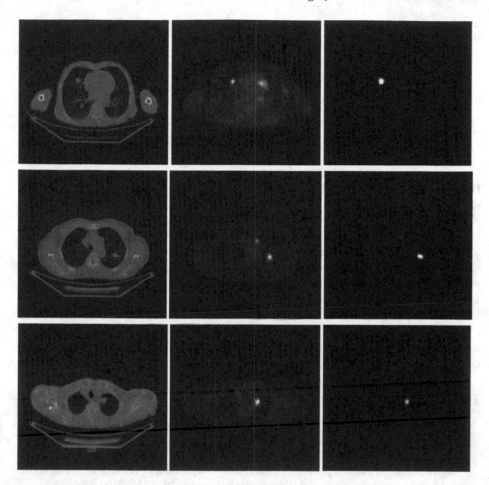

Fig. 8. Segmented results of lung nodules. The left image shows the original CT. The middle image is the reference PET image for lung nodule. The right image shows the predicted lung nodule for the original CT image on the left for lung cancer using our segmentation network.

Table 1. Performance comparison of the proposed cascaded encoder network with different classification network architectures for lung cancer detection

Network architectures	Precision	Recall	F1 score	Accuracy
Fully connected	92%	91%	91%	90.62%
Encoder-decoder with fully connected	26%	51%	34%	51.02%
Proposed	**98%**	**98%**	**98%**	**97.96%**

Table 2. Performance comparison of the proposed cascaded network classification with the state-of-the-arts

Network architectures	Precision	Recall	F1 score	Accuracy
Resnet50	71.25%	71.93%	71.57%	77.14%
VGG	75.94%	75.86%	75.33%	75.93%
Densenet	76.89%	76.47%	75.80%	76.50%
Proposed	**98%**	**98%**	**98%**	**97.96%**

6 Conclusion

We proposed two-stage cascaded architecture for the segmentation and classification of benign and malignant nodules for lung cancer detection. In the cascaded architecture, U-Net based segmentation network performed as a screening network and transfer the trained weights of the public data set of CT slices to the private CT slices that did not consisted ground truth for lung nodule localization. In addition the segmentation network improves the performance and robustness in classifying benign or malignant lung nodules. The experimental results suggested that our proposed encoder followed by fully connected layers classification network outperformed other classification networks for the identification of lung cancer.

References

1. Howlader, N., et al. (eds.): SEER Cancer Statistics Review, 1975–2016. National Cancer Institute, Bethesda, MD (2019). http://seer.cancer.gov/csr/1975_2016, based on November 2018 SEER data submission
2. Burns, D.M.: Primary prevention, smoking, and smoking cessation: implications for future trends in lung cancer prevention. Cancer **89**, 2506–2509 (2000)
3. Thun, M.J., et al.: Lung cancer occurrence in never-smokers: an analysis of 13 cohorts and 22 cancer registry studies. PLOS Med. **5**(9), e185 (2008). https://doi.org/10.1371/journal.pmed.0050185
4. Satcher, D., Thompson, T.G., Kaplan, J.P.: Women and smoking: a report of the surgeon general. Nicotine Tob. Res. **4**(1), 7–20 (2002)
5. Park, E.R., et al.: A snapshot of smokers after lung and colorectal cancer diagnosis. Cancer **12**, 3153–3164 (2012). https://doi.org/10.1002/cncr.26545/abstract
6. Diederich, S., Heindel, W., Beyer, F., Ludwig, K., Wormanns, D.: Detection of pulmonary nodules at multirow-detector CT: effectiveness of double reading to improve sensitivity at standard-dose and low-dose chest CT. Eur. Radiol. **15**, 14–22 (2004). https://doi.org/10.1007/s00330-004-2527-6
7. Bogoni, L., et al.: Impact of a computer-aided detection (CAD) system integrated into a picture archiving and communication system (PACS) on reader sensitivity and efficiency for the detection of lung nodules in thoracic CT exams. J. Digit. Imaging **25**, 771–781 (2012). https://doi.org/10.1007/s10278-012-9496-0
8. Sluimer, I.C., van Waes, P.F., Viergever, M.A., van Ginneken, B.: Computeraided diagnosis in high-resolution CT of the lungs. Med. Phys. **30**, 3081–3090 (2003). https://doi.org/10.1118/1.1624771

9. Helen, H., Jeongjin, L., Yeny, Y.: Automatic lung nodule matching on sequential CT images. Comput. Biol. Med. **38**(5), 623–634 (2008)
10. Ignatious, S., Joseph, R.: Computer aided lung cancer detection system. In: Global Conference on Communication Technologies (GCCT), pp. 555–558 (2015)
11. Greenspan, H., Summers, R.M., van Ginneken, B.: Deep learning in medical imaging: overview and future promise of an exciting new technique. IEEE Trans. Med. Imaging **35**(5), 1153–1159 (2016)
12. Kavitha, M.S., Yudistira, N., Kurita, T.: Multi instance learning via deep CNN for multi-class recognition of Alzheimer's disease. In: 2019 IEEE 11th International Workshop on Computational Intelligence and Applications (IWCIA), pp. 89–94 (2019)
13. Ardila, D., Kiraly, A.P., Bharadwaj, S., et al.: End-to-end lung cancer screening with three-dimensional deep learning on low-dose chest computed tomography. Nat. Med. **25**, 954–961 (2019)
14. Tekade, R., Rajeswari, K.: Lung cancer detection and classification using deep learning. In: Fourth International Conference on Computing Communication Control and Automation (ICCUBEA), pp. 1–5 (2018)
15. Kavitha, M.S., Kurita, T., Park, S.Y., Chien, S.I., Bae, J.S., Ahn, B.C.: Deep vector-based convolutional neural network approach for automatic recognition of colonies of induced pluripotent stem cells. PLoS One **12**(12), e0189974 (2017)
16. Ginneken, B.: Fifty years of computer analysis in chest imaging: rule-based, machine learning, deep learning. Radiol. Phys. Technol. **10**(1), 23–32 (2017). https://doi.org/10.1007/s12194-017-0394-5
17. The LUNA16 Challenge (2016). https://luna16.grand-challenge.org/
18. Ronneberger, O., Fischer, P., Brox, T.: U-Net: convolutional networks for biomedical image segmentation. In: Navab, N., Hornegger, J., Wells, W.M., Frangi, A.F. (eds.) MICCAI 2015. LNCS, vol. 9351, pp. 234–241. Springer, Cham (2015). https://doi.org/10.1007/978-3-319-24574-4_28
19. Xie, Y., Zhang, J., Xia, Y., Fulham, M., Zhang, Y.: Fusing texture, shape and deep model-learned information at decision level for automated classification of lung nodules on chest C.T. Inf. Fusion **42**, 102–110 (2018)
20. Lakshmanaprabu, S.K., NandanMohanty, S., Shankar, K., Arunkumar, N., Ramireze, G.: Optimal deep learning model for classification of lung cancer on CT images. Future Gener. Comput. Syst. **2019**(92), 374–382 (2019)

Hybrid Deep Learning and Data Augmentation for Disease Candidate Extraction

Van-Dung Hoang[1(✉)], Van-Thanh Hoang[2], and Kang-Hyun Jo[2]

[1] Quang Binh University, Dong Hoi, Vietnam
zunghv@gmail.com
[2] School of Electrical Engineering, Ulsan University, Ulsan, Korea
thanhhv@islab.ulsan.ac.kr, acejo@ulsan.ac.kr

Abstract. Nowadays, skin cancer is one of the most popular diseases which affected by ozone depletion, chemical environmental pollution and so on. It is very important for recognizing and treatments. There are many devices that support to capture high-quality skin image to be able for disease diagnose by expert systems. However, the difficult problem is that extracting region of interesting (ROI) for disease diagnosis. This paper presents an approach candidate diseased region extraction using hybrid deep learning of the Residual neural network (ResNet50) architecture and the Atrous convolutional neural network (ACNN). Then the ROI is fed to recognition system for diseased diagnoses. The imbalance of recall measures between classes affected the performance of existing models is deal with data augmentation technique. The proposed learning architecture is suitable for multi skin diseases segmentation and solved under fitting and avoided overfitting problems, achieved improving performance when used hybrid of learning models. Experimental results illustrated that the segmentation system based on deep feature processing combine with data augmentation reach high accuracy.

Keywords: Hybrid learning models · Diseases region extraction · Skin cancer diagnosis

1 Introduction

The skin cancer disease is a most popular health problem in over the world [1], with more than 5 million were diagnosed in each year. Melanoma is the most dangerous form of skin cancer, which is responsible for more than 9,000 deaths each year. A pigmented lesion appears on the surface of the skin, melanoma is the ability to detect early by examination through expert observation and diagnosis. It is also capable of automatic detection thanks to the ability to analyze images taken from skin tumors. Nowadays, there are many kinds of cameras have an ability to capture high-resolution images for detect skin lesions. As a result, many researchers have attempted to carry out their research on how to automate image analysis and disease diagnosis. Dermoscopy is a skin surface imaging microscopic technique technology. The visualization of the extent of deeper skin lesion is enhanced when surface reflections are removed. Numerous studies have demonstrated that, when used by dermatologists, this technique produces high diagnostic performance, when

© Springer Nature Singapore Pte Ltd. 2020
W. Ohyama and S. K. Jung (Eds.): IW-FCV 2020, CCIS 1212, pp. 274–286, 2020.
https://doi.org/10.1007/978-981-15-4818-5_21

compared to standard imaging [2]. In the near future, low-cost dermatoscope devices will be available to operate on smartphones, and the opportunity for automated dermatological diagnostic algorithms is due to a positive impact on health care. Recently, ISIC 2019 [3] has released the latest and largest dataset including 25,331 dermatological images of 8 different categories. This large data set helps solve the problem of missing labeled data for deep CNN training, promising to increase the performance of the algorithm. Melanocytic nevus, Basal cell carcinoma, Actinic keratosis, Benign keratosis, Dermatofibroma, Vascular lesion, and Squamous cell carcinoma. Besides, melanoma is the type of skin cancer with the highest mortality rate. There were nearly 60,000 deaths out of a total of more than 350,000 malignancies in 2015. Despite this highest mortality rate, melanoma can be cured up to 95% of cases if the cancer is detected in its early stages. Typically, skin cancer can be detected by a dermatologist using visual inspection of skin lesions and then pathological analysis if there is a suspicion. Automatic skin lesion classification using skin lesion images inspired the development of adaptive techniques from computer vision based on artificial intelligence. Pham et al. [4] introduced skin lesion classification from dermoscopy images using hand-crafted features. While Celebi et al. used classifier of Support Vector Machines (SVM) classifier; Barata et al. used SVM, k-Nearest Neighbor (kNN), AdaBoost and Bag of Features (BoF) as classifiers; Pham et al. compared the classification results of six classifiers (Support Vector Machine, Logistic Regression, Random Forest, AdaBoost, Balanced Bagging, and Balanced Random Forest) in combination with seven hand-crafted features methods and four data preprocessing steps on the two largest datasets of skin cancer. Recently, deep convolutional neural networks (CNN) have achieved excellent results in image recognition and exceeded human accuracy in some problems with large datasets. Many recent studies have used deep CNN for the classification of skin lesions [5–8] but there are still open challenges due to limited data and data imbalance problems.

Recently, there have been some method to extract disease region using the machine learning based segmentation technique. Authors in [9] studied the novel method by experimental therapy with induced pluripotent stem cells. However, functions of the proposed approach are still challenging. The traditional experimental approaches include assays testing on deoxyribonucleic acid and ribonucleic acid expression, immunolabeling, running gels, assessment of secreted proteins or other factors, and physiological tests. In the same field of research, there are some approaches proposed for segmentation of ROI. In order to automatically segment cells from absorbance images with high accuracy, The authors in [10] presented a method based on convolutional neural network for ROI segmentation. The supervised approach is must decide how to deal with the problem of millions of the coefficients of optimized CNN model and the coefficients of sufficiently optimize model. The study was investigated three basic approaches such as using generative adversarial network, performing transfer learning from already annotated common objects in context dataset for semantic segmentation with out-of-cell microscopy domain, and data augmentation technique was applied for driven the problem of imaging invariances. In another approach, the U-Net model [11] based on CNN models has been successfully applied to segmenting biological images. The proposed method includes of a contracting path to capture context and a symmetric expanding path. In that approach, the CNN model was trained with challenged large number of training segments are usually created by manual. In contrast, the model can be trained using very few images and also result high accuracy in comparison to the state of the art methods for segmentation of neuronal structures in electron microscopic stacks. Since CNN model was applied in the biomedical domains such as microscopy and medical images by experts subject matters. Usually, the expert's annotation data is limited with a small number of manually prepared samples.

For experiment, the ISIC2018 dataset was investigated and practiced. The lesion images were acquired with a variety of dermatoscope types, from all anatomic sites, or historical sample of patients presented for skin cancer screening, from several different institutions. Each lesion image contains exactly one main lesion; Other fiducial signs, smaller secondary lesions or other pigmented areas may be ignored. The paper [12] summarizes methods and validation results on the ISIC Challenge 2018. They presented a two-stage method to segment lesion regions from medical images based optimized training method and applied some part for post-process. Experimental results showed that the proposed approach outperformer on the task of lesion segmentation to state-of-the-art method. The article in [13] presents a method for skin cancer dataset processing. Disease images are divided into some types of medical criteria. This process consists of two parts, which include preprocess stage for image filter to remove free noise such as hair, and ruler marks. The second, deep learning architecture is improved based on U-Net architecture with 46-layered structure results high accuracy of lesion segmentation rate.

2 Proposed Segmentation Architecture

This study investigates a novel segmentation approach based on hybrid of deep learning for disease candidate extraction. The method includes some components: concatenate deep learning models, custom input output data size, and fully connected layers. In practice, disease candidates are diverse in shapes, images so that recognizing the boundary of disease region becomes a very challenging task. Here, background (normal skin area) and foreground (disease region) should be distinguished to reduce the complexity of recognition. The difficulty of disease region segmentation is potentially abnormal skin becoming infinite diverse as hair, reflective, dazzling, difference skin color. In this study, we propose a region of interesting (ROI) extraction based on hybrid deep neural network (HDNN) and data augmentation to enrich the training data. The overall of system architecture is illustrated in Fig. 1. The hybrid deep learning based on the residual neural network architecture (ResNet) and the Atrous convolutional neural network (ACNN) for skin image segmentation with full-scale Feature Maps. The ACNN also utilizes to reduced trained parameters.

In this approach, we combine of two learning models of ResNet and ACNN. Currently, ResNet50 is a classic neural network used as a backbone for many computer vision tasks. The fundamental breakthrough with ResNet was it allowed us to train extremely deep neural networks with 150 layers successfully. The parameters of the retrain model of ResNet from the layer 'res2a_branch2a' to the layer 'res5c_branch2c' is used for building this model. Prior to ResNet training very deep neural networks was difficult due to the problem of vanishing gradients. The input layer is changed to the size of 384 × 511 × 3 pixels as original image of data set. There are 16 inception blocks constructed based on the inheritance of the Resnet50. General architecture is shown in Fig. 1 in the part of "classification based on ResNet50 approach" and details of each inception block is illustrated in Fig. 2. The rest part of the architecture is build based on the Atrous convolutional neural network (ACNN) for semantic segmentation. The details of this part are shown in Fig. 3. Totally, there are 31 layers in this part as illustrated in Table 1.

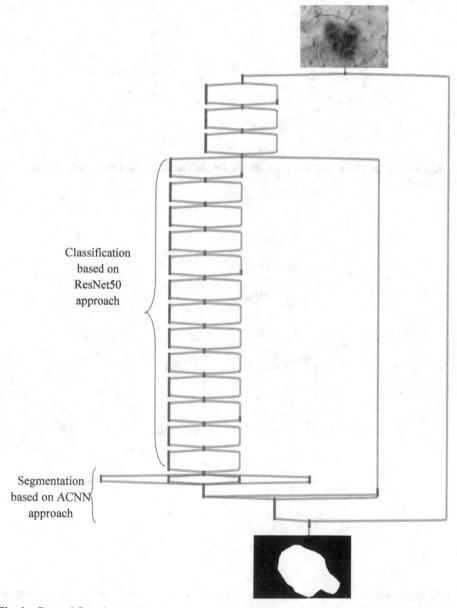

Fig. 1. General flowchart of hybrid machines based semantic segmentation for disease candidate extraction

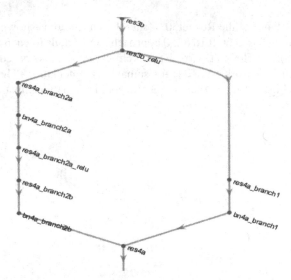

Fig. 2. Directed graph of one inception block inside classification DNN using the ResNet architecture

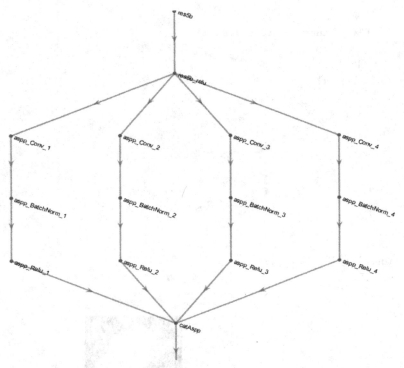

Fig. 3. Segmentation network using ACNN structure, which connected to the last activate of ResNet.

Table 1. Parameters of ACNN, which added to the last part of the system architecture.

Type of layer	Parameters
Depth concatenation	Depth concatenation of 4 channel inputs
Convolution	256 of $1 \times 1 \times 2048$ convolutions
Batch Normalization	Batch normalization with 256 channels
ReLU	Rectified linear unit
Convolution	256 of $3 \times 3 \times 2048$ convolutions
Batch Normalization	Batch normalization with 256 channels
ReLU	Rectified linear unit
Convolution	256 of $3 \times 3 \times 2048$ convolutions
Batch Normalization	Batch normalization with 256 channels
ReLU	Rectified linear unit
Convolution	256 of $3 \times 3 \times 2048$ convolutions
Batch Normalization	Batch normalization with 256 channels
ReLU	Rectified linear unit
Convolution	256 of $1 \times 1 \times 1024$ convolutions
Batch Normalization	Batch normalization with 256 channels
ReLU	Rectified linear unit
Transposed Convolution	256 of $8 \times 8 \times 256$ transposed convolutions
Crop 2D	center crop
Convolution	48 of $1 \times 1 \times 256$ convolutions
Batch Normalization	Batch normalization with 48 channels
ReLU	Rectified linear unit
Depth concatenation	Depth concatenation of 2 inputs
Convolution	256 of $3 \times 3 \times 304$ convolutions
Batch Normalization	Batch normalization with 256 channels
ReLU	Rectified linear unit
Convolution	256 of $3 \times 3 \times 256$ convolutions
Batch Normalization	Batch normalization with 256 channels
ReLU	Rectified linear unit
Convolution	2 of $1 \times 1 \times 256$ convolutions
Transposed Convolution	2 of $8 \times 8 \times 2$ transposed convolutions
Crop 2D	Center crop

3   Data Augmentation for Deep Learning

To deal with the natural situation, data augmentation task is applied for covering all situations of posed camera. The underlying concept of image augmentation is that the rotation, flipping, and other deformations can be applied to enhance data without changing and loosing characteristics and properties of data. Recently, Data Augmentation has been widely being used by not only natural image classification but also melanoma classification such as Matsunaga et al. [14], González-Díaz et al. [15], Menegola et al. [16–18], Esteva et al. [19], Codella, Nguyen et al. [20]. This is the easiest and most common method to mitigate overfitting problem of scarcity of labeled data in melanoma classification. The most importance concept of image augmentation is that the deformations applied to the annotated data do not change the semantic meaning of the labels. In melanoma segmentation, the authors apply three types of data augmentation.

In our experiments, we have applied several kinds of data augmentation as follows. Color normalization and balance: the facial images were collected in different resources, illumination conditions and from different types of devices. the skin lesion images are collected from different resources and are created by different types of device. Therefore, it is important to normalize the colors of the images when the authors use them for training and testing any system to improve performance of classification system [21, 22].

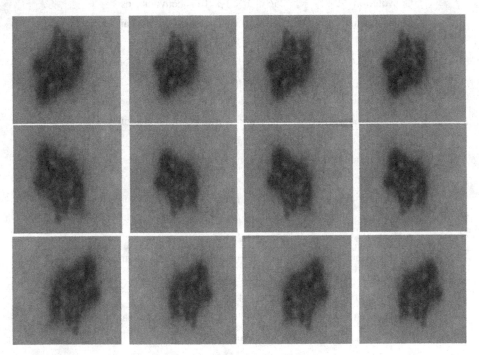

Fig. 4. Some examples of data augmentation.

Geometry transformations: affine transformations such as shearing, distorting and scaling randomly warp stroke data for image classification. Thus, affine transformations are very well suited to augment data for improving the overall performance and mitigating overfitting of the training task. We used various techniques for resampling such as rotation, stretching, shearing: random rotation with angle between $-10°$ and $10°$, random shearing with angle between $-10°$ and $10°$; random shearing stretching with stretch factor between $5°$ and $15°$; flipping is also applied in this situation because almost facial shapes are mirror. Data warping based on Specialists Knowledge: the fact that the melanoma specialist diagnosis is performed over the observation of the patterns around the lesion. In machine learning, affine transformations such as shearing, distorting and scaling randomly warp stroke data for image classification [23]. Thus, the warping processing is very well suited to augment data for improving performance and mitigating overfitting of melanoma classification. In current research, the data augmentation module combines these three types of augmentation in two steps. Firstly, the authors normalize input image by adding multiples a converting all pixels into $[-1.0, 1.0]$ range to create normalized data. Secondly, the authors combine cropping, scaling, distorting and horizontal, vertical flips processes in one step to augment the normalized data. In this step, the authors apply random parameters of each function to generate samples from original one. Figure 4 shows some results of data augmentation processing.

4 Evaluation

For evaluation the proposed approach, we use the ISIC2018 data of the task for boundary segmentation [3]. The ISIC challenge provides 2595 images and corresponding 2595 labeled images. This challenge is the largest standardized and comparative study in this field to date because it has not only the biggest number of training datasets. In this dataset, they did not release labeled images for testing dataset and evaluation dataset. Therefore, we used the original training data in our experiment for both tasks of training and evaluation processing. The dataset is separated to 70% for training and 30% for evaluation. In this experiment, we use pretrain ResNet [24] with reforming input and output layers for retraining in our training data. The input image of the first layer is $384 \times 511 \times 3$. Some specific parameters of layers are used 7×7, $3 \times 3 \times 128$, $1 \times 1 \times 128$, $1 \times 1 \times 256$ convolutional blocks with batch normalization and rectified linear units and are architecturally similar to ResNet, the network graph is illustrated in Figs. 1 and 2.

Output activation results of some special layers of the proposed model are illustrated in Fig. 5 for visualization and inspection of layer processing. In this study, the proposed approach was compared to the state-of-the-art method on the field of segmentation. The semantic segmentation based on the generative adversarial networks (GAN), such as an approach presented in [25]. The GAN model has resulted in high accuracy in many generative tasks of the real-world images.

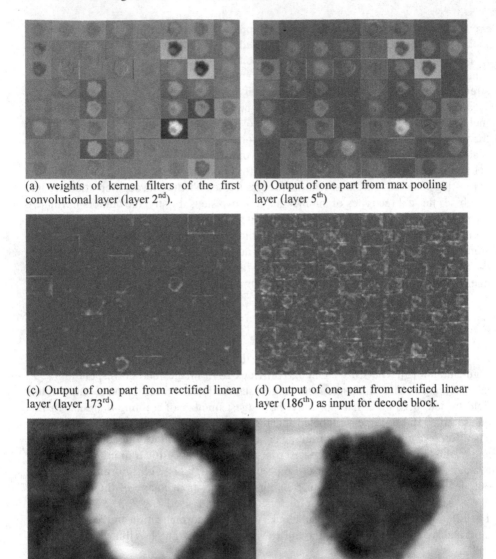

(a) weights of kernel filters of the first convolutional layer (layer 2nd).

(b) Output of one part from max pooling layer (layer 5th)

(c) Output of one part from rectified linear layer (layer 173rd)

(d) Output of one part from rectified linear layer (186th) as input for decode block.

(e) Output of one parts from crop 2D layer (layer 204th) for decode block as input data for segmentation processing.

Fig. 5. Activations results of some special layers using the proposed model

Some experimental results by practical disease candidate extractions from ISIC2018 dataset using our method, the state-of-the-art method based on GAN technique, and the ground truth labelling of disease regions are shown in Fig. 6.

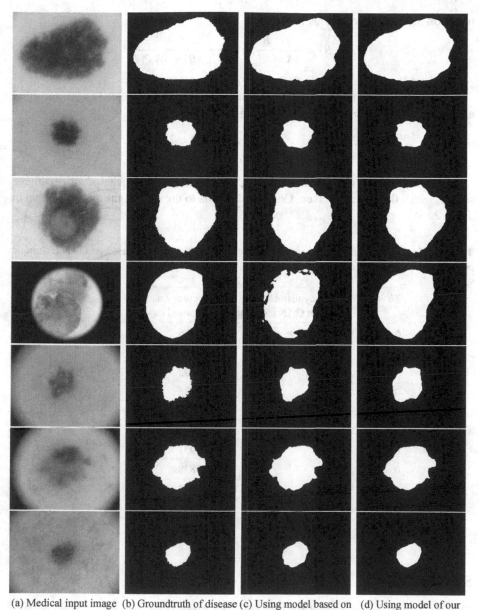

(a) Medical input image (b) Groundtruth of disease (c) Using model based on (d) Using model of our
                                          regions   GAN approach   method

Fig. 6. Some examples of segmentation results for disease candidate extraction

The accuracy metric of the predicted responses are scored using a threshold Jaccard index metric. For each image, a pixel-wise comparison of each prediction of disease candidate region with the corresponding ground truth of disease region is computed based on the Jaccard index J as follows

$$J(A, B) = \frac{|A \cap B|}{|A \cup B|} = \frac{|A \cap B|}{|A| + |B| - |A \cap B|} \tag{1}$$

If A and B are both empty, define $J(A, B) = 1$ and $0 \leq J(A, B) \leq 1$.

The final score of the disease region from each image is evaluated as Th threshold according to the Jaccard index the following

$$Score = \begin{cases} 1 & if \ J(A, B) < Th \\ 0 & otherwise \end{cases} \tag{2}$$

Accuracy of final metric value for the entire dataset is the mean of all per-image scores, which the system is taken. Compared results to the state of the arts are shown in Table 2.

Table 2. Compared results of our proposed approach and the method based on GAN technique correspondence to change Jaccard threshold

Th value	Accuracy using the CNN based on GAN technique	Accuracy use the proposed model
0.50	0.9961	0.9996
0.55	0.9954	0.9992
0.60	0.9934	0.9992
0.65	0.9904	0.9988
0.70	0.9873	0.9985
0.75	0.9788	0.9961
0.80	0.9549	0.9931
0.85	0.8917	0.9838
0.90	0.7074	0.9522
0.95	0.2032	0.7656

5   Conclusion

This paper presents a method for disease candidate region extraction. The essential approach is based on hybrid of segmentation and data augmentation, which supports for improving accuracy. The pretrained ResNet model and the ACNN architecture are combined with additional custom full connected layers for image segmentation. The problem of data unbalance, under fitting and overfitting problems are deal with augmentation technique, achieved improving performance when used hybrid of learning models. Experimental results illustrated that the extraction model, which trained using our architecture reach higher accuracy, outperformer to the state of the art while spends the same consuming time.

References

1. Schadendorf, D., et al.: Melanoma. Lancet **392**, 971–984 (2018)
2. Carli, P., et al.: Pattern analysis, not simplified algorithms, is the most reliable method for teaching dermoscopy for melanoma diagnosis to residents in dermatology. Br. J. Dermatol. **148**, 981–984 (2003)
3. Combalia, M., et al.: Bcn20000: dermoscopic lesions in the wild, arXiv preprint arXiv:1908. 02288 (2019)
4. Pham, T.C., et al.: A comparative study for classification of skin cancer. In: 2019 International Conference on System Science and Engineering (ICSSE), pp. 267–272 (2019)
5. Tschandl, P., et al.: Expert-level diagnosis of nonpigmented skin cancer by combined convolutional neural networks. JAMA Dermatol. **155**, 58–65 (2019)
6. Pham, T.-C., et al.: AI outperformed every dermatologist: improved dermoscopic melanoma diagnosis through customizing batch logic and loss function in an optimized Deep CNN architecture, arXiv, pp. 1–21 (2020)
7. Brinker, T.J., et al.: Comparing artificial intelligence algorithms to 157 German dermatologists: the melanoma classification benchmark. Eur. J. Cancer **111**, 30–37 (2019)
8. Pham, T.-C., Luong, C.-M., Visani, M., Hoang, V.-D.: Deep CNN and data augmentation for skin lesion classification. In: Nguyen, N.T., Hoang, D.H., Hong, T.-P., Pham, H., Trawiński, B. (eds.) ACIIDS 2018. LNCS (LNAI), vol. 10752, pp. 573–582. Springer, Cham (2018). https://doi.org/10.1007/978-3-319-75420-8_54
9. Jha, B.S., Bharti, K.: Regenerating retinal pigment epithelial cells to cure blindness: a road towards personalized artificial tissue. Curr. Stem Cell Rep. **1**, 79–91 (2015). https://doi.org/10.1007/s40778-015-0014-4
10. Majurski, M., et al.: Cell image segmentation using generative adversarial networks, transfer learning, and augmentations. In: Proceedings of the IEEE Conference on Computer Vision and Pattern Recognition Workshop (2019)
11. Ronneberger, O., Fischer, P., Brox, T.: U-Net: convolutional networks for biomedical image segmentation. In: Navab, N., Hornegger, J., Wells, William M., Frangi, Alejandro F. (eds.) MICCAI 2015. LNCS, vol. 9351, pp. 234–241. Springer, Cham (2015). https://doi.org/10.1007/978-3-319-24574-4_28
12. Qian, C., et al.: A two-stage method for skin lesion analysis, arXiv preprint arXiv:1809.03917 (2018)
13. Hasan, S.N., et al.: Skin lesion segmentation by using deep learning techniques. In: 2019 Medical Technologies Congress, pp. 1–4 (2019)
14. Matsunaga, K., et al.: Image classification of melanoma, nevus and seborrheic keratosis by deep neural network ensemble. ArXiv e-prints (2017)
15. González-Díaz, I.: Incorporating the knowledge of dermatologists to convolutional neural networks for the diagnosis of skin lesions. ArXiv e-prints (2017)
16. Menegola, A., et al.: Towards automated melanoma screening: exploring transfer learning schemes. ArXiv e-prints (2016)
17. Menegola, A., et al.: Knowledge transfer for melanoma screening with deep learning. ArXiv e-prints (2017)
18. Menegola, A., et al.: RECOD Titans at ISIC challenge 2017. ArXiv e-prints (2017)
19. Esteva, A., et al.: Dermatologist-level classification of skin cancer with deep neural networks. Nature **542**, 115–118 (2017)
20. Codella, N.C.F., et al.: Deep learning ensembles for melanoma recognition in dermoscopy images. IBM J. Res. Dev. **61**(4/5), 5:1–5:15 (2017)
21. Barata, C., et al.: Improving dermoscopy image classification using color constancy. IEEE J. Biomed. Health Inform. **19**, 1146–1152 (2014)

22. Ercal, F., et al.: Neural network diagnosis of malignant melanoma from color images. IEEE Trans. Biomed. Eng. **41**, 837–845 (1994)
23. Wong, S.C., et al.: Understanding data augmentation for classification: when to warp?. Presented at the Digital Image Computing: Techniques and Applications (DICTA), Gold Coast, QLD, Australia (2016)
24. He, K., et al.: Deep residual learning for image recognition. In: Proceedings of the IEEE Conference on Computer Vision and Pattern Recognition, pp. 770–778 (2016)
25. Luc, P., et al.: Semantic segmentation using adversarial networks, arXiv preprint arXiv:1611.08408 (2016)

Camera, 3D and Imaging

Multispectral Photometric Stereo Using Intrinsic Image Decomposition

Koumei Hamaen[1], Daisuke Miyazaki[1]([⊠]) [ID], and Shinsaku Hiura[2]

[1] Hiroshima City University, Hiroshima 731-3194, Japan
miyazaki@hiroshima-cu.ac.jp
[2] University of Hyogo, Kobe, Hyogo 651-2197, Japan
http://www.cg.info.hiroshima-cu.ac.jp/~miyazaki/

Abstract. One of the main problems faced by the photometric stereo method is that several measurements are required, as this method needs illumination from light sources from different directions. A solution to this problem is the color photometric stereo method, which conducts one-shot measurements by simultaneously illuminating lights of different wavelengths. However, the classic color photometric stereo method only allows measurements of white objects, while a surface-normal estimation of a multicolored object using this method is theoretically impossible. Therefore, it is necessary to convert a multi-colored object to a single-colored object before applying the photometric stereo. In this study, we employ the intrinsic image decomposition for conversion. Intrinsic image decomposition can produce the intrinsic image which is not affected by the reflectance. Since the intrinsic image is the image with white object, we can obtain the surface normal by applying the conventional photometric stereo algorithm to the intrinsic image. To demonstrate the effectiveness of this study, a measurement device that can realize the multispectral photometric stereo method with seven colors is employed instead of the classic color photometric stereo method with three colors.

Keywords: Photometric stereo · Color photometric stereo · Multispectral imaging

1 Introduction

Photometric stereo method estimates the normal by the brightness of pictures by changing the direction of the light source. Therefore, the photometric stereo method is not suitable for modeling a moving object. To measure the shape of a moving object, the color photometric stereo method, which employs several colored light sources, was developed. Such method involves placing light sources of red, green, and blue colors in three different directions, which simultaneously illuminate the target object. Common color photometric stereos suffer from the problem that they cannot be applied to the objects which have multiple kinds of albedo. This paper employs the intrinsic image decomposition in order to

© Springer Nature Singapore Pte Ltd. 2020
W. Ohyama and S. K. Jung (Eds.): IW-FCV 2020, CCIS 1212, pp. 289–304, 2020.
https://doi.org/10.1007/978-981-15-4818-5_22

overcome this problem. The intrinsic image decomposition decomposes an image into an illumination image and an albedo image. The decomposition is based on the Retinex theory, which explains the human perception that the strong edge is due to the albedo difference. The illumination image is independent to the albedo. Common color photometric stereos cannot be applied to the objects with multiple albedos, while our method can, since our method applies the intrinsic image decomposition beforehand.

2   Related Work

The photometric stereo method [35,43] estimates the normal of the surface of an object by illuminating the object and analyzing the resulting shadings on the object's surface. This method requires capturing three pictures with different light source directions. Therefore, it is impossible to measure a dynamic object. This problem can be resolved using the color photometric stereo method. In such method, lights are simultaneously illuminated from red, green, and blue light sources, and one picture photographed with an RGB color camera is captured. Such one-shot photograph enables the measurement of a dynamic object.

The color photometric stereo method [8,20,44] (also known as shape-from-color) was developed in the 1990s. Since then, various studies [1,3–7,10,13,14,18–21,29,32,33,40,41] have been conducted in this regard. However, many problems are inherent in the color photometric stereo method. Many researchers in the past have struggled with this method, and even till recently, it has been an ongoing problem. The principle problem of the color photometric stereo method is the fact that it can only be used with white objects. This is an inevitable problem as long as lights are illuminated from three colored light sources to estimate the surface normal.

Recently, various techniques have been proposed to apply the color photometric stereo method to multicolored objects. Roubtsova et al. [33] applied the color photometric stereo method to objects with arbitrary BRDF (bidirectional reflectance distribution function) by incorporating the Helmholtz Stereo method. However, the principle of this method does not allow for real-time measurement. Therefore, an optical flow is required to measure a dynamic object. Kim et al. [19] and Gotardo et al. [12] also tracked dynamic objects using optical flow, and estimated the surface shape of objects by utilizing several images taken at different times. Fyffe et al. [10] proposed a color photometric stereo method that employs six band cameras and three white color sources. This method pre-measures the reflectance of various objects to prepare a database, and calculated four bases. Using this technique, it is possible to obtain an analytic solution, as there are six unknowns and six equations. Anderson et al. [1] estimated the object color using the normal of multi-view stereo. Their technique incorporates the framework of region segmentation, where the number of the regions is automatically determined based on the Bayesian information criterion. Chakrabarti et al. [4] calculated the histogram of the object color candidates, chose only the limited number of colors that gained most votes, and evaluated the normal by postulating that the object is composed of these limited number of colors. Jiao et al. [18]

divided a picture into super pixel regions and estimated the normal by postulating that the object color inside each region is uniform. Miyazaki et al. [25] formulated a cost function of multispectral photometric stereo with several number of constraints, and obtained the surface normal by minimizing it.

In this paper, the problem faced by the color photometric stereo method is solved using a different approach from those used in previous studies. Most of color photometric stereo methods used three lights with red, green, and blue colors and observed the object with an RGB color camera. In our study, seven lights with different wavelengths are used to illuminate the object, which is then observed by a seven-band multispectral camera [25]. Conventional color photometric stereo suffers from multi-colored object, while our method overcomes this problem using the intrinsic image decomposition. Miyazaki et al. [25] suffers from the parameter tuning, since the adequate weights of each constraint of the cost function are required. On the other hand, our method is less affected by such problem, since the conventional photometric stereo can be applied, which does not need any parameter tuning, after the intrinsic image decomposition is applied.

3 Image Formulation

Although the fundamental theory is given in several number of literatures [28,30], we briefly explain the formulation of the problem. Suppose that we lit a single parallel light source (infinite-far point light source) whose spectral distribution is represented as delta function, the pixel brightness I_c can be represented as follows.

$$I_c = A_c \max(\mathbf{n} \cdot \mathbf{l}_c, 0). \tag{1}$$

$\mathbf{n}$ is a normal vector and $\mathbf{l}_c$ is the light source direction vector of channel c. Hereinafter, we call A_c albedo. Note that the camera sensitivity and light source brightness are included in A_c.

As shown in Fig. 1, this study conducts a photoshoot of a multicolored object using seven channels. Following Eq. (1), the brightness is obtained from this photoshoot as follows.

$$I_0 = A_0 \max(\mathbf{n} \cdot \mathbf{l}_0, 0),$$
$$I_1 = A_1 \max(\mathbf{n} \cdot \mathbf{l}_1, 0),$$
$$\vdots$$
$$I_6 = A_6 \max(\mathbf{n} \cdot \mathbf{l}_6, 0). \tag{2}$$

The surface normal $\mathbf{n}$ is a 3D vector; however, the degree-of-freedom is two because it is constrained to be a unit vector (such constraint reduces one degree-of-freedom). Albedo A_c is represented by seven parameters. There are seven equations, as shown in Eq. (2), and nine unknown parameters (A_0, A_1, $\ldots$, A_6, n_x, n_y, n_z, s.t., $n_x^2 + n_y^2 + n_z^2 = 1$, namely seven for albedo and two for

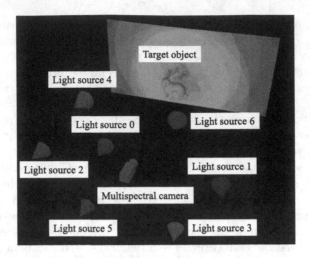

Fig. 1. Conceptual explanation of multispectral color photometric stereo. Target object is illuminated by multiple light sources whose wavelengths are different. One image is taken using multispectral camera.

surface normal). Therefore, color photometric stereo, without any assumption or constraint, is an ill-posed problem (Fig. 2).

The most commonly used assumption is to limit the color of the target objects to white ($A_0 = A_1 = \ldots = A_6$). If we set $\mathbf{s} = A_c\mathbf{n}$ and if we ignore the shadow, the surface normal $\mathbf{s}$ (scaled with albedo) can be directly solved.

$$
\begin{pmatrix} \mathbf{s} \end{pmatrix} = \begin{pmatrix} \mathbf{l}_0^\top \\ \mathbf{l}_1^\top \\ \vdots \\ \mathbf{l}_6^\top \end{pmatrix}^+ \begin{pmatrix} I_0 \\ I_1 \\ \vdots \\ I_6 \end{pmatrix}.
\tag{3}
$$

As is shown above, the color photometric stereo for white objects, or in other words, the conventional photometric stereo can directly solve the surface normal, without iterative optimization nor additional constraints such as smoothness constraints. However, this paper analyzes the methods with multi-colored objects. Therefore, we have to convert the image of multi-colored object to the image of single-colored object.

4   Multispectral Color Photometric Stereo Method

In this section, we describe our proposed method. The subsections are ordered in the same order as the processing step.

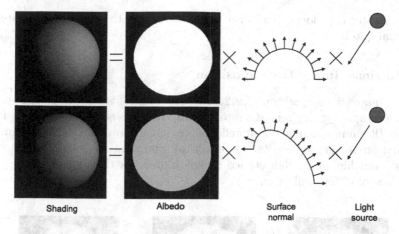

Fig. 2. Ambiguity problem of color photometric stereo due to the colored light source.

4.1   Channel Crosstalk

The 7-channel image captured by the system shown in Sect. 5.1 is contaminated by a so-called channel crosstalk. Therefore, we first remove the channel crosstalk beforehand, and use the processed image for input image. We skip to explain the process [25].

4.2   Edge of Multiple Albedos

The boundary of the regions where the albedo changes has large difference in observed brightness. We detect the boundary of multiple albedos using edge detection technique. Since we have to simply detect the brightness difference, we should use the edge detection algorithm which simply use the brightness difference without any additional post-processing technique. Therefore, Sobel filter [11] is one of the best choice for our purpose.

Since a single light source is illuminated for each channel, there is a shadow in the image. Edge cannot be detected in shadow region from a single channel image, however, we have 7 channels with different light source direction. Voting the Sobel edge of all channels makes the edge robust to noise. From the edge image of each channel $e_i(x, y)$, we robustly detect the edge $e(x, y)$ as follows.

$$e(x, y) = \begin{cases} \text{edge} & \text{if } \left| \bigcup_{i=0}^{6} e_i(x, y) \right| \geq 5 \\ \emptyset & \text{otherwise} \end{cases} \tag{4}$$

Note that an edge image is a binary image. The binary image is obtained from thresholding the brightness calculated by Sobel filter. The threshold is automatically calculated using Otsu method [11]. The adequate threshold might be different for each local area of the image, thus, the threshold is calculated for each local patch.

4.3   Intrinsic Image Decomposition

Intrinsic image decomposition [2,9,22,23,36,37,42,46] is known as an approach which decompose a single image into illumination image and reflectance image (Fig. 3). Illumination image and reflectance image are called intrinsic images. Illumination image represents the effect of illumination, shading, reflection, shadow, and highlight. Reflectance image represents the albedo, namely, the reflectance of diffuse reflection.

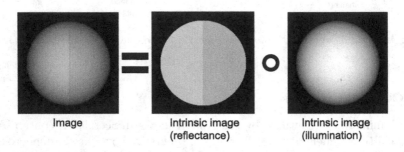

Image   Intrinsic image   Intrinsic image
               (reflectance)   (illumination)

Fig. 3. Intrinsic image decomposition which decompose an image into two intrinsic images which represent reflectance and illumination.

Unlike the conventional photometric stereo, color photometric stereo is impossible to be applied to an object with multiple albedo (reflectance). This is because that each light source has different color. Most of the existing techniques apply color photometric stereo to white objects. In order to overcome this problem, we calculate the illumination image from the captured image using the intrinsic image decomposition. Since the illumination image is independent to albedo, the image is suitable to be used for color photometric stereo.

The basic formulation of the intrinsic image decomposition is as follows (Fig. 4).

$$\nabla^2 I_{\text{out}}(x,y) = \begin{cases} 0 & \text{if } e(x,y) = \text{edge} \\ \nabla^2 I_{\text{in}}(x,y) & \text{otherwise} \end{cases}. \tag{5}$$

Here, $\nabla^2 I_{\text{out}} = 0$ is called Laplace equation, and represents the smoothness constraint. Also, $\nabla^2 I_{\text{out}} = \nabla^2 I_{\text{in}}$ is called Poisson equation, and represents the identity constraint which outputs the same image as input image. Equation (5) smoothly connects the boundary of different albedos, thus, the output image is seamless at the edge of different albedos.

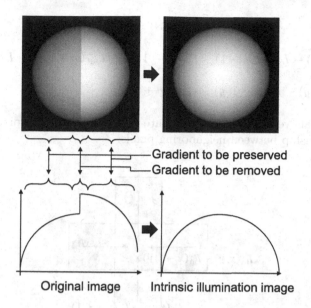

Fig. 4. Schematic example of intrinsic image decomposition based on Poisson image editing.

Discretization of $\nabla^2 I$ is as follows.

$$\nabla^2 I(x,y) = \frac{1}{4}\left(4I(x,y) - I(x,y-1) - I(x-1,y) - I(x+1,y) - I(x,y+1)\right).$$
(6)

Equation (6) is formed between the interest pixel and the four-neighbor pixels, and all five pixels should be either edge pixels or non-edge pixels. However, some pixels have both edge pixels and non-edge pixels in four-neighbor pixels. Suppose that the pixel in interest is p, and one of the neighboring pixel is q. Equation shown below is the same as Eq. (6), and is obtained from the average of $I_p - I_q$ for four-neighbor pixels, q_1, q_2, q_3, and q_4.

$$\nabla^2 I_p = \frac{1}{|\{q_1, q_2, q_3, q_4\}|}\left(4I_p - I_{q_1} - I_{q_2} - I_{q_3} - I_{q_4}\right).$$
(7)

The formulation should be adequately adjusted depending on the relationship between neighboring pixels. For example, if the pixel (x,y) is the non-edge pixel and the pixels $(x+1,y)$ and $(x,y-1)$ are the edge pixels, the formulation will be as follows (Fig. 5).

$$I_{\text{out}}(x,y) - I_{\text{out}}(x,y-1) = 0$$
$$I_{\text{out}}(x,y) - I_{\text{out}}(x-1,y) = I_{\text{in}}(x,y) - I_{\text{in}}(x-1,y)$$
$$I_{\text{out}}(x,y) - I_{\text{out}}(x+1,y) = 0$$
$$I_{\text{out}}(x,y) - I_{\text{out}}(x,y+1) = I_{\text{in}}(x,y) - I_{\text{in}}(x,y+1).$$

Putting the above formulae all together results in the following.

$$\frac{1}{4}\left(4I_{\text{out}}(x,y) - I_{\text{out}}(x,y-1) - I_{\text{out}}(x-1,y) - I_{\text{out}}(x+1,y) - I_{\text{out}}(x,y+1)\right)$$

$$= \frac{1}{4}\left(2I_{\text{in}}(x,y) - I_{\text{in}}(x-1,y) - I_{\text{in}}(x,y+1)\right). \tag{8}$$

As is done in above example, we formulate adequately for each pixel depending on the relationship between neighboring pixels.

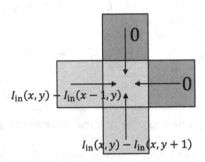

Fig. 5. Example of the equation holding at the boundary between edge region and non-edge region.

If we concatenate the formula for all pixels, we have a linear system shown below.

$$\begin{pmatrix} \vdots & \vdots & \vdots & \vdots & \vdots & \vdots & \vdots & \vdots & \vdots \\ \ldots & -1/4 & \ldots & -1/4 & 1 & -1/4 & \ldots & -1/4 & \ldots \\ \vdots & \vdots & \vdots & \vdots & \vdots & \vdots & \vdots & \vdots & \vdots \end{pmatrix} \begin{pmatrix} \vdots \\ I(x,y) \\ \vdots \end{pmatrix} = \begin{pmatrix} \vdots \\ i(x,y) \\ \vdots \end{pmatrix}, \tag{9}$$

where $i(x,y)$ depends on the condition of each pixel.

The structure of Eq. (9) is the same as $\mathbf{Ax} = \mathbf{b}$, and thus, we can obtain the closed-form solution $\mathbf{x} = \mathbf{A}^{-1}\mathbf{b}$ from the inverse of the matrix using sparse matrix library. We used Eigen library for sparse matrix library, and used LU decomposition for calculating the inverse of a matrix.

Our formulation use the natural boundary condition (Neumann condition) for the boundary condition of Poisson equation. The constraint condition is formulated for relative values between neighboring pixels. Therefore, the solution obtained has an ambiguity with a certain constant offset. We solve the ambiguity by calculating the offset value such that the output brightness will be as close as possible to the input brightness.

$$\text{offset} = \text{median}\left\{\bigcup\left(I_{\text{in}}(x,y) - \tilde{I}_{\text{out}}(x,y)\right)\right\}. \tag{10}$$

In order to avoid the influence of outlier, we calculated the offset using median of the difference between the input brightness I_{in} and the output brightness $\tilde{I}_{out}$. After that, the obtained constant value is added to all pixels.

$$\hat{I}_{out}(x, y) = \tilde{I}_{out}(x, y) + \text{offset}. \tag{11}$$

4.4 Photometric Linearization

The illumination image obtained in Sect. 4.3 has no albedo, and has solely the reflections. Conventional photometric stereo drastically degrades the estimation precision of surface normal if there is shadow and specular reflection in the image. The illumination image obtained by intrinsic image decomposition also includes shadow and specular reflection. An approach called photometric linearization [16,24,26,27,34,38,39,45] can remove the specular reflection. We skip to explain the detailed algorithm of photometric linearization.

4.5 Surface Normal Estimation

Since the albedo is canceled (Sect. 4.3), the severe problem of color photometric stereo, that it cannot be applied to multi-albedo objects, has been extinguished. Same as the most of the existing color photometric stereos which treat with white objects solely, we now have the intrinsic image of multi-colored object which looks like a single-colored object. As a result, the conventional photometric stereo can produce a closed-form solution of surface normal (Eq. (3)).

4.6 Calculating Height from Surface Normal

Surface normal is a differentiation of a shape. Such partial differentiation equation can be represented by Poisson equation. Integrating the Poisson equation, we obtain the height from the surface normal. We skip to explain the detail [15,17,31].

5 Experiment

5.1 Experimental Setup

The camera used for this experiment is an FD-1665 3CCD multi-spectral camera by FluxData, Inc., USA, as shown in Fig. 6. Figure 7 shows the spectral sensitivity of the camera. The light source directions were determined prior to the experiment by photographing a mirrored ball. The locations of the light sources and the camera were then left unchanged. The experiment was conducted in a darkroom. Figure 8 shows the experimental environment.

Fig. 6. Multispectral camera "FluxData FD-1665 (USA)."

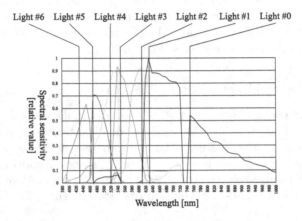

Fig. 7. Spectral sensitivity of multispectral camera and peak wavelength of each light sources.

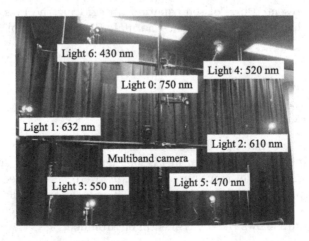

Fig. 8. Experimental setup with 7 light sources with different wavelengths and a single 7-band multispectral camera.

5.2   Experimental Result

First, we applied our method to simulationally-generated sphere. Input image is a single image with 7 channels, though we instead show 7 monochromatic images in Fig. 9(a). The sphere is consisted of several colored materials, and each light has different colors. Therefore, each material appears in different brightness for each channel, which is the fundamental problem of color photometric stereo. Using the edge image (Fig. 9(b)), intrinsic image can be calculated, which has no albedo difference (Fig. 9(c)). As a result, we can obtain the surface normal (Fig. 9(d)) easily using the basic algorithm of photometric stereo. Surface normal in Fig. 9(d) is represented in pseudo-color, where x, y, and z components are converted to red, green, and blue. Figure 9(e) shows the integrated height.

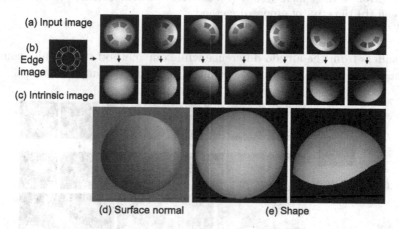

Fig. 9. The result of simulationally-generated sphere: (a) input image, (b) edge image, (c) intrinsic image, (d) surface normal, and (e) shape. (Color figure online)

The error of this result (Fig. 9) is shown in Fig. 10. Since this is a simulationally-generated data, we know the ground truth, and we can evaluate the estimation error. The error is represented as the angle between the surface normal of the ground truth and the surface normal of the proposed method. Figure 10(a) shows the error of conventional photometric stereo, which can only estimate white objects, and Fig. 10(b) shows the proposed method, which can be applied to multi-colored object. The average error of the conventional color photometric stereo was 0.0638 [rad], while that of our method was 0.0501 [rad]. This proves that our approach is adequate for color photometric stereo problem.

Next, we applied our method to real objects. First of all, a spherical object (Fig. 11(a)) is measured. After the edge detection (Fig. 11(b)), intrinsic image is calculated (Fig. 11(c)). The estimated shape is shown in Fig. 11(e). The estimated surface normal (Figs. 11(d) and 12(c)) is closer to the true surface normal (Fig. 12(a)) than to the surface normal calculated by conventional photometric stereo (Fig. 12(b)). The result shows that the conventional color photometric

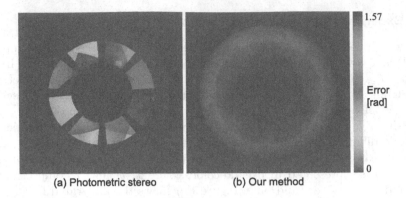

(a) Photometric stereo   (b) Our method

Fig. 10. Error of the sphere result: (a) the error of conventional color photometric stereo, and (b) the error of proposed method.

stereo suffers from the albedo difference while our method successfully connects the difference of albedo thanks to the intrinsic image decomposition.

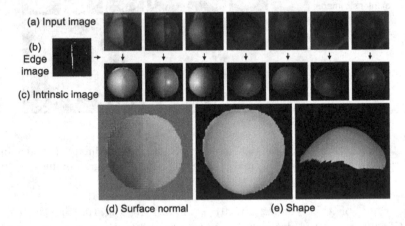

(d) Surface normal   (e) Shape

Fig. 11. The result of real sphere: (a) input image, (b) edge image, (c) intrinsic image, (d) surface normal, and (e) shape.

The bird object shown in Fig. 13(a) only has diffuse reflection, while the doll object shown in Fig. 14(a) has strong specular reflection. The edge image, the intrinsic image, the surface normal, and the shape are shown in Figs. 13(b) and 14(b), Figs. 13(c) and 14(c), Figs. 13(d) and 14(d), and Figs. 13(e) and 14(e), respectively. The shape in most part is successfully estimated, which empirically proves the usefulness of our method. However, some part which has strong specular reflection resulted in erroneous shape. Photometric linearization (Sect. 4.4) usually requires tens of hundreds of images, while our method has only 7 images. Assembling a hardware with more than 7 colored lights and with multispectral camera with more than 7 channels will be the future work of our hardware apparatus.

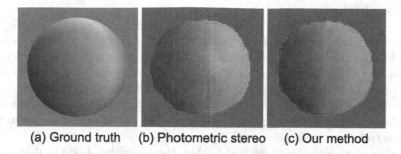

(a) Ground truth   (b) Photometric stereo   (c) Our method

Fig. 12. The surface normal result of real sphere: (a) ground truth, (b) conventional color photometric stereo, and (c) proposed method.

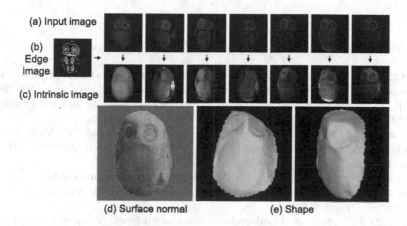

Fig. 13. The result of paper-made object: (a) input image, (b) edge image, (c) intrinsic image, (d) surface normal, and (e) shape.

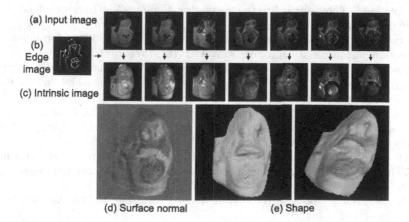

Fig. 14. The result of ceramic-made object: (a) input image, (b) edge image, (c) intrinsic image, (d) surface normal, and (e) shape.

6   Conclusion

In this study, surface normal estimation of multicolored objects was conducted by the multi-spectral color photometric stereo method using intrinsic image decomposition. Note that the conventional color photometric stereo method is an ill-posed problem for multicolored objects. Intrinsic image decomposition solved this problem. We employed the measurement hardware that illuminates the object with seven different spectra and captured the image by a seven-band multispectral camera.

The disadvantage of our method is that the algorithm is divided in several steps. The error of the previous step affects the succeeding processes. The future work will be to construct a unified framework which is not consisted of multiple processes.

References

1. Anderson, R., Stenger, B., Cipolla, R.: Color photometric stereo for multicolored surfaces. In: International Conference on Computer Vision, pp. 2182–2189 (2011)
2. Bell, M., Freeman, E.T.: Learning local evidence for shading and reflectance. In: IEEE International Conference on Computer Vision (2001)
3. Brostow, G.J., Stenger, B., Vogiatzis, G., Hernández, C., Cipolla, R.: Video normals from colored lights. IEEE Trans. Pattern Anal. Mach. Intell. **33**(10), 2104–2114 (2011)
4. Chakrabarti, A., Sunkavalli, K.: Single-image RGB photometric stereo with spatially-varying albedo. In: International Conference on 3D Vision, pp. 258–266 (2016)
5. Drew, M.S.: Reduction of rank-reduced orientation-from-color problem with many unknown lights to two-image known-illuminant photometric stereo. In: Proceedings of International Symposium on Computer Vision, pp. 419–424 (1995)
6. Drew, M.S.: Direct solution of orientation-from-color problem using a modification of Pentland's light source direction estimator. Comput. Vis. Image Underst. **64**(2), 286–299 (1996)
7. Drew, M.S., Brill, M.H.: Color from shape from color: a simple formalism with known light sources. J. Opt. Soc. Am. A: **17**(8), 1371–1381 (2000)
8. Drew, M., Kontsevich, L.: Closed-form attitude determination under spectrally varying illumination. In: IEEE Conference on Computer Vision and Pattern Recognition, pp. 985–990 (1994)
9. Funt, B.V., Drew, M.S., Brockington, M.: Recovering shading from color images. In: Sandini, G. (ed.) ECCV 1992. LNCS, vol. 588, pp. 124–132. Springer, Heidelberg (1992). https://doi.org/10.1007/3-540-55426-2_15
10. Fyffe, G., Yu, X., Debevec, P.: Single-shot photometric stereo by spectral multiplexing. In: IEEE International Conference on Computational Photography, pp. 1–6 (2011)
11. Gonzalez, R.C., Woods, R.E.: Digital Image Processing, p. 716. Addison Wesley, Reading (1993)
12. Gotardo, P.F.U., Simon, T., Sheikh, Y., Mathews, I.: Photogeometric scene flow for high-detail dynamic 3D reconstruction. In: IEEE International Conference on Computer Vision, pp. 846–854 (2015)

13. Hernandez, C., Vogiatzis, G., Brostow, G.J., Stenger, B., Cipolla, R.: Non-rigid photometric stereo with colored lights. In: IEEE International Conference on Computer Vision, p. 8 (2007)
14. Hernández, C., Vogiatzis, G., Cipolla, R.: Shadows in three-source photometric stereo. In: Forsyth, D., Torr, P., Zisserman, A. (eds.) ECCV 2008. LNCS, vol. 5302, pp. 290–303. Springer, Heidelberg (2008). https://doi.org/10.1007/978-3-540-88682-2_23
15. Horn, B.K.P., Brooks, M.J.: The variational approach to shape from shading. Comput. Vis. Graph. Image Process. **33**(2), 174–208 (1986)
16. Ikehata, S., Wipf, D., Matsushita, Y., Aizawa, K.: Photometric stereo using sparse Bayesian regression for general diffuse surfaces. IEEE Trans. Pattern Anal. Mach. Intell. **39**(9), 1816–1831 (2014)
17. Ikeuchi, K., Horn, B.K.P.: Numerical shape from shading and occluding boundaries. Artif. Intell. **17**(1–3), 141–184 (1981)
18. Jiao, H., Luo, Y., Wang, N., Qi, L., Dong, J., Lei, H.: Underwater multi-spectral photometric stereo reconstruction from a single RGBD image. In: Asia-Pacific Signal and Information Processing Association Annual Summit and Conference, pp. 1–4 (2016)
19. Kim, H., Wilburn, B., Ben-Ezra, M.: Photometric stereo for dynamic surface orientations. In: Daniilidis, K., Maragos, P., Paragios, N. (eds.) ECCV 2010. LNCS, vol. 6311, pp. 59–72. Springer, Heidelberg (2010). https://doi.org/10.1007/978-3-642-15549-9_5
20. Kontsevich, L., Petrov, A., Vergelskaya, I.: Reconstruction of shape from shading in color images. J. Opt. Soc. Am. A: **11**, 1047–1052 (1994)
21. Landstrom, A., Thurley, M.J., Jonsson, H.: Sub-millimeter crack detection in casted steel using color photometric stereo. In: International Conference on Digital Image Computing: Techniques and Applications, pp. 1–7 (2013)
22. Levin, A., Weiss, Y.: User assisted separation of reflections from a single image using a sparsity prior. IEEE Trans. Pattern Anal. Mach. Intell. **29**(9), 1647–1654 (2007)
23. Matsushita, Y., Nishino, K., Ikeuchi, K., Sakauchi, M.: Illumination normalization with time-dependent intrinsic images for video surveillance. IEEE Trans. Pattern Anal. Mach. Intell. **26**(10), 1336–1347 (2004)
24. Miyazaki, D., Ikeuchi, K.: Photometric stereo under unknown light sources using robust SVD with missing data. In: Proceedings of IEEE International Conference on Image Processing, pp. 4057–4060 (2010)
25. Miyazaki, D., Onishi, Y., Hiura, S.: Color photometric stereo using multi-band camera constrained by median filter and ollcuding boundary. J. Imaging **5**(7), 29 (2019). Article no. 64
26. Mori, T., Taketa, R., Hiura, S., Sato, K.: Photometric linearization by robust PCA for shadow and specular removal. In: Csurka, G., Kraus, M., Laramee, R.S., Richard, P., Braz, J. (eds.) VISIGRAPP 2012. CCIS, vol. 359, pp. 211–224. Springer, Heidelberg (2013). https://doi.org/10.1007/978-3-642-38241-3_14
27. Mukaigawa, Y., Ishii, Y., Shakunaga, T.: Analysis of photometric factors based on photometric linearization. J. Opt. Soc. Am. A: **24**(10), 3326–3334 (2007)
28. Nicodemus, F.E., Richmond, J.C., Hsia, J.J., Ginsberg, I.W., Limperis, T.: Geometrical considerations and nomenclature of reflectance. In: Wolff, L.B., Shafer, S.A., Healey, G. (eds.) Radiometry, pp. 940–145. Jones and Bartlett Publishers Inc. (1992)
29. Petrov, A.P., Kontsevich, L.L.: Properties of color images of surfaces under multiple illuminants. J. Opt. Soc. Am. A: **11**(10), 2745–2749 (1994)

30. Quéau, Y., Mecca, R., Durou, J.-D.: Unbiased photometric stereo for colored surfaces: a variational approach. In: IEEE Conference on Computer Vision and Pattern Recognition, pp. 4359–4368 (2016)

31. Quéau, Y., Durou, J.-D., Aujol, J.-F.: Normal integration: a survey. J. Math. Imaging Vis. **60**(4), 576–593 (2018). https://doi.org/10.1007/s10851-017-0773-x

32. Rahman, S., Lam, A., Sato, I., Robles-Kelly, A.: Color photometric stereo using a rainbow light for non-lambertian multicolored surfaces. In: Cremers, D., Reid, I., Saito, H., Yang, M.-H. (eds.) ACCV 2014. LNCS, vol. 9003, pp. 335–350. Springer, Cham (2015). https://doi.org/10.1007/978-3-319-16865-4_22

33. Roubtsova, N., Guillemaut, J.Y.: Colour Helmholtz Stereopsis for reconstruction of complex dynamic scenes. In: International Conference on 3D Vision, pp. 251–258 (2014)

34. Shum, H.-Y., Ikeuchi, K., Reddy, R.: Principal component analysis with missing data and its application to polyhedral object modeling. IEEE Trans. Pattern Anal. Mach. Intell. **17**(9), 854–867 (1995)

35. Silver, W.M.: Determining shape and reflectance using multiple images. Master's thesis, Massachusetts Institute of Technology (1980)

36. Tan, R.T., Ikeuchi, K.: Separating reflection components of textured surfaces using a single image. IEEE Trans. Pattern Anal. Mach. Intell. **27**(2), 178–193 (2005)

37. Tappen, M.F., Freeman, W.T., Adelson, E.H.: Recovering intrinsic images from a single image. IEEE Trans. Pattern Anal. Mach. Intell. **27**(9), 1459–1472 (2005)

38. Tibshirani, R.: Regression shrinkage and selection via the lasso. J. Roy. Stat. Soc. B **58**, 267–288 (1996)

39. Tomasi, C., Kanade, T.: Shape and motion from image streams under orthography: a factorization method. Int. J. Comput. Vis. **9**(2), 137–154 (1992). https://doi.org/10.1007/BF00129684

40. Vogiatzis, G., Hernández, C.: Practical 3D reconstruction based on photometric stereo. In: Cipolla, R., Battiato, S., Farinella, G.M. (eds.) Computer Vision: Detection, Recognition and Reconstruction. SCI, vol. 285, pp. 313–345. Springer, Heidelberg (2010). https://doi.org/10.1007/978-3-642-12848-6_12

41. Vogiatzis, G., Hernandez, C.: Self-calibrated, multi-spectral photometric stereo for 3D face capture. Int. J. Comput. Vis. **97**, 91–103 (2012). https://doi.org/10.1007/s11263-011-0482-7

42. Weiss, Y.: Deriving intrinsic images from image sequences. In: IEEE International Conference on Computer Vision (2001)

43. Woodham, R.J.: Photometric method for determining surface orientation from multiple images. Opt. Eng. **19**(1), 139–144 (1980)

44. Woodham, R.J.: Gradient and curvature from photometric stereo including local confidence estimation. J. Opt. Soc. Am. **11**, 3050–3068 (1994)

45. Wu, L., Ganesh, A., Shi, B., Matsushita, Y., Wang, Y., Ma, Y.: Robust photometric stereo via low-rank matrix completion and recovery. In: Kimmel, R., Klette, R., Sugimoto, A. (eds.) ACCV 2010. LNCS, vol. 6494, pp. 703–717. Springer, Heidelberg (2011). https://doi.org/10.1007/978-3-642-19318-7_55

46. Xie, X., Zheng, W., Lai, J., Yuen, P.C.: Face illumination normalization on large and small scale features. In: IEEE Conference on Computer Vision and Pattern Recognition (2008)

In-Plane Rotation-Aware Monocular Depth Estimation Using SLAM

Yuki Saito(✉)(iD), Ryo Hachiuma(✉)(iD), Masahiro Yamaguchi(✉),
and Hideo Saito(✉)(iD)

Department of Information and Computer Science, Keio University, Yokohama, Japan
{yusa19971015,ryo-hachiuma,yama-1467,hs}@keio.jp

Abstract. Estimating accurate depth from an RGB image in any environment is challenging task in computer vision. Recent learning based method using deep Convolutional Neural Networks (CNNs) have driven plausible appearance, but these conventional methods are not good at estimating scenes that have a pure rotation of camera, such as in-plane rolling. This movement imposes perturbations on learning-based methods because gravity direction is considered to be strong prior to CNN depth estimation (i.e., the top region of an image has a relatively large depth, whereas bottom region tends to have a small depth). To overcome this crucial weakness in depth estimation with CNN, we propose a simple but effective refining method that incorporates in-plane roll alignment using camera poses of monocular Simultaneous Localization and Mapping (SLAM). For the experiment, we used public datasets and also created our own dataset composed of mostly in-plane roll camera movements. Evaluation results on these datasets show the effectiveness of our approach.

Keywords: Monocular depth estimation · Simultaneous Localization and Mapping · Convolutional Neural Network

1 Introduction

Depth estimation from an RGB image, i.e., predicting the per-pixel distance to the camera, has many applications, such as Augmented Reality (AR) [1], autonomous driving [2], robot application [3], etc. Given a single image, recent efforts to estimate depths from a single image have yielded high-quality outputs by taking advantages of fully convolutional neural networks (CNNs) [4,5] and large amount of training data from indoor [6] and outdoor [7] scenes.

Monocular depth estimation using CNN implicitly assumes that the camera orientation along the roll direction (in-plane rotation[1]) is almost same in every input image. This is because a person generally takes a photograph with the vertical axis of the image parallel to the direction of gravity. According to this

---

[1] A rotary motion around an optical axis in camera coordinate system.

© Springer Nature Singapore Pte Ltd. 2020
W. Ohyama and S. K. Jung (Eds.): IW-FCV 2020, CCIS 1212, pp. 305–317, 2020.
https://doi.org/10.1007/978-981-15-4818-5_23

Fig. 1. CNN depth estimation in the in-plane rolled scene. (a) the input image, (b) the ground truth depth image. (c) the result using the conventional method, (d) the result using our proposed method. The pixels with large depth values are colored in red and the pixels with small depth values are colored in blue. (Color figure online)

implicit assumption, the orientation is a strong prior for inferring the depth information [8] in the monocular depth estimation using CNN. For example, the network implicitly learns that the lower side of the image is closer than the upper side of the image. This assumption is learned from the training dataset and is reasonable in its application to autonomous driving, because the position of the camera is fixed against the vehicle, and the camera itself does not move drastically. In contrast, when applied to AR or drone cameras, the user moves the smartphone/camera freely, and thus, this assumption collapses. Hence, when the camera rotates along in-plane direction, the accuracy of monocular depth estimation significantly drops. Figure 1(c) shows an failure example of monocular depth prediction. It is evident that the depth is not correctly estimated against the whole image because the input RGB image, Fig. 1(a), is rotated.

In order to overcome this crucial weakness of monocular depth prediction using CNN, we propose using the Simultaneous Localization and Mapping (SLAM) system to improve the accuracy when estimating monocular depth against a rolled image. Using the SLAM system, the 6 Degrees of Freedom (6DoF) camera trajectories are estimated from the RGB image sequences. As the camera pose consists of the translation and orientation of the camera with respect to the initial frame, we can extract the roll rotation angle from the camera pose. By using that angle, an RGB image can be transformed as if the camera was not rotated. Then, the transformed image is fed to the neural network to obtain the depth of the image. Finally, the predicted depth image is transformed inversely using the extracted angle. As a result, we can predict the accurate depth against the rolled image. Figure 1(d) shows the depth prediction result of our proposed method. It is evident that the structure of the scene can be more clearly inferred than the conventional depth prediction in Fig. 1(c). As this is the first work which tackles depth estimation against a roll-rotated image, we assume that the camera is not rotated in the initial frame. This is reasonable assumption because in most cases when pictures are taken, it is implicitly assumed that the direction of gravity is almost parallel to the vertical axis of the image.

In this paper, the sequences in which the camera is rotated in the roll direction are necessary for evaluating our proposed method. In the TUM RGB-D dataset [9], which is a public dataset for evaluating monocular depth estimation, there are three sequences in which the camera rotates along the roll-pitch-yaw direction. However, three sequences are not sufficient for evaluating the robustness of the method. Therefore, we recorded another dataset by ourselves. In this dataset, there are six sequences which are recorded at different indoor locations and the camera is rotated drastically in each sequence. In the experiments, we demonstrate the performance of our system on sequences from the TUM RGB-D dataset as well as the self-created dataset. As a result, our method significantly improved the depth estimation accuracy in two evaluation metrics on our dataset from the baseline method.

Although our method is simple and requires not an single RGB image but RGB image sequences, it significantly improves the depth estimation accuracy of the roll-rotated image using only RGB information. Our method needs neither any additional sensors like inertial measurement unit (IMU) [10] nor any cost for re-training the CNN network. Furthermore, as our method does not rely on a particular backbone of the depth estimation network or SLAM system and is not computationally high, it can be easily integrated into a real-time monocular dense reconstruction system using a depth prediction network, such as CNN-SLAM [11], DeepFusion [12], or CNN-MonoFusion [1].

There are three contributions in this paper. First, we first propose a method using the SLAM system for monocular depth estimation that is robust for in-plane rotation. Second, we created a dataset in which the sequences that were recorded by the camera were rotating in a roll direction. Third, our proposed method outperformed the baseline in two evaluation metrics on our dataset.

2   Related Work

2.1   In-Plane Rotation-Aware Prediction

While there are no previous work that regard on CNN depth estimation for overcoming the dependency of in-plane rotation, Toyoda et al. [13] have tried to reduce the dependency of in-plane rotation by selecting the most consistent pose from images rolled at various angles of wild motion video in Deep Neural Network (DNN) based pose estimation. There are rare scenes such that subjects are upside down in the real world and these rare data were not learned generally in datasets. Hence, to save the cost of training data again, they calculated roll angles using the output joint position probability. However, in terms of depth estimation, the confidence of the depth are not outputted typically. Furthermore, rotating images by every quantized roll angle is computationally expensive, which is a crucial problem for real-time applications like SLAM. Therefore, we use SLAM tracking to calculate the scenes' in-plane rotation angles, which is more precise and computationally cheap.

Kurz and Benhimane have proposed gravity-aware AR [14], in which the gravity direction measured with an IMU improves the accuracy of the camera pose estimation. This is related to our method because gravity direction is used to improve the accuracy of vision-based 3D sensing. Different from them, we propose an approach without relying on highly functional sensors. Our system can work only from RGB images.

2.2   SLAM with Monocular Depth Estimation

Enormous monocular SLAM or Visual Odometry approaches have been developed for motion estimation and are divided into feature-based methods [15,16] and direct methods [17–19]. However, they only provide sparse or semi-dense depth maps and cannot estimate camera poses accurately by pure rotational motions even in high-textured scenes.

In order to reconstruct dense 3D maps and improve the trajectory using these points, combining SLAM with CNN depth estimation have been proposed, which produced higher benchmark scores rather than conventional monocular systems. One of the most accurate SLAM/CNN network combination is CNN-SLAM [11] where CNN's learned depth maps are fused into direct SLAM framework. Though CNN-SLAM guarantees the strong estimation of accurate trajectory and dense maps, it does have CNN's inaccuracy against rotated inputs, because depth maps are produced by KeyFrames which are not created unless the camera translates over a certain distance. In addition, CNN-MonoFusion [1] evaluates 3D reconstruction models whose scenes have pure-rotational motion, such as TUM RGB-D dataset's *rpy* sequences [9]. There is no quantitative evaluations about CNN depth accuracy.

In contrast to these conventional approaches, we directly face the weakness of learning-based depth estimation and measure our refinement's efficiency from both qualitative and quantitative perspectives.

2.3   Learning Based Rotation Prediction

The learning-based approaches to predict camera rotation from a single RGB image have been proposed. Fischer et al. [20] constructed a network that directly regresses the orientation angle of an image. Moreover, Olmschenk et al. [21] proposed a method that estimates pitch and roll angles of the camera by using CNN from only an RGB image. However, these methods can only estimate a rough orientation angle which is insufficient in accuracy and have no geometric constraints (i.e., CNN outputs statistical likelihood values only based on learning data).

In another perspective, Xian et al. [22] estimated 2DoF camera orientation using both local and global scene representations extracted from an RGB image. Nevertheless, they verify the effectiveness of their method only with small roll angles, such as ±20° or ±50°.

Our method can estimate geometric aligned orientation angle without strong dependency on the scene environment. The roll angle is extracted accurately from the camera trajectory in our method by using ORB-SLAM [16], which is known to be able to estimate highly reliable camera poses. Furthermore, our approach can handle large roll angles.

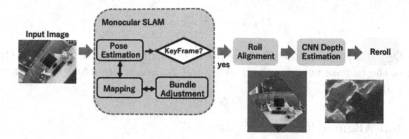

Fig. 2. Our framework overview.

3 Method

The overview of our method is shown in Fig. 2. First, We use monocular SLAM to obtain the camera poses of input RGB images. Second, we calculate transformation function $F(\theta)$ which transform the KeyFrame images against roll direction using SLAM camera poses. This transformation aims to set so that gravity vectors extracted from images are aligned to true gravity direction in the parallel scene. Third, CNN estimates the depth images of the input transformed images. At last, we reroll the CNN outputs in the reverse direction so that the final results have the same in-plane roll angles as the initial input images.

3.1 Camera Pose Estimation

To obtain accurate camera pose act as one of the most important roll in our system. Monocular SLAM or Visual Odometry can estimate precise camera poses based on multi-view geometry, but they suffer from pure rotational movement, including in-plane rotation. To keep tracking accuracy in such a difficult environment, we chose the feature-based RGB version of ORB-SLAM2 [23], which has state of the art accuracy in terms of pose estimation. Compared to other direct approaches [17, 18], this system has relatively low computational costs and is easy to combine with.

3.2 CNN Depth Estimation

We employ the same network architecture as CNN-MonoFusion [1]. This network is based on a Resnet50 model [24] following the work of Laina et al. [4]. Atrous convolution and up-projection layers are applied to broaden the field of view and prevent pooling loss. Also, a multi-scale skip-concat is introduced to unit high-level and low-level features. This network adopts *AdaBerhu* loss, which incorporates normalized depth to train the network using various indoor-scene datasets with different focal lengths. To obtain an absolute scale for images taken by the camera, whose intrinsic parameter is different from one at the training time, the output depth is converted to the SLAM scale, in the same manner as CNN-SLAM [11], using the following scaling:

$$D_{test} = \frac{f_{test}}{f_{tr}} D_{CNN}, \tag{1}$$

where D_{CNN} denotes the depth value predicted by the network, f_{test} is the focal length of the camera used for the SLAM, and f_{tr} is a reference focal length used at the training time.

3.3 Roll Alignment

We transformed input RGB images before and after applying CNN part for the same absolute angles, so all CNN inputs are parallel to the scenes. As mentioned in Sect. 1, we assumed that the initial Frame of SLAM will be parallel to the scene (i.e. the gravity direction of the subjects in the image matches the vertical axis in the camera coordinates).

We estimated the transformation $F_t(\theta)$ against the input RGB image I_t to obtain the depth image D_t using the camera pose. We set D_{test} in the previous section as D_t, and t denotes the timestep in the sequence. Note that the transformation $F_t(\theta)$ is an affine transformation.

The current camera pose $\mathbf{T}_t^{cw} \in \mathbb{R}^{4 \times 4}$ can be estimated using ORB-SLAM2 [23]; the pose is composed of the camera rotation $\mathbf{R}_t^{cw} \in \mathbb{R}^{3 \times 3}$ and camera translation $\mathbf{s}_t^{cw} \in \mathbb{R}^3$, which are relative to the initial frame. Camera rotation $\mathbf{R}^{cw}$ can be divided into three rotation matrices about xyz axes, as seen in the Eq. 2;

$$\mathbf{R}^{cw} = \mathbf{R}^{cw}(\psi)\mathbf{R}^{cw}(\phi)\mathbf{R}^{cw}(\theta), \tag{2}$$

where ψ is the pitch, ϕ is the yaw, and θ is the roll rotation. Focusing on in-plane rolling, $\mathbf{R}^{cw}(\theta)$ is expressed as a 3×3 matrix, as shown in the Eq. 3;

$$\mathbf{R}^{cw}(\theta) = \begin{pmatrix} \cos\theta & -\sin\theta & 0 \\ \sin\theta & \cos\theta & 0 \\ 0 & 0 & 1 \end{pmatrix}. \tag{3}$$

From this angle θ, we can obtain a 2×3 transformation matrix $F_t(\theta)$, as shown in the Eq. 4;

$$F_t(\theta) = \begin{pmatrix} \cos\theta & -\sin\theta & s_x \\ \sin\theta & \cos\theta & s_y \end{pmatrix}, \tag{4}$$

where s_x and s_y denotes translation vector to align the center of original image with the center of transformed image.

We applied the $F_t(\theta)$ affine transformation with bilinear interpolation so that CNN input would not lose its original pixels and have blank pixels which have no RGB data as few as possible. To prevent blank pixels from disturbing the CNN calculation, we altered their pixel values to zero in convolutional layer.

After getting CNN outputs, we reroll the depth image in the same manner in the inverse direction to obtain the same resolution depth images as the original KeyFrame RGB images.

TUM/frei1_rpy $\theta = 2$	TUM/frei1_rpy $\theta = 65$	Our/seq1 $\theta = -30$	Our/seq1 $\theta = 125$	Our/seq3 $\theta = -170$	Our/seq3 $\theta = -90$

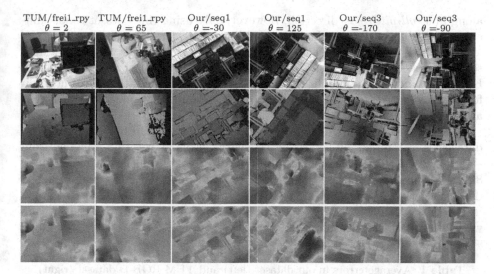

Fig. 3. Qualitative results on TUM RGB-D and our dataset. From top to bottom: the input image, the ground truth depth image, the predicted depth image by the baseline method, and the predicted depth image by our proposed method.

4 Experiment

4.1 Experiment Detail

In the experiments, we compared our proposed method to the baseline method that directly inputs the RGB image to the depth prediction network, which does not apply roll rectification using SLAM. Note that the depth prediction network is the same as the proposed method and the baseline method. The difference is that the proposed method transformed the input image. We evaluated our method from both qualitative and quantitative perspectives. This evaluation was carried out on a desktop PC with an Intel Core i7-7700 CPU at 3.60 GHz and a Nvidia GTX 1080Ti GPU.

For the depth prediction network, we employed the trained model from CNN-MonoFusion [1] which was publicly available[2]. The model is trained with both the NEAIR dataset [1] and the NYU Depth V2 dataset [6]. This network predicts the depth image with a resolution of half size of the input image, so that the depth image is rescaled as the same resolution of the input image.

4.2 Dataset

To evaluate our proposed method, we use three *rpy* sequences of a TUM RGB-D dataset [9], which is widely known and has a pure rotational camera movement captured by a Kinect V1 sensor. *rpy* is an abbreviation that the camera moves

---

[2] https://github.com/NetEaseAI-CVLab/CNN-MonoFusion.

along in a *roll-pitch-yaw* direction. However, only using this dataset is not sufficient for evaluating our method for the following reasons: (1) this dataset has a lot of ground truth depth images in which several pixels' values are zero because some scenes contain objects over 4.0 m away, which is the max depth range of Kinect V1 and (2) the number of frames at each in-plane roll angle is not uniformly distributed (e.g., the number of frames around 90° is much less than that around 0°).

Therefore, we recorded our own dataset using a Kinect V2 sensor. This dataset is composed of six sequences with in-plane rotation ranging from $-180 < \theta < 180$ with a uniform distribution. Each sequence is around 30 or 80 s, and the overall dataset contains 7,704 pairs of RGB images and aligned depth images with a resolution of 640×480 pixels. All sequences were recorded in indoor environments and we assumed that the max depth was 4.5 m within which the depth can be obtained accurately.

Table 1. Average errors in our dataset (left) and TUM RGB-D dataset (right)

	Abs_Rel ↓		RMSE ↓	
	Ours	Baseline	Ours	Baseline
seq1	**0.2372**	0.3260	**0.7865**	1.0565
seq2	**0.5161**	0.5929	**0.6557**	0.7321
seq3	**0.2745**	0.3425	**0.9406**	1.2068
seq4	**0.3590**	0.4225	**1.2818**	1.4601
seq5	**0.3687**	0.3930	1.9395	**1.9262**
seq6	**0.2614**	0.3339	**0.8769**	1.1095
ave	**0.3169**	0.3818	**1.0961**	1.2784

	Abs_Rel ↓		RMSE ↓	
	Ours	Baseline	Ours	Baseline
frei1_rpy	2.2482	**2.2380**	**1.0036**	1.0217
frei2_rpy	1.7147	**1.6586**	0.9486	**0.9285**
frei3_rpy	0.9190	**0.8557**	0.9062	**0.8672**
ave	1.6211	**1.5708**	0.9480	**0.9297**

5   Result

5.1   Qualitative Evaluation

Figure 3 shows the qualitative results on TUM RGB-D dataset and our dataset. When comparing our proposed method to the baseline, it is evident that the predicted depth is improved drastically as the structure of the scene can be predicted correctly. In the results of seq1 (in our dataset), our proposed method predicted that the ceiling was farther than the desk. However, the baseline method predicted that the ceiling has almost the same depth as the chair or desk.

In addition, Fig. 8 shows the crucial failure of conventional approach without in-plane roll refinement in a scene from the TUM frei2_rpy sequence. In Fig. 8(b), points of the teddy bear are located in front of the PC and the points of the wall, which should be far away from the desk and the PC, are sticking out. In contrast, Fig. 8(c) estimates that the points of teddy bear are in the back side of

PC and the points of wall are extended in the far side from the camera position like the ground truth model shown in Fig. 8(a).

As we mentioned in Sect. 1, objects which have relatively large depth, such as the ceiling and wall, tend to occupy the upper side, and those which have small depth, such as the floor, occupy the lower side of an image. Therefore, the CNN, which was trained on almost parallel scenes, hallucinates this natural perspective assumption regardless of input's camera pose. Our simple contrivance that incorporates camera poses can directly prevent this harmful characteristic.

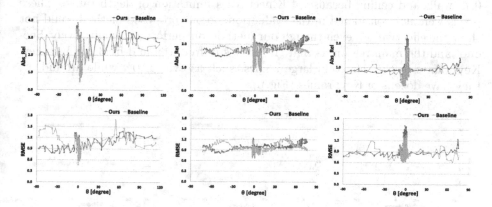

Fig. 4. The correlation between roll angle of frame pose and absolute relative error evaluated in the TUM dataset by Abs_Rel (top) and RMSE (bottom).

5.2   Quantitative Evaluation

We employ absolute relative error (Abs_Rel) and root mean squared error (RMSE) as the evaluation metrics, which means that the lower value is better. Table 1 left shows the results of the self-created dataset. From the Table 1, our proposed method outperformed the baseline method for both the Abs_Rel and the RMSE evaluation metrics.

Figure 5 shows the Abs_Rel of each sequence in our dataset. The horizontal axis shows the estimated roll angle and the vertical axis shows the Abs_Rel value. The errors around $\theta = 0$ do not show any difference between the error of the proposed method vs the baseline method. However, at the range $-45 < \theta < 45$, the baseline method outperformed ours, because the pixels, which are filled with zero disturb the performance slightly, as mentioned in Sect. 3.3. For larger θ, even though the error of the baseline method increased, the error of our proposed method does not depend on θ value. This shows the effectiveness of our proposed method.

Table 1 right shows the results of the TUM RGB-D dataset. In this dataset, our method does not outperform the baseline method. The Abs_Rel and RMSE

of each sequence is summarized in Fig. 4. However, from the predicted result of
the TUM frei1_rpy in Fig. 3, our proposed method correctly predicts the depth
of the floor which is located in the farther side rather than a table. Also, the
results in Fig. 7, which shows the average errors by 10° rolling angles in the TUM
dataset and our dataset, indicates our methods are not so far behind from the
baseline method.

There are two main explanations for the fact that our proposed method qualitatively predicted correct depth but quantitatively did not outperform. First,
scenes in frei2_rpy and frei3_rpy have ground truth depth data whose values are
0 in walls and ceiling because of Kinect V1's limitation of depth range. These
pixels were not considered in the evaluation, so our proposed method could not
show the effectiveness even though our method outperformed qualitatively. Second, and the main reason, is that the scenes in frei2_rpy and frei3_rpy have few
KeyFrames in the relatively large angles, such as over ±60°, while around 0°,
they have dozens of KeyFrames (Fig. 6).

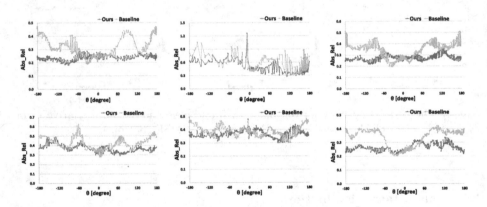

Fig. 5. The correlation between roll angle of frame pose and Abs_Rel evaluated in our
dataset.

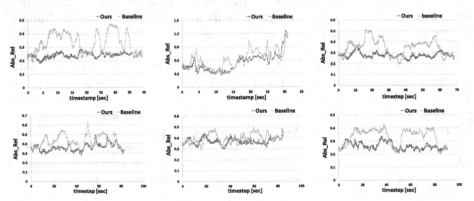

Fig. 6. Time series graph of Abs_Rel evaluated in our six sequences. .

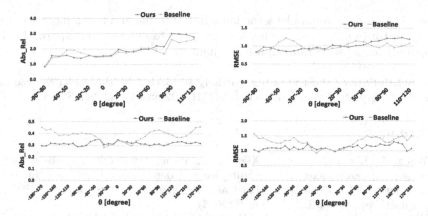

Fig. 7. The correlation between roll angle of frame and Abs_Rel or RMSE over all sequences in TUM and our datasets. Data is divided into bins by 10° and represented as average errors in the bins.

(a)   **(b)**   **(c)**

Fig. 8. Result of reprojected points using CNN predicted depth in a scene from TUM frei2_rpy. (a) result by ground truth depth, (b) result by depth of baseline approach, (c) result by depth of our proposed approach. The area circled with an orange marker indicates the location of the teddy bear in the scene. (Color figure online)

6   Conclusion

In this paper, we proposed a simple but effective method to estimate accurate depth for roll-rotated images by using the camera poses directly, which is extracted from the monocular SLAM system. Our method rotates the in-plane rolled image as if it was not roll-rotated before inputting to CNN and re-roll predicted depth image inversely after CNN. Although our approach is simple, we showed the effectiveness of this contrivance by evaluating both qualitatively and quantitatively in public and our own dataset for the in-plane rolling motion of the camera. Our system does not rely on the specific CNN architecture and can run only from RGB images.

We resolved the CNN's drawback that learning-based approach cannot handle the roll-rotated image because of the implicit disposition of learning data and the limitation of data argumentation. In the future work, we are going to get rid of the assumption of a parallel scene in an initial frame and find a more accurate gravity vector in a 2D image. Also, We are going to compare our approach with the trained model with random roll augmentation.

Acknowledgement. This work was partially supported by the Japan Science and Technology Agency (JST) under grant JPMJMI19B2 and JPMJCR1683.

References

1. Wang, J., Liu, H., Cong, L., Xiahou, Z., Wang, L.: CNN-MonoFusion: online monocular dense reconstruction using learned depth from single view. In: IEEE International Symposium on Mixed and Augmented Reality Adjunct (ISMAR-Adjunct), pp. 57–62. IEEE, Munich (2018)
2. Wang, Y., Chao, W., Garg, D., Hariharan, B., Campbell, M., Weinberger, K.: Pseudo-LiDAR from visual depth estimation: bridging the gap in 3D object detection for autonomous driving. In: Proceedings of the IEEE International Conference on Computer Vision, pp. 8445–8453. IEEE (2019)
3. Marcu, A., Costea, D., Licăreţ, V., Pîrvu, M., Sluşanschi, E., Leordeanu, M.: SafeUAV: learning to estimate depth and safe landing areas for UAVs from synthetic data. In: Leal-Taixé, L., Roth, S. (eds.) ECCV 2018. LNCS, vol. 11130, pp. 43–58. Springer, Cham (2019). https://doi.org/10.1007/978-3-030-11012-3_4
4. Laina, I., Rupprecht, C., Belagiannis, V., Tombari, F., Navab, N.: Deeper depth prediction with fully convolutional residual networks. In: International Conference on 3D Vision (3DV), pp. 11–20. IEEE (2016)
5. Fu, H., Gong, M., Wang, C., Batmanghelich, K., Tao, D.: Deep ordinal regression network for monocular depth estimation. In: Proceedings of the IEEE International Conference on Computer Vision, pp. 2002–2011. IEEE (2018)
6. Silberman, N., Hoiem, D., Kohli, P., Fergus, R.: Indoor segmentation and support inference from RGBD images. In: Fitzgibbon, A., Lazebnik, S., Perona, P., Sato, Y., Schmid, C. (eds.) ECCV 2012. LNCS, vol. 7576, pp. 746–760. Springer, Heidelberg (2012). https://doi.org/10.1007/978-3-642-33715-4_54
7. Uhrig, J., Schneider, N., Schneider, L., Franke, U., Brox, T., Geiger, A.: Sparsity invariant CNNs. In: International Conference on 3D Vision (3DV), pp. 11–20. IEEE (2017)
8. Mi, L., Wang, H., Tian, Y., Shavit, N.: Training-free uncertainty estimation for neural networks. arXiv preprint arXiv:1910.04858 (2019)
9. Sturm, J., Engelhard, N., Endres, F., Burgard, W., Cremers, D.: A benchmark for the evaluation of RGB-D SLAM systems. In: IEEE International Conference on Intelligent Robot Systems, pp. 573–580. IEEE (2012)
10. Grisettiyz, G., Stachniss, C., Burgard, W.: Improving grid-based SLAM with Rao-Blackwellized particle filters by adaptive proposals and selective resampling. In: IEEE International Conference on Robotics and Automation, pp. 2432–2437. IEEE (2005)
11. Tateno, K., Tombari, F., Laina, I., Navab, N.: CNN-SLAM: real-time dense monocular SLAM with learned depth prediction. In: Proceedings of the IEEE Conference on Computer Vision and Pattern Recognition, pp. 6243–6252. IEEE (2017)
12. Laidlow, T., Czarnowski, J., Leutenegger, S.: DeepFusion: real-time dense 3D reconstruction for monocular SLAM using single-view depth and gradient predictions. In: International Conference on Robotics and Automation, pp. 4068–4074. IEEE (2019)

13. Toyoda, K., Kono, M., Rekimoto, J.: Post-data augmentation to improve deep pose estimation of extreme and wild motions. arXiv preprint arXiv:1902.04250 (2019)
14. Kurz, D., Benhimane, S.: Gravity-aware handheld augmented reality. In: IEEE International Symposium on Mixed and Augmented Reality, pp. 111–120. IEEE (2011)
15. Klein, G., Murray, D.: Parallel tracking and mapping for small AR workspaces. In: Proceedings of the IEEE and ACM International Symposium on Mixed and Augmented Reality, pp. 225–234. IEEE (2007)
16. Mur-Artal, R., Montiel, J.M.M., Tardos, J.D.: ORB-SLAM: a versatile and accurate monocular SLAM system. IEEE Trans. Robot. **31**(5), 1147–1163 (2015)
17. Engel, J., Schöps, T., Cremers, D.: LSD-SLAM: large-scale direct monocular SLAM. In: Fleet, D., Pajdla, T., Schiele, B., Tuytelaars, T. (eds.) ECCV 2014. LNCS, vol. 8690, pp. 834–849. Springer, Cham (2014). https://doi.org/10.1007/978-3-319-10605-2_54
18. Engel, J., Koltun, V., Cremers, D.: Direct sparse odometry. IEEE Trans. Pattern Anal. Mach. Intell. **40**(3), 611–625 (2017)
19. Forster, C., Pizzoli, M., Scaramuzza, D.: SVO: fast semi-direct monocular visual odometry. In: International Conference on Robotics and Automation, pp. 15–22. IEEE (2014)
20. Fischer, P., Dosovitskiy, A., Brox, T.: Image orientation estimation with convolutional networks. In: Gall, J., Gehler, P., Leibe, B. (eds.) GCPR 2015. LNCS, vol. 9358, pp. 368–378. Springer, Cham (2015). https://doi.org/10.1007/978-3-319-24947-6_30
21. Olmschenk, G., Tang, H., Zhu, Z.: Pitch and roll camera orientation from a single 2D image using convolutional neural networks. In: 2017 14th Conference on Computer and Robot Vision, pp. 261–268. IEEE (2015)
22. Xian, W., Li, Z., Fisher, M., Eisenmann, J., Shechtman, E., Snavely, N.: UprightNet: geometry-aware camera orientation estimation from single images. In: Proceedings of the IEEE Conference on Computer Vision and Pattern Recognition, pp. 9974–9983. IEEE (2019)
23. Mur-Artal, R., Tardós, J.D.: ORB-SLAM2: an open-source SLAM system for monocular, stereo, and RGB-D cameras. IEEE Trans. Robot. **33**(5), 1255–1262 (2015)
24. He, K., Zhang, X., Ren, S., Sun, J.: Deep residual learning for image recognition. In: Proceedings of the IEEE Conference on Computer Vision and Pattern Recognition, pp. 770–778. IEEE (2016)

Uncalibrated Photometric Stereo Using Quadric Surfaces with Two Cameras

Takumi Nasu, Tsuyoshi Migita[✉], Takeshi Shakunaga,
and Norikazu Takahashi

Okayama University, Okayama, Japan
migita@cs.okayama-u.ac.jp

Abstract. Inverse rendering is a method for estimating object shapes and lighting conditions from a set of images. In the present paper, we propose an uncalibrated photometric stereo method that approximates the shapes of the target objects using quadric surfaces (ellipsoids or hyperboloids), and this shape representation allows us to use multiple cameras in order to reduce the GBR ambiguity. The proposed method uses the Levenberg-Marquardt method to minimize the differences between the input images and generated images calculated based on the estimated parameters and the image formation model. It is important to define each term in the cost function depending on the inside or outside of the contour of the estimated quadric surface and/or the target object. The proposed method has been verified on several sets of real images, namely, Vase, Grapes, and Snacks, and we found that the method required less than 100 iterations. On the other hand, there is room for improvement regarding the accuracy of the estimation by taking into account the shadows of the target objects and using a more advanced reflection model.

Keywords: Inverse rendering · Uncalibrated photometric stereo · Quadric surface · Multiple view images · Levenberg-Marquardt method

1 Introduction

Inverse rendering [1] is a method for obtaining information from a set of images, as opposed to computer graphics, which is a technique for generating images from information, such as object shapes and light sources. Typically, the input images for inverse rendering are taken from a fixed viewpoint but under different light source positions [2,3]. Retrieved information includes the shape and intrinsic color of the object or lighting conditions. Such a method can be used as a fundamental building block for various applications, including the realization of VR space, autonomous vehicles, object recognition/inspection, and photogrammetry.

An uncalibrated photometric stereo method [4] is a variant that simultaneously estimates both the shape of the object and the position of the light source from a set of images. It is well known that such methods suffer from

Supported by JSPS KAKENHI Grant Number 17K00239.

the GBR ambiguity, i.e., the estimated results are corrupted by some unknown linear transformation [5], and, in the present paper, we attempt to reduce the GBR ambiguity through the use of multiple cameras. To this end, we usually need feature correspondences across images. However, we can avoid this problem by using quadric surfaces (ellipsoids or hyperboloids) to approximate the shape of the object. In the present paper, we will verify that the proposed method can estimate quadric surfaces and light source directions with reduced GBR ambiguity from real images taken by two cameras. On the other hand, the fine structures on the surfaces of the objects cannot be well approximated, and a complementary method might be required in order to deal with these details, but this is not within the scope of the present paper.

2   Formulation

2.1   Inverse Rendering

First, we briefly describe the basic formulation of inverse rendering [4]. Let p be a vector consisting of parameters to be estimated, such as the shape of the object and the position of the light source. A complete description of p is presented in Sect. 4.2.

The vector p is estimated by searching for a parameter that best approximates the input images. Specifically, the vector p that minimizes $E(p)$ in the following expression is judged to be the best:

$$E(p) = \sum_{f,i} |r_{fi}|^2 = |r|^2, \tag{1}$$

where r is the residual vector and consists of the residual vectors for each pixel for each image (with pixel index i and image index f) as

$$r^t = (\cdots, r_{0,i}^t, r_{1,i}^t, \cdots, r_{fi}^t, \cdots, r_{F-1,i}^t, r_{0,i+1}^t, \cdots), \tag{2}$$

and

$$r_{fi} = e_{fi} - e'_{fi}, \tag{3}$$

which is the difference between the intensity calculated from the estimated parameters e_{fi} and that of the input image e'_{fi}. Here, f takes an integer in $0 \leq f \leq F - 1$, where F is the total number of images, whereas i is an integer in $0 \leq i \leq I - 1$, where I is the total number of effective pixels.

In the present paper, we modify this basic formulation to deal with quadric surfaces. Most importantly, the contour of the object in the image and that of the approximated quadric surface do not match. Therefore, we cannot calculate the difference when there is no corresponding pair (e_{fi}, e'_{fi}), and this often happens at pixels near the contours. On the other hand, if we can handle this issue properly, we can avoid exact correspondence matching across images with different viewpoints and can easily apply the method to multiple views with any number of cameras. The details of the modification are described in Sect. 4.5.

2.2   Quadric Surfaces and Coordinate Systems

The quadric surface equation we use is as follows:

$$\Phi = a'x^2 + b'y^2 + c'z^2 - 1 = 0, \tag{4}$$

where $(x, y, z)^t$ represents the coordinates of the point of interest in the object coordinate system (object coordinates), and a set of parameters (a', b', c') represents the shape of an ellipsoid when $b' > 0$ or a single-leaf hyperboloid when $b' < 0$. These shapes can be represented in a unified form, while the meanings of the parameters can easily be understood in the following form:

$$\Phi = \left(\frac{x}{a}\right)^2 \pm \left(\frac{y}{b}\right)^2 + \left(\frac{z}{c}\right)^2 - 1 = 0. \tag{5}$$

Note that, cylinders can also be represented, but it is not likely that the estimated b' is exactly zero. In addition, the Eq. (4) cannot exactly represent paraboloids or planes.

Using an orthographic camera at the coordinate origin, assuming the image coordinates are denoted by (u, v) and the depth of the pixel is denoted by w, the object coordinates $(x, y, z)^t$ are expressed as the following equation [6] using a rotation matrix R and the position $c = (c_x, c_y, c_z)^t$:

$$\begin{pmatrix} x \\ y \\ z \end{pmatrix} = R \begin{pmatrix} u - c_x \\ v - c_y \\ w - c_z \end{pmatrix}. \tag{6}$$

3   Image Generation Model

3.1   Reflection Model

We use the Lambertian reflection model [7], as usual in classical photometric stereo methods [2], and the intensity of each pixel is expressed as

$$e = \begin{cases} L^t N \cdot C & \text{if } L^t N > 0 \\ 0 & \text{otherwise} \end{cases} \tag{7}$$

where e is the intensity (a vector with three elements (r, g, b) ranging from 0 to 255), L is a three-dimensional unit vector pointing to the light source from the point of interest, hereinafter referred to as the light source vector, N is a unit normal vector at the point, and C is the intrinsic color of the point. When the inner product of L and N is negative, the pixel is black ($e = 0$) because the point is not lit by the light.

3.2   Contour of Quadric Surface

The contour of a quadric surface in the image can be determined by counting the number of real solutions w of a quadratic equation for each (u, v), because there exists real solution(s) w if a ray passing through pixel (u, v) intersects the

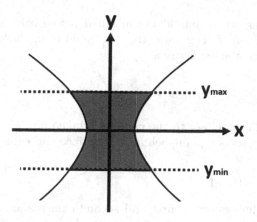

Fig. 1. Example of a contour of a truncated single-leaf hyperboloid

quadric surface. The number can be easily be determined by the discriminant D of the following quadratic equation, which combines (4) and (6):

$$\alpha w^2 + \beta w + \gamma = 0, \tag{8}$$

where

$$\alpha w^2 + \beta w + \gamma = (u\ v\ w\ 1) \begin{pmatrix} I \\ -c^t\ 1 \end{pmatrix} \begin{pmatrix} R^t \\ 1 \end{pmatrix} \begin{pmatrix} a' \\ b' \\ c' \\ -1 \end{pmatrix}.$$

$$\begin{pmatrix} R \\ 1 \end{pmatrix} \begin{pmatrix} I\ -c \\ 1 \end{pmatrix} \begin{pmatrix} u \\ v \\ w \\ 1 \end{pmatrix}. \tag{9}$$

When $D = \beta^2 - 4\alpha\gamma \geq 0$, the equation has one or two real solutions and pixel (u, v) is inside the contour. Otherwise, the equation has no real solutions and (u, v) is outside the contour.

In addition, we sometimes use 'truncated' ellipsoids or hyperboloids by constraining object coordinate y in a range $[y_{\min} : y_{\max}]$. Figure 1 shows an example of the contour of a truncated single-leaf hyperboloid.

3.3 Normal Vector of Quadric Surface

The normal at image coordinates (u, v) within the contour of the quadric surface can be obtained by partial differentiation of (4). In other words, the normal vector can be obtained by normalizing the following vector:

$$N = \begin{pmatrix} \frac{\partial}{\partial u} \\ \frac{\partial}{\partial v} \\ \frac{\partial}{\partial w} \end{pmatrix} \Phi \left(R \begin{pmatrix} u - c_u \\ v - c_v \\ w - c_w \end{pmatrix} \right). \tag{10}$$

Note that the unknown w should be obtained before calculating N by (10). When the discriminant D is greater than or equal to 0, the quadratic formula gives the real solution w explicitly as

$$w = \frac{-\beta + \sqrt{D}}{2\alpha},$$

(11)

where only the solution closer to the camera is taken into account, because the other solution represents a point behind the surface and cannot be observed.

3.4   Projection Model

If the image coordinates of the first and second cameras are denoted by (u, v) and (u', v') with corresponding depths w and w', these coordinates are related to some 3d point $(x_c, y_c, z_c)^t$ by the following equations:

$$\begin{pmatrix} u \\ v \\ w \end{pmatrix} = \begin{pmatrix} \ell & 0 & W/2 \\ & \ell & 0 & H/2 \\ & & 1 \end{pmatrix} \begin{pmatrix} x_c \\ y_c \\ z_c \\ 1 \end{pmatrix},$$

(12)

$$\begin{pmatrix} u' \\ v' \\ w' \end{pmatrix} = \begin{pmatrix} \ell' & 0 & W/2 \\ & \ell' & 0 & H/2 \\ & & 1 \end{pmatrix} \begin{pmatrix} & & & \Delta x \\ \Delta R & \Delta y \\ & & & \Delta z \\ 0^t & & 1 \end{pmatrix} \begin{pmatrix} x_c \\ y_c \\ z_c \\ 1 \end{pmatrix},$$

(13)

where ℓ and ℓ' are the focal lengths of the first and second cameras, respectively, W is the width of the image, H is the height of the image, ΔR and $(\Delta x, \Delta y, \Delta z)^t$ are the rotation matrix and translation vector, respectively, of the second camera relative to the first camera. Extending (13) to any number of cameras is easy, although we used two cameras in the present experiments.

Note that several equations for $(u, v, w)^t$ described in the present paper also hold for $(u', v', w')^t$, even if not explicitly stated.

4   Minimization Method

4.1   Levenberg-Marquardt Method

The Levenberg-Marquardt method [8,9] (hereinafter referred to as the LM method) is used to solve the nonlinear minimization problem of (1). In the method, the estimated parameter p is updated by the correction amount Δp, as follows:

$$p \leftarrow p - \Delta p,$$

(14)

where

$$\Delta p = (J^t J + D)^{-1} (J^t r),$$

(15)

and D is a diagonal matrix used as a regularization term to prevent the LM method from diverging. The details of the D are described in Sect. 4.6.

The matrix J is a Jacobian matrix:

$$J = \left(\frac{\partial r}{\partial p_0}, \frac{\partial r}{\partial p_1}, \cdots \right),\qquad(16)$$

with $p = (p_0, p_1, \cdots)^t$.

4.2   Elements of p

The vector p contains parameters for multiple objects, multiple light sources, and multiple cameras. All of these parameters are estimated simultaneously by iterations of (14). Then, the vector p consists of (a'_m, b'_m, c'_m) in (4), parameters of the rotation matrices R_m and translation vectors $(c_{mx}, c_{my}, c_{mz})^t$ for each object (m-th object), the light source vector of each input image $(L_0, L_1, \cdots, L_{F-1})$, and the parameters of the second camera (rotation matrix ΔR, focal length ℓ', and relative position $(\Delta x, \Delta y, \Delta z)^t$). A rotation matrix R is parametrized by a unit quaternion [10] as

$$R = \begin{pmatrix} q_0^2 + q_1^2 - q_2^2 - q_3^2 & 2(q_1 q_2 - q_0 q_3) & 2(q_1 q_3 + q_0 q_2) \\ 2(q_1 q_2 + q_0 q_3) & q_0^2 - q_1^2 + q_2^2 - q_3^2 & 2(q_2 q_3 - q_0 q_1) \\ 2(q_1 q_3 - q_0 q_2) & 2(q_2 q_3 + q_0 q_1) & q_0^2 - q_1^2 - q_2^2 + q_3^2 \end{pmatrix}.\qquad(17)$$

4.3   Finite Difference for a Jacobian

Each column of J is approximated by a finite difference as

$$\frac{\partial r}{\partial p_k} = \frac{r(p + \varepsilon b_k) - r(p - \varepsilon b_k)}{2\varepsilon},\qquad(18)$$

where b_k is a vector with the same dimension as p, where the value of the k-th row is 1, and the values of the other rows are 0. A single fixed value of ε may not be appropriate, since shape parameters (a', b', c'), rotation matrix R, translation vector c (the object index m is omitted here for simplicity), and light source vector L_f differ greatly in magnitude. Hence, each element is multiplied by a constant, so that the magnitudes of all elements become approximately even. As shown in (19), (a', b', c') and c are multiplied by different factors, s_1 or s_2, respectively, so that these scaled quantities have values near $[-1 : 1]$, which is the range of (q_0, q_1, q_2, q_3) and unit light source vectors:

$$p = (s_1 a', s_1 b', s_1 c', q_0, q_1, q_2, q_3, s_2 c_x, s_2 c_y, s_2 c_z, l_{00}, l_{01}, l_{02}, \cdots)^t.\qquad(19)$$

With such a normalization, $\varepsilon = 10^{-5}$ is appropriate for any element.

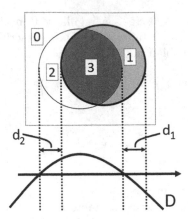

Fig. 2. Pixel distinction based on the contours of the input images and estimated quadric surfaces

4.4 Approximate Reflectance with Average Image

Since the target objects are often textured, the reflectance C in (7) is a function $C(u, v)$ and is not known in advance. Instead the function is approximated by the average of the input images. We denote the intensity of each pixel in the average image by m_i. Then, the reflectance C in (7) is $C(u, v) = m_i$, where (u, v) are the coordinates of the i-th pixel, and

$$m_i = \frac{\sum_f e'_{fi}}{F}. \tag{20}$$

4.5 Contour Mismatch

The i-th pixel is classified into one of four classes, as shown by the Venn diagram in Fig. 2, where the thick circle represents the contour of the target object in the input image, the thin circle represents the contour of the estimated quadric surface, and the pixel is classified based on whether it is in the former and/or latter contour(s). Then, the residual r_{fi} is defined differently for each class. For class 3, r_{fi} is defined as (3). For class 0, $r_{fi} = 0$. For classes 1 and 2, r_{fi} is defined as proportional to the discriminant D. The multiplicative factors are defined as follows in order to balance the magnitude of D and the differences given by (3):

$$r_{fi} = \begin{cases} D \cdot h_1 \cdot (1, 1, 1)^t & \text{for class-1} \\ D \cdot h_2 \cdot (1, 1, 1)^t & \text{for class-2} \end{cases} \tag{21}$$

where h_1 and h_2 are constants. The lower part of Fig. 2 illustrates a typical behavior of discriminant D with respect to coordinate u. The term d_1 represents the width of class-1 pixels, and d_2 represents that of class-2 pixels. Based on Fig. 2, as the width of d_1 or d_2 increases, the value of $|D|$ becomes larger. Therefore, the cost function is minimized when these contours are aligned as closely as possible, i.e., when the number of pixels classified as class-1 or -2 is minimized.

4.6 Diagonal Terms

The diagonal matrix D in (15) is defined as follows:

$$D = \mathrm{diag}(\mu_0, \mu_1, \cdots, \mu_{N-1}), \qquad (22)$$

where N is the dimension of p, and the number of elements in the matrix D is the same as the dimension of the parameter p. The diagonal matrix D is added to $J^t J$ in (15), so that $J^t J + D$ is not rank deficient and prevents the LM method from diverging. Furthermore, larger values of the diagonal elements of D correspond to smaller values of the correction amount Δp in (15). In other words, convergence is slow. Conversely, smaller diagonal element values of D correspond to larger values of correction Δp. In other words, convergence is fast. In the present paper, the values of the diagonal elements of D are determined manually in advance and gradually decrease upon iteration.

5 Experimental Results

5.1 Datasets

For evaluation of the proposed method, we use three sets of real images taken by two cameras (Figs. 3, 4, 7, 8, 11, and 12). The target object of Figs. 3 and 4 is a vase. Since the object is a solid of revolution, it can be used to verify the ability to reduce GBR ambiguity. The target object of Figs. 7 and 8 is a bunch of grapes. The target object of Figs. 11 and 12 is a pile of snacks. Although the objects are approximately sets of ellipsoids, which are seemingly ideal for the proposed method, estimation could be difficult because of non-Lambertian reflectance properties and shadows.

Figures 3, 7, and 11 show nine images taken from a fixed viewpoint under different lighting conditions. Figures 4, 8, and 12 show corresponding images of the same object under the same illumination, but by another camera from a different viewpoint. When photographing the vase, we placed the target object on a pedestal covered with a black cloth in a dark room and lit the object with an LED bulb that emits light only from one direction. Similarly, the grapes were placed on a sheet of black drawing paper, and the snacks were placed on a box made with black drawing paper. The images are of 93×181, 146×103, and 175×125 pixels, respectively.

5.2 Initial Values

Figures 5(a) and (b) are the average images created from Figs. 3 and 4, respectively. Figures 5(c) and (d) show the initial shapes for each camera as white curves superimposed on the average images. The initial value was manually given so that the quadric surfaces lie within the target object in the average images.

We can easily see that the object can be approximated by a combination of truncated ellipsoid(s) at convex part(s) and truncated hyperboloid(s) at concave part(s). Background pixels are manually blackened out to extract region(s) of the vase, grapes, or snacks. For grapes and snacks, grains are numbered from the left (e.g., Grape1, Grape2, ...).

The initial values of light source vectors were uniformly $(0,0,1)^t$, and those of the second camera were given such that these values approximate the actual configuration.

After some preliminary experiments, we determine the initial values of the diagonal matrix D, as shown in Tables 1, 2, and 3.

Table 1. Initial values of diagonal terms

	a'	b'	c'	q_0	q_1	q_2	q_3	c_x	c_y	c_z	L
Top of the vase	10^{11}	10^{11}	10^{10}	10^{15}	10^{15}	10^{15}	10^{15}	10^{13}	10^{13}	10^{13}	10^8
Middle of the vase	10^{10}	10^{11}	10^{11}	10^{15}	10^{15}	10^{15}	10^{15}	10^{14}	10^{14}	10^{13}	10^8
Grape1	10^9	10^9	10^{10}	10^9	10^9	10^9	10^9	10^8	10^8	10^8	10^8
Grape2	10^9	10^8	10^9	10^9	10^9	10^9	10^9	10^9	10^8	10^8	10^8
Grape3	10^{10}	10^9	10^{11}	10^9	10^9	10^9	10^9	10^{10}	10^9	10^9	10^8
Snack1	10^{10}	10^{10}	10^{10}	10^9	10^9	10^{10}	10^{12}	10^{11}	10^{12}	10^9	10^6
Snack2	10^9	10^9	10^{11}	10^9	10^{11}	10^{10}	10^9	10^{11}	10^{11}	10^{10}	10^6
Snack3	10^7	10^8	10^9	10^{11}	10^{11}	10^{10}	10^{10}	10^{12}	10^{12}	10^{12}	10^6

Table 2. Initial values of diagonal terms for the second camera

	Δq_0	Δq_1	Δq_2	Δq_3	Δx	Δy	Δz	f'
Vase	10^{16}	10^{16}	10^{15}	10^{15}	10^{10}	10^{11}	10^{10}	10^{11}
Grapes	10^{10}	10^{10}	10^{10}	10^{10}	10^8	10^8	10^8	10^9
Snacks	10^{11}	10^{11}	10^{11}	10^{11}	10^{11}	10^{11}	10^{10}	10^{10}

Table 3. Constant values h_1 and h_2

	h_1	h_2
Vase	10^5	10^5
Grapes	10^4	10^4
Snacks	10^4	10^4

5.3 Results

Vase. The white curves in Figs. 6(a) and (b) represent the estimated contour of the quadric surfaces. By comparing these figures with Figs. 5(c) and (d), we can see that the estimated contour moved closer to the contour of the target object, i.e., that the approximation accuracy is improved from the initial value.

Figure 6(d) shows the transition of the root mean square error, or RMSE, which is expressed as $||r'||/\sqrt{2F \cdot 3I'}$, where r' and I' are residuals and the number of pixels classified as class-3 only, respectively, when estimating the vase. Figure 6(d) shows that the RMSE decreased significantly up to the 30th iteration, and there was a notable drop around the 80th iteration. After that, the changes in RMSE and each element of the parameter p were relatively small. The average residual reached around 15, and there is no significant difference between estimated images and Figs. 3 or 4.

Figure 6(c) shows a comparison between the estimated image and the input image. The image on the left is the estimated image, and the image on the right is the input image. We can say that the light source vector was correctly estimated because the estimated shading pattern, e.g., which is the side in the shadow, is quite similar to that of the input image. Similar results were obtained for other lighting directions.

Figure 6(e) shows the estimated light source vectors. Positions of the light source were estimated at various positions around the origin O, even if these were initialized at the same point. Note that the distances of the light source could not be estimated in our directional lighting model.

The GBR ambiguity should be reduced by the proposed method. In order to verify this, the ratio $\sqrt{c'/a'}$ was calculated for two cases: when using two cameras (proposed) and when using only one camera (conventional). This ratio should be close to 1 because the x-z cross section of the target object is a circle. The calculated ratios are shown in Table 4, and we can confirm that the ratios are closer to 1 when using two cameras, i.e., that the GBR ambiguity was reduced.

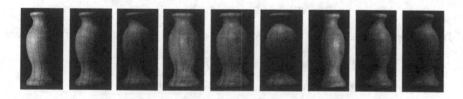

Fig. 3. Input images of Vase (first camera)

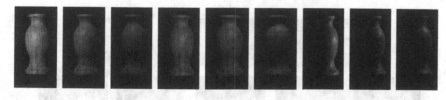

Fig. 4. Input images of Vase (second camera)

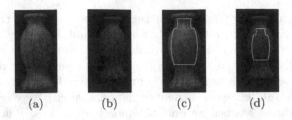

Fig. 5. Average images and initial shapes (Vase)

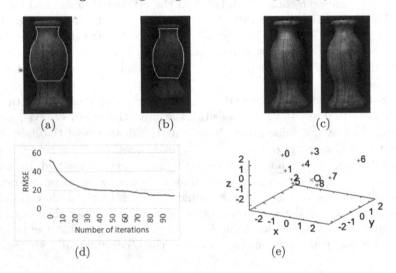

Fig. 6. Results for Vase

Table 4. Comparison between estimated results using two cameras and a single camera

	$\sqrt{1/a'}$	$\sqrt{1/c'}$	$\sqrt{c'/a'}$
Two cameras (Top)	19.87	16.69	1.19
Single camera (Top)	20.32	15.20	1.34
Two cameras (Middle)	35.70	29.63	1.20
Single camera (Middle)	35.87	25.29	1.42

Fig. 7. Input images of Grapes (first camera)

Fig. 8. Input images of Grapes (second camera)

Grapes. The white curves in Figs. 10(a) and (b) represent the estimated contours of the quadric surfaces. Comparing these figures with Figs. 9(c) and (d), we can see that the estimated contour moved closer to the contour of the target object.

Figure 10(d) shows the RMSE when estimating the grapes and that the changes in the RMSE become small as the number of iterations increases. In this case, the average residual did not fall below 30, which means there are noticeable differences between estimated images and Fig. 7 or 8. In fact, we can see that the estimated quadric surface and the contours of grains are relatively far away compared with the case in which the vase was estimated. In particular, Grape3 (the rightmost grain) shows the largest differences. There are two reasons for this. One reason is that the reflection of grapes is not sufficiently approximated by the Lambertian model. Another reason is that the shadows of other grains partially covered the grain.

Figure 10(c) shows the comparison of the estimated image and the input image. We can see that the actual shading pattern of the grape grains is quite different from the Lambertian model.

Figure 10(e) shows the estimated light source vectors. Looking at Fig. 10(e), we can see that the light source vectors were estimated as being close to each other as compared with the case of Vase. This is another aspect of the GBR ambiguity and was not sufficiently resolved, mainly because grapes are not ideal Lambertian objects. It is likely that this problem can be mitigated using some sophisticated reflectance models proposed for computer graphics, since the Lambertian model is too naïve for approximating real objects. Some graphics models can be combined with the proposed method, within the limitation that the model is differentiable. In addition, the parameter vector p should be extended to incorporate some new parameters into the model.

| (a) | (b) | (c) | (d) |

Fig. 9. Average images and initial shapes (Grapes)

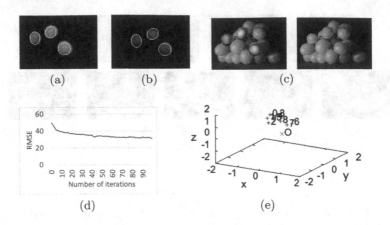

Fig. 10. Results for Grapes

Snacks. The white curves in Figs. 14(a) and (b) represent the estimated contours of the quadric surfaces. Comparing these figures with Figs. 13(c) and (d), we can see that the estimated contour moved closer to the contour of the target object.

Figure 14(d) shows the RMSE when estimating Snacks images and that the RMSE had almost converged around the 60th iteration. Although the average residual was around 30 and there are noticeable differences between the estimated images and Figs. 11 or 12, we can say that this estimation was better than that for Grapes because the estimated quadric surfaces were closer to the contour of the target objects than in the case of Grapes. However, some parts are not completely matched, such as in Snack1 (the leftmost grain). The reasons for this are that the estimated grains were partially covered by shadows of other grains and the shapes of these grains cannot be well approximated by quadric surfaces. On the other hand, the reflectance is much more Lambertian-like than for Grapes.

Figure 14(c) shows the estimated image and the input image. Looking at Snack1, the shade is somewhat different from the input image. The same applies to the other grains. This is likely improved if we can use a more complex shape model, say superquadrics [11], for example. For non-quadric models, the discriminant D is no longer applicable for defining the residual for class-1 and class-2 pixels, and should be replaced with some alternative, and much more complicated, definition.

Figure 14(e) shows estimated light source vectors. Looking at Fig. 14(e), we can see that the light source vector was properly estimated for the same reason as the case of Vase. Moreover, we can see that the distances between each light position are longer than in the case of Grapes, mainly because the reflectance is much more Lambertian-like than in the case of Grapes.

Fig. 11. Input images of Snacks (first camera)

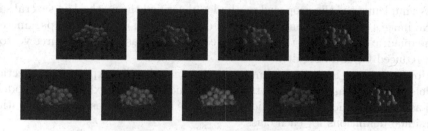

Fig. 12. Input images of Snacks (second camera)

(a)   (b)   (c)   (d)

Fig. 13. Average images and initial shapes (Snacks)

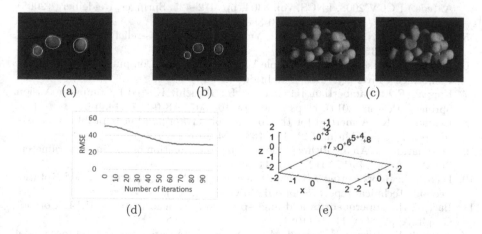

(a)   (b)   (c)

(d)   (e)

Fig. 14. Results for Snacks

6   Conclusions

In the present paper, we propose a method for parameter estimation of ellipsoids and single-leaf hyperboloids from images under various light sources with multiple cameras. The proposed method is to search for a set of parameters that minimizes the differences between the input images and estimated images calculated based on the parameters and the image formation model. In order to deal with quadrics, it is important to define residuals in the cost function depending on the inside or outside of the contour of the estimated quadric surface and/or the contour of the target object, and this allows us to easily use multiple-view images for photometric stereo.

We implemented the proposed method and verified the method on several sets of real images and found that the proposed method can estimate the parameters of the quadric surface(s) of the target object(s) as well as the light source vectors with reduced GBR ambiguity.

However, there is room for improvement, including incorporating reflection models [12] other than the Lambertian model and/or more flexible shape models, such as superquadrics, consideration of shadows and occlusions, and justification of residual definitions for each class.

References

1. Ramamoorthi, R., Hanrahan, P.: A signal-processing framework for inverse rendering. In: SIGGRAPH 2001, pp. 117–128 (2001)
2. Woodham, R.J.: Photometric method for determining surface orientation from multiple images. Opt. Eng. 19(I), 139–144 (1980)
3. Shi, B., Mo, Z., Wu, Z., Duan, D., Yeung, S.-K., Tan, P.: A benchmark dataset and evaluation for non-lambertian and uncalibrated photometric stereo. IEEE Trans. Pattern Anal. Mach. Intell. (TPAMI) 41(2), 271–284 (2019)
4. Migita, T., Ogino, S., Shakunaga, T.: Direct bundle estimation for recovery of shape, reflectance property and light position. In: Forsyth, D., Torr, P., Zisserman, A. (eds.) ECCV 2008. LNCS, vol. 5304, pp. 412–425. Springer, Heidelberg (2008). https://doi.org/10.1007/978-3-540-88690-7_31
5. Belhumeur, P.N., Kriegman, D.J., Yuille, A.L.: The bas-relief ambiguity. Int. J. Comput. Vis. 35(1), 33–44 (1999)
6. Hartley, R., Zisserman, A.: Multiple View Geometry in Computer Vison, 2nd edn. Cambridge University Press, Cambridge (2003)
7. Koppal, S.J.: Lambertian reflectance. In: Ikeuchi, K. (ed.) Computer Vision. Springer, Boston (2014). https://doi.org/10.1007/978-0-387-31439-6
8. Levenberg, K.: A method for the solution of certain non-linear problems in least squares. Q. Appl. Math. 2(2), 164–168 (1944)
9. Marquardt, D.: An algorithm for least-squares estimation of nonlinear parameters. SIAM J. Appl. Math. 11(2), 431–441 (1963)
10. Diebel, J.: Representing Attitude: Euler Angles, Unit Quaternions, and Rotation Vectors. Technical report, Stanford University (2006)
11. Barr, A.H.: Superquadrics and angle-preserving transformations. IEEE Comput. Graph. Appl. 1(1), 11–23 (1981)
12. Matusik, W., Pfister, H., Brand, M., McMillan, L.: A data-driven reflectance model. ACM Trans. Graph. 22(3), 759–769 (2003)

Gaussian Processes for Efficient Plane-Based Camera Calibration

Yuji Oyamada[✉]

Tottori University, Tottori, Japan
oyamada@tottori-u.ac.jp

Abstract. Camera calibration is a crucial pre-processing for 3D related computer vision applications. When non-expert calibration operators capture calibration images, they strongly require guidance what kind of images must be taken. In the literature, several types of supports have been proposed.

Focusing on the plane-based calibration method proposed by Zhang, this paper proposed to such non-expert calibration operators. The proposed method asks such operators to take calibration images with variety of position and orientation and the method takes a subset of good quality images. Thanks to Gaussian Process modeling, the proposed method can select a near optimum subset with some accuracy guarantee in the sense of submodularity. To enable this, we propose to use 4-point parameterized homography as a global image feature. We conduct a small experiment with both synthesized and a public dataset and validate the proposed method works.

Keywords: Camera calibration · Image selection · Gaussian Process · Submodular function maximization · Greedy algorithm

1 Introduction

Camera calibration estimates camera parameters that represent camera's internal structure and its lens property as well as its external property [22]. Calibration is a necessary pre-processing to recover 3D information from images such as multi-view stereo and visual SLAM.

Camera calibration requires reference objects whose shape in the real world is known. The 3D information of those reference objects are compared to its observation on images for camera parameter estimation. In the history of camera calibration, several types of reference objects have been used. Three-dimensional objects such as boxes are well used in 80s and 90s [18,20]. Those reference objects enable single-shot calibration, however they take time to measure their real shape and it is difficult to fill camera's view volume by such objects. Zhang proposed a 2D object-based [21] and a 1D object-based calibration [23] respectively. The 2D object-based method has been one of the most popular method because of its ease of use. The method is implemented in popular Computer Vision library

© Springer Nature Singapore Pte Ltd. 2020
W. Ohyama and S. K. Jung (Eds.): IW-FCV 2020, CCIS 1212, pp. 333–346, 2020.
https://doi.org/10.1007/978-981-15-4818-5_25

such as OpenCV [14] and MatLab toolbox [2]. We remind the readers the detail of the plane-based calibration method in Appendix A.

Researchers have paid attention to support non-expert calibration operators. Industrial software and mobile applications related to 3D reconstruction requires even non-expert persons to operate camera calibration. Without expertise on the operation, such operators have no ideas what kind of images they have to take for accurate calibration. One of the intuitive supports is visual guidance during image acquisition. Richardson et al. proposed a visual guidance that shows where operators must locate a reference plane on a computer monitor while they acquire images [17]. This support is very intuitive and thus even non-expert operators achieve as high accuracy as expert ones. Oyamada et al. proposed an indirect support from another aspect [15]. For accurate lens distortion estimation, reference objects must be located closer to image border but operators avoid locating reference objects from image border to keep it visible. This dilemma is solved by using random dot markers [19], each dot on a plane marker is tractable even under partial occlusion. Contrast to the previous type support, their support is indirect, however can relax the pressure on the operators. Last but not the least, it is another direct support to visualize both good and bad images such as one provided by Geiger et al. [4]. Non-expert operators can refer to those visualization especially when their calibration result is worse than expected.

1.1 Our Contribution

We aim to support such non-expert calibration operators those who have less knowledge on what kind of calibration images they should take. Contrast to the aforementioned existing methods, this paper proposes another type of support that relaxes pressure on non-expert operators during image acquisition. Assuming that huge number of images acquired by non-expert operators contain enough number of good quality images, our idea is to select a subset of those good quality images from all the acquired images. If the selected subset results as high accuracy as the result with all the acquired images, non-expert operators acquires as much pictures as they can without any hesitation. We regard this mental relaxation during image acquisition is another kind of indirect support for non-expert operators.

This subset selection problem is known as an NP-hard problem [7]. To accomplish the aim, we introduce a well-established solution for sensor location problems, greedy selection algorithm with Gaussian Processes modeling. The greedy selection algorithm gives a near-optimum solution with a constant factor approximation [12,13]. Following the existing procedure, the remaining problem is to derive an image feature that is an appropriate metric for evaluating the state of calibration images. We proposed to use 4-point parameterized homography [1] as global image feature and to derive a calibration image selection method based on the greedy selection algorithm.

To summarize this section, our contribution is that (1) we introduce the concept of sensor location problem for selecting good camera calibration images, (2) we propose to use 4-point parameterized homography as an image feature for a metric for calibration image selection, and (3) we validate the proposed method realizes efficient camera calibration that achieves as high quality as calibration with huge number of images.

2   Gaussian Processes for Solving Sensor Location Problems

This section introduces how Gaussian Processes (GPs) are used to solve sensor location problems. The readers those who expect further information can refer to a survey paper by Krause [7].

2.1   Gaussian Process Model

A Gaussian Process is a stochastic process that is applicable for regression [16]. Given a set of input data $\mathcal{X} = (\boldsymbol{x}_1, \ldots, \boldsymbol{x}_N)$, GP represents the joint distribution of the corresponding outputs $\mathcal{Y} = (\boldsymbol{y}_1, \ldots, \boldsymbol{y}_N)$ is a multi-variate Gaussian distribution with mean $\boldsymbol{\mu}$ and covariance $\boldsymbol{K}$ as

$$(\boldsymbol{y}_1, \ldots, \boldsymbol{y}_N) \sim \mathcal{N}(\boldsymbol{\mu}|\boldsymbol{K}), \tag{1}$$

$$\boldsymbol{\mu} = (\mu(\boldsymbol{x}_1), \ldots, \mu(\boldsymbol{x}_N)), \tag{2}$$

$$\boldsymbol{K} = \begin{bmatrix} k(\boldsymbol{x}_1, \boldsymbol{x}_1) & k(\boldsymbol{x}_1, \boldsymbol{x}_2) & \ldots & k(\boldsymbol{x}_1, \boldsymbol{x}_N) \\ k(\boldsymbol{x}_2, \boldsymbol{x}_1) & k(\boldsymbol{x}_2, \boldsymbol{x}_2) & \ldots & k(\boldsymbol{x}_2, \boldsymbol{x}_N) \\ \vdots & \vdots & \ddots & \vdots \\ k(\boldsymbol{x}_N, \boldsymbol{x}_1) & k(\boldsymbol{x}_N, \boldsymbol{x}_2) & \ldots & k(\boldsymbol{x}_N, \boldsymbol{x}_N) \end{bmatrix}, \tag{3}$$

where k denotes a kernel function. The kernel function that measures the similarity between two inputs is arbitrary for the target problem. One of the important properties of GPs is that we can predict conditional probability of a new input $\boldsymbol{x}'$ as $p(\boldsymbol{x}'|\mathcal{X})$ given some observation $\mathcal{D} = \{(\boldsymbol{x}_i, \boldsymbol{y}_i)\}, i = 1, \ldots, N$. Following the Gaussian distribution's formula, the conditional mean $\mu(\boldsymbol{x}' \mid \mathcal{X})$ and variance $\sigma^2(\boldsymbol{x}' \mid \mathcal{X})$ is derived as

$$\mu(\boldsymbol{x}' \mid \mathcal{X}) = \mu(\boldsymbol{x}') + \Sigma_{\boldsymbol{x}'\mathcal{X}} \Sigma_{\mathcal{X}\mathcal{X}}^{-1} \begin{bmatrix} \boldsymbol{x}_1 - \mu(\boldsymbol{x}_1) \\ \vdots \\ \boldsymbol{x}_N - \mu(\boldsymbol{x}_N) \end{bmatrix} \tag{4}$$

$$\sigma^2(\boldsymbol{x}' \mid \mathcal{X}) = k(\boldsymbol{x}', \boldsymbol{x}') - \Sigma_{\boldsymbol{x}'\mathcal{X}} \Sigma_{\mathcal{X}\mathcal{X}}^{-1} \Sigma_{\mathcal{X}\boldsymbol{x}'} \tag{5}$$

$$\Sigma_{\boldsymbol{x}'\mathcal{X}} = \begin{bmatrix} k(\boldsymbol{x}', \boldsymbol{x}_1) & \ldots & k(\boldsymbol{x}', \boldsymbol{x}_N) \end{bmatrix} \tag{6}$$

$$\Sigma_{\mathcal{X}\mathcal{X}} = \begin{bmatrix} k(\boldsymbol{x}_1, \boldsymbol{x}_1) & \ldots & k(\boldsymbol{x}_1, \boldsymbol{x}_N) \\ \vdots & \ddots & \vdots \\ k(\boldsymbol{x}_N, \boldsymbol{x}_1) & \ldots & k(\boldsymbol{x}_N, \boldsymbol{x}_N) \end{bmatrix} \tag{7}$$

$$\Sigma_{\mathcal{X}\boldsymbol{x}'} = \begin{bmatrix} k(\boldsymbol{x}', \boldsymbol{x}_1) \\ \vdots \\ k(\boldsymbol{x}', \boldsymbol{x}_N) \end{bmatrix}. \tag{8}$$

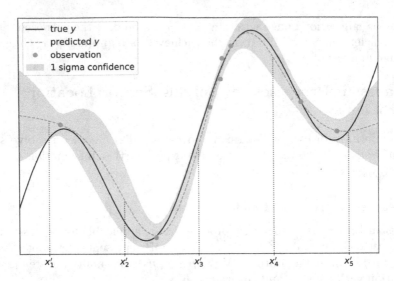

Fig. 1. 1D example of GP regression. Black curve represents true observation y, Blue dashed curve predicted mean $\mu(x)$, Blue dots observed data $\mathcal{X} = (x_1, \ldots, x_8)$, and Sky blue shaded area confidence intervals $\mu(x) \pm \sigma(x)$. (Color figure online)

As Eq. 5 shows, the uncertainty $\sigma(x' \mid \mathcal{X})$ is obtained only from the input data x' and $\mathcal{X}$ but does not need observation data $\mathcal{Y}$

Figure 1 shows an example of 1D GP regression. Blue dots represent the noisy observation data. The GP first estimates its parameters with the observation data $\{(x, y)\}$. Once the estimation is done, the GP can predict the conditional mean $\mu(x' \mid \mathcal{X})$ and covariance $\sigma(x' \mid \mathcal{X})$. The shaded area with sky blue color depicts confidence intervals $\mu(x) \pm \sigma(x)$. When the thickness of the shaded area is larger at x, the GP is has less confidence about the confidential mean. The figure has five candidate observation $\sigma(x_1'), \ldots, \sigma(x_5')$. The uncertainty on each candidate positions are 0.24, 0.44, 0.18, 0.26, 0.21 respectively. As the figure shows, x_2' has the largest uncertainty while x_3' the smallest.

2.2   Gaussian Processes for Sensor Location Problems

GP works a powerful tool for solving sensor location problems with submodular function maximization framework. [7]. Here, we introduce a portion of this technique that is a minimum requirement to understand the proposed method.

The task of sensor location problems is to find a subset of locations $\mathcal{S}$ from a ground set $\mathcal{V}$, which denotes all potential locations, by maximizing objective $f(\mathcal{S})$ that evaluates sensing quality of the selected locations $\mathcal{S}$ subject to some constraints such as the number of selected locations and sensing quality. This problem is known as an NP-hard problem.

One solution to tackle the NP-hard problem is to find a near optimal approximate solution such as greedy selection. The greedy algorithm is an iterative

Algorithm 1: Greedy algorithm conditioned by the size of subset $\mathcal{S}$.

1 $\mathcal{S} = \emptyset$;
2 **while** $|\mathcal{S}| < k$ **do**
3 $\quad$ $\hat{\imath} = \arg\max\limits_{i \in \mathcal{V} \setminus \mathcal{S}} f(\mathcal{S}, i)$;
4 $\quad$ $\mathcal{S} = \mathcal{S} \cup \{\hat{\imath}\}$;
5 **end**

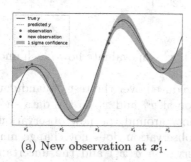
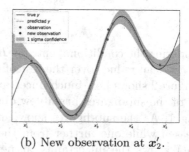

(a) New observation at x_1'. $\qquad\qquad$ (b) New observation at x_2'.

Fig. 2. How additional observation effects the uncertainty over potential area.

procedure, each of which selects a location that maximizes the objective at the iteration as shown in Algorithm 1.

When the objective f is monotonic and submodular, the greedy algorithm gives an approximation $\mathcal{S}_{\mathrm{greedy}}$ with constant factor [12, 13].

$$f(\mathcal{S}_{\mathrm{greedy}}) \geq \left(1 - \frac{1}{e}\right) \max_{|\mathcal{S}| \leq k} f(\mathcal{S}) \tag{9}$$

$$\text{subject to } f(A \cup \{s\}) \geq f(A) \tag{10}$$

$$f(A \cup \{s\}) - f(A) \geq f(B \cup \{s\}) - f(B) \forall A \subseteq B, s \notin B \tag{11}$$

where Eq. 10 describes the monotone constraint and Eq. 11 the submodularity constraint respectively.

Guestrin et al. proposed to use mutual information gain about the sensor location [5]. The mutual information for a subset $\mathcal{S}$ is defined as

$$f(\mathcal{S}) = H(\mathcal{S}) - H(\mathcal{S} \mid \overline{\mathcal{S}}) \tag{12}$$

$$H(\mathcal{S}) = \frac{1}{2} \log\left(2\pi e \sigma^2(\mathcal{S})\right), \tag{13}$$

where $H(\mathcal{S})$ denotes the entropy of $\mathcal{S}$ and $\overline{\mathcal{S}} = \mathcal{V} \setminus \mathcal{S}$ the complement of $\mathcal{S}$. So, the mutual information gain for a candidate $i \in \overline{\mathcal{S}}$ is rewritten as

$$f(\mathcal{S}, i) = f(\mathcal{S} \cup \{i\}) - f(\mathcal{S}) \tag{14}$$

$$= H(i \mid \mathcal{S}) - H(i \mid \overline{\mathcal{S}}.) \tag{15}$$

Table 1. The uncertainty of the 1D example of GP regression.

Location x_i'	$\sigma(x_i')$	$\sigma(\bar{x} \mid x_i')$
x_1'	0.24	230.54
x_2'	**0.44**	**193.22**
x_3'	0.18	235.19
x_4'	0.26	215.68
x_5'	0.21	225.29

Considering the conditional entropy $H(\mathcal{S} \mid \overline{\mathcal{S}})$, we can evaluate how much uncertainty we can reduce over the rest of candidates $\overline{\mathcal{S}}$.

Figure 2 shows how much uncertainty is reduced over the rest of candidates. Each of the sub-figures has a new observation at x_1' and x_2' to the data shown in Fig. 1. As the sub-figures show, uncertainty around the new observation is decreased while one further from the new observation does not change much. Table 1 shows the uncertainty at new observation $\sigma(x_i')$ and the uncertainty over rest of candidate positions $\sigma(\bar{x} \mid x_i')$ where $\bar{x}$ denote the rest of candidate positions. The uncertainty over entire area without new observation is 263.80 while one with any of new observation is smaller. This means that all of the new observation contributes to reduce the uncertainty. The largest uncertainty reduction is achieved with the new observation at x_2' where the uncertainty $\sigma(x_i')$ is also largest. Interest fact is that x_5' is less uncertainty than x_1' but obtains larger uncertainty reduction. This is the reason why we use mutual information rather than the uncertainty itself.

3   Proposed Method

We propose an image-set selection method based on Gaussian Processes to enable efficient plane-based camera calibration. The method is based on GP for sensor location problems by Guestrin et al. [5]. Our contribution is to propose an image feature that describes calibration images' location property and to validate the feature enables to select near optimal calibration image subset. Algorithm 2 shows brief overview of the method consisting of two steps. The first step (lines 1–3 in Algorithm 2) extracts a feature v for each image I. Contrast to typical local feature descriptors such as SIFT [9], the extracted feature is global. As written in Sect. 3.1, we propose several features and will evaluate their efficiency and effectiveness in Sect. 4 The second step (lines 4–8 in Algorithm 2) selects k images $\mathcal{S} = \{\hat{I}_1, \ldots, \hat{I}_k\}$ from the all N input images $\mathcal{V} = \{I_1, \ldots, I_N\}$. The selection procedure is same as a greedy selection for sensor location by Guestrin et al. [5]. In each selection i, the method selects an image $\hat{I}_i$ that maximizes an objective function among the remaining images $\mathcal{V} \setminus \mathcal{S}$. The objective function considers a kind of information gain from the extracted features.

Algorithm 2: The proposed method

Data: $\mathcal{V} = \{I_1, \ldots, I_N\}$: all captured images
Result: $\mathcal{S} = \{\hat{I}_1, \ldots, \hat{I}_k\}$: selected images
1 **for** $n = 1, \ldots, N$ **do**
2    $v_n = \text{ExtractImageFeature}(I_n)$;
3 **end**
4 $\mathcal{S} = \emptyset$;
5 **while** $|\mathcal{S}| < k$ **do**
6    $\hat{I} = \arg\max\limits_{i \in \mathcal{V} \setminus \mathcal{S}} f(\mathcal{S}, I_i)$;
7    $\mathcal{S} = \mathcal{S} \cup \{\hat{I}\}$;
8 **end**

3.1 Image Feature

The proposed method uses a vectorized 4-point parameterized homography [1] as global image feature. A homography H contains both intrinsic parameters and extrinsic parameters information as

$$H = K \begin{bmatrix} r_1 & r_2 & t \end{bmatrix}, \tag{16}$$

where K denotes the calibration matrix containing intrinsic parameters, r_1 and r_2 the first and second column vectors of rotation matrix $R = [r_1 \; r_2 \; r_3]$, and t the translation vector. Its 4-point parameterization H' is formulated as

$$H' = \begin{bmatrix} u_1 & u_2 & u_3 & u_4 \\ v_1 & v_2 & v_3 & v_4 \end{bmatrix} \simeq H \begin{bmatrix} 0 & 0 & 1 & 1 \\ 0 & 1 & 0 & 1 \\ 1 & 1 & 1 & 1 \end{bmatrix}. \tag{17}$$

The 4-point parameterized homography H' describes how a unit rectangle is distorted by the homography H. Figure 3 shows how pure translation and rotation distorts a unit rectangle and L_2 norm of the 4-point parameterized homography.

The benefit of the 4-point parameterization is the consistency of metric. The original 3×3 parameterization mixes the rotation and orientation information as shown in Eq. 16. If we use the 3×3 parameterization as input for GP, we have to balance the contribution of them. Imagine a situation that we have the following homographies

$$H = K \begin{bmatrix} r_1 & r_2 & t \end{bmatrix} \tag{18}$$

$$H_r = K \begin{bmatrix} r_1 + 1 & r_2 & t \end{bmatrix} \tag{19}$$

$$H_t = K \begin{bmatrix} r_1 & r_2 & t + 1 \end{bmatrix}, \tag{20}$$

where $1 = (1 \; 1 \; 1)^\top$. Both H_r and H_t have same L_2 distance from H but the difference from H occurs in different space, one in rotation the other in translation. When we use the original 3×3 parameterization with raw data,

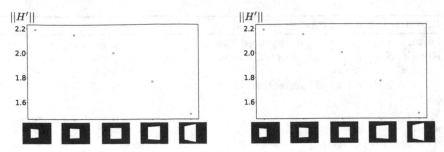

(a) Pure translation along z axis. From left to right, camera moves further from the image plane.

(b) Pure rotation around y axis. From left to right, camera rotates $-2\theta, \theta, 0, \theta, 2\theta$ degrees.

Fig. 3. How pure translation and rotation effects on a unit rectangle and 4-parameterized homography H'.

GP, or any regressor, cannot distinguish the difference in different spaces. This problem is usually tackled by balancing the contribution of these two factors. Instead of balancing them, we adapt the 4-point parameterization so that we can use homography as location variable of GP.

3.2   Kernel Function

The proposed method adapts a typical radial basis function (RBF kernel) as the kernel function as

$$k\left(\boldsymbol{x}_i, \boldsymbol{x}_j\right) = \exp\left(-\gamma||\boldsymbol{x}_i - \boldsymbol{x}_j||^2\right), \tag{21}$$

where γ is the hyper-parameter that balances the pairwise distance contribution. A smaller γ preserves slight pairwise difference more than larger ones. When γ is set too large, most of non-diagonal elements of the covariance matrix K_{ij} becomes negligible and thus the proposed method takes images according to their original order, namely the method takes $I_1, I_2, \ldots, I_k$.

With some small dataset, we have tuned the hyper-parameter γ and it is set to $\gamma = 10^{-5}$. We believe that the hyper-parameter is robust against the size of target because the criteria, 4-point parameterized homography, evaluates how the orientation and rotation of plane calibration target with a unit square. The variance of multiple homographies must be robust against dataset size.

4   Experimental Results

To validate the proposed method, we conducted experiments with synthetic and real data. The experiment with synthetic data is to confirm that 4-point parameterized homography is an appropriate feature (Sect. 4.1) while the one with real data is to validate the method works as expected (Sect. 4.2).

4.1   Experiments with Synthetic Data

We conducted a quantitative evaluation with synthetic data. Specifically, we tested the behavior of the greedy selection algorithm with different image features. For data synthesis, we first generated pure rotation r and then computed its corresponding homography H and its 4-point parameterization H' by using Eq. 16 and Eq. 17 respectively. Next, we applied the greedy selection algorithm with different image features.

In this experiment, we synthesized rotation vectors on a spherical grid. The azimuth angle is uniformly sampled 18 times from 0.0 to 2.0π radian while the elevation angle θ is uniformly sampled 6 times from 0.0 to 0.5π radian, 128 rotation vectors were synthesized in total. The focal length f was set to 600.0 and the principal point (c_x, c_y) was set to (640.0, 480.0). As image features, we tested rotation vector r, homography H, and 4-point parameterized one H'.

Figure 4 plots the selected location using different image features when the number of selected locations k is 27. Each selected location is computed by applying the corresponding rotation to a unit vector $(0, 0, 1)^\top$. As the figure shows, different image features result not exactly but similar selection. As an evaluation metric, we compute circular variance, which represents how data is spread on a circle/sphere [10], for the selected locations. For the selected locations $x_1, \ldots, x_k$ on a sphere, their circular variance R is computed as

$$R = 1 - \frac{1}{k} \left| \sum_i x_i \right|. \tag{22}$$

The circular variance ranges from 0.0 to 1.0 and larger value represents the locations are more spread. In this experiment, the circular values for r, H, H' are 0.42, 0.41, 0.39 respectively. Same as qualitative result, the circular variance is not exactly same but similar.

4.2   Experiments with Real Data

We conducted a quantitative evaluation with a public dataset. In this experiment, we used OpenCV left camera images shown in Fig. 5. For varying number of selected images $k = 3, \ldots, 6$, the proposed method selects a subset S and ran calibration with the selected subset. The evaluation metric is the reprojection error of calibration optimization[1]. As mentioned above, we use radial basis function kernel with $\gamma = 10^{-5}$ as its hyper-parameter (Eq. 21). For comparison, we also implemented the proposed method with original homography, 3×3 representation and random selection method. The proposed method with original homography uses same kernel function. The random selection method selects images with uniform probability. To cancel the bias, random selection was executed for 100 times for each k and the mean and standard deviation of reprojection error is computed.

---

[1] We cannot evaluate the calibration parameters because the dataset does not contain that information unfortunately.

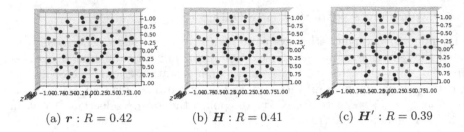

(a) $r : R = 0.42$ (b) $H : R = 0.41$ (c) $H' : R = 0.39$

Fig. 4. The selected location using different image features under pure rotation from bird-view. Red and black circles denote selected and deselected locations. R in each sub-caption denotes the circular variance for each case. (Color figure online)

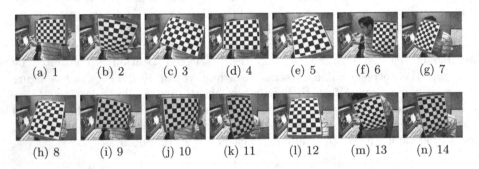

(a) 1   (b) 2   (c) 3   (d) 4   (e) 5   (f) 6   (g) 7

(h) 8   (i) 9   (j) 10   (k) 11   (l) 12   (m) 13   (n) 14

Fig. 5. All the images of OpenCV left. Each sub-caption denotes the index of the image.

Figures 6 and 7 show the selected images using H and H'. The difference is 4-th and 5-th selected images are swapped but the other ones are same. This result shows that homography expression does not differ the selection much.

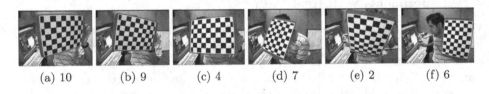

(a) 10   (b) 9   (c) 4   (d) 7   (e) 2   (f) 6

Fig. 6. The selected images using H.

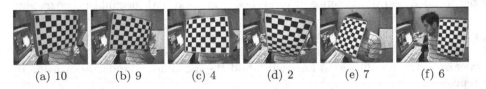

(a) 10   (b) 9   (c) 4   (d) 2   (e) 7   (f) 6

Fig. 7. The selected images using H'.

Figure 8 shows reprojection error with respect to the number of selected images k. The reprojection error of both homography representations results similar reprojection error and the error is smaller than one obtained with all images, we regard the result as an evidence that the proposed method supports calibration effectively and efficiently. The random selection results slight larger mean reprojection error than the greedy selection ones for all k. Considering its standard deviation, we can say the proposed greedy selection selects a subset with good image quality in the sense of calibration result.

From those results, we can say that the proposed method works better than random selection with respect to reprojection error. However, the benefit of using 4-point parameterized homography is weakly shown. We should also note that further evaluation with ground truth value is required.

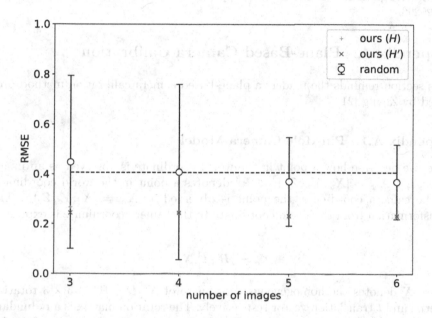

Fig. 8. Reprojection error w.r.t. k. The horizontal dashed line: RMSE with all 14 images. Red +: RMSE by our method with $\boldsymbol{H}$. Blue x: RMSE by our method with $\boldsymbol{H'}$. White circle with error bar: RMSE of random selection. (Color figure online)

5   Conclusion

In this paper, we aimed to support non-expert camera calibration operators who have less knowledge on what kind of calibration images are supposed to be taken. We introduced a well-established solution for sensor location problem, greedy selection algorithm with GP modeling. To select good quality images in the sense of camera calibration, we proposed to use 4-point parameterized homography as global image feature. As the experimental result showed, the proposed method worked with a small dataset.

There still remain several cues to realize practical quality method. In algorithmic sense, the proposed method should have auto-tuning scheme for hyperparameter of the kernel function. We set the hyper-parameter with small portion of data but are not sure the tuning is fine for variety of cameras and lenses. It is also important to introduce another criteria to stop the iteration rather than the number of selected images. To realize it, we have to investigate hidden relation between the value of mutual information and calibration quality. In experimental sense, we have a lot of things to complete. Some simulation experiments are absolutely essential to validate the proposed method.

Acknowledgements. This work was supported by JSPS KAKENHI Grant Number 19K20296.

Appendix A   Plane-Based Camera Calibration

This section reminds the readers a plane-based camera calibration method proposed by Zhang [21].

Appendix A.1   Pin-Hole Camera Model

Here, we describe how a point in the world coordinate is observed as an image point. Let $\boldsymbol{X}_w = [X_w, Y_w, Z_w]^\top \in \mathbb{R}^3$ denotes a point in the world coordinate. In the camera coordinate, the point is observed as $\boldsymbol{X}_c = [X_c, Y_c, Z_c]^\top$. The transformation from the world coordinate to the camera coordinate is expressed as

$$\tilde{\boldsymbol{X}}_c = \left[\boldsymbol{R} \mid \boldsymbol{t} \right] \tilde{\boldsymbol{X}}_w \tag{23}$$

where $\tilde{X}$ denotes the homogeneous coordinate of X, $\boldsymbol{R} \in \mathbb{R}^{3 \times 3}$ 3×3 rotation matrix, and $\boldsymbol{t}$ translation vector respectively. The rotation matrix is a redundant representation of rotation vector $\boldsymbol{r} \in \mathbb{R}^3$. The homogeneous coordinate of a point is described by its tilde as $\tilde{\boldsymbol{x}} = [\boldsymbol{x}^\top, 1]^\top$. Following a polynomial lens distortion model [3,20], the point is observed on the canonical frame as

$$\boldsymbol{x}_d = \boldsymbol{x}_n + \boldsymbol{d}_{\mathrm{rad}} + \boldsymbol{d}_{\mathrm{tan}}, \tag{24}$$

$$\boldsymbol{x}_n = \begin{bmatrix} x_n \\ y_n \end{bmatrix} = \frac{1}{Z_c} \begin{bmatrix} X_c \\ Y_c \end{bmatrix} \tag{25}$$

$$\boldsymbol{d}_{\mathrm{rad}} = \begin{bmatrix} (\delta_1 r^2 + \delta_2 r^4 + \delta_5 r^6) x_n \\ (\delta_1 r^2 + \delta_2 r^4 + \delta_5 r^6) y_n \end{bmatrix}, \tag{26}$$

$$\boldsymbol{d}_{\mathrm{tan}} = \begin{bmatrix} 2\delta_3 x_n y_n + \delta_4 (3x_n^2 + y_n^2) \\ 2\delta_4 x_n y_n + \delta_3 (x_n^2 + 3y_n^2) \end{bmatrix}, \tag{27}$$

$$r = \sqrt{x_n^2 + y_n^2}, \tag{28}$$

where $\boldsymbol{\delta} = [\delta_1, \ldots, \delta_5]^\top$ denotes lens distortion parameters and $\boldsymbol{d}_{\text{rad}}$ and $\boldsymbol{d}_{\text{tan}}$ denote the radial distortion and tangential distortion vector respectively. The final pixel coordinate $\boldsymbol{x}$ is described using a calibration matrix $\boldsymbol{K} \in \mathbb{R}^{3 \times 3}$ as

$$\boldsymbol{K} = \begin{bmatrix} f_x & \theta & o_x \\ 0 & f_y & o_y \\ 0 & 0 & 1 \end{bmatrix}, \tag{29}$$

$$\tilde{\boldsymbol{x}} = \boldsymbol{K}\tilde{\boldsymbol{x}}_d, \tag{30}$$

where $[f_x, f_y]^\top$ denotes the focal length along x and y axes respectively, θ the skew parameter, and $[o_x, o_y]^\top$ the principle point.

Appendix A.2 Plane-Based Camera Calibration

Zhang proposed a user friendly plane-based camera calibration method [23].

We first prepare a plane calibration object that has $N(\geq 4)$ points $\{\boldsymbol{X}_n = (X_n, Y_n)\}^2$ on its surface. For calibration, we take $M(\geq 3)$ images $\{\boldsymbol{I}_m\}$ with different orientation. For each input image $\boldsymbol{I}_m$, we first extract N feature points $\{\boldsymbol{x}_{n,m}\}$ on the target and compute the homography $\boldsymbol{H}_m$ describing a 2D-2D transformation from the reference target to the input image plane as

$$\boldsymbol{x}_{n,m} = \boldsymbol{H}_m \boldsymbol{X}_n. \tag{31}$$

The homography can be decomposed into

$$\boldsymbol{H} = \boldsymbol{K} \begin{bmatrix} \boldsymbol{r}_1 & \boldsymbol{r}_2 & \boldsymbol{t} \end{bmatrix}, \tag{32}$$

where $\boldsymbol{r}_1$ and $\boldsymbol{r}_2$ denotes the first and second column vectors of rotation matrix $\boldsymbol{R}$. From M homographies $\{\boldsymbol{H}_m\}$, we estimate the intrinsic parameter $\boldsymbol{K}$ using orthogonality of vanishing points obtained from homographies [6]. Once the intrinsic parameters are estimated, we compute the extrinsic parameters $\{\boldsymbol{r}_m, \boldsymbol{t}_m\}$ given $\boldsymbol{K}$ and $\boldsymbol{H}_m$ by solving Perspective-n-Points problem. Lastly, we optimize all the parameters by non-linear least squares [8,11].

References

1. Baker, S., Datta, A., Kanade, T.: Parameterizing homographies. Technical report. CMU-RI-TR-06-11, Carnegie Mellon University (2006)
2. Bouguet, J.Y.: Camera calibration toolbox for matlab (2004)
3. Faugueras, O.D., Toscani, G.: The calibration problem for stereoscopic vision. In: IEEE Conference on Computer Vision and Pattern Recognition (CVPR), pp. 15–20 (1986)
4. Geiger, A., Moosmann, F., Car, Ö., Schuster, B., Stiller, C.: Camera and Range Sensor Calibration Toolbox: Frequently Made Mistakes. http://www.cvlibs.net/software/calibration/mistakes.php

---

² We omit the 3rd dimension because all points lie on a plane.

5. Guestrin, C., Krause, A., Singh, A.P.: Near-optimal sensor placements in gaussian processes. In: International Conference on Machine Learning (ICML) (2005)
6. Hartley, R., Zisserman, A.: Estimation - 2D projective transformations, chap. 4. In: Multiple View Geometry in Computer Vision, 2 edn, pp. 87–131. Cambridge University Press (2003)
7. Krause, A., Golovin, D.: Submodular function maximization. In: Tractability: Practical Approaches to Hard Problems. Cambridge University Press, February 2014
8. Levenberg, K.: A method for the solution of certain non-linear problems in least squares. Q. Appl. Math. **2**, 164–168 (1944)
9. Lowe, D.G.: Distinctive image features from scale-invariant keypoints. Int. J. Comput. Vis. **60**(2), 91–110 (2004)
10. Mardia, K.V., Jupp, P.E.: Directional Statistics. Probability and Statistics. Wiley, Hoboken (1999)
11. Marquardt, D.W.: An algorithm for least-squares estimation of nonlinear parameters. J. Soc. Ind. Appl. Math. **11**(2), 431–441 (1963)
12. Nemhauser, G.L., Wolsey, L.A.: Best algorithms for approximating the maximum of a submodular set function. Math. Oper. Res. **3**(3), 177–188 (1978)
13. Nemhauser, G.L., Wolsey, L.A., Fisher, M.L.: An analysis of approximations for maximizing submodular set functions—I. Math. Program. **14**(1), 265–294 (1978)
14. OpenCV: OpenCV: Camera calibration and 3D reconstruction (calib3d module)
15. Oyamada, Y., Fallavollita, P., Navab, N.: Single camera calibration using partially visible calibration objects based on random dots marker tracking algorithm. In: IEEE ISMAR 2012 Workshop on Tracking Methods and Applications (TMA) (2012)
16. Rasmussen, C., Williams, C.: Gaussian Processes for Machine Learning. Adaptive Computation and Machine Learning. MIT Press, Cambridge (2006)
17. Richardson, A., Strom, J., Olson, E.: AprilCal: assisted and repeatable camera calibration. In: IEEE/RSJ International Conference on Intelligent Robots and Systems (IROS) (2013)
18. Tsai, R.Y.: A versatile camera calibration technique for high-accuracy 3D machine vision metrology using off-the-shelf TV cameras and lenses. IEEE Trans. Robot. Autom. **3**(4), 323–344 (1987)
19. Uchiyama, H., Saito, H.: Random dot markers. In: IEEE Virtual Reality Conference, pp. 271–272 (2011)
20. Weng, J., Cohen, P., Herniou, M.: Camera calibration with distortion models and accuracy evaluation. IEEE Trans. Pattern Anal. Mach. Intell. **14**(10), 965–980 (1992)
21. Zhang, Z.: A flexible new technique for camera calibration. IEEE Trans. Pattern Anal. Mach. Intell. **22**(11), 1330–1334 (2000)
22. Zhang, Z.: Camera Calibration, chap. 2, pp. 5–43. Prentice Hall (2004)
23. Zhang, Z.: Camera calibration with one-dimensional objects. IEEE Trans. Pattern Anal. Mach. Intell. **26**(7), 892–899 (2004)

Leveraging Pyramidal Feature Hierarchy
for 3D Reconstruction

Fairuz Safwan Mahad(✉)📵, Masakazu Iwamura📵, and Koichi Kise📵

Graduate School of Engineering, Osaka Prefecture University,
1-1 Gakuen-cho, Naka, Sakai, Osaka 599-8531, Japan
fsafwan88@gmail.com, {masa,kise}@cs.osakafu-u.ac.jp

Abstract. Most state-of-the-art 3D reconstruction methods with CNNs
have focused on completion and generalization of the reconstructed 3D
models. Although the reconstructed 3D models may look complete,
mostly lose out in detail causing a wider gap between the reconstructed
3D model and the groundtruth. We propose a method that adapts a pyramidal hierarchical-based network. Our strategy is to focus on improving
the reconstruction of the detailed parts which comprise of thin and fine
parts of the 3D models. Improving the detailed parts of the 3D model
helps improve the accuracy and the overall shape of the 3D model resulting in a reconstructed 3D model which looks closer to the groundtruth.
The advantage of using a pyramidal hierarchical-based network is that it
builds a feature pyramid which considers high-level semantics at different scales. This builds a network that is tailored to focus on the detailed
parts of the 3D model while considering the overall shape of the 3D
model.

Keywords: Computer vision · 3D reconstruction · Deep learning

1 Introduction

3D reconstruction is an ill-posed problem which researchers have addressed for
decades. The goal of 3D reconstruction is to reconstruct a 3D model from a
given input. Ideally, the reconstructed 3D model has to look exactly the same
as the input. However, this is far from easy to achieve as there are various
challenges to overcome in 3D reconstruction. Conventional methods such as [7,
28, 32] reconstruct 3D models based on feature point correspondences. However,
these methods are ineffective if there is a large baseline between viewpoints
which makes finding feature point correspondences even more challenging or in
the worst case, it fails. A typical solution is to acquire more viewpoints but this
is not always convenient in most cases. Other disadvantages include occlusion
and error in point correspondences.

In recent years, researches such as [4, 6, 12–16, 18, 26, 29, 30, 34–36] have
started utilizing convolutional neural networks (CNNs) to reconstruct 3D models and have achieved considerable success. Unlike the conventional methods,

W. Ohyama and S. K. Jung (Eds.): IW-FCV 2020, CCIS 1212, pp. 347–362, 2020.
https://doi.org/10.1007/978-981-15-4818-5_26

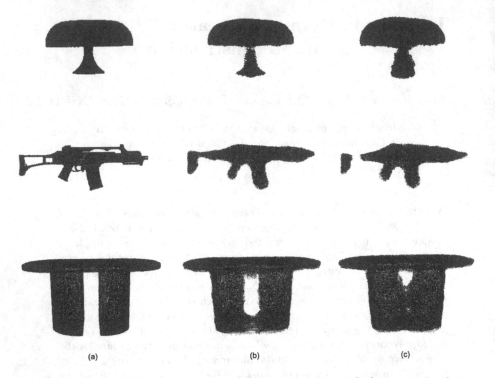

Fig. 1. Reconstructed 3D models of our proposed method and [33] from 20 depth map images with different viewpoints. (a) groundtruth. (b) Our results. (c) Soltani et al. [33].

CNNs-based methods do not require any feature point correspondences which conveniently overcomes one of the main problems in the conventional methods. However, these methods focus on the completion and generalization of the 3D models. The reconstructed 3D model often suffers from the loss in detail and resolution. Methods such as [20,33] have focused on achieving high resolution 3D models. Despite the high resolution 3D reconstructed models, they suffer from the loss in details as shown in Fig. 1(c). The mentioned detailed parts refer to the fine parts of the 3D models such as the stand of a lamp, the tip of a rifle, the stand of a chair or table. We saw a niche in further enhancing the quality of the reconstructed 3D model by focusing on the reconstruction of the detailed parts.

In this paper, we propose a simple yet effective way to further enhance the quality of the reconstructed models. Our network architecture is based on a pyramidal hierarchical-based network concept shown in Fig. 2 from [21]. [21] builds a multi-scale feature map where each feature map is made up of high-level semantic features with different spatial resolution. By leveraging the semantically strong features extracted at different levels, the reconstruction quality of the detailed parts of the 3D model can be further improved. [21] is actually designed for object detection but with a slight improvement we demonstrate that it is able

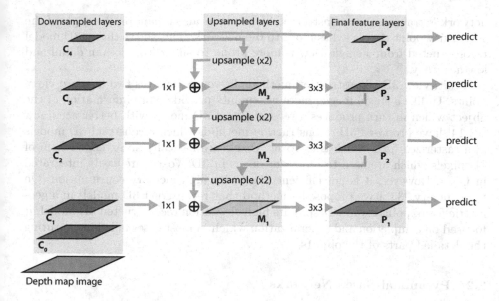

Fig. 2. Network architecture of Lin et al. [21].

to extract useful features at different scales with the purpose of enhancing the quality of the reconstructed 3D model as shown in Fig. 1. Our proposed method is an improved implementation of [33].

Our contributions are listed as follows:

- Implements a pyramidal hierarchical-based network in encoder
- Improves reconstruction of detailed parts which comprise of thin and fine parts of the 3D model
- Improves the overall shape and accuracy of the 3D reconstructed models.

2 Related Work

2.1 Single-View and Multi-view 3D Reconstruction Networks

3D reconstruction methods can be categorized in either single-view or multi-view. In a single-view 3D reconstruction method [6, 13, 15, 16, 18, 20, 29, 30, 34–36], a single image is required as input in order to reconstruct a 3D model. A single image is easily obtainable and can be convenient in certain cases. However, there are several downsides to it. A single-view 3D reconstruction is an ill-pose problem. Since only a single viewpoint is fed as input to the network, the network will estimate the unseen viewpoints of the object. In most cases, this produce a wider dissimilarity gap between the groundtruth and the reconstructed 3D model. Furthermore, apart from relying heavily on how well the network is trained, the reconstructed 3D model is also reliant on the angle of the single viewpoint that is fed as input to the network. This shows that a 3D model reconstructed from a single-view is more prone to suffer from loss in detail and low accuracy.

Multi-view 3D reconstruction methods however, involves two or more viewpoints. Unlike a single image, more viewpoints provide more information of the object which in turn produces a reconstructed 3D model with better accuracy. [12,14] have proposed 3D reconstruction methods which reconstruct 3D models in a rasterized form which is in voxel. Voxels are basically an extended form of 2D pixels which are used to represent pixels in 3D. Voxels are easily integrated in CNN. However, it is not efficient due to its high memory consumption. On the contrary, [33] have proposed a method that reconstruct 3D models in a geometric form, point clouds. Despite its high resolution reconstructed 3D model, it focused on completion and generalization which in most cases failed in capturing the detailed parts of the objects.

2.2   Pyramidal-Based Networks

Exploiting features extracted from different layers or in other words, multi-scale layers have been practiced since the early days of neural networks. This technique is especially common in addressing issues such as detection and segmentation. Methods such as [8,9,23,24,27,31] focused on segmentation while [1,2,11,19,22] focused on detection. There are also other method such as [25] that deals with pose estimation. Methods such as [8,11,25,27,31] have progressed even further by implementing skip connections that connects features from previous layers to current layers which achieved promising results. Although all of these methods adopt pyramidal-based architectures, [21] in particular stood out from the rest as predictions are made independently at all levels.

3   Approach

Our proposed method is an improved implementation of Soltani et al. [33]. [33] is a 3D shape synthesizing network that estimates a set of depth map and silhouettes. The network is trained from a collection of depth map images rendered from the ShapeNet dataset [3] using 20 pre-defined camera positions. The method takes in either 20 depth map or 20 silhouette images as input. It outputs the same number of depth map and silhouette images which amounts to a total of 40 output images. These output images are used to obtain a final 3D reconstructed model. In order to do so, each output depth map image is used to generate a group of point clouds. Accumulating all the groups of point clouds forms an initial 3D model. The output silhouette images are used to further

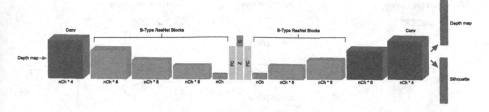

Fig. 3. Network architecture of Soltani et al. [33].

refine the initial 3D model by removing noisy points which ends up creating a final reconstructed 3D model with high resolution. Furthermore, [33] can be trained in three different ways. It can work with 20 views, a single view or 20 views with 15 to 18 of them being randomly zero out. However, the trained network cannot work with all of the three settings simultaneously. It can only be trained on any one of the three settings at a time. In other words, one would need to train three different networks in order to work with all three settings. In this paper, we will only train our network on the first setting which is working with 20 views. An overview of the network architecture of [33] is shown in Fig. 3. It implements a deep generative network, Variational Autoencoder (VAE) [17]. Both the encoder and decoder are made up of ResNet blocks [10]. Although it is able to reconstruct a high resolution 3D model, the network is designed for completion and generalization. It learns single-scaled features. Following the nature of the network, most of the detailed parts are being left out and not reconstructed.

Our goal is to further enhance the quality of the reconstructed 3D model. In order to do so, our strategy is to focus more on capturing features at tight spots such as small and thin parts of the object. This improves the quality of the reconstructed 3D model hence improving its accuracy. For this purpose, we implemented the multi-scale layered network with skip connections from [21] as shown in Fig. 2, in the encoder part of the VAE network structure used in [33]. According to [21], the multi-scale upsampled layers are made up of semantically stronger features than the downsampled layers which is the main advantage of using pyramidal-based networks. Figure 2 shows that [21] utilizes every output level $\{P_1, P_2, P_3, P_4\}$ to make predictions independently. Our proposed network architecture shown in Fig. 4 adapts similar concept but with two distinct differences. Firstly, [21] considers every output level $\{P_1, P_2, P_3, P_4\}$ independently while our proposed network concatenates the final feature maps $\{P_2, P_4\}$ producing a final merged feature map followed by a fully-connected layer. Secondly, our proposed network is implemented in the encoder of a VAE structure.

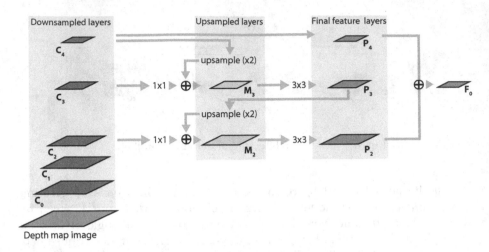

Fig. 4. Our proposed network architecture.

3.1 Network Architecture

Figure 4 shows the network architecture of our proposed method which we adapted from [21]. It features bottom-up and top-down pathways with skip connections. All blocks in both the bottom-up and top-down pathways are made up of ResNet blocks [10]. The network starts with a bottom-up pathway by scaling down the input image to feature maps of sizes $\{110^2, 53^2, 25^2, 11^2, 4^2\}$ which we denote them as $\{C_0, C_1, C_2, C_3, C_4\}$ respectively. The bottom-up pathway ends with C_4 as its last layer.

The top-down pathway begins by first upsampling the last layer which is C_4 back to a feature map of size 11^2. The layer C_3 (which is of the same spatial size as the upsampled layer from C_4) from the bottom-up pathway is associated with the upsampled layer with a 1×1 convolution. Similar to [21], the features in the upsampled layer and the skip connection layer are then concatenated which produce a feature map denoted as M_3. The layer M_3 goes through a 3×3 convolution which acts as an anti-aliasing measure to reduce the aliasing effect caused by sampling the layers, producing a final feature map for this level denoted as $\{P_3\}$. This iterates until we have the final features maps denoted as $\{P_2, P_3, P_4\}$. It is to note that $\{P_4\}$ is the same layer as $\{C_4\}$. Finally, we concatenate the final feature maps $\{P_2, P_4\}$ to produce a final merged feature map denoted as $\{F_0\}$ followed by a fully connected layer. In order to concatenate the final feature maps $\{P_2\}$ and $\{P_4\}$, we had to further downsample the layer $\{P_2\}$ in order to match the size of layer $\{P_4\}$. We did not include $\{P_3\}$ in the final merged feature map in order to reduce the number of parameters. The same reason applies to not further upsampling the layer $\{P_2\}$ to spatial size of $\{110^2, 53^2\}$. Our proposed network architecture is implemented only in the encoder of the VAE structure of [33]. We used the same decoder structure as [33].

The network in [33] can be trained either in an unsupervised manner or conditionally. For our purpose, we will train our network using the unsupervised method. Therefore, we use the same loss function as Equation (1) in [33].

4 Experiments

We evaluated our proposed method against Soltani et al. [33]. Similar to [33], we trained our network using the ShapeNet dataset [3]. The ShapeNet dataset consists of 57 object categories such as aeroplane, car, table, chair, vase. It involved a total of 56,652 3D models. Each 3D model was first rendered into 20 depth map images with distinct views. All 3D models are rendered with the same set of pre-defined camera angles. Each rendered depth map image was of size 224 × 224. In order to evaluate our method against Soltani et al. [33], we used the same dataset distribution as [33] which was 92.5% and 7.5% for training and validation respectively. We also used their pre-trained model which was used to produce the results in [33]. We present our results qualitatively and quantitatively.

4.1 Qualitative Evaluation

In this section, we present our qualitative results. We reconstructed the 3D models from the test dataset and compared our results against the groundtruth and Soltani et al. [33]. The reconstructed 3D models are all represented in point cloud form and rendered using [5]. Figure 5 shows the results for several categories such as bench, car, guitar and table. The results in Fig. 5 show that the proposed method is able reconstruct a denser model as compared to [33]. Furthermore, it is able to capture the overall shape of the 3D model better as compared to [33]. These results in a 3D reconstructed model looking much closer to the groundtruth. Apart from reconstructing parts that could not be reconstructed by [33] such as in row 2 and 3 of Fig. 5, it can also be observed that our proposed method is able to eliminate the incorrectly reconstructed parts such as in the first row in Fig. 5. This proves that concatenating the multiple-level features from the deepest layer (top-most layer of the pyramid) and the lowest layer of the feature pyramid is effective in refining parts of the reconstructed 3D model. The contributing factor lies in the multiple-level feature maps, $\{P_2\}$ and $\{P_4\}$, which have features from different levels. Concatenating features extracted on different levels allows the network to learn both coarse and fine details of the image.

However, our proposed method failed under certain circumstances. As shown in Fig. 6, our proposed method could not cope with reconstructing 3D models with complicated shapes. It especially did not work well for objects with uncommon shapes such as in row 2 and 3. Our goal is to improve the reconstruction of the fine parts of the 3D models. Therefore, although our results in Fig. 6 are better shaped than Soltani et al. [33], they are still considered a failure as the fine parts are not reconstructed.

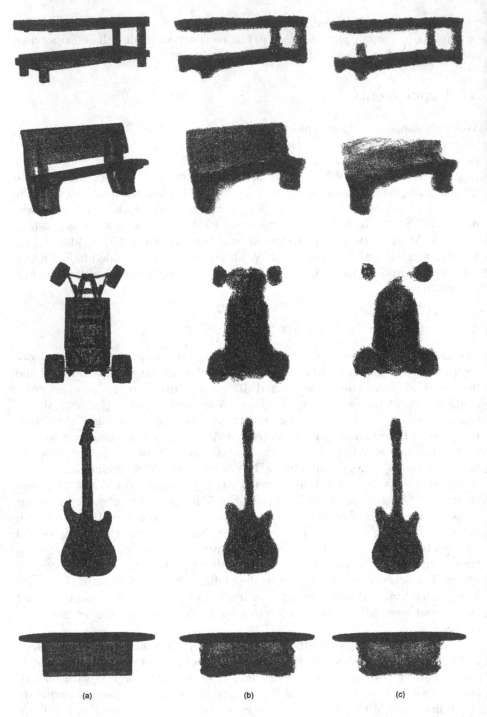

Fig. 5. Qualitative results depicting 3D reconstructed models for success cases. (a) groundtruth. (b) Our results. (c) Soltani et al. [33].

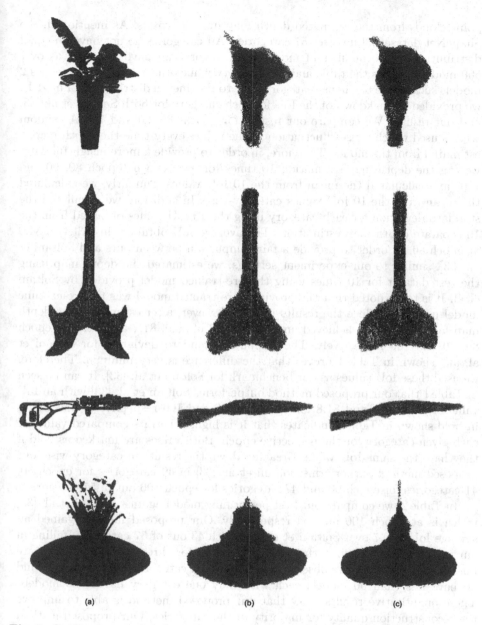

(a)   (b)   (c)

Fig. 6. Qualitative results depicting 3D reconstructed models for failure cases. (a) groundtruth. (b) Our results. (c) Soltani et al. [33].

4.2 Quantitative Evaluation

In this section, we compare our results against Soltani et al. [33] quantitatively. We used the same evaluation metric as Soltani et al. [33] which is Intersection-over-Union (IoU) in order to provide a fair comparison between the results of ours and Soltani et al. [33]. The IoU is computed by converting the projected point clouds from the estimated depth map into 3D voxels. As mentioned, the ShapeNet dataset [3] involves 57 categories. All categories do not have an equal distribution of the number of models. A category can have as many as over 500 models such as the table and car category while others can have as few as 2 models such as the birdhouse category. Due to the uneven distribution of models, we provided a breakdown of the IoU for each category for both Soltani et al. [33] and our results. We compare our results for epochs 80, 90 and 100. A random seed is used which causes fluctuation in the values every time the depth map is estimated from the model. Therefore, in order to provide a more insightful data, we ran the depth map estimation 10 times for each epoch (epoch 80, 90 and 100) and calculated the mean from the 10 IoU values. Similarly, we calculated the mean from the 10 IoU values category-wise. In addition, we calculated the standard deviation for each category using the 10 IoU values obtained from the 10 separate depth map estimation. The average IoU obtained in [33] was 84.0 at epoch 80. In order to provide a fair comparison between ours and Soltani et al. [33], similar to our experiment settings, we estimated the depth map using the test dataset for 10 times using the pre-trained model provided by Soltani et al. It is to be noted that the provided pre-trained model was the exact same model used to produce the results in [33]. However, after estimating the depth map for 10 times, we achieved an average IoU of 80.9, 81.1 and 81.0 for epoch 80, 90 and 100 respectively. The computed standard deviation for Soltani et al. [33] shown in Table 1 proves that the difference is very minimal. Therefore, we used these IoU values as our benchmark for Soltani et al. [33]. It can be seen in Table 1 that our proposed method outperforms Soltani et al. [33] with an IoU value of 81.5, 81.6 and 81.8 for epoch 80, 90 and 100 respectively. The values in bold shown in Table 1 indicates that it is higher than its compared value for each given category for the respective epoch. Both values are marked as bold if they have the same IoU value. Breaking down the results in category-wise, our proposed method outperforms Soltani et al. [33] in 40 categories for epoch 80, 41 categories for epoch 90 and 47 categories for epoch 100 out of 57 categories.

In Table 2, we compare our best performing model against Soltani et al. [33] which is at epoch 100 and 90 respectively. Our proposed method gained an average IoU of 0.7 over Soltani et al. [33] with 43 out of 57 categories falling in our favour while achieving the same IoU values for three categories which are bus, display and rifle. We observed that all eleven categories that we fell behind all have less than 50 models each with only one category having 85 models. These quantitative results show that our proposed method is able to improve the reconstruction quality for majority of the categories. Our proposed method is able improve the quality of the reconstruction while focusing on both shape completion and also on the fine parts of the models. The improvement in IoU in categories such as chair, lamp and table as shown in Table 2 further supports this claim. However, not all categories with fine parts excelled with our proposed method. Our proposed method caused a decline in IoU values in categories such as tower, motorcycle and faucet. This is due to the complex shapes that these categories have. On top of the complexity of the shapes, these categories have very few models for the network to train with which weakens the effectiveness of the proposed method.

Table 1. IoU comparison between [33] and ours. "#M" indicates #Model.

Category	#M	Epoch 80		Epoch 90		Epoch 100	
		[33]	Ours	[33]	Ours	[33]	Ours
Aeroplane	304	72.3 ±0.001	**72.8** ±0.002	72.4 ±0.001	**72.7** ±0.001	72.2 ±0.001	**72.6** ±0.001
Bag	8	78.8 ±0.007	**80.2** ±0.007	79.0 ±0.006	**80.6** ±0.006	79.0 ±0.006	**79.7** ±0.004
Basket	11	84.0 ±0.007	**85.3** ±0.007	83.8 ±0.005	**84.5** ±0.006	83.8 ±0.006	**84.7** ±0.005
Bathtub	62	87.7 ±0.003	**88.8** ±0.003	87.7 ±0.004	**87.8** ±0.004	88.1 ±0.004	**88.3** ±0.003
Bed	10	75.6 ±0.009	**78.5** ±0.007	76.0 ±0.006	**77.2** ±0.005	75.9 ±0.005	**77.6** ±0.004
Bench	132	78.1 ±0.002	**78.6** ±0.002	78.2 ±0.003	**78.3** ±0.002	78.1 ±0.002	**78.6** ±0.003
Bicycle	6	**43.6** ±0.013	43.5 ±0.013	**43.2**±0.01	38.6 ±0.012	**43.2** ±0.011	40.3 ±0.01
Birdhouse	2	81.4 ±0.033	**86.6** ±0.03	83.7 ±0.033	**85.9**±0.018	82.9 ±0.021	**87.3** ±0.027
Bookshelf	39	73.3 ±0.003	**75.8** ±0.006	73.7 ±0.008	**74.6** ±0.006	73.8 ±0.007	**74.4** ±0.003
Bottle	35	92.5 ±0.003	**92.6** ±0.003	**92.7** ±0.002	91.5 ±0.003	92.7 ±0.002	**93.0** ±0.002
Bowl	13	93.6 ±0.004	**93.7** ±0.006	**93.5** ±0.004	92.5 ±0.005	**93.8** ±0.005	93.4 ±0.006
Bus	82	**91.2** ±0.002	90.9 ±0.002	**91.1** ±0.001	**91.1** ±0.002	91.3 ±0.002	**91.8** ±0.002
Cabinet	115	90.7 ±0.001	**91.6** ±0.002	90.8 ±0.002	**91.2** ±0.002	90.9 ±0.002	**91.4** ±0.002
Camera	8	67.5 ±0.004	**68.2** ±0.008	68.1 ±0.006	**69.9** ±0.008	67.9 ±0.005	**69.8** ±0.009
Can	8	94.7 ±0.007	**95.3** ±0.005	**94.7** ±0.004	94.1 ±0.005	**94.8** ±0.007	94.6 ±0.006
Cap	3	**79.2** ±0.01	77.1 ±0.02	**81.0** ±0.018	79.2 ±0.027	78.6 ±0.011	**80.5** ±0.01
Car	554	82.6 ±0.001	**82.7** ±0.001	**82.5** ±0.001	82.4 ±0.001	82.7 ±0.001	**82.8** ±0.001
Cellphone	45	91.6 ±0.005	**92.4** ±0.003	91.7 ±0.003	91.6 ±0.004	92.4 ±0.004	**92.6** ±0.003
Chair	491	77.5 ±0.001	**78.2** ±0.001	**77.7** ±0.001	77.3 ±0.001	77.5 ±0.001	**78.6** ±0.001
Clock	40	**80.4** ±0.004	79.8 ±0.004	80.1 ±0.004	**81.2** ±0.005	80.5 ±0.004	**82.3** ±0.006
Dishwasher	8	93.4 ±0.005	**94.8** ±0.002	**94.0** ±0.004	93.1 ±0.006	**94.4** ±0.005	93.5 ±0.005
Display	81	**86.3** ±0.002	86.0 ±0.004	86.5 ±0.003	**86.6** ±0.002	86.4 ±0.002	**87.6** ±0.004
Faucet	47	**66.0** ±0.007	64.6 ±0.007	**66.8** ±0.009	65.6 ±0.007	**66.8** ±0.008	**66.8** ±0.008
File cabinet	18	92.4 ±0.003	**92.6** ±0.004	**92.8** ±0.004	92.2 ±0.006	**92.6** ±0.005	92.0 ±0.005
Flowerpot	42	65.5 ±0.002	**66.4** ±0.003	65.5 ±0.003	**65.8** ±0.003	65.5 ±0.002	**66.1** ±0.004
Guitar	65	78.3 ±0.006	**79.7** ±0.005	78.4 ±0.004	**79.3** ±0.004	78.3 ±0.004	**81.9** ±0.003
Headphone	5	55.4 ±0.009	**55.6** ±0.015	55.6 ±0.01	**60.3** ±0.005	55.1 ±0.007	**62.6** ±0.012
Helmet	16	**75.5** ±0.003	**75.5** ±0.002	**75.4** ±0.002	75.1 ±0.003	75.3 ±0.004	**75.9** ±0.004
Keyboard	5	**87.9** ±0.013	87.3 ±0.007	87.8 ±0.009	**91.4** ±0.009	88.1 ±0.01	**90.9** ±0.008
Knife	42	78.3 ±0.007	**78.8** ±0.011	**79.4** ±0.006	78.4 ±0.015	78.7 ±0.006	**79.2** ±0.008
Lamp	181	67.2 ±0.003	**68.2** ±0.004	**67.8** ±0.003	67.0 ±0.005	67.3 ±0.005	**68.4** ±0.005
Laptop	34	96.6 ±0.001	**96.9** ±0.003	96.8 ±0.002	**97.0** ±0.003	96.7 ±0.002	**97.3** ±0.001
Letterbox	7	**70.1** ±0.011	68.2 ±0.01	70.1 ±0.007	**71.6** ±0.006	69.8 ±0.013	**72.5** ±0.009
Microphone	6	62.1 ±0.007	**65.2** ±0.053	**62.8** ±0.008	62.1 ±0.033	62.5 ±0.008	**68.8** ±0.009
Microwave	11	**93.8** ±0.003	93.2 ±0.006	93.6 ±0.003	**93.7** ±0.003	93.4 ±0.004	**94.2** ±0.004
Motorcycle	28	**75.4** ±0.004	75.0 ±0.004	**75.4** ±0.003	74.8 ±0.003	75.0 ±0.006	**75.8** ±0.003
Mug	17	84.4 ±0.006	**84.6** ±0.004	**84.2** ±0.004	83.0 ±0.003	**84.4** ±0.004	84.0 ±0.002
Piano	13	79.4 ±0.003	**80.3** ±0.005	79.4 ±0.004	**80.1** ±0.005	79.2 ±0.005	**80.6** ±0.007
Pillow	6	86.9 ±0.012	**87.8** ±0.014	**86.9** ±0.009	84.0 ±0.009	**86.7** ±0.01	86.5 ±0.013
Pistol	19	84.4 ±0.007	**85.3** ±0.008	84.7 ±0.006	**85.8** ±0.004	84.5 ±0.006	**86.8** ±0.007
Printer	18	79.1 ±0.007	**81.3** ±0.005	79.2 ±0.007	**80.8** ±0.008	79.3 ±0.006	**80.7** ±0.004
Remote control	4	90.9 ±0.009	**92.3** ±0.005	89.4 ±0.268	**91.2** ±0.012	**91.0** ±0.006	89.6 ±0.005
Rifle	171	**77.5** ±0.003	**77.5** ±0.003	**77.6** ±0.003	77.0 ±0.003	77.2 ±0.003	**78.2** ±0.003
Rocket	7	72.4 ±0.01	**73.1** ±0.011	**73.2** ±0.012	71.0 ±0.012	71.8 ±0.015	**72.3** ±0.011

(continued)

Table 1. (*continued*)

Category	#M	Epoch 80		Epoch 90		Epoch 100	
		[33]	Ours	[33]	Ours	[33]	Ours
Ship	147	**79.3** ±0.003	79.2 ±0.001	**79.5** ±0.002	78.9 ±0.003	79.3 ±0.001	**80.2** ±0.002
Skateboard	18	78.9 ±0.017	**80.5** ±0.013	**80.7** ±0.009	79.8 ±0.012	80.0 ±0.013	**82.0** ±0.009
Sofa	242	87.2 ±0.001	**87.3** ±0.001	**87.1** ±0.001	86.9 ±0.001	87.1 ±0.001	**87.2** ±0.001
Speaker	121	84.1 ±0.003	**84.3** ±0.002	**84.1** ±0.002	**84.1** ±0.002	84.0 ±0.002	**84.4** ±0.002
Stove	8	88.2 ±0.009	**88.8** ±0.005	88.5 ±0.006	**88.9** ±0.006	88.5 ±0.006	**90.4** ±0.008
Table	652	**84.6** ±0.001	**84.6** ±0.001	**84.8** ±0.001	84.4 ±0.001	84.5 ±0.001	**85.3** ±0.001
Telephone	92	92.8 ±0.006	**93.1** ±0.003	92.5 ±0.006	**93.0** ±0.002	93.0 ±0.005	**93.5** ±0.004
Tower	12	**76.3** ±0.005	74.8 ±0.006	**76.4** ±0.006	75.6 ±0.005	**76.5** ±0.007	**76.5** ±0.005
Train	25	84.2 ±0.005	**85.0** ±0.005	84.0 ±0.005	**84.6** ±0.003	84.3 ±0.007	**85.9** ±0.005
Trashcan	28	**85.4** ±0.005	**85.4** ±0.002	85.2 ±0.004	**85.4** ±0.004	85.5 ±0.003	**85.6** ±0.005
Vase	38	82.0 ±0.004	**83.2** ±0.004	**82.4** ±0.004	82.0 ±0.002	82.1 ±0.004	**83.6** ±0.003
Vessel	85	**81.0** ±0.002	80.5 ±0.003	**81.1** ±0.003	80.2 ±0.002	81.2 ±0.002	**81.5** ±0.003
Washing machine	17	93.0 ±0.002	**93.2** ±0.003	92.4 ±0.277	**93.0** ±0.003	93.0 ±0.003	**93.2** ±0.003
Average		80.9	81.5	81.1	81.6	81.0	81.8

Table 2. IoU comparison between the best performance models for [33] and ours.

Category	#Model	[33] of epoch 90	Ours of epoch 100	Our gain
Aeroplane	304	72.4 ±0.001	**73.2** ±0.001	0.8
Bag	8	79.0 ±0.006	**80.2** ±0.004	1.2
Basket	11	83.8 ±0.005	**85.3** ±0.005	1.5
Bathtub	62	87.7 ±0.004	**89.1** ±0.003	1.4
Bed	10	76.0 ±0.006	**79.2** ±0.004	3.2
Bench	132	78.2 ±0.003	**79.2** ±0.003	1.0
Bicycle	6	43.2 ±0.01	**43.8** ±0.01	0.6
Birdhouse	2	83.7 ±0.033	**88.6** ±0.027	4.9
Bookshelf	39	73.7 ±0.008	**76.2** ±0.003	2.5
Bottle	35	92.7 ±0.002	**92.8** ±0.002	0.1
Bowl	13	93.5 ±0.004	**94.2** ±0.006	0.7
Bus	82	**91.1** ±0.001	**91.1** ±0.002	0.0
Cabinet	115	90.8 ±0.002	**91.6** ±0.002	0.8
Camera	8	68.1 ±0.006	**69.0** ±0.009	0.9
Can	8	94.7 ±0.004	**95.3** ±0.006	0.6
Cap	3	**81.0** ±0.018	77.9 ±0.01	−3.1
Car	554	82.5 ±0.001	**82.8** ±0.001	0.3
Cellphone	45	91.7 ±0.003	**92.5** ±0.003	0.8
Chair	491	77.7 ±0.001	**78.7** ±0.001	1.0
Clock	40	**80.1** ±0.004	79.9 ±0.006	−0.2

(*continued*)

Table 2. (*continued*)

Category	#Model	[33] of epoch 90	Ours of epoch 100	Our gain
Dishwasher	8	94.0 ±0.004	**94.3** ±0.005	0.3
Display	81	**86.5** ±0.003	**86.5** ±0.004	0.0
Faucet	47	**66.8** ±0.009	65.2 ±0.008	−1.6
Filecabinet	18	**92.8** ±0.004	92.5 ±0.005	−0.3
Flowerpot	42	65.5 ±0.003	**66.6** ±0.004	1.1
Guitar	65	78.4 ±0.004	**80.2** ±0.003	1.8
Headphone	5	55.6 ±0.01	**56.8** ±0.012	1.2
Helmet	16	75.4 ±0.002	**75.8** ±0.004	0.4
Keyboard	5	87.8 ±0.009	**88.2** ±0.008	0.4
Knife	42	**79.4** ±0.006	79.0 ±0.008	−0.4
Lamp	181	67.8 ±0.003	**68.5** ±0.005	0.7
Laptop	34	96.8 ±0.002	**97.3** ±0.001	0.5
Letterbox	7	**70.1** ±0.007	68.1 ±0.009	−2.0
Microphone	6	62.8 ±0.008	**63.0** ±0.009	0.2
Microwave	11	**93.6** ±0.003	93.5 ±0.004	−0.1
Motorcycle	28	**75.4** ±0.003	75.3 ±0.003	−0.1
Mug	17	84.2 ±0.004	**84.6** ±0.002	0.2
Piano	13	79.4 ±0.004	**80.8** ±0.007	1.4
Pillow	6	86.9 ±0.009	**88.8** ±0.013	1.9
Pistol	19	84.7 ±0.006	**85.6** ±0.007	0.9
Printer	18	79.2 ±0.007	**82.0** ±0.004	2.8
Remote control	4	89.4 ±0.268	**92.0** ±0.005	2.6
Rifle	171	**77.6** ±0.003	**77.6** ±0.003	0.0
Rocket	7	**73.2** ±0.012	72.8 ±0.011	−0.4
Ship	147	79.5 ±0.002	**79.8** ±0.002	0.3
Skateboard	18	80.7 ±0.009	**80.9** ±0.009	0.2
Sofa	242	87.1 ±0.001	**87.6** ±0.001	0.5
Speaker	121	84.1 ±0.002	**84.3** ±0.002	0.2
Stove	8	88.5 ±0.006	**88.9** ±0.008	0.4
Table	652	84.8 ±0.001	**85.2** ±0.001	0.4
Telephone	92	92.5 ±0.006	**93.1** ±0.004	0.6
Tower	12	**76.4** ±0.006	75.9 ±0.005	−0.5
Train	25	84.0 ±0.005	**85.1** ±0.005	1.1
Trashcan	28	85.2 ±0.004	**85.5** ±0.005	0.3
Vase	38	82.4 ±0.004	**83.7** ±0.003	1.3
Vessel	85	**81.1** ±0.003	80.8 ±0.003	−0.3
Washing machine	17	92.4 ±0.277	**93.3** ±0.003	0.9
Average		**81.1**	**81.8**	0.7

4.3 Conclusion

In order to improve the accuracy and overall shape of the 3D model, we focus on reconstructing the detailed parts of the 3D models that most state-of-the-art 3D reconstruction methods with CNNs have overlooked. We presented a simple yet effective way to improve the quality of the reconstructed 3D model by leveraging the advantage of a pyramidal hierarchical-based network. We show that building a feature pyramid of high-level semantics with different scales and concatenating the layers is able to reconstruct a denser 3D model while improving the reconstruction of the detailed parts. We demonstrated that our proposed method outperformed the state-of-the-art method in most categories and also in terms of overall IoU. However, our proposed method is not fully able to cope with the reconstruction of 3D models with uncommon and complex shapes.

References

1. Bell, S., Lawrence Zitnick, C., Bala, K., Girshick, R.: Inside-outside net: detecting objects in context with skip pooling and recurrent neural networks. In: Proceedings of the IEEE Conference on Computer Vision and Pattern Recognition, pp. 2874–2883 (2016)
2. Cai, Z., Fan, Q., Feris, R.S., Vasconcelos, N.: A unified multi-scale deep convolutional neural network for fast object detection. In: Leibe, B., Matas, J., Sebe, N., Welling, M. (eds.) ECCV 2016. LNCS, vol. 9908, pp. 354–370. Springer, Cham (2016). https://doi.org/10.1007/978-3-319-46493-0_22
3. Chang, A.X., et al.: ShapeNet: an information-rich 3D model repository. arXiv preprint arXiv:1512.03012 (2015)
4. Choy, C.B., Xu, D., Gwak, J.Y., Chen, K., Savarese, S.: 3D-R2N2: a unified approach for single and multi-view 3D object reconstruction. In: Leibe, B., Matas, J., Sebe, N., Welling, M. (eds.) ECCV 2016. LNCS, vol. 9912, pp. 628–644. Springer, Cham (2016). https://doi.org/10.1007/978-3-319-46484-8_38
5. Cignoni, P., Callieri, M., Corsini, M., Dellepiane, M., Ganovelli, F., Ranzuglia, G.: MeshLab: an open-source mesh processing tool. In: Scarano, V., Chiara, R.D., Erra, U. (eds.) Eurographics Italian Chapter Conference. The Eurographics Association (2008). https://doi.org/10.2312/LocalChapterEvents/ItalChap/ItalianChapConf2008/129-136
6. Fan, H., Su, H., Guibas, L.J.: A point set generation network for 3D object reconstruction from a single image. In: Proceedings of the IEEE Conference on Computer Vision and Pattern Recognition, pp. 605–613 (2017)
7. Furukawa, Y., Ponce, J.: Accurate, dense, and robust multiview stereopsis. IEEE Trans. Pattern Anal. Mach. Intell. 32(8), 1362–1376 (2009)
8. Ghiasi, G., Fowlkes, C.C.: Laplacian pyramid reconstruction and refinement for semantic segmentation. In: Leibe, B., Matas, J., Sebe, N., Welling, M. (eds.) ECCV 2016. LNCS, vol. 9907, pp. 519–534. Springer, Cham (2016). https://doi.org/10.1007/978-3-319-46487-9_32
9. Hariharan, B., Arbeláez, P., Girshick, R., Malik, J.: Hypercolumns for object segmentation and fine-grained localization. In: Proceedings of the IEEE Conference on Computer Vision and Pattern Recognition, pp. 447–456 (2015)

10. He, K., Zhang, X., Ren, S., Sun, J.: Deep residual learning for image recognition. In: Proceedings of the IEEE Conference on Computer Vision and Pattern Recognition, pp. 770–778 (2016)

11. Honari, S., Yosinski, J., Vincent, P., Pal, C.: Recombinator networks: learning coarse-to-fine feature aggregation. In: Proceedings of the IEEE Conference on Computer Vision and Pattern Recognition, pp. 5743–5752 (2016)

12. Ji, M., Gall, J., Zheng, H., Liu, Y., Fang, L.: SurfaceNet: an end-to-end 3D neural network for multiview stereopsis. In: Proceedings of the IEEE International Conference on Computer Vision, pp. 2307–2315 (2017)

13. Kanazawa, A., Tulsiani, S., Efros, A.A., Malik, J.: Learning category-specific mesh reconstruction from image collections. In: Ferrari, V., Hebert, M., Sminchisescu, C., Weiss, Y. (eds.) ECCV 2018. LNCS, vol. 11219, pp. 386–402. Springer, Cham (2018). https://doi.org/10.1007/978-3-030-01267-0_23

14. Kar, A., Häne, C., Malik, J.: Learning a multi-view stereo machine. In: Advances in Neural Information Processing Systems, pp. 365–376 (2017)

15. Kato, H., Harada, T.: Learning view priors for single-view 3D reconstruction. In: Proceedings of the IEEE Conference on Computer Vision and Pattern Recognition, pp. 9778–9787 (2019)

16. Kato, H., Ushiku, Y., Harada, T.: Neural 3D mesh renderer. In: Proceedings of the IEEE Conference on Computer Vision and Pattern Recognition, pp. 3907–3916 (2018)

17. Kingma, D.P., Welling, M.: Auto-encoding variational bayes. arXiv preprint arXiv:1312.6114 (2013)

18. Kong, C., Lin, C.H., Lucey, S.: Using locally corresponding CAD models for dense 3D reconstructions from a single image. In: Proceedings of the IEEE Conference on Computer Vision and Pattern Recognition, pp. 4857–4865 (2017)

19. Kong, T., Yao, A., Chen, Y., Sun, F.: HyperNet: towards accurate region proposal generation and joint object detection. In: Proceedings of the IEEE Conference on Computer Vision and Pattern Recognition, pp. 845–853 (2016)

20. Lin, C.H., Kong, C., Lucey, S.: Learning efficient point cloud generation for dense 3D object reconstruction. In: Thirty-Second AAAI Conference on Artificial Intelligence (2018)

21. Lin, T.Y., Dollár, P., Girshick, R., He, K., Hariharan, B., Belongie, S.: Feature pyramid networks for object detection. In: Proceedings of the IEEE Conference on Computer Vision and Pattern Recognition, pp. 2117–2125 (2017)

22. Liu, W., et al.: SSD: single shot multibox detector. In: Leibe, B., Matas, J., Sebe, N., Welling, M. (eds.) ECCV 2016. LNCS, vol. 9905, pp. 21–37. Springer, Cham (2016). https://doi.org/10.1007/978-3-319-46448-0_2

23. Liu, W., Rabinovich, A., Berg, A.C.: Parsenet: looking wider to see better. arXiv preprint arXiv:1506.04579 (2015)

24. Long, J., Shelhamer, E., Darrell, T.: Fully convolutional networks for semantic segmentation. In: Proceedings of the IEEE conference on computer vision and pattern recognition, pp. 3431–3440 (2015)

25. Newell, A., Yang, K., Deng, J.: Stacked hourglass networks for human pose estimation. In: Leibe, B., Matas, J., Sebe, N., Welling, M. (eds.) ECCV 2016. LNCS, vol. 9912, pp. 483–499. Springer, Cham (2016). https://doi.org/10.1007/978-3-319-46484-8_29

26. Niu, C., Li, J., Xu, K.: Im2Struct: recovering 3D shape structure from a single RGB image. In: Proceedings of the IEEE Conference on Computer Vision and Pattern Recognition, pp. 4521–4529 (2018)

27. Pinheiro, P.O., Lin, T.-Y., Collobert, R., Dollár, P.: Learning to refine object segments. In: Leibe, B., Matas, J., Sebe, N., Welling, M. (eds.) ECCV 2016. LNCS, vol. 9905, pp. 75–91. Springer, Cham (2016). https://doi.org/10.1007/978-3-319-46448-0_5

28. Pons, J.P., Keriven, R., Faugeras, O.: Modelling dynamic scenes by registering multi-view image sequences. In: 2005 IEEE Computer Society Conference on Computer Vision and Pattern Recognition (CVPR 2005), vol. 2, pp. 822–827. IEEE (2005)

29. Pontes, J.K., Kong, C., Eriksson, A., Fookes, C., Sridharan, S., Lucey, S.: Compact model representation for 3D reconstruction. arXiv preprint arXiv:1707.07360 (2017)

30. Pontes, J.K., Kong, C., Sridharan, S., Lucey, S., Eriksson, A., Fookes, C.: Image2Mesh: a learning framework for single image 3D reconstruction. In: Jawahar, C.V., Li, H., Mori, G., Schindler, K. (eds.) ACCV 2018. LNCS, vol. 11361, pp. 365–381. Springer, Cham (2019). https://doi.org/10.1007/978-3-030-20887-5_23

31. Ronneberger, O., Fischer, P., Brox, T.: U-Net: convolutional networks for biomedical image segmentation. In: Navab, N., Hornegger, J., Wells, W.M., Frangi, A.F. (eds.) MICCAI 2015. LNCS, vol. 9351, pp. 234–241. Springer, Cham (2015). https://doi.org/10.1007/978-3-319-24574-4_28

32. Snavely, N., Seitz, S.M., Szeliski, R.: Photo tourism: exploring photo collections in 3D. In: ACM Transactions on Graphics (TOG), vol. 25, pp. 835–846. ACM (2006)

33. Soltani, A.A., Huang, H., Wu, J., Kulkarni, T.D., Tenenbaum, J.B.: Synthesizing 3D shapes via modeling multi-view depth maps and silhouettes with deep generative networks. In: Proceedings of the IEEE Conference on Computer Vision and Pattern Recognition, pp. 1511–1519 (2017)

34. Sun, Y., Liu, Z., Wang, Y., Sarma, S.E.: Im2Avatar: Colorful 3D reconstruction from a single image. arXiv preprint arXiv:1804.06375 (2018)

35. Tulsiani, S., Zhou, T., Efros, A.A., Malik, J.: Multi-view supervision for single-view reconstruction via differentiable ray consistency. In: Proceedings of the IEEE Conference on Computer Vision and Pattern Recognition, pp. 2626–2634 (2017)

36. Wang, N., Zhang, Y., Li, Z., Fu, Y., Liu, W., Jiang, Y.-G.: Pixel2Mesh: generating 3D mesh models from single RGB images. In: Ferrari, V., Hebert, M., Sminchisescu, C., Weiss, Y. (eds.) ECCV 2018. LNCS, vol. 11215, pp. 55–71. Springer, Cham (2018). https://doi.org/10.1007/978-3-030-01252-6_4

Inverse Lighting from Cast Shadows Under Unknown Radiometric Response Function

Takuto Nakashima, Ryo Matsuoka[iD], and Takahiro Okabe[✉][iD]

Department of Artificial Intelligence, Kyushu Institute of Technology, Iizuka, Japan
okabe@ai.kyutech.ac.jp

Abstract. Inverse lighting is a technique for estimating the illumination distribution of a scene from a single image. Conventionally, inverse lighting assumes either a linear radiometric response function or a convex scene without cast shadows. Unfortunately, however, consumer cameras usually have unknown and nonlinear radiometric response functions, and then the existing methods do not work well for images such as Internet photos taken by using those cameras. Moreover, it is known that the high-frequency components of an illumination distribution cannot be recovered from diffuse reflection components without cast shadows. In this paper, we propose a method for jointly estimating both an illumination distribution and a radiometric response function from cast shadows. Specifically, our proposed method represents the illumination distribution and the response function by using Haar wavelets with the sparseness constraint and polynomials respectively, and then estimates their coefficients. We conducted a number of experiments by using both synthetic and real images, and confirmed that our method works better than the existing methods. In addition, we showed that masking pixels near edges makes the joint estimation robust for real images with approximate geometry.

Keywords: Inverse lighting · Cast shadows · Radiometric response function · Haar wavelets · Spherical harmonics

1 Introduction

The appearance of an object depends on the shape and reflectance of the object as well as the illumination distribution of a scene. Inverse lighting [6] is a technique for estimating the illumination distribution of a scene from a single input image with known shape and reflectance. Illumination recovery is important for applications to Augmented Reality (AR) and Mixed Reality (MR); it enables us to superimpose photometrically consistent synthetic objects onto real scenes and real images [1,11]. Inverse lighting is important also as a building block of multi-view inverse rendering [4,13,15,16]; it jointly estimates the detailed shape, reflectance, and illumination from multiple images such as Internet photos.

© Springer Nature Singapore Pte Ltd. 2020
W. Ohyama and S. K. Jung (Eds.): IW-FCV 2020, CCIS 1212, pp. 363–375, 2020.
https://doi.org/10.1007/978-981-15-4818-5_27

Conventionally, inverse lighting assumes either a linear radiometric response function or a convex scene. The former means that a pixel value is proportional to a radiance value. Unfortunately, however, consumer cameras usually have unknown and nonlinear radiometric response functions [3]. Therefore, the existing methods assuming a linear response function [6,9,10,12] do not work well for images, in particular Internet photos, taken by using those cameras with unknown and nonlinear radiometric response functions.

The latter means that there are no shadows cast by one object onto another in the scene. It is known that the high-frequency components of an illumination distribution cannot be recovered from diffuse reflection components [10], but can be recovered from cast shadows [9]. Ohta and Okabe [8] propose a method for jointly estimating both the illumination distribution of a scene and the radiometric response function of a camera from diffuse reflection components, and therefore their method can recover only the low-frequency components of an illumination distribution. In addition, they tested their method only on synthetic images with accurate geometry, and then its effectiveness on real images with approximate geometry is questionable.

To cope with those limitations, we propose a method for jointly estimating both the illumination distribution of a scene and the radiometric response function of a camera from cast shadows. Specifically, our proposed method represents the illumination distribution and the response function by using Haar wavelets with the sparseness constraint and polynomials respectively, and then estimates their coefficients. We conducted a number of experiments using both synthetic and real images, and confirmed that our method works better than the existing methods. In addition, we empirically show that masking the pixels near the edges in an input image makes the joint estimation robust for real images with approximate geometry.

The main contributions of this study are twofold. First, we propose a method for jointly estimating both an illumination distribution and a radiometric response function from cast shadows; it enables us to estimate the high-frequency components of the illumination distribution from a single input image captured by using a consumer camera with an unknown and nonlinear response function. Second, through the experiments using both synthetic and real images, we experimentally confirmed that our method works better than the existing methods. Specifically, we showed the effectiveness of the joint estimation and the use of Haar wavelets with the sparseness constraint. In addition, we showed that the joint estimation from real images with approximate geometry becomes robust when the pixels near the edges in an input image are removed from the estimation.

2   Proposed Method

In this section, we propose a method for jointly estimating both the illumination distribution of a scene and the radiometric response function of a camera from a single input image. Our proposed method assumes that the shape and reflectance of a scene are known, and the scene is illuminated by distant light sources in a similar manner to the conventional inverse lighting. We discuss how to make the joint estimation robust for real images with approximate geometry.

2.1 Illumination Distribution

According to the above distant illumination assumption, we describe the intensity of the incident light ray from the direction (θ, ϕ) to a scene as $L(\theta, \phi)$. Here, θ and ϕ are the zenith and azimuth angles in the spherical coordinate system centered at the scene. Hereafter, we call $L(\theta, \phi)$ the illumination distribution of the scene.

We can represent an illumination distribution as a linear combination of basis functions. It is known that low-degree spherical harmonics can be used for the basis functions of an illumination distribution when a scene of interest is convex and obeys the Lambert model [10]. On the other hand, it is known that a large number of spherical harmonics are required when a scene is not convex and cast shadows are observed [14].

Ng *et al.* [7] show that an illumination distribution can approximately be represented by using a small number of Haar wavelets sparsely. Okabe *et al.* [9] make use of Haar wavelets for inverse lighting from cast shadows, and show that Haar wavelets work better than spherical harmonics for the basis functions of an illumination distribution. Therefore, our proposed method represents an illumination distribution by using Haar wavelets as

$$L(\theta, \phi) = \sum_{n=1}^{N} \alpha_n H_n(\theta, \phi), \tag{1}$$

where $H_n(\theta, \phi)$ and α_n are the n-th basis function of Haar wavelets and the corresponding n-th coefficient.

Based on the assumption of known shape and reflectance, we can synthesize the basis images; the n-th basis image is the image of the scene when the illumination distribution is equal to the n-th basis function of Haar wavelets $H_n(\theta, \phi)$. We denote the p-th $(p = 1, 2, 3, \ldots, P)$ pixel value in the n-th basis image by R_{np}. According to the superposition principle, the p-th pixel value of a single input image I_p $(p = 1, 2, 3, \ldots, P)$ is described as

$$I_p = \sum_{n=1}^{N} \alpha_n R_{np}. \tag{2}$$

2.2 Radiometric Response Function

The radiance values of a scene are converted to pixel values via in-camera processing. As mentioned in Sect. 1, the relationship between radiance values and pixel values is described by a radiometric response function. Consumer cameras often apply nonlinear radiometric response functions for converting radiance values to pixel values in order to improve perceived image quality [3]. In general, the response function depends on cameras themselves as well as camera settings.

Let us denote a response function by f, and assume that a radiance value I is converted to a pixel value I' by using the response function as $I' = f(I)$. Since the response function is strictly increasing, there exists the inverse of f, i.e. an inverse response function g. The inverse response function converts a pixel value I' to a radiance value I as $I = g(I')$, and therefore has 255 degrees of freedom for 8-bit images. Such a high degree of freedom could make the joint estimation of an illumination distribution and a response function from a single image intractable.

Accordingly, we make use of the polynomial representation for a radiometric response function [5]. Specifically, our proposed method represents the inverse response function $g(I'_p)$ as

$$I_p = g(I'_p) = I'_p + I'_p(I'_p - 1) \sum_{m=1}^{M} \beta_m I'^{M-m}_p, \tag{3}$$

where $(M + 1)$ is the degree of polynomial and β_m is the m-th coefficient. Both the radiance values and pixel values are normalized so that $0 \leq I_p \leq 1$ and $0 \leq I'_p \leq 1$. The polynomial representation in Eq. (3) automatically satisfies the boundary conditions: $g(0) = 0$ and $g(1) = 1$. Since the inverse response function is also strictly increasing, the coefficients β_m have to satisfy

$$g\left(\frac{I'}{255}\right) < g\left(\frac{I'+1}{255}\right), \tag{4}$$

where $I' = 0, 1, 2, \ldots, 254$ for 8-bit images.

2.3   Joint Estimation

Substituting Eq. (3) into the left-hand side of Eq. (2), we obtain

$$I'_p + I'_p(I'_p - 1) \sum_{m=1}^{M} \beta_m I'^{M-m}_p = \sum_{n=1}^{N} \alpha_n R_{np}, \tag{5}$$

i.e. a single constraint on the coefficients of the illumination distribution α_n and those of the response function β_m per pixel. Therefore, our proposed method estimates the coefficients of the illumination distribution and those of the response function by minimizing the following cost function

$$\frac{1}{P}\sum_{p=1}^{P}\left[I'_p + I'_p(I'_p - 1)\sum_{m=1}^{M}\beta_m I'^{M-m}_p - \sum_{n=1}^{N}\alpha_n R_{np}\right]^2 + \frac{w}{N}\sum_{n=1}^{N}|\alpha_n|_1 \tag{6}$$

with respect to α_n and β_m subject to the strictly increasing constraint in Eq. (4) and the non-negativity constraint on the illumination distribution[1]. Here, the

[1] The non-negativity constraint is represented by the linear constraints on the coefficients of the illumination distribution α_n.

first term measures the discrepancy between the radiance values predicted by the inverse response function and the illumination distribution, and the second term measures the sparseness of the coefficients for the illumination distribution. Once the coefficients of the illumination distribution α_n and those of the response function β_m are obtained, we can compute the illumination distribution and the response function by substituting them into Eq. (1) and Eq. (3).

2.4 Joint Estimation with Approximate Geometry

The performance of inverse lighting depends on the accuracy of the given geometry of a scene. Unfortunately, however, inverse lighting is often used with approximate geometry; it is used for a previously captured image in a passive manner where the geometry is given manually [12], and for a building block of multi-view inverse rendering where detailed shape is unknown and to be estimated [4,13,15,16].

Accordingly, in order to make the joint estimation with approximate geometry robust against inaccurate geometry, we propose to mask the pixels near the edges in an input image out of the estimation. The example of the edges and mask are shown in Fig. 5. The reason why the pixels near the edges are removed is that the edges correspond to the discontinuity in depths and surface normals and the sharp shadow boundaries caused by the occluding objects, and therefore their pixel values computed from the given geometry significantly change due to slight noises in the geometry.

3 Experiments

To confirm the effectiveness of our proposed method, we conducted qualitative and quantitative evaluation by using both synthetic and real images.

3.1 Comparison Using Synthetic Images

We compared the following four methods.

- **HW + RF (Our Proposed Method)** jointly estimates the illumination distribution of a scene and the inverse response function (RF) of a camera from a single input image. Haar wavelets (HW) are used for the basis functions of the illumination distribution.
- **HW** assumes that the inverse response function is linear and estimates only the illumination distribution by using Haar wavelets in a similar manner to the existing technique [9].
- **L-SH + RF** [8] jointly estimates the illumination distribution and the inverse response function. It assumes a convex scene, and therefore low-degree spherical harmonics (L-SH) up to the second degree are used for the basis functions of the illumination distribution.
- **H-SH + RF** jointly estimates the illumination distribution and the inverse response function. High-degree spherical harmonics (H-SH) are used.

Fig. 1. The images of four scenes synthesized by using the HDR radiance maps. Each one is used as input for inverse lighting.

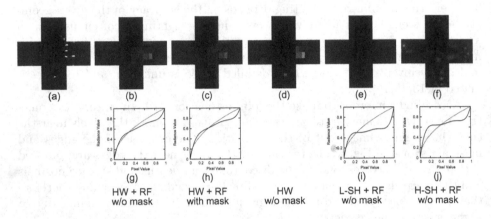

Fig. 2. The results of the first scene: (a) the ground truth of the illumination distribution, and those estimated by using (b) HW + RF w/o mask, (c) HW + RF with mask, (d) HW, (e) L-SH + RF, and (f) H-SH + RF respectively, and the corresponding inverse response functions estimated by using (g) HW + RF w/o mask, (h) HW + RF with mask, (i) L-SH + RF, and (j) H-SH + RF respectively, where the ground truth (dotted line) is superimposed.

For HW + RF and HW, the illumination distribution is represented by the Vertical Cross Cube Format (cube map) whose resolution is $N = 1280$ ($= 256 \times 5$). For L-SH + RF and H-SH + RF, the degrees of spherical harmonics are 2 and 35, $i.e.$ $N = 9$ and $N = 1296$ respectively. We empirically set the degree of the polynomial to $(M + 1) = 5$. For HW + RF and HW, we used CVX [2] for optimization, and set the weight, which controls the balance between the data term and the sparseness term in Eq. (6), to $w = 10^{-2}$. We show how the performance of our method depends on the value of the weight w later in Subsect. 3.3.

As shown in Fig. 1, we tested four images synthesized by using the HDR radiance maps [1]. In Fig. 1(a), two polyhedrons on a plane[2] are illuminated by the radiance map of "Galileo's Tomb", and its radiance values are converted by a convex upward inverse response function. In Fig. 1(b), (c), and (d), one

---

[2] The geometry of the scene is the same as that of the real images in the next subsection.

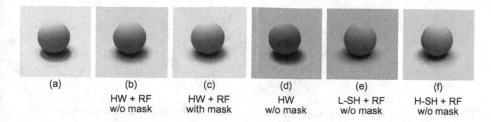

(a)	(b)	(c)	(d)	(e)	(f)
	HW + RF	HW + RF	HW	L-SH + RF	H-SH + RF
	w/o mask	with mask	w/o mask	w/o mask	w/o mask

Fig. 3. The relighting images by using (a) the ground truth of the illumination distribution, and those estimated by using (b) HW + RF w/o mask, (c) HW + RF with mask, (d) HW, (e) L-SH + RF, and (f) H-SH + RF respectively.

Table 1. The RMSEs of the relighting images in Fig. 3 and those of the estimated inverse response function in Fig. 2 for the four scenes shown in Fig. 1(a), (b), (c), and (d).

Method	Mask	Relighting image				Response function			
		(a)	(b)	(c)	(d)	(a)	(b)	(c)	(d)
HW + RF	w/o	0.056	**0.055**	0.051	**0.077**	0.077	**0.078**	**0.067**	**0.019**
HW + RF	w	**0.031**	0.101	0.063	0.079	**0.070**	0.091	0.110	0.021
HW	w/o	0.233	0.164	0.094	0.186	-	-	-	-
L-SH + RF	w/o	0.176	0.177	**0.048**	0.085	0.186	0.247	0.118	0.034
H-SH + RF	w/o	0.093	0.151	0.097	0.422	0.121	0.580	0.210	0.176

of the conditions is different from (a); (b) a convex downward inverse response function, (c) the radiance map of "Eucalyptus Grove", and (d) a sphere on a plane are used instead respectively. We added zero-mean Gaussian noises, whose standard deviation is $\sigma = 0.01$ for pixel values normalized to $[0, 1]$, to those synthetic images.

Figure 2 shows the results of the first scene: (a) the ground truth of the illumination distribution, and those estimated by using (b) HW + RF w/o mask, (c) HW + RF with mask, (d) HW, (e) L-SH + RF, and (f) H-SH + RF respectively. We show the corresponding inverse response functions estimated by using HW + RF w/o mask, HW + RF with mask, L-SH + RF, and H-SH + RF in (g), (h), (i), and (j) respectively, where the ground truth (dotted line) is superimposed on each result. In order to evaluate the effectiveness of the estimated illumination distribution for applications to AR and MR, we synthesized the relighting images of a scene different from that of the input image. Figure 3 shows the relighting images by using (a) the ground truth of the illumination distribution, and those estimated by using (b) HW + RF w/o mask, (c) HW + RF with mask, (d) HW, (e) L-SH + RF, and (f) H-SH + RF respectively. Table 1 summarizes the RMSEs of the relighting images in Fig. 3 and those of the estimated inverse response function in Fig. 2 for the four scenes shown in Fig. 1(a), (b), (c), and (d).

Fig. 4. The real input images of a scene captured with different response functions.

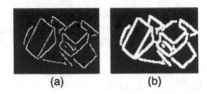

Fig. 5. The edges and mask for the real image in Fig. 4(a).

Effectiveness of Mask

Comparing the results of HW + RF, *i.e.* our proposed method, without and with mask in Figs. 2, 3, and Table 1, we can see that the proposed method without mask works better than that with mask. This is because the geometry of a scene is accurate for synthetic images, and therefore the use of the mask would lose the clues for estimating the high-frequency details of illumination distributions. Hence, we did not use the mask for evaluating the performance of the other methods: HW, L-SH + RF, and H-SH + RF. It is worth noting that the degradation of the performance due to the mask is relatively small.

Effectiveness of Joint Estimation

Comparing the results of HW + RF, *i.e.* our proposed method with those of HW in Figs. 2, 3, and Table 1, we can see that our method works better than HW both qualitatively and quantitatively. In particular, the brightness of the relighting image in Fig. 3(d) is distorted due to the assumption of a linear inverse response function. Those results show that the effectiveness of the joint estimation of an illumination distribution and an inverse response function. The reason why the estimated inverse response function in Fig. 2(g) deviates from the ground truth when pixel values are large is that the number of bright pixels is small in the input image in Fig. 1(a), and therefore the constraints from those pixels are loose.

Effectiveness of Haar Wavelets

Comparing the results of HW + RF, *i.e.* our proposed method with those of L-SR + RF [8] in Figs. 2, 3, and Table 1, we can see that our method works better than L-SH + RF both qualitatively and quantitatively. Moreover, our method works better than H-SH + RF, *i.e.* even when we increase the degree of spherical harmonics from 2 ($N = 9$) to 35 ($N = 1296$). Specifically, the RMSEs of our method using Haar wavelets are significantly smaller than those of the methods

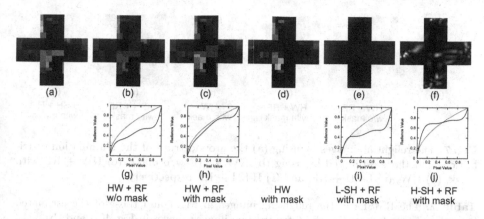

Fig. 6. The results for the first real image: (a) the ground truth of the illumination distribution, and those estimated by using (b) HW + RF w/o mask, (c) HW + RF with mask, (d) HW, (e) L-SH + RF, and (f) H-SH + RF respectively, and the corresponding inverse response functions estimated by using (g) HW + RF w/o mask, (h) HW + RF with mask, (i) L-SH + RF, and (j) H-SH + RF respectively, where the ground truth (dotted line) is superimposed.

using spherical harmonics. Those results show that Haar wavelets are effective for representing illumination distributions.

Hence, we can conclude that our proposed method works better than the existing/closely-related methods. In particular, we confirmed the effectiveness of both the joint estimation and Haar wavelets.

3.2 Comparison Using Real Images

In order to show the effectiveness of our proposed method for real images, we compared our method with the other three methods by using real images in a similar manner to the previous subsection. Figure 4 shows the real input images of a scene captured by the same Point Grey camera (Chameleon) with different settings in response functions. Figure 5 shows (a) the edges extracted by using the Canny edge detector and (b) the mask for the real input image in Fig. 4(a).

Figure 6 shows the results for the first real image: (a) the ground truth of the illumination distribution, and those estimated by using (b) HW + RF w/o mask, (c) HW + RF with mask, (d) HW, (e) L-SH + RF, and (f) H-SH + RF respectively. Here, we consider the illumination distribution estimated from the image with a linear response function by using HW with mask as the ground truth. We show the corresponding inverse response functions estimated by using HW + RF w/o mask, HW + RF with mask, L-SH + RF, and H-SH + RF in (g), (h), (i), and (j) respectively, where the ground truth (dotted line) is superimposed on each result. Figure 7 shows the relighting images by using (a) the ground truth of the illumination distribution, and those estimated by using (b) HW + RF w/o mask, (c) HW + RF with mask, (d) HW, (e) L-SH + RF, and

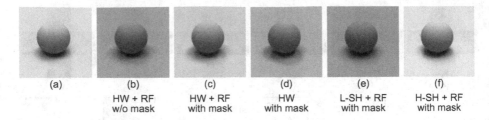

(a)	(b)	(c)	(d)	(e)	(f)
	HW + RF w/o mask	HW + RF with mask	HW with mask	L-SH + RF with mask	H-SH + RF with mask

Fig. 7. The relighting images by using (a) the ground truth of the illumination distribution, and those estimated by using (b) HW + RF w/o mask, (c) HW + RF with mask, (d) HW, (e) L-SH + RF, and (f) H-SH + RF respectively.

Table 2. The RMSEs of the relighting images in Fig. 7 and those of the estimated inverse response function in Fig. 6 for the two images shown in Fig. 4(a) and (b).

Method	Mask	Relighting image (a)	Relighting image (b)	Response function (a)	Response function (b)
HW + RF	w/o	0.206	0.036	0.231	0.095
HW + RF	w	**0.082**	**0.031**	**0.080**	**0.033**
HW	w	0.229	0.219	-	-
L-SH + RF	w	0.235	0.201	0.217	0.256
H-SH + RF	w	0.247	0.280	0.125	0.549

(f) H-SH + RF respectively. Table 2 summarizes the RMSEs of the relighting images in Fig. 7 and those of the estimated inverse response function in Fig. 6 for the two real images shown in Fig. 4(a) and (b).

Effectiveness of Mask

Comparing the results of HW + RF, *i.e.* our proposed method, without and with mask in Figs. 6, 7, and Table 2, we can see that the proposed method with mask works significantly better than that without mask. Those results show the effectiveness of the mask when estimating from real images with approximate geometry. Therefore, we used the mask for evaluating the performance of the other methods: HW, L-SH + RF, and H-SH + RF.

Effectiveness of Joint Estimation

Comparing the results of HW + RF, *i.e.* our proposed method with those of HW in Figs. 6, 7, and Table 2, we can see that our method works better than HW both qualitatively and quantitatively. Those results are consistent with the results for synthetic images. The reason why the estimated inverse response function in Fig. 6(h) deviates from the ground truth when pixel values are large is that the number of bright pixels is small in the input image in Fig. 4(a), and therefore the constraints from those pixels are loose.

Fig. 8. The input images for the sensitivity analysis. We added zero-mean Gaussian noises with the standard deviation (a) $\sigma = 0$, (b) $\sigma = 0.01$, (c) $\sigma = 0.02$, and (d) $\sigma = 0.04$ respectively.

Table 3. The RMSEs of the relighting images synthesized from the illumination distributions estimated for various combinations of σ and w.

$\sigma \backslash w$	0	10^{-4}	10^{-3}	10^{-2}	10^{-1}
0	**0.012**	**0.012**	0.018	0.106	0.399
0.01	0.134	0.123	0.071	**0.056**	0.383
0.02	0.175	0.170	0.151	**0.065**	0.260
0.04	0.203	0.197	0.178	0.155	**0.064**

Effectiveness of Haar Wavelets

Comparing the results of HW + RF, *i.e.* our proposed method with those of L-SR + RF [8] in Figs. 6, 7, and Table 2, we can see that our method works better than L-SH + RF both qualitatively and quantitatively. Moreover, our method works better than H-SH + RF, *i.e.* even when we increase the degree of spherical harmonics from 2 ($N = 9$) to 35 ($N = 1296$). Those results are also consistent with the results on synthetic images.

Hence, we can conclude that our proposed method works better than the existing/closely-related methods. In particular, we confirmed the effectiveness of the mask for real images with approximate geometry in addition to the effectiveness of the joint estimation and Haar wavelets.

3.3 Sensitivity Analysis

The performance of our proposed method depends on the value of the weight w in Eq. (6) as well as noises. Accordingly, we studied the sensitivity of our method to the value of the weight w and noises by using synthetic images. Specifically, we added zero-mean Gaussian noises with varying standard deviation σ to the synthesized image of the first scene as shown in Fig. 8, and then estimated the illumination distribution and the inverse response function with varying weight w. Table 3 summarizes the RMSEs of the relighting images synthesized from the illumination distributions estimated for various combinations of σ and w.

We can see that the sparseness term, *i.e.* non-zero weight w is not always necessary when using noiseless image in Fig. 8(a). On the other hand, we can see that the sparseness term works well when Gaussian noises are added to the input image. In particular, the performance of our proposed method is not sensitive to the value of the weight, and $w = 10^{-2}$ is the best for realistic noise levels such as $\sigma = 0.01$ and $\sigma = 0.02$.

4 Conclusion

In this paper, we proposed a method for jointly estimating both the illumination distribution of a scene and the radiometric response function of a camera from cast shadows in a single input image. Specifically, our proposed method represents the illumination distribution and the response function by using Haar wavelets with the sparseness constraint and polynomials respectively, and then estimates their coefficients. We conducted a number of experiments using both synthetic and real images, and confirmed that our method works better than the existing methods. Incorporating our method into multi-view inverse rendering [4,13,15,16] is one of the directions of our future work.

Acknowledgments. This work was supported by JSPS KAKENHI Grant Number JP17H00744.

References

1. Debevec, P.: Rendering synthetic objects into real scenes: bridging traditional and image-based graphics with global illumination and high dynamic range photography. In: Proceedings of the ACM SIGGRAPH1998, pp. 189–198 (1998)
2. Grant, M., Boyd, S.: CVX: Matlab software for disciplined convex programming, version 2.1 (2014). http://cvxr.com/cvx
3. Grossberg, M., Nayar, S.: What is space of camera response functions? In: Proceedings of the IEEE CVPR2003, pp. 602–609 (2003)
4. Kim, K., Torii, A., Okutomi, M.: Multi-view inverse rendering under arbitrary illumination and albedo. In: Leibe, B., Matas, J., Sebe, N., Welling, M. (eds.) ECCV 2016. LNCS, vol. 9907, pp. 750–767. Springer, Cham (2016). https://doi.org/10.1007/978-3-319-46487-9_46
5. Lee, J.Y., Matsushita, Y., Shi, B., Kweon, I.S., Ikeuchi, K.: Radiometric calibration by rank minimization. IEEE TPAMI **35**(1), 144–156 (2013)
6. Marschner, S., Greenberg, D.: Inverse lighting for photography. In: Proceedings of the IS&T/SID Fifth Color Imaging Conference, pp. 262–265 (1997)
7. Ng, R., Ramamoorthi, R., Hanrahan, P.: All-frequency shadows using non-linear wavelet lighting approximation. In: Proceedings of the ACM SIGGRAPH2003, pp. 376–381 (2003)
8. Ohta, S., Okabe, T.: Does inverse lighting work well under unknown response function? In: Proceedings of the VISAPP2015, pp. 652–657 (2015)
9. Okabe, T., Sato, I., Sato, Y.: Spherical harmonics vs. Haar wavelets: basis for recovering illumination from cast shadows. In: Proceedings of the IEEE CVPR 2004, pp. I-50–57 (2004)
10. Ramamoorthi, R., Hanrahan, P.: A signal-processing framework for inverse rendering. In: Proceedings of the ACM SIGGRAPH2001, pp. 117–128 (2001)
11. Sato, I., Sato, Y., Ikeuchi, K.: Acquiring a radiance distribution to superimpose virtual objects onto a real scene. IEEE TVCG **5**(1), 1–12 (1999)

12. Sato, I., Sato, Y., Ikeuchi, K.: Illumination from shadows. IEEE TPAMI **25**(3), 290–300 (2003)
13. Shan, Q., Adams, R., Curless, B., Furukawa, Y., Seitz, S.: The visual Turing test for scene reconstruction. In: Proceedings of the IEEE 3DV, pp. 25–32 (2013)
14. Sloan, P.P., Kautz, J., Snyder, J.: Precomputed radiance transfer for real-time rendering in dynamic, low-frequency lighting environments. In: Proceedings of the ACM SIGGRAPH 2002, pp. 527–536 (2002)
15. Wu, C., Wilburn, B., Matsushita, Y., Theobalt, C.: High-quality shape from multi-view stereo and shading under general illumination. In: Proceedings of the IEEE CVPR 2011, pp. 969–976 (2011)
16. Zollhöfer, M., et al.: Shading-based refinement on volumetric signed distance functions. ACM TOG **34**(4), 1–14 (2015)

Author Index

Printed in the United States
By Bookmasters